CAMBRIDGE
UNIVERSITY PRESS

Cambridge Lower Secondary Mathematics

LEARNER'S BOOK 9

Lynn Byrd, Greg Byrd & Chris Pearce

CAMBRIDGE
UNIVERSITY PRESS

University Printing House, Cambridge CB2 8BS, United Kingdom

One Liberty Plaza, 20th Floor, New York, NY 10006, USA

477 Williamstown Road, Port Melbourne, VIC 3207, Australia

314–321, 3rd Floor, Plot 3, Splendor Forum, Jasola District Centre, New Delhi – 110025, India

103 Penang Road, #05-06/07, Visioncrest Commercial, Singapore 238467

Cambridge University Press is part of the University of Cambridge.

It furthers the University's mission by disseminating knowledge in the pursuit of education, learning and research at the highest international levels of excellence.

www.cambridge.org
Information on this title: www.cambridge.org/9781108783774

First published 2014
Second edition 2021

20 19 18 17 16 15

Printed in Malaysia by Vivar Printing

A catalogue record for this publication is available from the British Library

ISBN 978-1-108-78377-4 Paperback + Digital Access (1 year)
ISBN 978-1-108-74651-9 Digital Edition (1 year)
ISBN 978-1-108-74647-2 eBook

Projects and their accompanying teacher guidance have been written by the NRICH team. NRICH is an innovative collaboration between the Faculties of Mathematics and Education at the University of Cambridge, which focuses on problem solving and on creating opportunities for students to learn mathematics through exploration and discussion.
https://nrich.maths.org

Introduction

Welcome to Cambridge Lower Secondary Mathematics Stage 9

The *Cambridge Lower Secondary Mathematics* course covers the Cambridge Lower Secondary Mathematics curriculum framework and is divided into three stages: 7, 8 and 9.

During your course, you will learn a lot of facts, information and techniques. You will start to think like a mathematician. This book covers all you need to know for Stage 9.

The curriculum is presented in four content areas:

- Number
- Algebra
- Geometry and measures
- Statistics and probability.

This book has 15 units, each related to one of the four content areas. However, there are no clear dividing lines between these areas of mathematics; skills learned in one unit are often used in other units. The book encourages you to understand the concepts that you need to learn, and gives opportunity for you to practise the necessary skills.

Many of the questions and activities are marked with an icon that indicates that they are designed to develop certain *thinking and working mathematically* skills.

There are eight characteristics that you will develop and apply throughout the course:

- Specialising – testing ideas against specific criteria;
- Generalising – recognising wider patterns;
- Conjecturing – forming questions or ideas about mathematics;
- Convincing – presenting evidence to justify or challenge a mathematical idea;
- Characterising – identifying and describing properties of mathematical objects;
- Classifying – organising mathematical objects into groups;
- Critiquing – comparing and evaluating ideas for solutions;
- Improving – refining your mathematical ideas to reach more effective approaches or solutions.

Your teacher can help you develop these skills, and you will also develop your ability to apply these different strategies.

We hope you will find your learning interesting and enjoyable.

Lynn Byrd, Greg Byrd and Chris Pearce

Contents

How to use this book

In this book you will find lots of different features to help your learning.

Questions to find out what you know already.

Getting started

1 Write

a 12^2 b $\sqrt{81}$ c 5^3 d $\sqrt[3]{64}$

2 $2^8 = 256$

Use this fact to work out the value of

a 2^9 b 2^7

3 Here is a multiplication: $15^5 \times 15^2$

a Write the correct answer from this list: 15^7 15^{10} 30^7 30^{10}

b Write the answer to $15^5 \div 15^2$ in index form.

What you will learn in the unit.

In this section you will …

- learn about the difference between rational numbers and irrational numbers
- use your knowledge of square numbers to estimate square roots
- use your knowledge of cube numbers to estimate cube roots.

Important words to learn.

Key words

irrational number

rational number

surd

Step-by-step examples showing how to solve a problem.

Worked example 1.1

Do not use a calculator for this question.

a Show that $\sqrt{90}$ is between 9 and 10.

b N is an integer and $\sqrt[3]{90}$ is between N and $N + 1$. Find the value of N.

Answer

a $9^2 = 81$ and $10^2 = 100$

$81 < 90 < 100$ — This means 90 is between 81 and 100.

So $\sqrt{81} < \sqrt{90} < \sqrt{100}$

And so $9 < \sqrt{90} < 10$

b $4^3 = 64$ and $5^3 = 125$

$64 < 90 < 125$ and so

$\sqrt[3]{64} < \sqrt[3]{90} < \sqrt[3]{125}$

So $4 < \sqrt[3]{90} < 5$ and $N = 4$

These questions help you to develop your skills of thinking and working mathematically.

10 a Explain why the number 65×10^4 is **not** in standard form.

b Write 65×10^4 in standard form.

c Write 48.3×10^6 in standard form.

These investigations, to be carried out with a partner or in a group, will help develop skills of thinking and working mathematically.

Think like a mathematician

6 Work with a partner to answer this question.
So far in this unit you have used the formula $A = \pi r^2$
In questions **1**, **4a** and **4b**, you found the area when you were given the radius.
In questions **2**, **4c** and **4d**, you found the area when you were given the diameter.
Can you write a formula to work out the area which uses *d* (diameter) instead of *r* (radius)?
Write your formula in its simplest form.
Test your formula on questions **4c** and **4d**. Does it work?
Compare your formula with other pairs of learners in the class.

Questions to help you think about how you learn.

Look back at this exercise.

a How confident do you feel in your understanding of this section?

b What can you do to increase your level of confidence?

This is what you have learned in the unit.

Summary checklist

- [ ] I can use square numbers and cube numbers to estimate square roots and cube roots.
- [ ] I can say whether a square root or the cube root of a positive integer is rational or irrational.

Questions that cover what you have learned in the unit.

Check your progress

1 Work out the circumference of these circles. Use the π button on your calculator.
Give your answers correct to two decimal places (2 d.p.).
a diameter = 12.5 cm b radius = 3.4 m

2 Work out the area of these circles. Use the π button on your calculator.
Give your answers correct to three significant figures (3 s.f.).
a diameter = 12.5 cm b radius = 3.4 m

3 Work out the area of this compound shape.
Use the π button on your calculator.
Give your answer correct to one decimal place (1 d.p.).

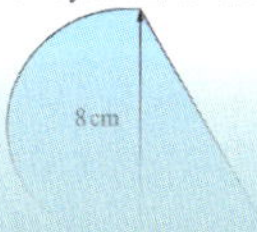

At the end of several units, there is a project for you to carry out, using what you have learned. You might make something or solve a problem.

Cutting tablecloths

Imagine a square piece of cloth 1 metre by 1 metre that could be altered to make a tablecloth for a rectangular table.
You could cut off a strip 20% of the way along the square, rotate it, and attach it to the other edge to make a rectangle. There would be a little bit of cloth left over!

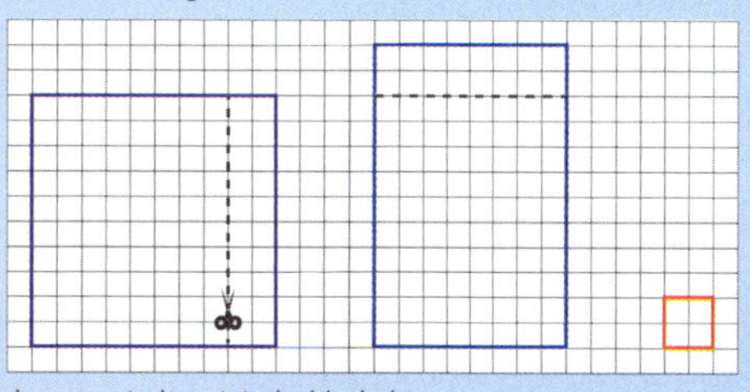

- The purple square is the original tablecloth.
- The blue rectangle is the new tablecloth.
- The red piece shows the cloth that is left over.

Look at the diagram.

- What percentage of the original cloth has been used to make the new tablecloth?

Instead of cutting off a 20% strip, you could cut a 10% strip, or a 15% strip, or a different percentage.

› Acknowledgements

The authors and publishers acknowledge the following sources of copyright material and are grateful for the permissions granted. While every effort has been made, it has not always been possible to identify the sources of all the material used, or to trace all copyright holders. If any omissions are brought to our notice, we will be happy to include the appropriate acknowledgements on reprinting.

Thanks to the following for permission to reproduce images:

Cover image: ori-artiste/Getty Images

Inside: Unit 1 Mohamad Faizal Ramli/EyeEm/GI; Bernt Ove Moss/GI; Ernest Andrei; Unit 2 Adrienne Bresnahan/GI; Brian Ach/GI; Feellife/GI; Abstract Aerial Art/GI; Image by Chris Winsor/GI; Unit 3 AlpamayoPhoto/GI; M.Arai/GI; © Razvan Ciuca/GI; Mint Images/GI; Images By Tang Ming Tung/GI; Grassetto/GI; Alexander Spatari/GI; Focus on Sport/GI; Witthaya Prasongsin/GI; SolStock/GI; Mr.Cole_Photographer/GI; Dddb/GI; Unit 4 Nick Brundle Photography/GI; DEA Picture Library/De Agostini/GI; AaronAmat/GI; Daniel Milchev/GI; Andrew Brookes/GI; RobinOlimb/GI; Unit 5 Adrienne Bresnahan/GI; hanohiki/GI; ExpressIPhoto/GI; OsakaWayne Studios/GI; Paula Daniëlse/GI; Unit 6 Sean Gladwell/GI; Mark Edward Atkinson/GI; Henrik Sorensen/GI; Rubberball/GI; Hello World/GI;Unit 7 Westend61/GI; MirageC/GI; Westend61/GI; Kevin Horgan/GI; Skarie20/GI;Yevgen Romanenko/GI; Suriyo Hmun Kaew/GI; Pictafolio/GI; Studiocasper/GI; Unit 8 Epoxydude/GI; Christian Lagarek/Science Photo Library/GI; Westend61/GI; Weng Hock Goh/GI; Unit 9 Oxygen/GI; Konstik/GI; © Jackie Bale/GI; Silentfoto/GI; Nora Carol Photography/GI; Unit 10 Somyot Techapuwapat/GI; Monty Rakusen/GI; Gary John Norman/GI; EujarimPhotography/GI; John Eder/GI; Unit 11 Abstract Aerial Art/GI; Hybrid Images/GI; Brianbalster/GI; RealPeopleGroup/GI; Heidi Harting/GI; Westend61/GI; Alan Schein/GI; Jose A.Bernat Bacete/GI; rezkrr/GI; Unit 12 Peter Dazeley/GI; ImageJournal-Photography/GI; Riou/GI; Helen Camacaro/GI; Unit 13 Ask Goldstein/GI; Roman Becker/GI; Christopher Daley/GI; Busà Photography/GI; Unit 14 Abstract Aerial Art/GI; Unit 15 Gary John Norman/GI; Irin717/GI; Dougal Waters/GI; PhotoStock-Israel/GI; Peter Dowell(peterocks)/GI; Omersukrugoksu/GI; Joseph Van Os/GI; Maskot/GI; John P Kelly/GI

Key: GI= Getty Images.

1 Number and calculation

Getting started

1 Write as a number:

a 12^2 b $\sqrt{81}$ c 5^3 d $\sqrt[3]{64}$

2 $2^8 = 256$

Use this fact to work out the value of

a 2^9 b 2^7

3 Here is a multiplication: $15^5 \times 15^2$

a Write the correct answer from this list: 15^7 15^{10} 30^7 30^{10}

b Write the answer to $15^5 \div 15^2$ in index form.

4 Look at these numbers: 4 -4.5 3000 $17\frac{3}{20}$ $\sqrt{225}$

a Which of these numbers are integers?

b Which of these numbers are rational numbers?

5 Write one million as a power of 10.

1, 4, 9 and 16 are the first four square numbers. They have integer square roots.

$1^2 = 1$ and $\sqrt{1} = 1$ $\quad$ $2^2 = 4$ and $\sqrt{4} = 2$

$3^2 = 9$ and $\sqrt{9} = 3$ $\quad$ $4^2 = 16$ and $\sqrt{16} = 4$

What about $\sqrt{2}$? Is there a rational number n for which $n^2 = 2$? Remember that you can write a rational number as a fraction.

$\left(1\frac{1}{2}\right)^2 = 1\frac{1}{2} \times 1\frac{1}{2} = 2\frac{1}{4}$ so $\sqrt{2}$ must be a little less than $1\frac{1}{2}$.

A closer answer is $1\frac{5}{12}$ because $\left(1\frac{5}{12}\right)^2 = 2\frac{1}{144}$.

An even closer answer is $1\frac{169}{408}$ because $\left(1\frac{169}{408}\right)^2 = 2\frac{1}{166464}$.

Do you think you can find a fraction which gives an answer of **exactly** 2 when you square it?

A calculator gives the answer $\sqrt{2} = 1.414213562$. This is a rational number because you can write it as a fraction: $1\frac{414213562}{1000000000}$.

Is $1.414213562 \times 1.414213562$ **exactly** 2?

In this unit, you will look at numbers such as $\sqrt{2}$.

1.1 Irrational numbers

In this section you will …

- learn about the difference between rational numbers and irrational numbers
- use your knowledge of square numbers to estimate square roots
- use your knowledge of cube numbers to estimate cube roots.

Key words

irrational number

rational number

surd

Integers are whole numbers. For example, 13, −26 and 100 004 are integers.

You can write **rational numbers** as fractions. For example, $9\frac{3}{4}$, $-3\frac{4}{15}$ and $18\frac{5}{11}$ are rational numbers.

You can write any fraction as a decimal.

$9\frac{3}{4} = 9.75 \qquad -3\frac{4}{15} = -3.26666666... \qquad 18\frac{5}{11} = 18.4545454...$

The fraction either terminates (for example, 9.75) or it has recurring digits (for example, −3.266666666666… continues with 6s and 18.45454545454… continues with the digits 4 and 5 repeating).

There are many square roots and cube roots that you cannot write as fractions. When you write these fractions as decimals, they do not terminate and there is no recurring pattern. For example, a calculator gives the answer $\sqrt{7} = 2.645751...$ The calculator answer is **not** exact. The decimal does **not** terminate and there is **no** recurring pattern. Therefore, $\sqrt{7}$ is **not** a rational number.

Numbers that are not rational are called **irrational numbers**. $\sqrt{7}$, $\sqrt{23}$, $\sqrt[3]{10}$ and $\sqrt[3]{45}$ are irrational numbers. Irrational numbers that are square roots or cube roots are called **surds**.

There are also numbers that are irrational but are not square roots or cube roots. One of these irrational numbers is called pi, which is the Greek letter π. Your calculator will tell you that $\pi = 3.141592...$ You will meet π later in the course.

Tip

The set of rational numbers includes integers.

Tip

Square roots of negative numbers do **not** belong to the set of rational or irrational numbers. You will learn more about these numbers if you continue to study mathematics to a higher level.

Worked example 1.1

Do not use a calculator for this question.

a Show that $\sqrt{90}$ is between 9 and 10.

b N is an integer and $\sqrt[3]{90}$ is between N and $N + 1$. Find the value of N.

Answer

a $9^2 = 81$ and $10^2 = 100$

$81 < 90 < 100$ — This means 90 is between 81 and 100.

So $\sqrt{81} < \sqrt{90} < \sqrt{100}$

And so $9 < \sqrt{90} < 10$

b $4^3 = 64$ and $5^3 = 125$

$64 < 90 < 125$ and so

$\sqrt[3]{64} < \sqrt[3]{90} < \sqrt[3]{125}$

So $4 < \sqrt[3]{90} < 5$ and $N = 4$

Exercise 1.1

1 Write whether each of these numbers is an integer or an irrational number. Explain how you know.

a $\sqrt{9}$ b $\sqrt{19}$ c $\sqrt{39}$ d $\sqrt{49}$ e $\sqrt{99}$

2 a Write the rational numbers in this list.

$\sqrt{1}$ $7\frac{5}{12}$ -38 $\sqrt{160}$ $-\sqrt{2.25}$ $-\sqrt{35}$

b Write the irrational numbers in this list.

$0.3333\ldots$ -16 $\sqrt{200}$ $\sqrt{1.21}$ $\frac{23}{8}$ $\sqrt[3]{343}$

3 Write whether each of these numbers is an integer or a surd. Explain how you know.

a $\sqrt{100}$ b $\sqrt[3]{100}$ c $\sqrt{1000}$

d $\sqrt[3]{1000}$ e $\sqrt{10\,000}$ f $\sqrt[3]{10\,000}$

4 Is each of these numbers rational or irrational? Give a reason for each answer.

a $2+\sqrt{2}$ b $\sqrt{2+2}$

c $4+\sqrt[3]{4}$ d $\sqrt[3]{4+4}$

5 Find

a two irrational numbers that add up to 0

b two irrational numbers that add up to 2.

Think like a mathematician

6 a Use a calculator to find

i $\sqrt{8}\times\sqrt{2}$ ii $\sqrt{3}\times\sqrt{12}$ iii $\sqrt{20}\times\sqrt{5}$ iv $\sqrt{2}\times\sqrt{18}$

b What do you notice about your answers?

c Find another multiplication similar to the multiplications in part **a**.

d Find similar multiplications using cube roots instead of square roots.

7 Without using a calculator, show that

a $7<\sqrt{55}<8$ b $4<\sqrt[3]{100}<5$

8 Without using a calculator, find an irrational number between

a 4 and 5 b 12 and 13.

9 Without using a calculator, estimate

a $\sqrt{190}$ to the nearest integer

b $\sqrt[3]{190}$ to the nearest integer.

10 a Use a calculator to find

i $(\sqrt{2}+1)\times(\sqrt{2}-1)$ ii $(\sqrt{3}+1)\times(\sqrt{3}-1)$ iii $(\sqrt{4}+1)\times(\sqrt{4}-1)$

b Continue the pattern of the multiplications in part **a**.

c Generalise the results to find $(\sqrt{N}+1)\times(\sqrt{N}-1)$ where N is a positive integer.

d Check your generalisation with further examples.

11 Here is a decimal: 5.020 020 002 000 020 000 020 000 002…

Arun says:

a Is Arun correct? Give a reason for your answer.

b Compare your answer with a partner's. Do you agree? If not, who is correct?

In this exercise, you have looked at the properties of rational and irrational numbers.

a Are the following statements true or false?

i The sum of two integers is always an integer.

ii The sum of two rational numbers is always a rational number.

iii The sum of two irrational numbers is always an irrational number.

b Here is a calculator answer: 3.646 153 846

The answer is rounded to 9 decimal places.

Can you decide whether the number is rational or irrational?

Summary checklist

- [ ] I can use square numbers and cube numbers to estimate square roots and cube roots.
- [ ] I can say whether the square root or the cube root of a positive integer is rational or irrational.

1.2 Standard form

In this section you will …

- learn to write large and small numbers in standard form.

Key words

scientific notation

standard form

Look at these numbers:

$4.67 \times 10 = 46.7$

$4.67 \times 10^2 = 467$

$4.67 \times 10^3 = 4670$

$4.67 \times 10^6 = 4\,670\,000$

Tip

4.67×10^2 is the same as 4.67×100 or $4.67 \times 10 \times 10$

You can use powers of 10 in this way to write large numbers. For example, the average distance to the Sun is 149 600 000 km. You can write this as 1.496×10^8 km. This is called **standard form**. You write a number in standard form as $a \times 10^n$ where $1 \leqslant a < 10$ and n is an integer.

You can write small numbers in a similar way, using negative integer powers of 10. For example:

$4.67 \times 10^{-1} = 0.467$

$4.67 \times 10^{-2} = 0.0467$

$4.67 \times 10^{-3} = 0.00467$

$4.67 \times 10^{-6} = 0.000\,004\,67$

Tip

Think of 4.67×10^{-1} as $4.67 \div 10$

Small numbers occur often in science. For example, the time for light to travel 5 metres is 0.000 000 017 seconds. In standard form, you can write this as 1.7×10^{-8} seconds.

Tip

Standard form is also sometimes called **scientific notation**.

Worked example 1.2

Write these numbers in standard form.

a 256 million **b** 25.6 billion **c** 0.000 025 6

Answer

a 1 million = 1 000 000 or 10^6

So 256 million = 256 000 000 = 2.56×10^8

b 1 billion = 1 000 000 000 or 10^9

So 25.6 billion = 25 600 000 000 = 2.56×10^{10}

c 0.000 025 6 = 2.56×10^{-5}

Tip

Notice that in every case the decimal point is placed after the 2, the first non-zero digit.

Exercise 1.2

1 Write these numbers in standard form.

a 300 000 b 320 000

c 328 000 d 328 710

2 Write these numbers in standard form.

a 63 000 000 b 488 000 000

c 3 040 000 d 520 000 000 000

3 These numbers are in standard form. Write each number in full.

a 5.4×10^3 b 1.41×10^6

c 2.337×10^{10} d 8.725×10^7

4 Here are the distances of some planets from the Sun.

Write each distance in standard form.

Planet	Mercury	Mars	Uranus
Distance (km)	57 900 000	227 900 000	2 870 000 000

5 Here are the areas of four countries.

Country	China	Indonesia	Russia	Kazakhstan
Area (km^2)	9.6×10^6	1.9×10^6	1.7×10^7	2.7×10^6

a Which country has the largest area?

b Which country has the smallest area?

c Copy and complete this sentence with a whole number:

The largest country is approximately … times larger than the smallest country.

6 Write these numbers in standard form.

a 0.000 007 b 0.000 812

c 0.000 066 91 d 0.000 000 205

7 These numbers are in standard form. Write each number in full.

a 1.5×10^{-3} b 1.234×10^{-5}

c 7.9×10^{-8} d 9.003×10^{-4}

8 The mass of an electron is 9.11×10^{-31} kg.

This is 0.000…911 kg.

a How many zeros are there between the decimal point and the 9?

b Work out the mass of 1 million electrons.

Give the answer in kilograms in standard form.

9 Here are four numbers:

$w = 9.81 \times 10^{-5}$	$x = 2.8 \times 10^{-4}$	$y = 9.091 \times 10^{-5}$	$z = 4 \times 10^{-4}$

a Which number is the largest?

b Which number is the smallest?

10 a Explain why the number 65×10^4 is **not** in standard form.

b Write 65×10^4 in standard form.

c Write 48.3×10^6 in standard form.

11 Write these numbers in standard form.

a 15×10^{-3} b 27.3×10^{-4} c 50×10^{-9}

12 Do these additions. Write the answers in standard form.

a $2.5 \times 10^6 + 3.6 \times 10^6$ b $4.6 \times 10^5 + 1.57 \times 10^5$ c $9.2 \times 10^4 + 8.3 \times 10^4$

13 Do these additions. Write the answers in standard form.

a $4.5 \times 10^{-6} + 3.1 \times 10^{-6}$ b $5.12 \times 10^{-5} + 2.9 \times 10^{-5}$

c $9 \times 10^{-8} + 7 \times 10^{-8}$

14 a Multiply these numbers by 10. Give each answer in standard form.

i 7×10^5 ii 3.4×10^6

iii 4.1×10^{-5} iv 1.37×10^{-4}

b Generalise your results from part **a**.

c Describe how to multiply or divide a number in standard form by 1000.

What are the advantages of writing numbers in standard form?

Summary checklist

☐ I can write large and small numbers in standard form.

1.3 Indices

In this section you will ...

- use positive, negative and zero indices
- use index laws for multiplication and division.

This table shows powers of 3.

3^2	3^3	3^4	3^5	3^6
9	27	81	243	729

When you move one column to the **right**, the index **increases** by 1 and the number multiplies by 3.

$9 \times 3 = 27$ $27 \times 3 = 81$ $81 \times 3 = 243$, and so on.

When you move one column to the **left**, the index **decreases** by 1 and the number divides by 3. You can use this fact to extend the table to the left:

3^{-4}	3^{-3}	3^{-2}	3^{-1}	3^0	3^1	3^2	3^3	3^4	3^5	3^6
$\frac{1}{81}$	$\frac{1}{27}$	$\frac{1}{9}$	$\frac{1}{3}$	1	3	9	27	81	243	729

$9 \div 3 = 3$ $3 \div 3 = 1$ $1 \div 3 = \frac{1}{3}$ $\frac{1}{3} \div 3 = \frac{1}{9}$ $\frac{1}{9} \div 3 = \frac{1}{27}$, and so on.

You can see from the table that $3^1 = 3$ and $3^0 = 1$.

Also: $3^{-1} = \frac{1}{3}$ $3^{-2} = \frac{1}{3^2}$ $3^{-3} = \frac{1}{3^3}$, and so on.

In general, if n is a positive integer then $3^{-n} = \frac{1}{3^n}$. These results are not only true for powers of 3. They apply to any positive integer.

For example: $5^{-2} = \frac{1}{5^2} = \frac{1}{25}$ $8^{-3} = \frac{1}{8^3} = \frac{1}{512}$ $6^0 = 1$

In general, if a and n are positive integers then $a^0 = 1$ and $a^{-n} = \frac{1}{a^n}$.

Tip

The index is the small red number.

Tip

$3^0 = 1$ seems strange but it fits the pattern.

Exercise 1.3

1 Write each number as a fraction.

a 4^{-1} b 2^{-3} c 9^{-2}

d 6^{-3} e 10^{-4} f 2^{-5}

2 Here are five numbers: 2^{-4} 3^{-3} 4^{-2} 5^{-1} 6^0

List the numbers in order of size, smallest first.

3 Write these numbers as powers of 2.

a $\frac{1}{2}$ b $\frac{1}{4}$ c 64

d $\frac{1}{64}$ e 1 f 8^{-1}

4 Write each number as a power of 10.

a 100 b 1000 c 1

d 0.1 e 0.001 f 0.000 001

5 Write $\frac{1}{64}$

a as a power of 64 b as a power of 8

c as a power of 4 d as a power of 2.

6 a Write $\frac{1}{81}$ as a power of a positive integer.

b How many different ways can you write the answer to part **a**?

7 When $x = 6$, find the value of

a x^2 b x^{-2} c x^0 d x^{-3}

8 Write m^{-2} as a fraction when

a $m = 9$ b $m = 15$ c $m = 1$ d $m = 20$

9 $y = x^2 + x^{-2}$ and x is a positive number.

a Write y as a mixed number when

i $x = 1$ ii $x = 2$ iii $x = 3$

b Find the value of x when

i $y = 25.04$ ii $y = 100.01$

10 a Write the answer to each multiplication as a power of 3.

i $3^2 \times 3^3$ ii $3^4 \times 3^5$

iii $3^6 \times 3^4$ iv 3×3^5

b In part **a** you used the rule $3^a \times 3^b = 3^{a+b}$ when the indices are positive integers.

In the following multiplications, a or b can be negative integers.

Show that the rule still gives the correct answers.

i $3^2 \times 3^{-1}$ ii $3^{-2} \times 3$

iii $3^3 \times 3^{-1}$ iv $3^{-1} \times 3^{-1}$

v $3^{-2} \times 3^{-1}$

c Write two examples of your own to show that the rule works.

d Give your work to a partner to check.

> **Tip**
>
> Write out the numbers and multiply.

11 Write the answer to each multiplication as a power of 5.

a $5^4 \times 5^2$ b $5^4 \times 5^{-2}$

c $5^{-4} \times 5^2$ d $5^{-4} \times 5^{-2}$

12 Write the answer to each multiplication as a single power.

a $6^{-3} \times 6^{2}$ b $7^{5} \times 7^{-2}$

c $11^{-4} \times 11^{-6}$ d $4^{-6} \times 4^{2}$

13 Find the value of x in each case.

a $2^{5} \times 2^{x} = 2^{9}$ b $3^{x} \times 3^{-2} = 3^{4}$

c $4^{x} \times 4^{-3} = 4^{-5}$ d $12^{-3} \times 12^{x} = 12^{2}$

Think like a mathematician

14 a Write as a single power:

i $2^5 \div 2^3$ ii $4^5 \div 4^2$ iii $5^6 \div 5^5$ iv $2^{10} \div 2^7$

b The rule for part **a** is that $n^a \div n^b = n^{a-b}$ when the indices a and b are positive integers.

Write some examples to show that this rule also works for indices that are negative integers.

c Give your examples to a partner to check.

15 Write the answer to each division as a single power.

a $6^{2} \div 6^{5}$ b $9^{3} \div 9^{4}$

c $15^{2} \div 15^{6}$ d $10^{3} \div 10^{8}$

16 Write the answer to each division as a single power.

a $2^{2} \div 2^{-3}$ b $8^{5} \div 8^{-2}$

c $5^{-4} \div 5^{2}$ d $12^{-3} \div 12^{-5}$

17 Write down

a 8^2 as a power of 2 b 8^{-2} as a power of 2

c 27^2 as a power of 3 d 27^{-2} as a power of 3

e 27^2 as a power of 9 f 27^{-2} as a power of 9.

Summary checklist

- [ ] I can understand positive, negative and zero indices.
- [ ] I can use the addition rule for indices to multiply powers of the same number.
- [ ] I can use the subtraction rule for indices to divide powers of the same number.

Check your progress

1 Write whether each number is rational or irrational.

a $\sqrt{4}$ b $\sqrt{5}$ c $\sqrt{6.25}$

d $\sqrt{62.5}$ e $\sqrt{625}$

2 Write whether each number is rational or irrational. Give a reason for each answer.

a $\sqrt{3^2+4^2}$ b $\sqrt{9}+\sqrt{7}$

3 Without using a calculator, find an integer n such that $n < \sqrt[3]{50} < n+1$.

4 Write each number in standard form.

a 86 000 000 000 b 0.000 006 45

5 Write these numbers in order of size, smallest first.

$A = 9 \times 10^{-4}$ $B = 6 \times 10^{-3}$ $C = 8 \times 10^{-5}$ $D = 7.5 \times 10^{-4}$

6 Write each number as a fraction.

a 7^{-2} b 3^{-4} c 2^{-7}

7 Write each number as a power of 5.

a 125 b 1 c 0.04

8 Write the answer to each calculation as the power of a single number.

a $6^8 \times 6^{-3}$ b $12^{-2} \times 12^{-3}$

c $4^2 \div 4^8$ d $15^{-4} \div 15^{-6}$

2 Expressions and formulae

Getting started

1. Sara thinks of a number, x. She divides the number by 3, then adds 7.
   Write an expression for the number Sara gets.
2. Copy and complete
   a $3^2 \times 3^4 = 3^{\square}$ b $\frac{5^{12}}{5^9} = 5^{\square}$ c $(7^2)^5 = 7^{\square}$
3. Expand
   a $x(x + 2)$ b $3y(4y - 7w)$
4. Factorise
   a $4x + 12$ b $4x^2 + 14x$
5. Work out
   a $\frac{3}{4} + \frac{2}{3}$ b $2\frac{1}{2} - 1\frac{3}{10}$
6. a Use the formula $F = ma$ to work out F when $m = 10$ and $a = 2.5$.
   b Rearrange the formula $F = ma$ to make a the subject.
   c Use your formula in part **b** to work out a when $F = 72$ and $m = 12$.

You might not be surprised that computer programmers, scientists, engineers and statisticians all use algebra in their jobs. But you might be surprised at some other jobs that also need algebra.

Cooks and chefs prepare food for other people. They work in all sorts of places, from cafés and restaurants to international business headquarters. They need to plan menus and adapt recipes for the number of people they are feeding. They must work out quantities of ingredients, their cost and the price their customers will pay for the food. They use algebra when they deal with ingredients and prices.

Farm and ranch managers deal with the day-to-day activities of a ranch or farm. They use algebra when they manage the farm accounts and write yearly business plans. If they grow crops, they need to plan how much fertiliser to apply and when to put it on the crops. They might use quite complicated algebra, as they need to consider lots of different things such as soil type, crop to be grown, type of fertiliser, cost of fertiliser, etc.

Whatever job you do, you never know when algebra will be there to help you!

2.1 Substituting into expressions

In this section you will ...

- use the correct order of operations in algebraic expressions.

Key word

counter-example

When you substitute numbers into expressions, remember the correct order of operations:

- Work out brackets and indices before divisions and multiplications.
- Always work out additions and subtractions last.

Tip

Examples of indices are 4^2, 7^3, $(-2)^2$ and $(-3)^3$.

Worked example 2.1

a Work out the value of the expression $5a - 6b$ when $a = 4$ and $b = -3$.

b Work out the value of the expression $3x^2 - 2y^3$ when $x = -5$ and $y = 2$.

c Work out the value of the expression $p\left(5 - \frac{4q}{p}\right)$ when $p = 2$ and $q = -3$.

Answer

a $5a - 6b = 5 \times 4 - 6 \times -3$	Substitute $a = 4$ and $b = -3$ into the expression.
$= 20 - -18$	Work out the multiplications first: $5 \times 4 = 20$ and $6 \times -3 = -18$.
$= 20 + 18$ $= 38$	Subtracting -18 is the same as adding 18.
b $3x^2 - 2y^3 = 3 \times (-5)^2 - 2 \times 2^3$	Substitute $x = -5$ and $y = 2$ into the expression.
$= 3 \times 25 - 2 \times 8$	Work out the indices first: $(-5)^2 = -5 \times -5 = 25$ and $2^3 = 2 \times 2 \times 2 = 8$.
$= 75 - 16$	Then work out the multiplications. $3 \times 25 = 75$ and $2 \times 8 = 16$.
$= 59$	Finally work out the subtraction.
c $p\left(5 - \frac{4q}{p}\right) = 2\left(5 - \frac{4 \times -3}{2}\right)$	Substitute $p = 2$ and $q = -3$ into the expression.
$= 2(5 - -6)$	Work out the term in brackets first. Start with the fraction.
	$4 \times -3 = -12$; $-12 \div 2 = -6$.
$= 2 \times (5 + 6)$ $= 2 \times 11$	Subtracting -6 is the same as adding 6.
$= 22$	Finally, multiply the value of the term in brackets by 2; $2 \times 11 = 22$.

Tip

In part **a**, there are no brackets and no indices, so first deal with any divisions and multiplications and then with any additions and subtractions.

Exercise 2.1

1 Copy and complete the workings to find the value of each expression when $x = 3$ and $y = 5$.

a $x - 2y = 3 - 2 \times 5$
$= 3 - \square$
$= \square$

b $x^3 + xy = 3^3 + 3 \times 5$
$= \square + \square$
$= \square$

c $y^2 - \frac{10x}{y} = (5)^2 - \frac{10 \times 3}{5}$
$= \square - \frac{30}{5}$
$= \square - \square$
$= \square$

2 Work out the value of each expression when $a = -2$, $b = 3$, $c = -4$ and $d = 6$.

a	$b + d$	b	$a + 2b$	c	$2d - b$	d	$4b + 2a$
e	$bd - 10$	f	$d^2 + ab$	g	$\frac{d}{2} - a$	h	$20 + b^3$
i	$ab + cd$	j	$\frac{bc}{d} + a$				

Think like a mathematician

3 Work with a partner to answer this question.

a The expression $ab - \frac{c}{d}$ has a value of 24. Write values for a, b, c and d when
   i a, b, c and d are all positive numbers
   ii a, b, c and d are all negative numbers
   iii a, b, c and d are a mixture of positive and negative numbers.

b Discuss the methods you used, and the values you found, with other learners in your class.

c Look at the Thinking and Working Mathematically characteristics. Which characteristics do you think you have used here?

4 This is part of Pierre's homework.

<u>Question</u>

Work out the value of each expression when $x = -3$ and $y = -2$.

a $x^2 + xy$ b $y^3 - \frac{6x}{y}$

<u>Answer</u>

a $-3^2 + -3 \times -2 = -9 + 6$
$= -3$

b $(-2)^3 - \frac{6 \times -3}{-2} = 8 - \frac{-18}{-2}$
$= 8 - 9$
$= -1$

a Look at Pierre's answers. Do you think his working and answers are correct?

Give a reason for your answer.

b Discuss your answers to part **a** with other learners in your class.

Do you agree or disagree with the other learners?

If you made a mistake, do you understand the mistake you made?

If other learners made a mistake, explain to them the mistake they made.

Think like a mathematician

5 Work with a partner to answer this question.

The expression $x^2 + y$ has a value of 15.

Write down three pairs of integer values for x and y when

a x and y are both positive numbers

b x and y are both negative numbers

c x is negative and y is positive, or vice versa.

Discuss the methods you used, and the values you found, with other learners in your class.

6 Copy and complete the workings to find the value of each expression when $m = 2$ and $p = -4$.

a $4(m+2p) = 4(2+2\times-4)$
$= 4(2-\square)$
$= 4\times\square$
$= \square$

b $p^3 - 3mp = (-4)^3 - 3\times2\times-4$
$= \square + \square$
$= \square$

c $\left(\frac{p}{m}\right)^5 + (p)^3 = \left(\frac{-4}{2}\right)^5 + (-4)^3$
$= (\square)^5 - \square$
$= \square - \square$
$= \square$

7 Work out the value of each expression when $w = 5$, $x = 2$, $y = -8$ and $z = -1$.

a $3(w + x)$ **b** $x(2w - y)$ **c** $3w - z^3$ **d** $(2x)^3$

e $x^2 + y^2$ **f** $\frac{wx}{z} + y$ **g** $2(x^3 - z^2)$ **h** $25 - 2w^2$

i $w + z(2x - y)$ **j** $(3z)^4 - z^7$

Activity 2.1

Work with a partner for this activity.

With your partner, choose different values for the letters *m* and *p*.

Write three expressions that use *m* and *p*, similar to those in Question **6**, and work out the values of your expressions. You can make your expressions as easy or as difficult as you like but they must have whole number answers.

Write your expressions on a piece of paper, then swap your piece of paper with another pair of learners in your class.

Work out the values of each other's expressions. Swap back and mark each other's work.

Discuss any mistakes that have been made.

8 This is part of Dai's homework.

<u>Question</u>

Use a counter-example to show that the statement $2x^2 = (2x)^2$ is not true $(x \neq 0)$.

<u>Answer</u>

Let $x = 3$, so $2x^2 = 2 \times 3^2 = 2 \times 9 = 18$ and

$(2x)^2 = (2 \times 3)^2 = 6^2 = 36$

$18 \neq 36$, so $2x^2 \neq (2x)^2$.

Tip

A **counter-example** is just one example that shows a statement is not true.

Use a counter-example to show that these statements are not true $(x \neq 0, y \neq 0)$.

a $3x^2 = (3x)^2$ **b** $(-y)^4 = -y^4$ **c** $2(x + y) = 2x + y$

9 Work out the value of each expression.

a $4(x^2 - 1) + \frac{x^3}{4} + 12$ when $x = 2$

b $\frac{3y - 5}{2} + 2y^3 - \frac{21}{y}$ when $y = 3$

10 Show that $5a^2 - 9(b - a) + \frac{2}{b^5} + 7ab = \frac{-5a}{b} - 6a^3 - (ab)^4 + \frac{9}{b^2 - a^3}$ when $a = -2$ and $b = -1$.

Look back at the questions in this exercise.

- Which questions did you find easy to answer? Why?
- Which questions did you find difficult to answer? Why?
- Do you feel confident using the correct order of operations?
- Do you feel confident substituting negative numbers into expressions?
- What can you do to improve your skills in this topic?

Summary checklist

☐ I can use the correct order of operations in algebraic expressions.

2.2 Constructing expressions

In this section you will …

- use letters to represent numbers
- use the correct order of operations in algebraic expressions.

Key word

in terms of

In algebraic expressions, letters represent unknown numbers. You often need to construct algebraic expressions to help you solve problems. Suppose you want to work out the price of tickets for a day out. You might choose to let a represent the price of an adult's ticket and c represent the price of a child's ticket.

- You can write the total price for an adult's ticket and a child's ticket as $a + c$.
- You can write the difference between the price of an adult's ticket and a child's ticket as $a - c$.
- You can write the total price of tickets for 2 adults and 2 children as $2(a + c)$ or $2a + 2c$.

These expressions are written **in terms of** a and c.

Worked example 2.2

a Ahmad thinks of a number, n.

Write an expression, in terms of n, for the number Ahmad gets when he

i divides the number by 3, then subtracts 6

ii adds 3 to the number, then multiplies the result by 4

iii multiplies the number by itself, then halves the result

iv square roots the number then adds 5.

b The diagram shows a rectangle. Write an expression in terms of x for

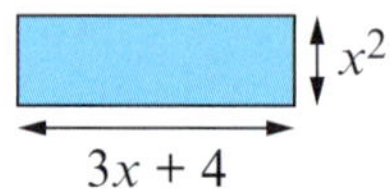

i the perimeter

ii the area.

Write each expression in its simplest form.

Answer

a i $\frac{n}{3} - 6$	Divide n by 3, then subtract 6. Write $n \div 3$ as $\frac{n}{3}$.
ii $4(n + 3)$	Add 3 to n, then multiply the result by 4. Write $n + 3$ inside brackets to show this must be done before multiplying by 4.
iii $\frac{n^2}{2}$	Multiply n by itself to give $n \times n$; write this as n^2. Then divide the result by 2. Write $n^2 \div 2$ as $\frac{n^2}{2}$.
iv $\sqrt{n} + 5$	Square root n. Then add 5.
b i $3x + 4 + 3x + 4 + x^2 + x^2$	Add together the lengths of the four sides to work out the perimeter.
$= 2x^2 + 6x + 8$	Simplify the expression by collecting like terms.
ii $x^2(3x + 4)$	Multiply the length by the width to work out the area.
$= 3x^3 + 4x^2$	Simplify the expression by multiplying out the bracket.

Exercise 2.2

1 Kara thinks of a number, n.

Write the correct expression from the cloud for the number Kara gets when she:

a adds five to the number

b multiplies the number by five, then subtracts five

c divides the number by five, then adds five

d adds five to the number, then multiplies by five

e subtracts five from the number, then divides by five

f subtracts the number from five.

$5 - n$ $\quad 5(n + 5)$

$5n - 5$ $\quad \frac{n-5}{5}$

$n + 5$ $\quad \frac{n}{5} + 5$

2 Luis thinks of a number, x.

Write an expression, in terms of x, for the number Luis gets when he:

- **a** multiplies the number by 7
- **b** subtracts the number from 20
- **c** multiplies the number by 2, then adds 9
- **d** divides the number by 6, then subtracts 4
- **e** multiplies the number by itself
- **f** divides 100 by the number
- **g** subtracts 7 from the number, then multiplies the result by 5
- **h** square roots the number
- **i** cubes the number
- **j** cube roots the number
- **k** multiplies the number by 3, squares the result, then adds 7
- **l** multiplies the number by 2, cubes the result, then subtracts 100.

> **Tip**
>
> Remember that you write the cube root like this $\sqrt[3]{}$

3 Write an expression for **i** the perimeter and **ii** the area of each rectangle.

Write each expression in its simplest form.

a

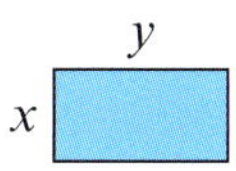

b

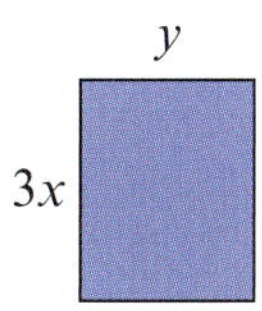

c

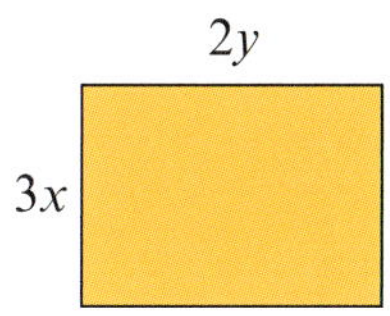

d

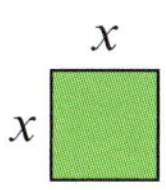

e

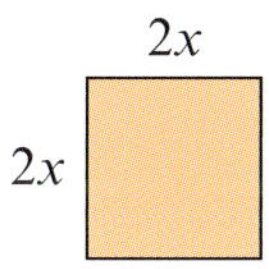

f

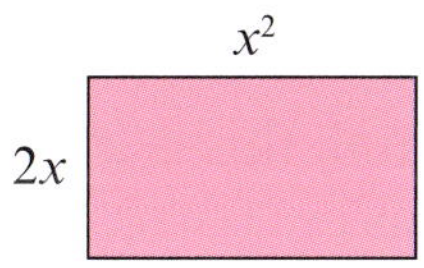

4 This is part of Mia's homework.

> Question
>
> Write an expression for the perimeter and area of this rectangle.
>
> Write each answer in its simplest form.
>
> 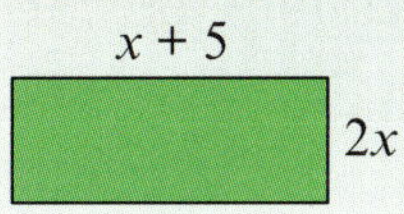
>
>
> Answer
>
> Perimeter $= x + 5 + 2x + x + 5 + 2x$
>
> $= 6x + 10$
>
> Area $= 2x(x + 5)$
>
> $= 2x^2 + 10x$

a Read what Sofia says.

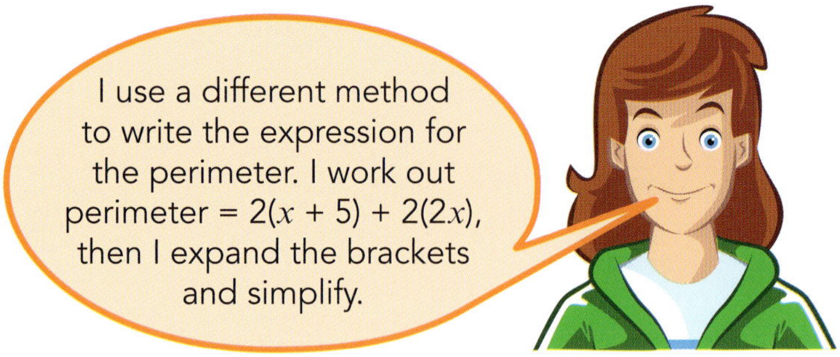

Show that Sofia's method will give the correct expression for the perimeter.

b Critique each method. Whose method do you prefer to use to write the expression for the perimeter? Explain why.

c When $x = 3$, copy and complete these workings:

length of rectangle $= x + 5 = 3 + 5 = \square$

width of rectangle $= 2x = 2 \times 3 = \square$

perimeter $= 2 \times$ length $+ 2 \times$ width $= 2 \times \square + 2 \times \square = \square$

area $=$ length $\times$ width $= \square \times \square = \square$

d When $x = 3$, copy and complete these workings:

perimeter $= 6x + 10 = 6 \times 3 + 10 = \square$

area $= 2x^2 + 10x = 2 \times 3^2 + 10 \times 3 = \square + \square = \square$

e What do you notice about your answers for the perimeter and area in parts **c** and **d**?

Do you think this is a good method to use to check your expressions are correct?

Explain your answer.

5 Write an expression for **i** the perimeter and **ii** the area of each rectangle.
Write each expression in its simplest form.

iii Then use the values given, and the method from Question **4**, to check your expressions are correct.

a

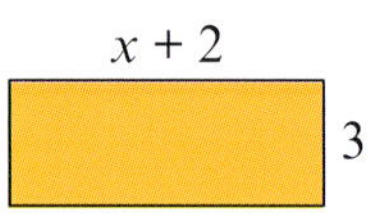

$x = 4$

b

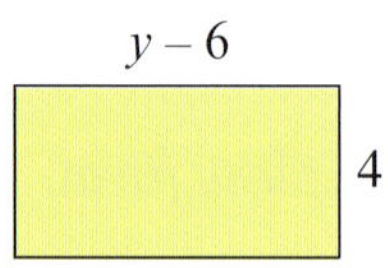

$y = 10$

c

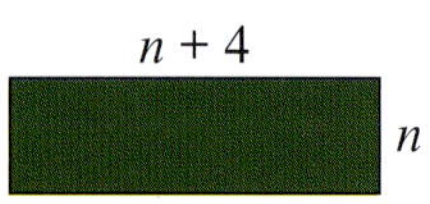

$n = 6$

d

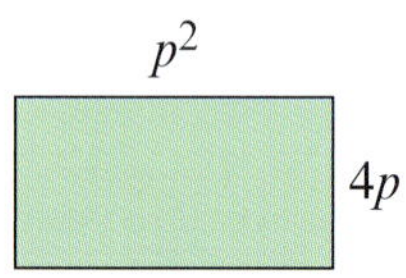

$p = 2$

Think like a mathematician

6 Work with a partner to answer these questions.

Alicia and Razi have rods of four different colours.

The blue rods have a length of $x + 1$.

The red rods have a length of $x + 2$.

The green rods have a length of $2x + 1$.

The yellow rods have a length of $3x$.

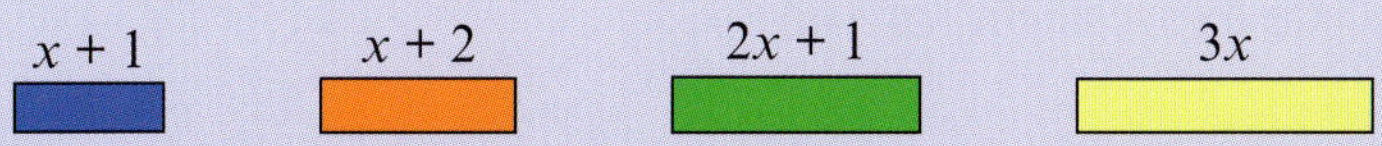

Alicia shows Razi that the total length of 3 red rods and 5 yellow rods is the same as 6 green rods and 2 yellow rods, like this.

$$\begin{aligned}3 \text{ red} + 5 \text{ yellow} &= 3(x + 2) + 5(3x)\\ &= 3x + 6 + 15x\\ &= 18x + 6\end{aligned}$$

$$\begin{aligned}6 \text{ green} + 2 \text{ yellow} &= 6(2x + 1) + 2(3x)\\ &= 12x + 6 + 6x\\ &= 18x + 6\end{aligned}$$

a Show that

i the total length of 2 red rods and 2 yellow rods is the same as 4 green rods

ii the total length of 3 red rods and 3 yellow rods is the same as 6 green rods

iii the total length of 4 red rods and 4 yellow rods is the same as 8 green rods.

b What do your answers to part **a** tell you about the connection between the number of red and yellow rods and the number of green rods?

c Show that

i the total length of 6 red rods and 2 yellow rods is the same as 12 blue rods

ii the total length of 9 red rods and 3 yellow rods is the same as 18 blue rods

iii the total length of 12 red rods and 4 yellow rods is the same as 24 blue rods.

d What do your answers to part **c** tell you about the connection between the number of red and yellow rods and the number of blue rods?

e Discuss your answers to parts **b** and **d** with other learners in your class.

7 The diagram shows a triangle.

The lengths of the sides of the triangle are written as expressions.

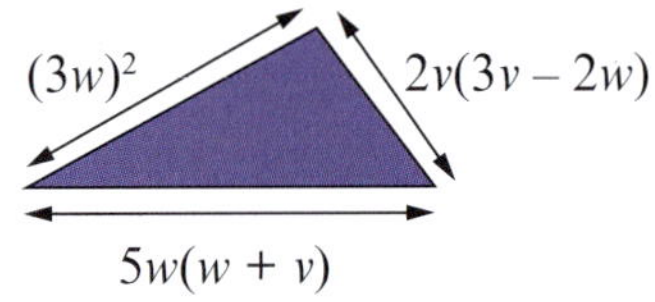

a Work out the lengths of the sides of the triangle when $w = 2$ and $v = 3$.

b Use your answers to part **a** to work out the perimeter of the triangle when $w = 2$ and $v = 3$.

c Write an expression for the perimeter of the triangle.

Show that the expression can be simplified to $14w^2 + vw + 6v^2$.

d Substitute $w = 2$ and $v = 3$ into the expression for the perimeter from part **c**.

Check that your answers to parts **b** and **d** are the same.

Think like a mathematician

8 Work with a partner to answer this question.

The diagram shows a quadrilateral.

The lengths of the sides of the quadrilateral are written as expressions.

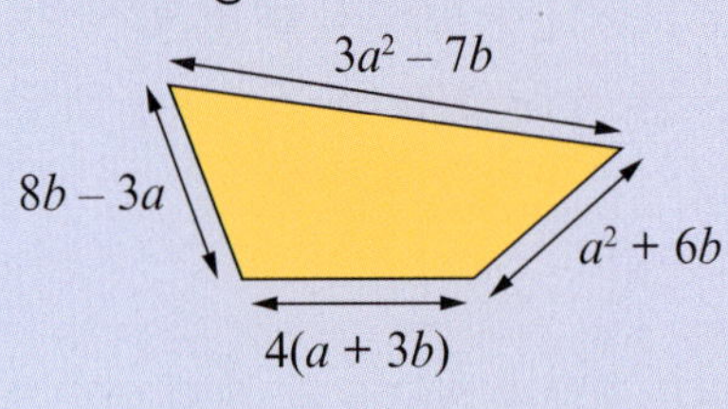

a Work out the lengths of the sides of the quadrilateral when $a = -5$ and $b = 2$.

b Use your answers to part **a** to work out the perimeter of the quadrilateral when $a = -5$ and $b = 2$.

c Write an expression for the perimeter of the quadrilateral.

Show that the expression can be simplified to $a + 4a^2 + 19b$.

d Use the expression in part **c** to work out the perimeter of the quadrilateral when $a = -5$ and $b = 2$.

Are your answers to parts **b** and **d** the same? If not, check your working.

e Work out the perimeter of the quadrilateral when $a = 4$ and $b = -3$.

f Is your answer to part **e** a valid measurement for the perimeter? Explain your answer.

Discuss your answer with other learners in your class.

9 **a** Write an expression for the perimeter of this rectangle.

b Show that the expression can be simplified to $2(2x^2 + 9)$.

c Read what Arun says.

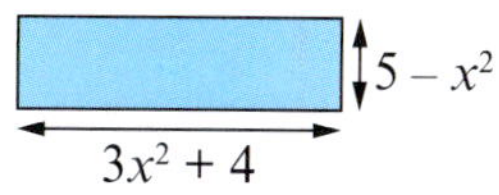

Tip

You might need to remind yourself how to factorise expressions.

Is Arun correct? Explain your answer. Show your working.

10 **a** A square has an area of $25\,\text{cm}^2$. Show that the perimeter of the square is 20 cm.

b A square has an area of $49\,\text{cm}^2$. Work out the perimeter of the square.

c A square has an area of $x\,\text{cm}^2$. Write an expression for the perimeter of the square.

Use your working for parts **a** and **b** to help you.

11 **a** A cube has side length x cm. Write an expression for the volume of the cube.

b A cube has a volume of $y\,\text{cm}^3$. Write an expression for the side length of the cube.

Summary checklist

- [ ] I can use letters to represent numbers.
- [ ] I can use the correct order of operations in algebraic expressions.

2.3 Expressions and indices

In this section you will …

- use the laws of indices in algebraic expressions.

You already know how to use the laws of indices for multiplication and division of numbers. You can also use these rules with algebraic expressions.

- When you **multiply** powers of the same variable, you **add** the indices. $x^a \times x^b = x^{a+b}$
- When you **divide** powers of the same variable, you **subtract** the indices. $x^a \div x^b = x^{a-b}$
- When you simplify the power of a power, you **multiply** the indices. $(x^a)^b = x^{a \times b}$

Worked example 2.3

Simplify each expression.

a $x^2 \times x^3$ **b** $y^7 \div y^4$ **c** $(z^3)^4$ **d** $6w^4 + 2w^4$

Answer

a $x^2 \times x^3 = x^{2+3}$
$= x^5$

To multiply, add the indices.
$2 + 3 = 5$, so the answer is x^5.

b $y^7 \div y^4 = y^{7-4}$
$= y^3$

To divide, subtract the indices.
$7 - 4 = 3$, so the answer is y^3.

c $(z^3)^4 = z^{3\times4}$
$= z^{12}$

To simplify the power of a power, multiply the indices.
$3 \times 4 = 12$, so the answer is z^{12}.

d $6w^4 + 2w^4 = 8w^4$

$6w^4$ and $2w^4$ are like terms, so add 6 and 2 together.
The index stays the same.

Exercise 2.3

1 Copy and complete.

a $x^4 \times x^5 = x^{4+5}$
$= x^{\square}$

b $y^2 \times y^4 = y^{2+4}$
$= y^{\square}$

c $u^8 \div u^6 = u^{8-6}$
$= u^{\square}$

d $w^5 \div w = w^{5-1}$
$= w^{\square}$

e $(g^3)^2 = g^{3\times2}$
$= g^{\square}$

f $(h^5)^{12} = h^{5\times12}$
$= h^{\square}$

g $5m^3 + 3m^3 = \square m^3$

h $8n^2 - n^2 = \square n^2$

2 Simplify each expression.

a $m^8 \times m^6$ **b** $n^9 \times n^3$ **c** $p^6 \times p$ **d** $q^9 \div q^4$

e $r^6 \div r^3$ **f** $t^7 \div t^2$ **g** $(x^7)^3$ **h** $(y^2)^5$

i $(z^3)^4$ **j** $3t^7 + 2t^7$ **k** $8g^2 - 3g^2$ **l** $3h^9 + h^9 - 5h^9$

Think like a mathematician

3 Arun, Sofia and Zara simplify the expression $x^2 \div x^2$.
Read what they say.

- **a** What do you think?
  Do you agree with Arun, Sofia, Zara or none of them?
- **b** Discuss your answer with other learners in the class.
- **c** Following your discussions, write down the correct simplified expression for $x^2 \div x^2$.
- **d** What can you say about the answers when you simplify these expressions?

  $x^5 \div x^5$ $\quad y^4 \div y^4$ $\quad a^b \div a^b$ $\quad c^d \div c^d$

  Explain your answer.

Tip

You could try different values for x and work out numerical answers first.

4 This is part of Kai's homework.
Use Kai's method to simplify these expressions:

- **a** $3x^2 \times 2x^3$
- **b** $4y^4 \times 3y^5$
- **c** $6z^2 \times 5z^5$
- **d** $2m^4 \times 2m^3$
- **e** $4n^6 \times n^7$
- **f** $p^2 \times 8p$

Question

Simplify the expression $6x^2 \times 3x^4$.

Answer

$$6x^2 \times 3x^4 = 6 \times x^2 \times 3 \times x^4$$
$$= 6 \times 3 \times x^2 \times x^4$$
$$= 18 \times x^{2+4}$$
$$= 18x^6$$

Think like a mathematician

5 Harsha and Sasha simplify the expression $6x^5 \div 3x^2$ as shown.

Harsha's method
$6x^5 \div 3x^2$
$6 \div 3 = 2$ and $x^5 \div x^2 = x^{5-2} = x^3$
So the answer is $2x^3$

Sasha's method
$\frac{{}^2\not{6}x^5}{{}^1\not{3}x^2} = 2x^{5-2} = 2x^3$
So the answer is $2x^3$

a Critique Harsha's and Sasha's methods. Whose method do you prefer? Why? Can you think of a better method to use?

b Do you prefer to write a division expression using a division sign ($6x^5 \div 3x^2$) or as a fraction $\left(\frac{6x^5}{3x^2}\right)$? Why?

c Discuss your answers to parts **a** and **b** with other learners in your class.
Discuss how you could simplify expressions such as $4x^5 \div 6x^3$, $12y^7 \div 8y^6$ and $6z^9 \div 36z^4$.
For these expressions, would Harsha's method or Sasha's method be easier to use?

6 Simplify each expression.

a $6q^{10} \div 2q^6$ **b** $9r^9 \div 3r^5$ **c** $15t^7 \div 5t$

d $\frac{8u^7}{4u^2}$ **e** $\frac{2v^6}{v^2}$ **f** $\frac{5w^7}{w^6}$

7 Which answer is correct, **A**, **B**, **C** or **D**?

		A	B	C	D
a	Simplify $\frac{6x^6}{12x^3}$	$2x^2$	$2x^3$	$\frac{1}{2}x^2$	$\frac{1}{2}x^3$
b	Simplify $\frac{4y^8}{10y^2}$	$\frac{2}{5}y^6$	$\frac{2}{5}y^4$	$2\frac{1}{2}y^6$	$2\frac{1}{2}y^4$
c	Simplify $\frac{25k^3}{15k^2}$	$\frac{3}{5}k$	$\frac{3}{5}k^{1.5}$	$\frac{5}{3}k$	$\frac{5}{3}k^{1.5}$
d	Simplify $\frac{20m^6}{6m^6}$	$3\frac{1}{3}m$	$3\frac{1}{3}$	$\frac{3}{10}m$	$\frac{3}{10}$

8 Marcus and Arun simplify the expression $(3x^2)^3$. Read what they say.

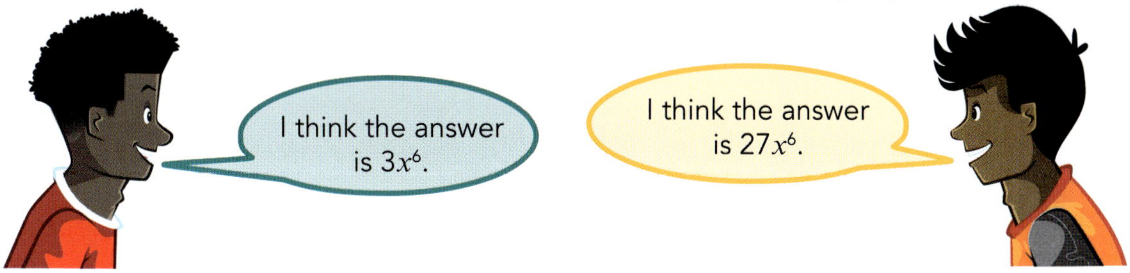

a Who is correct, Marcus or Arun? Explain why.

b Simplify these expressions.

i $(4x^5)^2$ ii $(5y^4)^3$ iii $(2z^7)^4$

Activity 2.3

a Make a copy of this spider diagram.

b In each empty circle, write an expression that simplifies to the expression in the centre circle.

Use expressions similar to those in questions **4**, **6** and **8**.

c Swap your spider diagram with a partner's diagram and mark each other's work.

Discuss any mistakes that have been made.

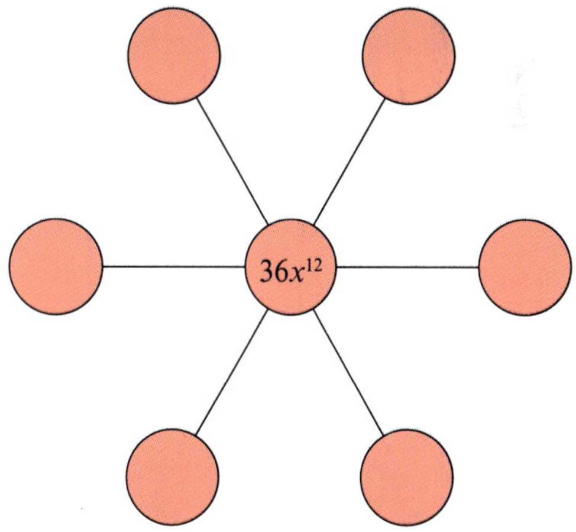

9 Simplify these expressions.

Write your answers using a negative power and a fraction.

Part **a** has been done for you.

a $q^4 \div q^7 = q^{4-7} = q^{-3} = \frac{1}{q^3}$ b $r^3 \div r^5$

c $t^7 \div t^{12}$ d $v^6 \div v^7$

Tip

Remember the rules for negative indices:

$2^{-1} = \frac{1}{2^1}$, $2^{-2} = \frac{1}{2^2}$, $2^{-3} = \frac{1}{2^3}$, etc.

10 Here are six rectangular cards and seven oval cards.

The expressions on the rectangular cards have been simplified to give the expressions on the oval cards.

A $5y^6 \div 10y^8$ B $3y^2 \div 9y^7$ C $4y^4 \div 6y^8$

D $\frac{9y^4}{12y^7}$ E $\frac{15y^2}{10y^6}$ F $\frac{15y}{12y^3}$

i $\frac{2}{3y^4}$ ii $\frac{1}{6y^7}$ iii $\frac{1}{2y^2}$ iv $\frac{1}{3y^5}$

v $\frac{5}{4y^2}$ vi $\frac{3}{2y^4}$ vii $\frac{3}{4y^3}$

a Match each rectangular card with the correct oval card.

b There is one oval card left. Write an expression that simplifies to give the expression on this card.

In this section, you have used the rules for indices in algebraic expressions. In Unit 1, you used the rules for indices with numbers. Do you find it easier to use the rules for indices with expressions or with numbers, or is there no difference? Why?

Summary checklist

☐ I can use the laws of indices in algebraic expressions.

2.4 Expanding the product of two linear expressions

In this section you will …

- expand two brackets.

Key words

brackets

difference of two squares

expand

perfect square

When you multiply together two expressions in **brackets**, you must multiply each term in the first pair of brackets by each term in the second pair of brackets.

Worked example 2.4

Expand and simplify these expressions.

a $(x + 2)(x + 3)$ **b** $(y + 8)(y - 4)$

Answer

a $(x + 2)(x + 3)$

First, multiply the x in the first brackets by the x in the second brackets to give x^2.

Then, multiply the x in the first brackets by the 3 in the second brackets to give $3x$.

Then, multiply the 2 in the first brackets by the x in the second brackets to give $2x$.

Finally, multiply the 2 in the first brackets by the 3 in the second brackets to give 6.

$= x^2 + 3x + 2x + 6$ Write each term as you work it out.

$= x^2 + 5x + 6$ Collect like terms, $3x + 2x = 5x$, to simplify your answer.

b $(y + 8)(y - 4)$

First, multiply the y in the first brackets by the y in the second brackets to give y^2.

Then, multiply the y in the first brackets by the -4 in the second brackets to give $-4y$.

Then, multiply the 8 in the first brackets by the y in the second brackets to give $8y$.

Finally, multiply the 8 in the first brackets by the -4 in the second brackets to give -32.

$= y^2 - 4y + 8y - 32$ Write each term as you work it out.

$= y^2 + 4y - 32$ Collect like terms, $-4y + 8y = 4y$, to simplify your answer.

Exercise 2.4

1 Copy and complete these multiplications.

a $(x + 4)(x + 1) = x^2 + 1x + \square x + \square$
$= x^2 + \square x + \square$

b $(x - 3)(x + 6) = x^2 + 6x - \square x - \square$
$= x^2 + \square x - \square$

c $(x + 2)(x - 8) = x^2 - \square x + \square x - \square$
$= x^2 - \square x - \square$

d $(x - 4)(x - 1) = x^2 - \square x - \square x + \square$
$= x^2 - \square x + \square$

2 Expand and simplify.

a $(x + 3)(x + 7)$ b $(x + 1)(x + 10)$
c $(x + 5)(x - 3)$ d $(x - 4)(x + 8)$
e $(x - 7)(x - 2)$ f $(x - 12)(x - 2)$

Think like a mathematician

3 Sofia and Zara discuss the different methods they use to expand two brackets. Read what they say.

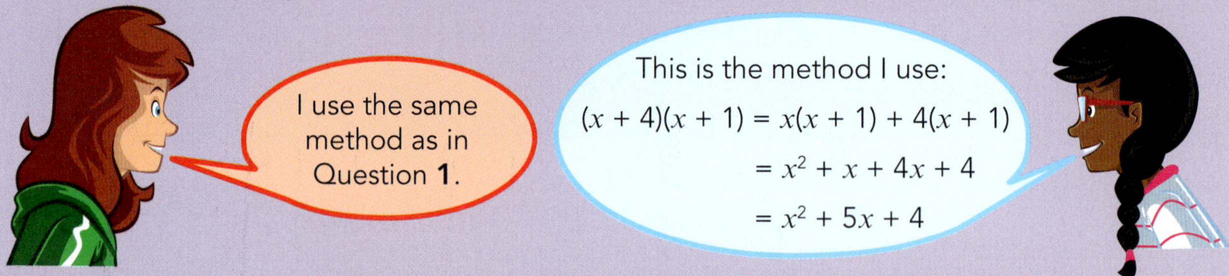

a Critique Zara's method. Do you prefer Zara's method or Sofia's method? Why?
b Can you think of another method you can use to expand two brackets?
c Discuss your answers to parts **a** and **b** with other learners in your class.

4 Expand and simplify these expressions. Use your favourite method.

a $(y + 2)(y + 4)$ b $(z + 6)(z + 8)$
c $(m + 4)(m - 3)$ d $(a - 9)(a + 2)$
e $(p - 6)(p - 5)$ f $(n - 10)(n - 20)$

Think like a mathematician

5 Work with a partner to answer this question.

a Look at this expansion. $(x + 5)(x + 4) = x^2 + 5x + 4x + 20 = x^2 + 9x + 20$
How would the expansion change if the red + sign changed to − ?

b Here is the expansion again. $(x + 5)(x + 4) = x^2 + 5x + 4x + 20 = x^2 + 9x + 20$
How would the expansion change if the red + sign changed to − ?

c Here is the expansion again. $(x + 5)(x + 4) = x^2 + 5x + 4x + 20 = x^2 + 9x + 20$
How would the expansion change if both of the + signs changed to − signs?

d Write down the missing signs (+ or −) in these expansions.
In each expression, the number represented by A **is greater than** the number represented by B. C is the **sum** of A and B in each equation, and D is the **product** of A and B in each equation.

i $(x + \text{A})(x + \text{B}) = x^2 \square \text{C}x \square \text{D}$
ii $(x + \text{A})(x - \text{B}) = x^2 \square \text{C}x \square \text{D}$
iii $(x - \text{A})(x + \text{B}) = x^2 \square \text{C}x \square \text{D}$
iv $(x - \text{A})(x - \text{B}) = x^2 \square \text{C}x \square \text{D}$

Discuss your answers to these questions with other learners in your class.

6 Which is the correct expansion of the expression, **A**, **B** or **C**?
Use what you have learned from Question **5** to help you.

a	$(w + 9)(w + 3) =$	A	$w^2 + 12w - 27$	B	$w^2 - 12w + 27$	C	$w^2 + 12w + 27$
b	$(x + 7)(x - 5) =$	A	$x^2 + 2x - 35$	B	$x^2 - 2x + 35$	C	$x^2 - 2x - 35$
c	$(y - 8)(y + 6) =$	A	$y^2 - 2y + 48$	B	$y^2 - 2y - 48$	C	$y^2 + 2y - 48$
d	$(z - 4)(z - 5) =$	A	$z^2 - 9z + 20$	B	$z^2 - 9z - 20$	C	$z^2 + 9z + 20$

7 Copy and complete each expansion.

a $(x + 2)^2 = (x + 2)(x + 2)$
$= x^2 + 2x + \square x + \square$
$= x^2 + \square x + \square$

b $(x - 3)^2 = (x - 3)(x - 3)$
$= x^2 - 3x - \square x + \square$
$= x^2 - \square x + \square$

8 a Expand and simplify each expression.

i $(y + 5)^2$ ii $(z + 1)^2$ iii $(m + 8)^2$
iv $(a - 2)^2$ v $(p - 4)^2$ vi $(n - 9)^2$

b Look carefully at your answers to part **a**.
Use these answers to complete the general expansion: $(x + a)^2 = x^2 + \square x + \square$

Tip

Use the same method as in Question 7.

Tip

This type of expansion is called a perfect square.

9 **a** Show that when you expand and simplify $(x + 3)(x - 3)$ you will have an expression with only two terms.

b Expand and simplify these expressions.

i $(x + 2)(x - 2)$ **ii** $(x - 5)(x + 5)$ **iii** $(x + 7)(x - 7)$

c What do you notice about your answers in part **b**?

d Use your answer to part **c** to write the simplified expansion of $(x - 10)(x + 10)$.

e Look carefully at your answers to this question so far.

Use these answers to complete the general expansion: $(x + a)(x - a) = x^2 - \square$

> **Tip**
>
> This type of expansion is called the difference of two squares.

Activity 2.4

Work with a partner on this activity.

Here is part of a number grid.

Look at the red block of four squares, and follow these steps.

1	2	3	4	5
6	7	8	9	10
11	12	13	14	15
16	17	18	19	20
21	22	23	24	25
26	27	28	29	30
31	32	33	34	35
36	37	38	39	40

① Multiply the number in the bottom left square by the number in the top right square: $9 \times 5 = 45$

② Multiply the number in the top left square by the number in the bottom right square: $4 \times 10 = 40$

③ Subtract the second answer from the first: $45 - 40 = 5$

a Repeat these three steps with the blue block of four squares.

b Repeat these three steps with the green block of four squares.

c What do you notice about your answers to parts **a** and **b**?

d Here is a general block of four squares from the same number grid.

n	

Copy the block of four squares and write an expression, in terms of n, in each of the other squares to represent the missing numbers.

e Repeat the three steps with the block of four squares in part **d**.

What do you notice about your answer?

Now you have completed this activity, compare your answers with other learners in your class. Discuss any differences in your answers and explain any mistakes that have been made.

Summary checklist

☐ I can expand two brackets.

2.5 Simplifying algebraic fractions

In this section you will …

- simplify algebraic fractions.

Key word

algebraic fraction

An **algebraic fraction** is a fraction that contains an unknown variable, or letter. For example, $\frac{x}{4}$, $\frac{y}{2}$, $\frac{8}{z}$, $\frac{2a}{3}$ and $\frac{5}{4b}$ are all algebraic fractions.

You can write the fraction $\frac{x}{4}$ (say 'x over 4') as $\frac{1}{4}x$ (say 'one-quarter of x').

You can write the fraction $\frac{2a}{3}$ (say '$2a$ over 3') as $\frac{2}{3}a$ (say 'two-thirds of a').

To add and subtract algebraic fractions, use the same method as for normal fractions.

- If the denominators are the same, simply add or subtract the numerators.
- If the denominators are different, write the fractions as equivalent fractions with the same denominator, then add or subtract the numerators.
- Cancel your answer to its simplest form.

Worked example 2.5

Simplify these expressions.

a $\frac{x}{6} + \frac{x}{6}$ **b** $\frac{4}{y} - \frac{5}{2y}$ **c** $\frac{n}{5} + \frac{2}{3p}$

Answer

a $\frac{x}{6} + \frac{x}{6} = \frac{x + x}{6}$ — The denominators are the same, so add the numerators.

$= \frac{2x}{6}$ — Cancel the fraction to its simplest form.

$= \frac{x}{3}$ — Write $\frac{1x}{3}$ as $\frac{x}{3}$

b $\frac{4}{y} - \frac{5}{2y} = \frac{8}{2y} - \frac{5}{2y}$ — The denominators are different, so change $\frac{4}{y}$ to $\frac{8}{2y}$

$= \frac{8 - 5}{2y}$ — The denominators are now the same, so subtract the numerators.

$= \frac{3}{2y}$ — $\frac{3}{2y}$ cannot be simplified, so leave it as it is.

Continued

c $\frac{n}{5}+\frac{2}{3p}=\frac{n\times 3p}{5\times 3p}+\frac{2\times 5}{3p\times 5}$

Find equivalent fractions which have a common denominator.

$=\frac{3np}{15p}+\frac{10}{15p}$

The denominators are now the same, so add the numerators.

$=\frac{3np+10}{15p}$

$\frac{3np+10}{15p}$ cannot be simplified, so leave it as it is.

Exercise 2.5

Throughout this exercise, give each answer as a fraction in its simplest form.

1 Simplify these expressions.

a $\frac{x}{5}+\frac{x}{5}$ b $\frac{x}{7}+\frac{3x}{7}$ c $\frac{3}{x}+\frac{5}{x}$

d $\frac{2x}{3}+\frac{x}{3}$ e $\frac{7x}{15}-\frac{x}{15}$ f $\frac{11}{x}-\frac{7}{x}$

2 Simplify these expressions. The first two have been started for you.

a $\frac{2y}{5}+\frac{3y}{10}=\frac{\square y}{10}+\frac{3y}{10}=\frac{\square y}{10}$ b $\frac{2}{5y}-\frac{1}{25y}=\frac{\square}{25y}-\frac{1}{25y}=\frac{\square}{25y}$ c $\frac{y}{2}+\frac{y}{4}$

d $\frac{y}{2}-\frac{y}{8}$ e $\frac{2}{3y}+\frac{5}{9y}$ f $\frac{4y}{7}-\frac{5y}{14}$

3 Copy and complete these additions and subtractions.

a $\frac{a}{2}+\frac{a}{5}=\frac{5a}{10}+\frac{\square a}{10}$
$=\frac{5a+\square a}{10}$
$=\frac{\square a}{10}$

b $\frac{b}{4}+\frac{b}{3}=\frac{3b}{12}+\frac{\square b}{12}$
$=\frac{3b+\square b}{12}$
$=\frac{\square b}{12}$

c $\frac{5}{7c}+\frac{2}{5c}=\frac{25}{35c}+\frac{\square}{35c}$
$=\frac{25+\square}{35c}$
$=\frac{\square}{35c}$

d $\frac{5d}{6}-\frac{3d}{5}=\frac{\square d}{30}-\frac{\square d}{30}$
$=\frac{\square d-\square d}{30}$
$=\frac{\square d}{30}$

e $\frac{7e}{8}-\frac{2e}{3}=\frac{\square e}{24}-\frac{\square e}{24}$
$=\frac{\square e-\square e}{24}$
$=\frac{\square e}{24}$

f $\frac{9}{10f}-\frac{3}{4f}=\frac{\square}{20f}-\frac{\square}{20f}$
$=\frac{\square-\square}{20f}$
$=\frac{\square}{20f}$

4 Here are some algebraic fraction cards.
The red cards are question cards. The blue cards are answer cards.

A	$\frac{9x}{10} - \frac{13x}{20}$	B	$\frac{x}{6} + \frac{x}{3}$	C	$\frac{2x}{7} + \frac{3x}{14}$	D	$\frac{11x}{18} - \frac{13x}{36}$
E	$\frac{7x}{9} - \frac{5x}{18}$	F	$\frac{x}{12} + \frac{x}{6}$	G	$\frac{x}{30} + \frac{3x}{10}$		
i	$\frac{x}{4}$	ii	$\frac{x}{2}$				

a Which question cards match answer card **i**? Show your working.
b Which question cards match answer card **ii**? Show your working.
c Which question card does not match either of the answer cards?
Work out the answer to this card.

Think like a mathematician

5 Work with a partner to answer this question.
This is part of Su-Lin's homework.

Question
Simplify $\frac{x}{2} + \frac{y}{6}$

Answer
$$\frac{x}{2} + \frac{y}{6} = \frac{3x}{6} + \frac{y}{6} = \frac{3x + y}{6} = \frac{{}^1\cancel{3}x + y}{{}^2\cancel{6}} = \frac{x + y}{2}$$

a Substitute $x = 1$ and $y = 2$ into $\frac{x}{2} + \frac{y}{6}$ and work out the answer.
b Substitute $x = 1$ and $y = 2$ into $\frac{x+y}{2}$ and work out the answer.
c Use your answers to parts **a** and **b** to show that Su-Lin's answer is incorrect.
d Look back at Su-Lin's solution and explain the mistake she has made.
Write the correct answer.
e Discuss your answers to parts **a** to **d** with other learners in your class.
f Use what you have learned to decide if these simplified fractions are correct or incorrect.
If they are incorrect, work out the correct answer.

i $\frac{2x}{3} + \frac{y}{9} = \frac{6x}{9} + \frac{y}{9} = \frac{6x + y}{9}$

ii $\frac{2x}{5} - \frac{y}{10} = \frac{4x}{10} - \frac{y}{10} = \frac{{}^2\cancel{4}x - y}{{}^5\cancel{10}} = \frac{2x - y}{5}$

iii $\frac{11x}{14} - \frac{2}{7} = \frac{11x}{14} - \frac{4}{14} = \frac{11x - 4}{14}$

iv $\frac{9x}{20} - \frac{2}{5} = \frac{9x}{20} - \frac{8}{20} = \frac{9x - {}^2\cancel{8}}{{}^5\cancel{20}} = \frac{9x - 2}{5}$

6 **a** Simplify these expressions.

i $\frac{a}{5}+\frac{b}{5}$ **ii** $\frac{5a}{12}+\frac{3b}{4}$ **iii** $\frac{2a}{15}+\frac{3}{5}$

iv $\frac{a}{4}+\frac{3}{b}$ **v** $\frac{3a}{10}+\frac{4}{b}$ **vi** $\frac{4a}{9}+\frac{3}{2b}$

b For each expression in part **a**, choose values for a and b.

Substitute your values into the questions and work out the numerical answers.

Substitute your values into your algebraic answer and work out the numerical answers.

Check your numerical answers match, to show your algebraic expressions are correct.

> **Tip**
>
> **iv** $\frac{a}{4}+\frac{3}{b}$
>
> $=\frac{a\times b}{4\times b}+\frac{3\times 4}{b\times 4}=\dots$

Activity 2.5

Work with a partner for this activity.

Here are eight fractions cards labelled A to H.

A	$\frac{3x}{5}$	B	$\frac{4y}{3}$	C	$\frac{7z}{8}$	D	$\frac{m}{8}$
E	$\frac{7k}{12}$	F	$\frac{4p}{9}$	G	$\frac{1}{2}$	H	$\frac{5h}{4}$

Take it in turns to ask your partner to add or subtract two of the cards.

For example, you could say 'C + F' or 'H – B'. You can choose.

Work out the answer yourself and mark your partner's work.

Discuss any mistakes that have been made. Do this twice each.

Think like a mathematician

7 Work with a partner to answer this question.

This is part of Iain's homework.

> Question
>
> Simplify $\frac{6x+2}{2}$
>
> Answer
>
> $\frac{6x+2}{2}=\frac{2(3x+1)}{2}=\frac{\cancel{2}^{1}(3x+1)}{\cancel{2}^{1}}=3x+1$

Continued

a Substitute $x = 3$ into $\frac{6x+2}{2}$ and work out the answer.

b Substitute $x = 3$ into $3x + 1$ and work out the answer.

c Use your answers to parts **a** and **b** to show that Iain's answer is correct.

d Look back at Iain's solution and explain why his method works.

e Read what Arun says:

Show that when $x = 3$, Arun's answer is incorrect.
Explain why his method is incorrect.

f Discuss your answers to parts **a** to **e** with other learners in your class.
How will you convince them about your findings if your answers are different?

8 Simplify these expressions. Make sure you factorise the numerator before you cancel with the denominator.

a $\frac{6x+3}{3}$ **b** $\frac{5x+10}{5}$ **c** $\frac{6x-9}{3}$ **d** $\frac{8x-20}{4}$

Tip

In Question **9**, simplify each fraction separately, then add the answers together.

9 Show that $\frac{6x-4}{2} + \frac{20x+25}{5}$ simplifies to $7x + 3$.

10 This is how Shania and Taylor simplify the fraction $\frac{6x+18}{3}$.

Shania

Fully factorise $6x + 18 = 6(x + 3)$

$$\frac{6x+18}{3} = \frac{6(x+3)}{3}$$
$$= \frac{{}^{2}\cancel{6}(x+3)}{{}^{1}\cancel{3}}$$
$$= 2(x+3)$$

Taylor

The denominator is 3, so take out a factor of 3: $6x + 18 = 3(2x + 6)$

$$\frac{6x+18}{3} = \frac{3(2x+6)}{3}$$
$$= \frac{{}^{1}\cancel{3}(2x+6)}{{}^{1}\cancel{3}}$$
$$= 2x+6$$

a Show that Shania's answer is equivalent to Taylor's answer.

b Critique both methods. Whose method do you prefer, Shania's or Taylor's? Explain why.

c Simplify these fractions. Use your favourite method.

i $\frac{10x + 30}{5}$ **ii** $\frac{12x + 24}{6}$ **iii** $\frac{16x - 48}{4}$ **iv** $\frac{6 - 18x}{2}$

While answering the questions in this exercise, you have used skills you have learned before.

Make a list of the skills you have used while simplifying these algebraic fractions (for example, one skill you have used is factorising expressions).

If you are not sure of the other skills, look back through the questions in the exercise.

Summary checklist

☐ I can simplify algebraic fractions.

2.6 Deriving and using formulae

In this section you will ...

- write and use formulae
- change the subject of a formula.

Key words

changing the subject

subject of a formula

A formula is a mathematical rule that shows the relationship between two or more variables. For example, a formula that is often used in physics is: $v = u + at$

In this formula, v is the **subject of the formula**. It is written on its own, on one side of the equation.

Depending on the information you are given and the variable you want to find, you might need to rearrange the formula. This is called **changing the subject** of the formula. For example, if you know the values of v, a and t in the formula $v = u + at$ and you want to work out the value of u, you would rearrange the equation as shown.

$$v = u + at$$
$$u + at = v$$
$$u = v - at$$

This makes u the subject of the formula.

Tip

You usually write the subject of the formula (in this example, v) on the left-hand side of the equation.

If you know the values of v, u and a in the formula $v = u + at$ and you want to work out the value of t, you would rearrange the equation as shown.

This makes t the subject of the formula.

$$v = u + at$$
$$u + at = v$$
$$at = v - u$$
$$t = \frac{v - u}{a}$$

Worked example 2.6

a Each day, Li is paid a fixed wage W dollars, and an extra R dollars per hour he works. Write a formula for the total pay, P dollars, Li earns when he works H hours one day.

b Use the formula in part **a** to work out P when $W = 60$, $H = 8\frac{1}{4}$ and $R = 4.80$.

c Rearrange the formula in part **a** to make H the subject.

d Use your answer to part **c** to work out H when $P = 91$, $W = 65$ and $R = 5.20$.

Answer

a $P = W + HR$

pay (P) = fixed wage (W) + number of hours (H) × rate of pay (R)

Remember to write $H \times R$ as HR.

b $P = 60 + 8.25 \times 4.80$

$= \$99.60$

Substitute $W = 60$, $H = 8.25$ and $R = 4.80$ into the formula.

Work out the answer and remember the units ($).

c $P - W = HR$

To make H the subject, use inverse operations.

Start by subtracting W from P.

$\frac{P - W}{R} = H$

Now divide by R.

$H = \frac{P - W}{R}$

Now rewrite the formula with H as the subject on the left-hand side.

d $H = \frac{91 - 65}{5.20}$

Substitute $P = 91$, $W = 65$ and $R = 5.20$ into the formula.

$= 5$ hours

Work out the answer and remember the units (hours).

Exercise 2.6

1 a Write a formula for the number of seconds, S, in any number of minutes, M.

 b Use your formula in part **a** to work out S when $M = 15$.

 c Rearrange your formula in part **a** to make M the subject.

 d Use your formula in part **c** to work out M when $S = 1350$.

2 a Use the formula $F = ma$ to work out the value of

 i F when $m = 12$ and $a = 5$

 ii F when $m = 26$ and $a = -3$.

 b Rearrange the formula $F = ma$ to make m the subject.
 Work out the value of m when $F = 30$ and $a = 2.5$.

 c Rearrange the formula $F = ma$ to make a the subject.
 Work out the value of a when $F = -14$ and $m = 8$.

Think like a mathematician

3 Work with a partner to answer these questions.

 a Copy and complete this table showing the number of faces, edges and vertices of 3D shapes.

3D shape	Number of faces	Number of vertices	Number of edges
cube			
cuboid			
triangular prism			
triangular-based pyramid			
square-based pyramid			

 b Write a formula that connects the number of faces (F), vertices (V) and edges (E).
 Check your formula works for the shapes in the table.

 c Make V the subject of your formula.
 Work out V when

 i $E = 10$ and $F = 6$ ii $E = 12$ and $F = 7$.

Tip

Make a sketch of each shape to help you.

Tip

You studied Euler's formula in Stage 8.

Continued

d Can you identify the shapes in parts **ci** and **cii**?

e Make F the subject of your formula.
Work out F when $E = 5$ and $V = 7$.
What does your value of F tell you?

f Compare and discuss your answers to parts **a** to **e** with other pairs in your class.

Tip

Compare your answers to parts **ci** and **cii** with the shapes in the last two rows of the table in part **a**.

4 Amy is x years old. Ben is 2 years **older than** Amy.
Alice is six years **younger than** Amy.

a Write an expression for Ben's age and Alice's age in terms of x.

b Write a formula for the total age, T, of Amy, Ben and Alice.

c Use your formula in part **b** to work out T when $x = 19$.

d Rearrange your formula in part **b** to make x the subject.

e Use your formula in part **d** to work out x when $T = 62$.

5 Use the formula $v = u + at$ to work out the value of

a v when $u = 7$, $a = 10$, $t = 8$

b v when $u = 0$, $a = 5$, $t = 25$

c u when $v = 75$, $a = 4$, $t = 12$

d u when $v = 97$, $a = 6$, $t = 8.5$

e t when $v = 80$, $u = 20$, $a = 6$

f a when $v = 72$, $u = 34$, $t = 19$.

Tip

In parts **c** to **f** start by changing the subject of the formula.

6 Adrian buys and sells paintings.
He uses the formula shown to work out the percentage profit he makes.

$$\text{Percentage profit} = \frac{\text{selling price} - \text{cost price}}{\text{cost price}} \times 100$$

Work out Adrian's percentage profit on each of these paintings.

a Cost price \$250, selling price \$300

b Cost price \$120, selling price \$192

c Cost price \$480, selling price \$1080

7 In some countries, the mass of a person is measured in stones (S) and pounds (P).

The formula to convert a mass from stones and pounds to kilograms is shown.

$K = \frac{5(14S + P)}{11}$ where: K is the number of kilograms
S is the number of stones
P is the number of pounds.

Work out the mass, in kilograms, of a person with a mass of

a 10 stones and 3 pounds b 7 stones and 10 pounds
c 15 stones and 1 pound d 9 stones.

Tip

9 stones exactly means 9 stones and 0 pounds.

Think like a mathematician

8 Work with a partner to answer this question.

a Make x the subject of each of these formulae.
Write down if A, B or C is the correct answer.

i	$y = 2x + z$	A	$x = \frac{y+z}{2}$	B	$x = \frac{y-z}{2}$	C	$x = \frac{y}{2} - z$
ii	$y = \frac{5x}{2} - 3h$	A	$x = \frac{2y+3h}{5}$	B	$x = \frac{2y-6h}{5}$	C	$x = \frac{2(y+3h)}{5}$
iii	$y = 6 + \frac{x}{7k}$	A	$x = 7k(y-6)$	B	$x = 7ky - 6$	C	$x = 7k(y+6)$
iv	$y = \frac{x-m}{3n}$	A	$x = 3ny - m$	B	$x = \frac{3ny}{m}$	C	$x = 3ny + m$
v	$y = w - 7x$	A	$x = \frac{w-y}{7}$	B	$x = \frac{y+w}{7}$	C	$x = \frac{y-w}{7}$

b Discuss with your partner and with other learners in the class.
Explain what mistakes have been made to get the incorrect answers.

9 Make t the subject of each of these formulae.

a $m = 7t + 9$ b $k = \frac{t}{5} - m$ c $p = \frac{h+t}{v}$ d $q = \frac{5t - w}{9}$

10 The diagram shows a shape made from a square and a rectangle.

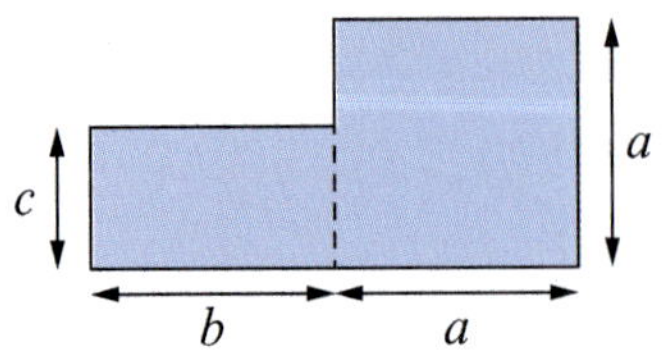

a Write a formula for the area (A) of the shape.

b Work out A when $a = 6$, $b = 3$ and $c = 4.5$.

c Show that you can rearrange your formula to give $a = \sqrt{A - bc}$.

d Work out a when $A = 80$, $b = 8$ and $c = 2$.

11 The formula for the area of a circle is $A = \pi r^2$

a Work out the area of a circle with radius 5 cm.
Use the π button on your calculator.
Write your answer correct to 3 significant figures (3 s.f.).

b Make r the subject of the formula.

c Work out the radius of a circle with an area of $122.7\ \text{cm}^2$.
Write your answer correct to 3 significant figures (3 s.f.).

12 Simon uses the formula $V = l^3$ to work out the volume of a cube.

a Make l the subject of the formula.

b Simon works out that the volumes of two different cubes are $64\ \text{cm}^3$ and $216\ \text{cm}^3$.
Work out the difference in the side length of the cubes.

13 Sasha uses the relationship shown to change between temperatures in degrees Fahrenheit (°F) and temperatures in degrees Celsius (°C).

Sasha thinks that 30 °C is higher than 82 °F.

Is she correct? Show how you worked out your answer.

> $5F = 9C + 160$
> where: F is the temperature in degrees Fahrenheit (°F)
> C is the temperature in degrees Celsius (°C)

14 A doctor uses the formula in the box to calculate a patient's body mass index (BMI).

A patient is described as underweight if their BMI is below 18.5.

> $\text{BMI} = \frac{m}{h^2}$
> where: m is the mass in kilograms
> h is the height in metres.

a Tina's mass is 48.8 kg and her height is 1.56 m. Is she underweight?
Explain your answer. Show your working.

b Stephen's height is 1.80 m and his mass is 68.5 kg. He wants to have a BMI of 20.
How many kilograms must he lose to reach a BMI of 20? Show your working.

Summary checklist

- [ ] I can write and use formulae.
- [ ] I can change the subject of a formula.

Check your progress

1 Work out the value of each expression when $x = 3$, $y = 5$ and $z = -2$.

a $x(3y + z)$ **b** $(2x)^2 + y^3$ **c** $\frac{(x + y)}{4} - 5z$

2 Write an expression for the perimeter and area of this rectangle.
Write each answer in its simplest form.

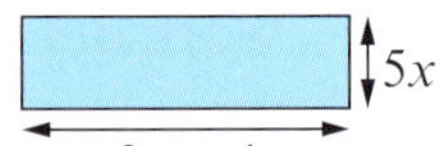

3 Simplify each expression.

a $x^2 \times x^3$ **b** $q^8 \div q^2$ **c** $(h^2)^5$

d $3m^7 \times 5m^2$ **e** $\frac{12u^5}{6u^3}$ **f** $4p^2 - p^2$

4 Expand and simplify each expression.

a $(x + 2)(x + 5)$ **b** $(x - 3)(x + 4)$ **c** $(x + 6)(x - 9)$

d $(x - 10)(x - 4)$ **e** $(x - 8)(x + 8)$ **f** $(x - 6)^2$

5 Simplify each expression.

a $\frac{x}{3} + \frac{x}{3}$ **b** $\frac{y}{5} - \frac{y}{15}$ **c** $\frac{3x}{5} - \frac{y}{20}$ **d** $\frac{9x - 15}{3}$

6 **a** Use the formula $x = y^2 + 5z$ to work out the value of x when $y = 4$ and $z = 3$.

b Make z the subject of the formula. Work out the value of z when $x = 55$ and $y = 5$.

c Make y the subject of the formula. Work out the value of y when $x = 46$ and $z = 2$.

3 Decimals, percentages and rounding

Getting started

1 Work out

a	80×0.1	**b**	325×0.1	**c**	600×0.01	**d**	85×0.01
e	$9 \div 0.1$	**f**	$62.5 \div 0.1$	**g**	$7 \div 0.01$	**h**	$0.32 \div 0.01$

2 Which card, **A**, **B**, **C** or **D**, gives the correct answer to 0.08×120?
Show your working.

A	B	C	D
96	9.6	960	0.096

3 Work out

a $46.2 \div 3$ **b** $128 \div 0.2$

4 **a** Increase \$300 by 15%

b Decrease \$300 by 20%

5 Use a calculator to work out the area of a circle with radius 4.5 cm.
Give your answer correct to three significant figures.

The world record for the fastest growing plant belongs to a certain type of bamboo. Bamboo is a member of the grass family. The plant produces new shoots (culms) in the spring, and these grow into canes. The canes increase in height and diameter for about 60 days. They then stop growing. The fastest growing bamboo can grow at a rate of 0.9 m per day, which is equivalent to 0.000 04 km/h. Over time, the roots of the plant spread out. Each spring the new canes grow larger in height and diameter than the previous spring. This is due to the increase in the underground system of roots. Finally, after several years, the maximum size for that particular type of bamboo is reached.

A new bamboo shoot (culm)

The number of new canes that grow each year also increases. In the first year, there is one cane. In the second year, there are usually three canes. In the third year, there are nine canes and in the fourth year there are 27 canes. This is a 200% increase in the number of canes each year for the first four years. For the next four years, the number of canes increases, on average, by 120% each year.

This information about bamboo includes decimals and percentages. To make the information easier to read and understand, a lot of the values are rounded. In this unit, you will work with decimals and percentages and discuss the values that rounded numbers can take.

3.1 Multiplying and dividing by powers of 10

In this section you will …

- multiply numbers by 10 to the power of any positive or negative number.

Look at this section of the decimal place-value table.

…	thousands	hundreds	tens	units	•	tenths	hundredths	thousandths	…
…	1000	100	10	1	•	$\frac{1}{10}$	$\frac{1}{100}$	$\frac{1}{1000}$	…

You can write the numbers 10, 100, 1000, … as positive powers of 10.

You can write the numbers $\frac{1}{10}$, $\frac{1}{100}$, $\frac{1}{1000}$, … as negative powers of 10.

Look at this pattern of numbers, written as powers of 10. Is there a link between the powers and the values?

…, $1000 = 10^3$, $100 = 10^2$, $10 = 10^1$, $1 = 10^0$, $\frac{1}{10} = 10^{-1}$, $\frac{1}{100} = 10^{-2}$, $\frac{1}{1000} = 10^{-3}$, …

Tip

Note: You can write the decimal 0.1 as $\frac{1}{10}$ or 10^{-1}.

You can write the decimal 0.01 as $\frac{1}{100}$ or 10^{-2}.

This pattern continues as the numbers get bigger and smaller.

For example, $10\,000 = 10^4$ and $\frac{1}{10\,000} = 10^{-4}$, $100\,000 = 10^5$ and $\frac{1}{100\,000} = 10^{-5}$.

It is important to remember these two key points:

1 **Multiplying** a number by $\frac{1}{10}$, $\frac{1}{100}$, $\frac{1}{1000}$, … is the same as **dividing** the same number by 10, 100, 1000, …

2 **Dividing** a number by $\frac{1}{10}$, $\frac{1}{100}$, $\frac{1}{1000}$, … is the same as **multiplying** the same number by 10, 100, 1000, …

Worked example 3.1

Work out

a 2.5×10^3 **b** 12×10^{-2} **c** $365 \div 10^4$ **d** $0.45 \div 10^{-3}$

Answer

a $10^3 = 1000$

$2.5 \times 1000 = 2500$

Start by writing 10^3 as 1000.
Rewrite the multiplication as 2.5×1000 and work out the answer.

b $10^{-2} = \frac{1}{100}$

$12 \times \frac{1}{100} = 12 \div 100$

$= 0.12$

Start by writing 10^{-2} as $\frac{1}{100}$
Multiplying 12 by $\frac{1}{100}$ is the same as dividing 12 by 100.
Work out the answer.

c $10^4 = 10\,000$

$365 \div 10\,000 = 0.0365$

Start by writing 10^4 as 10 000.
Rewrite the division as $365 \div 10\,000$ and work out the answer.

d $10^{-3} = \frac{1}{1000}$

$0.45 \div \frac{1}{1000} = 0.45 \times 1000$

$= 450$

Start by writing 10^{-3} as $\frac{1}{1000}$
Dividing 0.45 by $\frac{1}{1000}$ is the same as multiplying 0.45 by 1000.
Work out the answer.

Exercise 3.1

1 Match each decimal with the correct fraction and power of 10.
The first one has been done for you: **a**, **D** and **ii**.

	Decimal		Fraction		Power of 10
a	0.1	**A**	$\frac{1}{1000}$	**i**	10^{-2}
b	0.001	**B**	$\frac{1}{10\,000}$	**ii**	10^{-1}
c	0.000 01	**C**	$\frac{1}{100}$	**iii**	10^{-4}
d	0.01	**D**	$\frac{1}{10}$	**iv**	10^{-5}
e	0.0001	**E**	$\frac{1}{100\,000}$	**v**	10^{-3}

2 Copy and complete

a $3.2 \times 10^3 = 3.2 \times 1000 = \ldots$

b $3.2 \times 10^2 = 3.2 \times 100 = \ldots$

c $3.2 \times 10^1 = 3.2 \times \ldots = \ldots$

d $3.2 \times 10^0 = 3.2 \times 1 = \ldots$

e $3.2 \times 10^{-1} = 3.2 \div 10 = \ldots$

f $3.2 \times 10^{-2} = 3.2 \div 100 = \ldots$

g $3.2 \times 10^{-3} = 3.2 \div \ldots = \ldots$

h $3.2 \times 10^{-4} = 3.2 \div \ldots = \ldots$

3 Look at your answers to Question **2**. Compare all your answers with the number you started with, 3.2. Arun makes this conjecture.

a Is Arun correct? Use specialising to explain your answer.

b Copy and complete these generalising statements:

i When you multiply a number by 10 to a negative power, the answer is always .... than the number you started with.

ii When you multiply a number by 10 to the power zero, the answer is always .... as the number you started with.

iii When you multiply a number by 10 to a positive power, the answer is always .... than the number you started with.

4 Work out

a 13×10^2

b 7.8×10^3

c 24×10

d 8.55×10^4

e 6.5×10^1

f 0.08×10^5

g 17×10^0

h 8×10^{-1}

i 8.5×10^{-2}

j 4500×10^{-4}

k 32×10^{-3}

l 125×10^{-2}

Tip

Remember:

$10^0 = 1$

$10^1 = 10$

5 Copy and complete

a $320 \div 10^3 = 320 \div 1000 = \ldots$

b $320 \div 10^2 = 320 \div 100 = \ldots$

c $320 \div 10^1 = 320 \div \ldots = \ldots$

d $320 \div 10^0 = 320 \div 1 = \ldots$

6 Work out

a $27 \div 10$

b $450 \div 10^3$

c $36 \div 10^2$

d $170 \div 10^4$

e $0.8 \div 10^1$

f $2480 \div 10^5$

g $9 \div 10^0$

h $0.25 \div 10^2$

Think like a mathematician

7 Work with a partner to answer these questions.

This is how Cesar and Domonique work out $2.6 \div 10^{-2}$.

Cesar

$$10^{-2} = \frac{1}{10^2} = \frac{1}{100}$$

$$2.6 \div \frac{1}{100} = 2.6 \times \frac{100}{1}$$

$$= 2.6 \times 100$$

$$= 260$$

Domonique

$$2.6 = 2\frac{6}{10} = \frac{26}{10} = \frac{26}{10^1} = 26 \times 10^{-1}$$

$$26 \times 10^{-1} \div 10^{-2} = 26 \times \frac{10^{-1}}{10^{-2}}$$

$$= 26 \times 10^{-1 - -2}$$

$$= 26 \times 10^1 = 260$$

- **a** Do you understand how Cesar's method and Domonique's method work?
- **b** Try using both of their methods to work out
  - **i** $6.8 \div 10^{-3}$
  - **ii** $0.07 \div 10^{-4}$
- **c** Whose method do you prefer? Explain why.
- **d** Can you think of a better method to use to divide a decimal by 10 to a negative power?
- **e** Discuss your answers to parts **a** to **d** with other learners in your class.

8 Copy and complete

- **a** $3.2 \div 10^3 = 3.2 \div 1000 = \ldots$
- **b** $3.2 \div 10^2 = 3.2 \div 100 = \ldots$
- **c** $3.2 \div 10^1 = 3.2 \div \ldots = \ldots$
- **d** $3.2 \div 10^0 = 3.2 \div 1 = \ldots$
- **e** $3.2 \div 10^{-1} = 3.2 \times 10 = \ldots$
- **f** $3.2 \div 10^{-2} = 3.2 \times 100 = \ldots$
- **g** $3.2 \div 10^{-3} = 3.2 \times \ldots = \ldots$
- **h** $3.2 \div 10^{-4} = 3.2 \times \ldots = \ldots$

9 Look at your answers to Question **8**. Compare all your answers with the number you started with, 3.2. Zara makes this conjecture.

a Is Zara correct? Use specialising to explain your answer.

b Copy and complete these generalising statements:

i When you divide a number by 10 to a negative power, the answer is always .... than the number you started with.

ii When you divide a number by 10 to the power zero, the answer is always .... as the number you started with.

iii When you divide a number by 10 to a positive power, the answer is always .... than the number you started with.

10 Work out

a $0.25 \div 10^{-1}$ b $4.76 \div 10^{-4}$

c $0.07 \div 10^{-3}$ d $0.085 \div 10^{-2}$

11 Copy this table, which contains a secret coded message.

					S !
3 3.3	0.3 3.3 300	300 33 6 6	0.6 0.3 0.33 3.3 0.3 33	300 0.06 33	60 33 0.03 600 33 300

Work out the answers to the calculations in the code box.

Find the answer in your secret code table.
Write the letter from the code box above the number in your table.

For example, the first calculation is 0.6×10^2.

$0.6 \times 10^2 = 60$, so write S above 60 in the table as shown.

What is the secret coded message?

$0.6 \times 10^2 = \text{S}$	$60 \times 10^{-1} = \text{L}$
$0.06 \div 10^{-1} = \text{A}$	$600 \div 10^0 = \text{R}$
$60 \times 10^{-3} = \text{H}$	$33 \div 10^1 = \text{O}$
$0.33 \times 10^0 = \text{Y}$	$300 \times 10^{-3} = \text{N}$
$300 \div 10^4 = \text{C}$	$3300 \times 10^{-2} = \text{E}$
$0.3 \div 10^{-3} = \text{T}$	$300 \div 10^2 = \text{D}$

Think like a mathematician

12 Work with a partner to answer these questions.

a Work out

i 4×10^2 ii 4×10^1 iii 4×10^0

iv 4×10^{-1} v 4×10^{-2} vi 4×10^{-3}

b Use specialising to answer this question.
When you multiply a number by 10^{-4}, is the answer larger or smaller than when you multiply the same number by 10^{-3}?

Continued

c Which word, smaller or larger, is missing from this generalising sentence?

> When you multiply a number by 10^x, the smaller the power, the ……… the answer.

d Work out

i	$12 \div 10^2$	**ii**	$12 \div 10^1$	**iii**	$12 \div 10^0$
iv	$12 \div 10^{-1}$	**v**	$12 \div 10^{-2}$	**vi**	$12 \div 10^{-3}$

e Use specialising to answer this question.
When you divide a number by 10^{-4}, is the answer larger or smaller than when you divide the same number by 10^{-3}?

f Which word, smaller or larger, is missing from this generalising sentence?

> When you divide a number by 10^x, the smaller the power, the ……… the answer.

g Discuss your answers to parts **b**, **c**, **e** and **f** with other learners in your class.

13 Work out the missing power in each question in these spider diagrams.
In each part, all the questions in the outer shapes should give the answer in the centre shape.

a

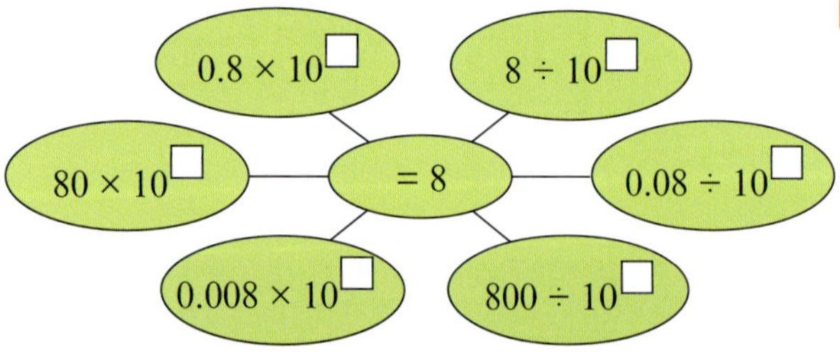

b

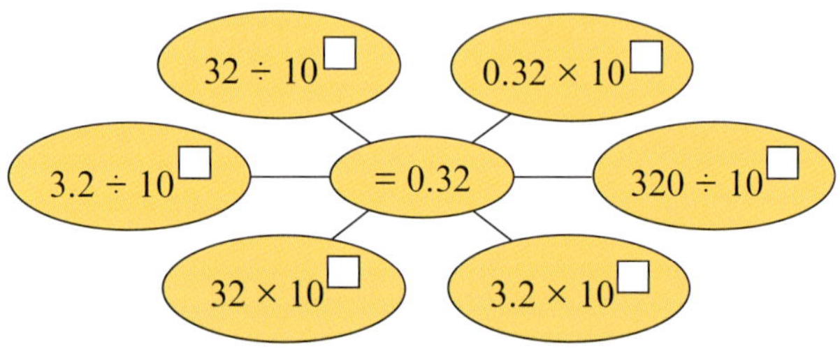

Activity 3.1

Here are four number cards, four multiplication cards and four division cards.
Work with a partner to answer this question.

3.25	0.98	$\times 10^3$	$\times 10^{-2}$	$\div 10^{-3}$	$\div 10^4$
68.1	590	$\times 10^{-4}$	$\times 10^5$	$\div 10^{-1}$	$\div 10^0$

Continued

a Take it in turns, twice each, to choose one number card and one multiplication card. Ask your partner to work out the answer. Mark each other's work and discuss any mistakes that have been made.

b Take it in turns, twice each, to choose one number card and one division card. Ask your partner to work out the answer. Mark each other's work and discuss any mistakes that have been made.

In Activity 3.1, did you get the multiplication questions and the division questions correct?

If you didn't, do you understand the mistakes you made?

Discuss with your partner ways to remember the methods for these types of question.

Summary checklist

- [ ] I can multiply and divide numbers by 10 to the power of any positive or negative number.

3.2 Multiplying and dividing decimals

In this section you will ...

- estimate, multiply and divide decimals by integers and decimals.

Key word

equivalent calculation

When you multiply or divide a number by a decimal, use the place value of the decimal to work out an **equivalent calculation**. For simple questions, you can do this 'in your head', or mentally. For more difficult questions, you will need to write down the steps in your working.

Worked example 3.2

Work out

a 12×0.6 **b** 0.3×0.15 **c** $-16 \div 0.4$ **d** $9.6 \div -0.12$ **e** $\frac{36 \times 0.5}{0.2 \times 4.5}$

Answer

a $12 \times 6 = 72$	Ignore the decimal point and work out $12 \times 6 = 72$. The answer 72 is 10 times bigger than the actual answer, because 6 is 10 times bigger than 0.6.
$12 \times 0.6 = 7.2$	Divide 72 by 10 to get 7.2
b $3 \times 15 = 45$	Ignore the decimal points and work out $3 \times 15 = 45$.
$0.3 \times 0.15 = 0.045$	$3 \times 15 = 45 \rightarrow 0.3 \times 15 = 4.5 \rightarrow 0.3 \times 0.15 = 0.045$
c $\frac{-16 \times 10}{0.4 \times 10}$	Think of the division as a fraction. Multiply the top and the bottom of the fraction by 10 to eliminate the decimal from the division.
$\frac{-160}{4} = -40$	This makes an equivalent calculation, which is much easier to do.
d $\frac{9.6 \times 100}{-0.12 \times 100}$	Again, think of the division as a fraction. Multiply the top and the bottom of the fraction by 100 to eliminate the decimal.
$\frac{960}{-12} = -80$	As before, this makes an equivalent calculation, which is much easier to do.
e $36 \times 0.5 = 18$	Work out the answer to the numerator first. Since 0.5 is the same as one half, work out $\frac{1}{2} \times 36 = 18$.
$2 \times 4.5 = 9$	Now work out the denominator: $2 \times 4.5 = 9$
So $0.2 \times 4.5 = 0.9$	2 is 10 times bigger than 0.2, so divide 9 by 10 to get 0.9
$\frac{36 \times 0.5}{0.2 \times 4.5} = \frac{18}{0.9}$	Rewrite the fraction using the numerator and denominator you just worked out.
$\frac{18 \times 10}{0.9 \times 10}$	Multiply the top and the bottom of the fraction by 10 to eliminate the decimal.
$\frac{180}{9} = 20$	This makes an equivalent calculation, which is much easier to do.

Exercise 3.2

1 Work out mentally

a 8×0.2 b 8×-0.7 c -0.6×9 d -0.4×-15

e 6×0.05 f -22×0.03 g 0.12×30 h 0.11×-4

2 Copy and complete

a 0.08×0.2 $8 \times 2 = \ldots$ $8 \times 0.2 = \ldots$ $0.08 \times 0.2 = \ldots$

b 0.4×0.007 $4 \times 7 = \ldots$ $4 \times 0.007 = \ldots$ $0.4 \times 0.007 = \ldots$

3 Sort these cards into groups that have the **same** answer.

A 3×0.05 B 30×0.05 C 0.3×0.05 D 0.005×3

E 500×0.03 F 5×0.03 G 0.3×5 H 0.3×0.5

I 0.003×5 J 0.005×30 K 0.03×0.5 L 0.5×3

4 Work out mentally

a $4 \div 0.2$ b $-25 \div 0.5$ c $12 \div -0.4$ d $-60 \div -0.1$

e $2 \div 0.05$ f $28 \div -0.07$ g $-24 \div -0.12$ h $-45 \div 0.15$

5 Copy and complete.

a $0.81 \div 0.09$ $\frac{0.81 \times 100}{0.09 \times 100} = \frac{81}{\square} = \square$ b $6.4 \div 0.004$ $\frac{6.4 \times 1000}{0.004 \times 1000} = \frac{\square}{\square} = \square$

6 Which answer is correct, **A**, **B**, **C** or **D**?

a $0.8 \div 0.02 =$ A 0.04 B 0.4 C 4 D 40

b $4.5 \div 0.5 =$ A 0.9 B 9 C 90 D 900

c $0.09 \div 0.003 =$ A 0.3 B 3 C 30 D 300

d $3.6 \div 0.006 =$ A 0.6 B 6 C 60 D 600

Think like a mathematician

7 a Work out mentally

i 8×0.1 ii 8×0.3 iii 8×0.5

iv 8×0.7 v 8×0.9 vi 8×1.1

b Use your answers to part **a** to answer these questions.

i When you multiply a number by 0.8, do you expect the answer to be larger or smaller than your answer when you multiply the same number by 0.7?

ii When you multiply a number by a decimal between 0 and 1, do you expect the answer to be larger or smaller than the number you started with?

Continued

c Work out mentally

i	$12 \div 0.2$	ii	$12 \div 0.4$	iii	$12 \div 0.6$
iv	$12 \div 0.8$	v	$12 \div 1.0$	vi	$12 \div 1.2$

d Use your answers to part **c** to answer these questions.

i When you divide a number by 0.7, do you expect your answer to be larger or smaller than when you divide the same number by 0.6?

ii When you divide a number by a decimal between 0 and 1, do you expect the answer to be larger or smaller than the number you started with?

e Discuss your answers to parts **a** to **d** with other learners in your class.

8 Write 'True' or 'False' for each of these statements.

a $5.729 \times 0.62 > 5.729$ b $4.332 \div 0.95 > 4.332$

c $12.664 \times 1.002 < 12.664$ d $45.19 \div 1.45 < 45.19$

Tip

For Question **8**, do not work out the answers to the multiplications and divisions, but use your answers to Question **7**.

9 This is part of Hassan's homework.

Question

Work out $\dfrac{24 \times 0.25}{0.2 \times 0.6}$

Answer

numerator $= \frac{1}{4}$ *of* $24 = 6$ *denominator* $= 0.2 \times 0.6 = 1.2$

$6 \div 1.2 = 60 \div 12 = 5$

Is Hassan correct? Explain your answer. Show your working.

10 Work out

a $\dfrac{48 \times 0.5}{0.04 \times 3}$ b $\dfrac{120 \times 0.3}{0.2 \times 1.5}$

c $\dfrac{84 \times 0.25}{35 \times 0.002}$ d $\dfrac{120 \times 0.4 \times 0.1}{0.8 \times 0.15}$

11 Here are six rectangular question cards and seven oval answer cards.

A	$-6 \times -8 \times 0.5$	B	$0.3 \times -4 \times 20$	C	$-6 \times -2 \times -0.02$
D	$\dfrac{12 \times 0.04}{-0.2}$	E	$\dfrac{1.44}{20 \times 0.3}$	F	$\dfrac{-320 \times 0.6}{-80}$

i 2.4   ii 0.024   iii 0.24   iv 24

v −24   vi −0.24   vii −2.4

a Match each question card with the correct answer card.

b There is one answer card left over. Write a question card to go with that answer card.

c Ask a partner to check that your question gives the correct answer.

Think like a mathematician

12 Work with a partner to answer this question.
Here is a calculation: $28 \times 0.57 = 15.96$
What other calculations can you deduce from this calculation?
Discuss your answers with other learners in your class.

13 a Work out 123×57.

b Use your answer to part **a** to write the answers to these calculations.

i 12.3×57	ii 123×5.7	iii 12.3×5.7
iv 1.23×5.7	v 12.3×0.57	vi 0.123×0.57

14 Hugo uses these methods to estimate and work out the answer to this question.

Question
Work out 0.23 × 37.8
Estimate
Round 0.23 to 0.2 and 37.8 to 40 → 0.2 × 40 = 8
Answer
378 × 20 = 378 × 2 × 10 = 756 × 10 = 7560
378 × 3 = 1134
7560 + 1134 = 8694
0.23 × 37.8 = 8694 ÷ 1000 = 8.694
8.694 is close to 8, so this answer is probably correct.

a Critique Hugo's methods.

b Can you improve his methods? If you can, write down your method(s).

c Estimate and work out the answers to these calculations.
Use your favourite methods.

i 4.35×27.5 ii $11.78 \div 0.19$ iii $\frac{64 \times 3.6}{0.012}$

15 The diagram shows a rectangle. The area of the rectangle is $0.171\,m^2$.

a Estimate the length of the rectangle.

b Work out the length of the rectangle.

c Compare your answers to parts **a** and **b**.
Do you think your answer to part **b** is correct?
Explain why.

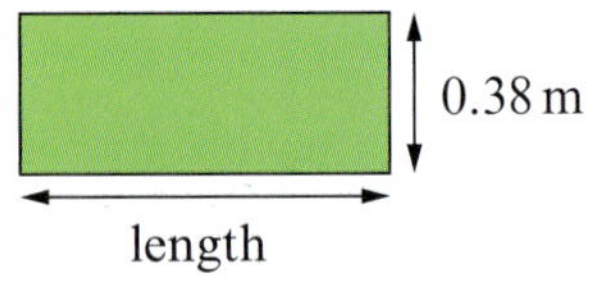

Summary checklist

☐ I can estimate, multiply and divide decimals by integers and decimals.

3.3 Understanding compound percentages

In this section you will …

- use and understand compound percentages.

Key word

compound percentage

You already know how to work out a percentage increase and decrease using a multiplier. For example:

When a price of \$300 is increased by 20%, the new price is $300 \times \boxed{1.2} = \$360$.

The multiplier is 1.2 because $100\% + 20\% = 120\% = \frac{120}{100} = 1.2$

When a price of \$300 is decreased by 20%, the new price is $300 \times \boxed{0.8} = \$240$.

The multiplier is 0.8 because $100\% - 20\% = 80\% = \frac{80}{100} = 0.8$

A **compound percentage** change is when a percentage increase or decrease is followed by another percentage increase or decrease.

Worked example 3.3

The value of a new car is \$12 000.

In the first year, the value of the car decreases by 20%.

In the second year, the value of the car decreases by 15%.

Work out the value of the car at the end of the second year.

Answer

$100\% - 20\% = 80\%$	In the first year, the value of \$12 000 decreases by 20%.
$= 0.8$	So the multiplier is 0.8
$12\,000 \times 0.8 = \$9600$	At the end of the first year, the value of the car is \$9600
$100\% - 15\% = 85\%$	In the second year, the value of \$9600 decreases by 15%.
$= 0.85$	So the multiplier is 0.85
$9600 \times 0.85 = \$8160$	At the end of the second year, the value of the car is \$8160

Exercise 3.3

Tip

Remember:

for an increase, add the percentage on to 100%

for a decrease, subtract the percentage from 100%.

1 Copy and complete the workings for these compound percentage changes.

a \$200 increased by 10%, then increased by 15%.

$200 \times 1.1 = 220 \quad \rightarrow \quad 220 \times 1.15 = \$\ldots$

b \$200 decreased by 10%, then decreased by 15%.

$200 \times 0.9 = \ldots \quad \rightarrow \quad \ldots \times \ldots = \$\ldots$

c \$200 increased by 20%, then decreased by 5%.

$200 \times \ldots = \ldots \quad \rightarrow \quad \ldots \times \ldots = \$\ldots$

Think like a mathematician

2 Work with a partner to answer this question.
The value of a gold coin is $800. It has a 10% increase in value followed by a 10% decrease in value. Read what Marcus and Sofia say.

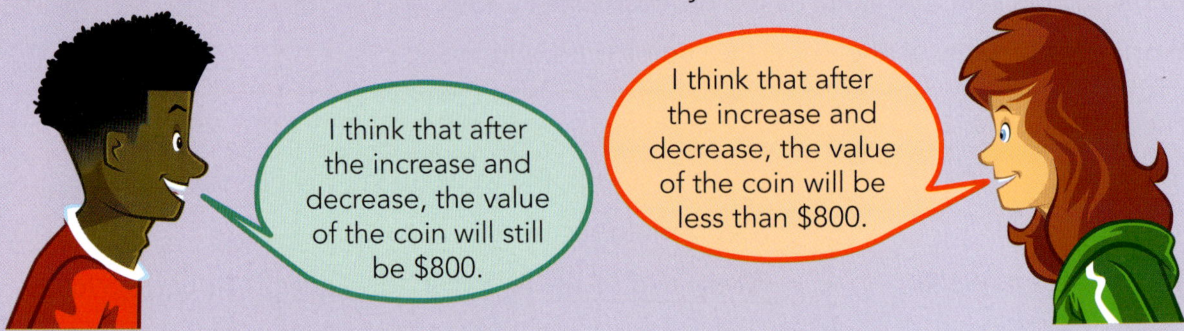

a Who do you think is correct, Marcus or Sofia? Explain why.

b Work out who is correct. Explain the mistake the other person has made.

c If the gold coin has a 10% decrease in value followed by a 10% increase in value, do you think the final value of the coin will be more or less than $800? Explain why.
Check your answer by working out the new value of the coin.

d Discuss your answers to parts **a**, **b** and **c** with other learners in your class.

3 **a** Work out these compound percentage changes.

- **i** 60 increased by 20%, then decreased by 20%
- **ii** 60 decreased by 20%, then increased by 20%

b Which sign, <, > or = is missing from this sentence?
60 increased by 20%, then decreased by 20% □ 60 decreased by 20%, then increased by 20%

c Without doing any calculations, decide which sign, <, > or = is missing from each sentence.

- **i** 72 decreased by 15%, then increased by 15% □ 72 increased by 15%, then decreased by 15%
- **ii** 140 increased by 8%, then decreased by 8% □ 140 decreased by 8%, then increased by 8%

Think like a mathematician

4 Work with a partner to answer this question.
Anil, Raj and Mari use different methods to work out 50 increased by 20%, then increased by 10%. This is what they write.

Continued

Anil	Raj	Mari
First increase: $50 \times 1.2 = 60$	*Both increases:*	*Multiplier:* $1.2 \times 1.1 = 1.32$
Second increase: $60 \times 1.1 = 66$	$50 \times 1.2 \times 1.1 = 66$	*Final value:* $50 \times 1.32 = 66$

Discuss with your partner:

a What is the difference between Anil's method and Raj's method?
b What is the difference between Raj's method and Mari's method?
c Whose method is easiest to use if you have a calculator?
d Whose method is easiest to use if you do not have a calculator?
e Whose method do you prefer? Explain why.

Use a calculator for the rest of the questions in this exercise.

5 **a** Work out the final value after these compound percentage increases.
Use Raj's method from Question **4**.
  i 120 increased by 25%, then increased by 30%.
  ii 40 increased by 15%, then increased by 40%.

b Work out the final value after these compound percentage increases.
Use Mari's method from Question **4**.
  i 400 increased by 50%, then increased by 5%.
  ii 90 increased by 12%, then increased by 8%.

> **Tip**
>
> Remember that in part **b i** the multiplier for a 5% increase is 1.05.

6 Mari uses the train company 'GoRail' to travel to work.
In 2018, GoRail increased the cost of a ticket by 7%.
In 2019, GoRail increased the cost of a ticket by 5%.

a Use Mari's method from Question **4** to work out the multiplier for the compound percentage increase.

b In 2017, Mari buys a ticket for $60.
How much will this ticket cost her in 2019?

7 **a** Work out the final value after these compound percentage decreases.
Use Raj's method from Question **4**.
  i 100 decreased by 10%, then decreased by 20%.
  ii 80 decreased by 25%, then decreased by 12%.

b Work out the final value after these compound percentage decreases.
Use Mari's method from Question **4**.
  i 600 decreased by 50%, then decreased by 5%.
  ii 76 decreased by 30%, then decreased by 9%.

8 Mari buys a new motorbike.
In the first year, the value of the motorbike decreases by 18%.
In the second year, the value of the motorbike decreases by 12%.

a Use Mari's method from Question **4** to work out the multiplier for the compound percentage decrease.

b Mari pays $6400 for her motorbike.
What will be the value of her motorbike after two years?

9 The rectangular cards show percentage changes. The oval cards show multipliers.

A	20% increase then 10% decrease	**B**	18% increase then 30% decrease
C	12% decrease then 20% increase	**D**	40% decrease then 35% increase
E	15% increase then 32% decrease	**F**	5% decrease then 8% increase

i 1.056   ii 0.782   iii 1.08   iv 0.826   v 1.026

a Match each oval card with the correct rectangular card.

b There is one rectangular card left over.
Work out the multiplier that goes with this card.

Tip

For card **A**, the multiplier is $1.2 \times 0.9 = \ldots$

10 An investor invests \$5000 in a bank account. The investor gets 4% of the money in their account added to this account at the end of each year. The investor works out how much they will have in their account at the end of each year for five years.

This is what they write:

End of year	Calculation	Amount
1	5000×1.04	\$5200.00
2	$5000 \times 1.04 \times 1.04$	\$5408.00
3	$5000 \times 1.04 \times 1.04 \times 1.04$	\$5624.32
4	$5000 \times 1.04 \times 1.04 \times 1.04 \times 1.04$	\$5849.29
5	$5000 \times 1.04 \times 1.04 \times 1.04 \times 1.04 \times 1.04$	\$6083.26

a Read what Zara says.

Is Zara correct? Explain your answer.

b For the end of year 3, instead of writing $5000 \times 1.04 \times 1.04 \times 1.04$, what calculation could the investor write?

c For the end of year 4, instead of writing $5000 \times 1.04 \times 1.04 \times 1.04 \times 1.04$, what calculation could the investor write?

d The investor writes the calculation $5000 \times (1.04)^8$ to work out how much money they have in their account. For how many years have they invested the money? Explain how you worked out your answer.

e What calculation could the investor write to work out how much money they would have at the end of:

- **i** 12 years
- **ii** 20 years
- **iii** n years?

f After how many years will the investor have more than \$9000 in their account?

Show how you worked out your answer.

11 The population of a town is 10 000 people.

The population is predicted to decrease at a steady rate of 10% per year.

a Write down a calculation to work out the population of the town after

i 1 year **ii** 2 years **iii** 3 years.

b What does the calculation $10\,000 \times (0.9)^5$ represent?

c What does the calculation $10\,000 \times (0.9)^{10}$ represent?

d After how many years does the population of the town first fall below 6000 people?

Show how you worked out your answer.

e Write a calculation to work out the population of the town after n years.

Activity 3.3

Work with a partner to answer this question.

Here are two calculation cards.

A 800×1.15^4 **B** 500×0.95^8

a What situations could these calculations represent?

b Discuss and compare your situations in part **a** with those of other learners in your class.

Were all of the situations realistic? Who described the best situations?

Are you happy with the situations you described, or could you have thought of something better?

Summary checklist

☐ I can use and understand compound percentages.

3.4 Understanding upper and lower bounds

In this section you will …

- work out upper and lower bounds.

Key words

lower bound

upper bound

You already know how to round numbers to a given number of decimal places or significant figures. When you are given a number that has already been rounded, have you ever wondered what the original number was, before it was rounded? Read this information about the Super Bowl:

The Super Bowl is an American football game played to decide the champion of the National Football League (NFL). It is one of the most widely watched sporting events in the world. The Super Bowl in 1979 holds the record for the highest number of fans actually in the stadium at 104 000 (to the nearest 1000).

How many fans were actually in the stadium? It is impossible to know the exact number of fans from the information given. However, you can work out the smallest number of fans there could have been. This is called the **lower bound**. You can also work out the greatest number of fans there could have been. This is called the **upper bound**.

Tip

For the rounded number of fans 104 000:

lower bound = 103 500 fans

upper bound = 104 499 fans

Worked example 3.4

A whole number is rounded to the nearest 10. The answer is 80.

a List the integer values the number could be.

b What is the

i lower bound **ii** upper bound?

Answer

a 75, 76, 77, 78, 79, 80, 81, 82, 83, 84	These are the only whole numbers that round to 80 (to the nearest 10).
b i 75	This is the smallest whole number that rounds up to 80 (to the nearest 10).
ii 84	This is the largest whole number that rounds down to 80 (to the nearest 10).

Exercise 3.4

1 All of these whole numbers have been rounded to the nearest 10. For each part write

i a list of the integer values the number could be

ii the lower bound

iii the upper bound.

a 30 **b** 90 **c** 270 **d** 850

2 A number with one decimal place is rounded to the nearest whole number. The answer is 12.

Copy and complete these sentences.

a The numbers with one decimal place that round to 12 are 11.5, 11.6, 11.7, …, …, …, …, …, …, …

b The lower bound is …

c The upper bound is …

3 This is part of Aashi's homework.
There are marks on her work, covering some of the numbers.

> <u>Question</u>
> Increase $42 by %. Round your answer to the nearest whole number.
> <u>Solution</u>
> 42 × 1 = = $55 (to the nearest whole number)

The number she rounds to $55 has one decimal place.

a Write
  i a list of the numbers with one decimal place that round to 55
  ii the lower bound
  iii the upper bound.

b The question is 'Increase $42 by 30%'.
  What are the numbers covered by the marks in Aashi's solution?

Think like a mathematician

4 Work with a partner to answer this question.
A decimal number is rounded to the nearest whole number. The answer is 8.
Read what Arun and Zara say.

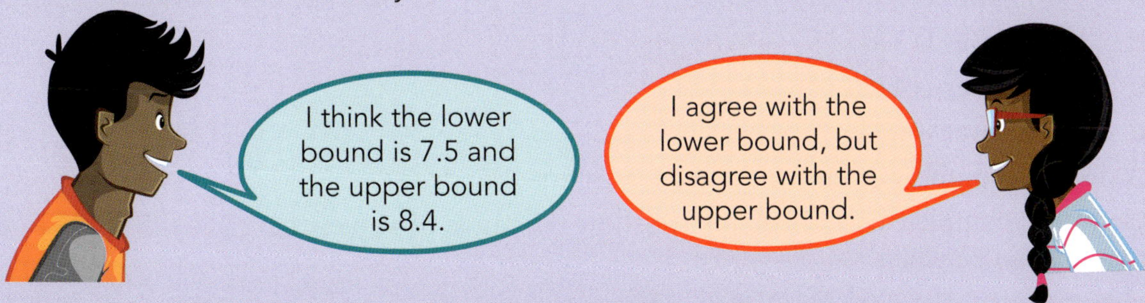

a Do you agree with the lower bound of 7.5? Explain why.

b Zara knows that the upper bound is not 8.4 but she has not said what she thinks it is.
  What do you think the upper bound is? Explain your answer.

c Discuss your answers to parts **a** and **b** with other learners in the class.

Think like a mathematician

5 Work with a partner to answer this question.

Sofia and Marcus are discussing the answers to Question **4**.

Read what they say.

- **a** Who do you think has written the inequality in the better way, Sofia or Marcus? Explain why.
- **b** Can you think of another way to write the inequality?
- **c** Discuss your answers to parts **a** and **b** with other learners in the class.

6 A decimal number is rounded to the nearest whole number.

Write an inequality to show the range of values the number can be when

- **a** the answer is 4
- **b** the answer is 12
- **c** the answer is 356
- **d** the answer is 670.

7 A decimal number is rounded to the nearest ten.

Copy and complete each inequality to show the range of values the number can be when

- **a** the answer is 20 $15 \leqslant x <$ ...
- **b** the answer is 340 ... $\leqslant x < 345$
- **c** the answer is 4750 ... $\leqslant x <$ ...
- **d** the answer is 6300 ... $\leqslant x <$ ...

8 A decimal number is rounded to the nearest one hundred.

Copy and complete each inequality to show the range of values the number can be when

- **a** the answer is 300 $250 \leqslant x <$ ...
- **b** the answer is 1900 ... $\leqslant x < 1950$
- **c** the answer is 4700 ... $\leqslant x <$ ...
- **d** the answer is 8000 ... $\leqslant x <$ ...

> **Tip**
>
> Use Marcus' method of writing the inequality from Question **5**. So for part **a** the answer is $3.5 \leqslant x <$ ... .

Think like a mathematician

9 Work with a partner to answer this question.

Look back at your answers to questions **6**, **7** and **8**.

What do you notice about the methods you use to work out the lower and upper bounds?

a Copy and complete these generalising sentences.

i When you round to the nearest whole number, the lower and upper bounds will be … below and above the rounded number.

ii When you round to the nearest ten, the lower and upper bounds will be … below and above the rounded number.

iii When you round to the nearest one hundred, the lower and upper bounds will be … below and above the rounded number.

b Can you describe a general rule to explain how you work out the lower and upper bounds of a rounded number?

10 Vihaan works out the circumference of this pond to be 1560 cm, correct to the nearest 10 cm.

a Write

i the lower bound of the circumference

ii the upper bound of the circumference.

b Write an inequality to show the range of values the circumference could have.

11 Saarya works out the mean height of the members in their netball team to be 172 cm, correct to the nearest centimetre.

a Write

i the lower bound of the mean height

ii the upper bound of the mean height.

b Write an inequality to show the range of values the mean height could have.

12 The rectangular cards show a range of values that a rounded number can be.

The oval cards show the degree of accuracy of the rounding.

The hexagonal cards show the rounded numbers.

Match each rectangular card with the correct oval and hexagonal card.

A	$1550 \leqslant x < 1650$	B	$550 \leqslant x < 650$	C	$55 \leqslant x < 65$
D	$15.5 \leqslant x < 16.5$	E	$155 \leqslant x < 165$	F	$164.5 \leqslant x < 165.5$

i	nearest 100	ii	nearest 10	iii	nearest 1

a	16	b	60	c	160
d	165	e	1600	f	600

Summary checklist

☐ I can work out upper and lower bounds.

Check your progress

1 Work out

a 7.45×10^4 b 12×10^0 c 46×10^{-3}

d 5.9×10^1 e $7280 \div 10^5$ f $0.5 \div 10^{-1}$

g $0.037 \div 10^{-3}$ h $18 \div 10^0$

2 Work out

a 8×-0.2 b 0.12×30 c -0.4×0.007

d $-60 \div -0.1$ e $6 \div 0.02$ f $0.81 \div 0.09$

g $-3 \times -5 \times 0.5$ h $\frac{1.32}{30 \times 0.4}$

3 Use your calculator to work out the final value after \$240 is increased by 30%, then decreased by 15%.

4 A painting has a value of \$20 000.

The value is predicted to increase at a steady rate of 8% per year.

a Write a calculation to work out the value of the painting after

i 1 year ii 2 years iii 3 years.

b What does the calculation $\$20\,000 \times (1.08)^5$ represent?

c What does the calculation $\$20\,000 \times (1.08)^{20}$ represent?

d After how many years does the value of the painting first go above \$30 000?

Show how you worked out your answer. You can use a calculator.

e Write a calculation to work out the value of the painting after n years.

5 Alexi works out the area of a soccer pitch to be $7200\,m^2$, correct to the nearest $100\,m^2$.

a Write

i the lower bound of the area of the soccer pitch

ii the upper bound of the area of the soccer pitch.

b Write the range of values the area of the soccer pitch could have.

Project 1

Cutting tablecloths

Imagine a square piece of cloth 1 metre by 1 metre that could be altered to make a tablecloth for a rectangular table.

You could cut off a strip 20% of the way along the square, rotate it, and attach it to the other edge to make a rectangle. There would be a little bit of cloth left over!

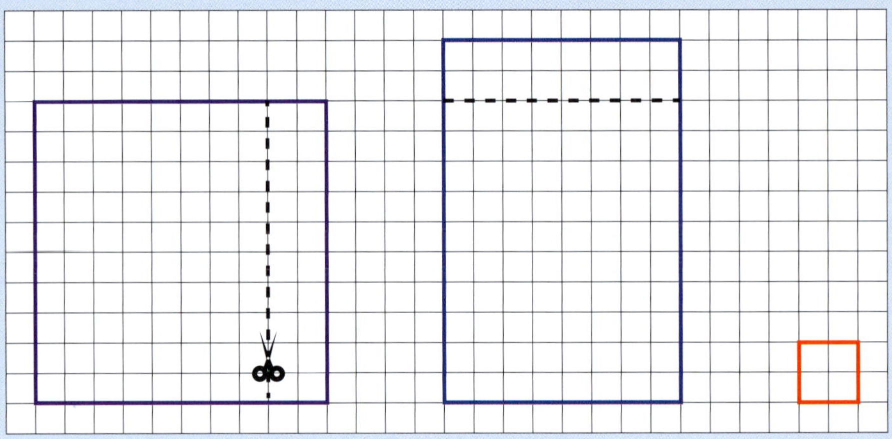

- The purple square is the original tablecloth.
- The blue rectangle is the new tablecloth.
- The red piece shows the cloth that is left over.

Look at the diagram.

- What percentage of the original cloth has been used to make the new tablecloth?

Instead of cutting off a 20% strip, you could cut a 10% strip, or a 15% strip, or a different percentage.

Choose some percentages to try. For each example, think about the following questions:

- What percentage of the original tablecloth is used to make the new tablecloth?
- What percentage of the original tablecloth is wasted?
- Is there a quick way to work out the percentage of cloth used and wasted, if you know what percentage strip was cut off?

Then answer these questions.

- To make a rectangular tablecloth in this way, with an area of 75% of the original cloth, what percentage strip would you need to cut off?
- To make a rectangular tablecloth in this way, with an area of 50% of the original cloth, what percentage strip would you need to cut off?

4 Equations and inequalities

Getting started

1 Solve these equations.

a $3x + 7 = 22$ b $2x - 8 = 10$

c $\frac{y}{5} + 3 = 8$ d $2y + 2 = y + 27$

2 For the inequality $4 < y \leqslant 7$, write

a the smallest integer that y could be

b the largest integer that y could be

c a list of the integer values that y could be.

3 Copy and complete these equivalent inequalities.

a $x > 5$ is equivalent to $2x > \ldots$ b $x < 9$ is equivalent to $\ldots x < 36$

c $y \geqslant 8$ is equivalent to $y + 5 \geqslant \ldots$ d $y \leqslant -6$ is equivalent to $y - 5 \leqslant \ldots$

The Rhind Papyrus is a famous document kept in the British Museum in London. It was written in Egypt in 1650 BCE. It is a list of 84 practical problems and their solutions. It shows how the people of Ancient Egypt carried out mathematical calculations. Some of the problems are easy to solve using algebra. However, this technique was not known at that time in Egypt. They wrote their problems and solutions in words, rather than using symbols.

In this unit you will use algebra to solve problems; hopefully, this will make them much easier to solve!

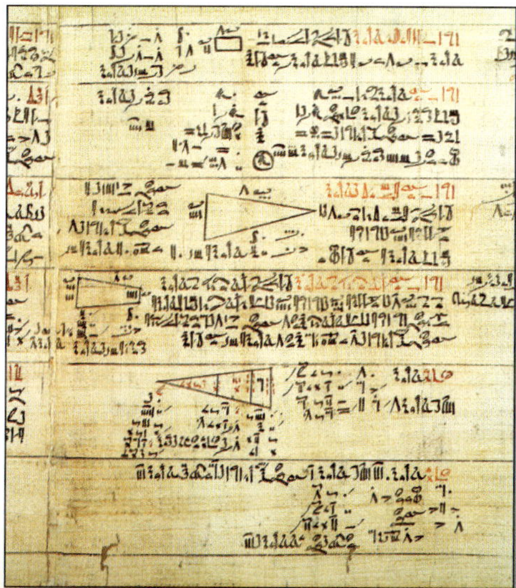

4.1 Constructing and solving equations

In this section you will ...

- write and solve equations.

Key words

construct (algebra)

sector

solve

When you are given a problem to **solve**, you can **construct**, or write, an equation to help you solve the problem.

Worked example 4.1

Write an equation to represent each problem, then solve your equations.

a Xavier thinks of a number. He doubles the number, then adds 3. Then he doubles the result. The answer is 70. What number did Xavier think of first?

b 120 sweets are shared between some children. Each child gets 8 sweets. How many children are there?

Answer

a Call the number x	You can use any letter.
$2x + 3$	Double it and add 3.
$2(2x + 3) = 70$	Double $2x + 3$ is 70. Now solve the equation.
$2x + 3 = 35$	Divide both sides by 2.
$2x = 32$	Subtract 3 from both sides.
$x = 16$	Divide both sides by 2. The number is 16.
b Call the number of children c	You can use any letter.
$\frac{120}{c} = 8$	Write the equation. Now solve the equation.
$120 = 8c$	Multiply by c, to remove c from the denominator.
$\frac{120}{8} = c$	Divide both sides by 8.
$c = 15$	There are 15 children.

Exercise 4.1

1 Copy and complete the workings to solve these equations.

a $8x - 14 = -30$

$8x = -30 + 14$

$8x = \square$

$x = \dfrac{\square}{8}$

$x = \square$

b $5(3 - 2x) = 9$

$\square - 10x = 9$

$-10x = 9 - \square$

$-10x = \square$

$x = \dfrac{\square}{-10} = \dfrac{\square}{\square}$

c $\dfrac{2y}{3} - 5 = 11$

$\dfrac{2y}{3} = 11 + 5$

$\dfrac{2y}{3} = \square$

$2y = \square \times \square$

$2y = \square$

$y = \dfrac{\square}{2} = \square$

d $6y + 7 = 22 - 3y$

$6y + 3y = 22 - 7$

$9y = \square$

$y = \dfrac{\square}{9}$

$y = \dfrac{\square}{\square}$

$y = \square\dfrac{\square}{\square}$

2 Solve these equations.

a $2x + 14 = -8$ **b** $-2x + 8 = 14$ **c** $12 - 2y = 4$

d $-4 = 12 - 2y$ **e** $a - 15 = 4a + 3$ **f** $5 + 3a = -3 - 5a$

g $3x + 6 = 20 - 4x$ **h** $z + 11 = 35 - 5z$

3 Here is an equation: $2(x + 12) = 4x - 6$

a Solve the equation by first multiplying out the brackets.

b Solve the equation by first dividing both sides by 2.

c Critique each method in parts **a** and **b**. Can you improve these methods?

Which is your favourite method? Explain why.

Think like a mathematician

4 Work with a partner to answer this question.

This is part of Shen's homework.

Question

Solve the equation $2(x + 8) = 3(6 - x)$

Answer

$2x + 8 = 18 - 3x$

$-x + 8 = 18$

$x = 26$

a How can you use the answer to show that Shen's working is incorrect?

b Work through Shen's solution. Explain all the mistakes he has made.

c Work out the correct answer, and show how to check that your answer is correct.

d Discuss your answers to parts **a**, **b** and **c** with other learners in your class.

5 Jacob and Zander solve the equation $10(x - 4) = 5x + 25$

a Jacob starts to solve the equation by multiplying out the brackets.

Complete Jacob's solution.

b Zander starts to solve the equation by dividing both sides of the equation by 5.

Complete Zander's solution.

c Critique Jacob and Zander's methods. Whose method do you prefer? Explain why.

6 Copy and complete the workings to solve these equations.

a $\frac{42}{c} = 7$

$42 = 7c$

$\frac{42}{\square} = c$

$c = \square$

b $\frac{12}{d} = 15$

$12 = 15d$

$\frac{12}{\square} = d$

$d = \frac{12}{\square} = \frac{\square}{\square}$

c $\frac{21}{e+2} = 7$

$21 = 7(e+2)$

$\frac{21}{\square} = e + 2$

$\square = e + 2$

$\square - 2 = e$

$e = \square$

7 Solve these equations. Check each of your answers by substituting the answer back into the equation.

a $\frac{81}{a} = 3$ b $\frac{9}{b} = 21$ c $\frac{32}{c+5} = 4$ d $\frac{10}{d-9} = 5$

Think like a mathematician

8 Work with a partner to answer this question.

This is how Steffan and Heidi solve the equation $\frac{17}{c+2} = 3$

Steffan

$17 = 3(c + 2)$

$\frac{17}{3} = c + 2$

$5\frac{2}{3} = c + 2$

$5\frac{2}{3} - 2 = c$

$c = 3\frac{2}{3}$

Heidi

$17 = 3(c + 2)$

$17 = 3c + 6$

$17 - 6 = 3c$

$11 = 3c$

$\frac{11}{3} = c$

$c = 3\frac{2}{3}$

Continued

a Critique Steffan's and Heidi's methods. Whose method do you prefer? Explain why.

b Can you improve their methods?

c Discuss your answers to parts **a** and **b** with other learners in the class.

d Try solving these equations using your favourite method.

i $\frac{9}{x-12}=4$ ii $\frac{2}{7-x}=5$ iii $\frac{8}{x+1}=10$

e Is your favourite method still your favourite method? Explain your answer.

9 Adeline is A years old.

a Write an expression for

i Adeline's age in 10 years' time

ii Adeline's age 6 years ago.

b Use the information from Adeline to write an equation for A.

c Solve the equation to find Adeline's age now.

10 The sides of a triangle, in centimetres, are $2(x + 3)$, $7x - 5$ and $5(7 - x)$.

The perimeter of the triangle is 48 cm.

a Write an equation for x.

b Solve your equation to find the value of x.

c Work out the lengths of the three sides of the triangle.

11 This equilateral triangle and this rectangle have equal perimeters.

a Write an equation to show this.

b Solve the equation.

c Find the lengths of the sides of the shapes.

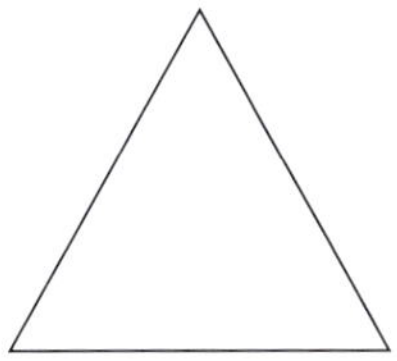

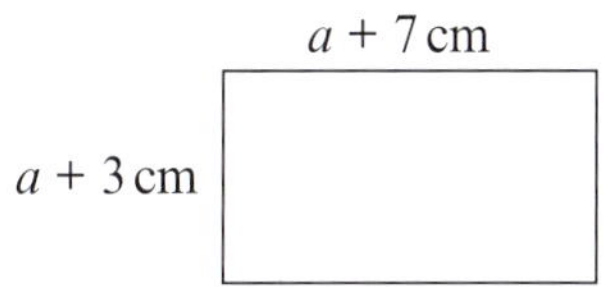

12 Su draws a pie chart with x equal size sectors.
She works out that the angle of each sector is 24°.

a Which two of these equations represent the situation?

A $360x = 24$ B $\frac{360}{x} = 24$ C $\frac{x}{360} = 24$

D $24x = 360$ E $\frac{24}{x} = 360$

b Solve all of the equations in part **a**.
Use your answers to decide if you chose the correct two equations in part **a**.

13 There are y learners in class 9T. Mrs Leclerc shares 85 pencils between the learners in class 9T. Each learner gets five pencils.

a Write an equation to represent this situation. Do not solve your equation.

There are 2 more learners in class 9S than in class 9T. Mrs Leclerc shares 152 pencils between the learners in class 9S. They each get eight pencils.

b Write an equation to represent this situation.

c Solve both of your equations to find the number of learners in class 9T.

d In part **c**, is the value for y the same in both of your equations? If not, check to see where you have made a mistake.

Activity 4.1

Work in a group of three or four. For each part of this question

i individually write an equation to represent the situation

ii compare the equation you have written with the equations written by the other members of your group. Decide who has written the correct equation in the easiest way

iii solve the equation you chose in part **ii**.

a Xavier thinks of a number. He multiplies the number by 5, then adds 12. The answer is the same as when he multiplies his number by 10 and then subtracts 8. What number did he think of?

b Anders thinks of a number. He subtracts 5, then multiplies the result by 12. The answer is the same as when he adds 1 to the number, then multiplies the result by 4. What number did he think of?

c Sasha thinks of a number. She multiplies her number by 5, then subtracts 4. The answer is the same as 2 times the number plus 20. What number did Sasha think of?

d Alicia thinks of a number. She adds 7 to the number, then divides 75 by the result. The answer is 5. What number did Alicia think of?

e Jake thinks of a number. He doubles the number, then divides 126 by the result. The answer is 9. What number did Jake think of?

14 The diagram shows the sizes of the two equal angles in an isosceles triangle.

a Write an equation to represent the situation.

b Solve your equation to find the value of x.

c Work out the size of all three of the angles in the triangle.

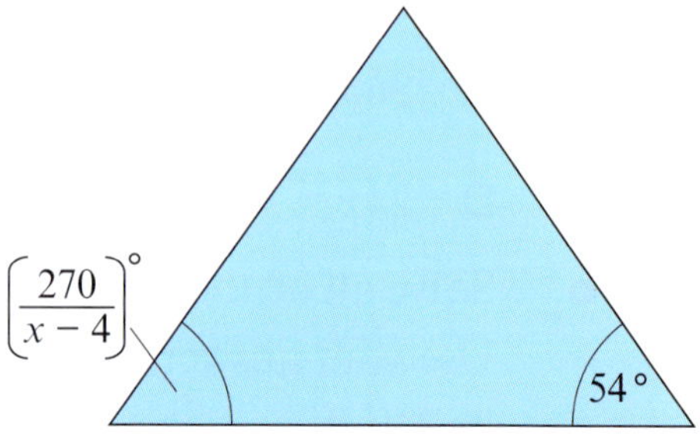

15 **a** Write a problem to represent each equation.

i $x + 2(x + 1) + 3(x + 2) + 4(x + 3) = 80$ **ii** $6(3a - 4) = 3(4a - 3)$ **iii** $\frac{180}{x - 5} = 15$

b Solve the equations in part **a**.

Summary checklist

- [ ] I can understand and solve equations.
- [ ] I can write and solve equations.

4.2 Simultaneous equations

In this section you will …

- solve simultaneous equations.

Key words

method of elimination

method of substitution

simultaneous equations

The sum of two numbers is 37. The difference between the two numbers is 13. What are the numbers?

Call the numbers x and y. Then: $x + y = 37$ and $x - y = 13$

Now you have **two** equations and **two** unknowns. These are **simultaneous equations**. You need to find the values of x and y that solve **both** equations simultaneously. There is only one value for x and one value for y for which both of the equations are true.

In this case, $x = 25$ and $y = 12$ because $25 + 12 = 37$ and $25 - 12 = 13$.

Worked example 4.2

Solve these simultaneous equations:

$y = 3x + 1$ and $y = x + 9$

Answer

Step 1 $3x + 1 = x + 9$	You know from the first equation that $y = 3x + 1$, so you can use the **method of substitution** and substitute the y in the second equation with $3x + 1$.
$3x - x = 9 - 1$	Rearrange the equation to get the xs on one side and the numbers on the other side.
$2x = 8$ $x = \frac{8}{2} = 4$	Solve as normal to find the value of x.

Continued

Step 2 $y = 3x + 1$ $= 3 \times 4 + 1$ $= 13$	Substitute $x = 4$ into either of the equations to find the value of y.
Step 3 $y = x + 9$ $= 4 + 9$ $= 13$	Substitute $x = 4$ into the other equation to check you get the same value for y. If you don't get the same value, you have made a mistake.
Step 4 $x = 4$ $y = 13$	Clearly write your answers at the end of your working.

Exercise 4.2

1 Copy and complete the workings to solve the equations $y = 5x - 3$ and $y = 2x + 15$

Step 1: Work out x.

$5x - 3 = 2x + 15$

$5x - \square = 15 + \square$

$\square x = \square$

$x = \dfrac{\square}{\square} = \square$

Step 2: Work out y.

$y = 5x - 3$

$= 5 \times \square - 3$

$= \square - 3$

$= \square$

Step 3: Check values are correct.

$y = 2x + 15$

$= 2 \times \square + 15$

$= \square + 15$

$= \square$

Step 4: Write the answers: $x = \square$ and $y = \square$

2 Solve the simultaneous equations $y = 2x - 1$ and $y = x + 4$

3 Solve the simultaneous equations $y = x + 9$ and $y = 3x + 1$

4 Solve the simultaneous equations $y = 9 - 2x$ and $y = x - 12$

Think like a mathematician

5 a Copy and complete the tables of values for each equation.

$y = 3x + 1$

x	0	3	6
y			

$y = x + 9$

x	0	3	6
y			

Continued

b On graph paper, draw a coordinate grid from 0 to 6 on the x-axis and from 0 to 20 on the y-axis.

Plot the points from your tables on the grid and draw the straight lines $y = 3x + 1$ and $y = x + 9$.

c Write the coordinates of the points where your two lines intersect.

d What do you notice about your answers to part **c**, and the solution to the simultaneous equations in Worked example 4.2?

e Discuss your answer to part **d** with other learners in your class.

In general, what can you say about the solution of two simultaneous equations and the coordinates of the point where the lines of the two equations intersect?

6 **a** Solve these simultaneous equations using

i a graphical method

ii an algebraic method.

$y = 3x$ and $y = x + 4$

b Check that your answers to part **ai** and **aii** are the same.

c Which method do you prefer, the graphical or the algebraic method? Explain why.

Tip

For the graphical method, use the same method as in Question **5**. For the algebraic method, use the same method as in questions **1** to **4**.

Think like a mathematician

7 Work with a partner to answer these questions.

a Solve these simultaneous equations.

i $y = 3x + 1$ and $5x = y + 3$

ii $x = 4y - 2$ and $y + x = 8$

b Discuss the methods you used in part **a** with other learners in your class.

Critique the various methods and decide which method is easiest to use.

8 Sergio and Fausta solve the simultaneous equations $x + 3y = 25$ and $4x = 3y + 10$. They both use the method of substitution, but their methods are slightly different. This is what they write:

Sergio	Fausta
Rearrange $x + 3y = 25 \rightarrow x = 25 - 3y$	Rearrange $x + 3y = 25 \rightarrow 3y = 25 - x$
Substitute $x = 25 - 3y$ into $4x = 3y + 10$	Substitute $3y = 25 - x$ into $4x = 3y + 10$
$4(25 - 3y) = 3y + 10$	$4x = 25 - x + 10$
$100 - 12y = 3y + 10$	$5x = 35$
$100 - 10 = 3y + 12y$	$x = \frac{35}{5} = 7$
$90 = 15y$	Substitute $x = 7$ into $3y = 25 - x$
$y = \frac{90}{15} = 6$	$3y = 25 - 7$
Substitute $y = 6$ into $x = 25 - 3y$	$3y = 18$
$x = 25 - 3 \times 6 = 25 - 18 = 7$	$y = \frac{18}{3} = 6$
Check in second equation:	Check in second equation:
$4 \times 7 = 3 \times 6 + 10 \rightarrow 28 = 28$ ✓	$4 \times 7 = 3 \times 6 + 10 \rightarrow 28 = 28$ ✓
$x = 7$ and $y = 6$	$x = 7$ and $y = 6$

a Use Sergio's method to solve these simultaneous equations.

i $x + 2y = 17$ and $3x = 4y + 11$

ii $2x + y = 28$ and $4y = x + 22$

Tip

For part **i**, rearrange $x + 2y = 17$ to get $x = \ldots$ For part **ii**, rearrange $2x + y = 28$ to get $y = \ldots$ OR rearrange $4y = x + 22$ to get $x = \ldots$

b Use Fausta's method to solve these simultaneous equations.

i $x + 2y = 8$ and $5x = 2y + 4$

ii $3x + 2y = 28$ and $3y = 3x + 12$

Tip

For part **i**, rearrange $x + 2y = 8$ to get $2y = \ldots$ For part **ii**, rearrange $3x + 2y = 28$ to get $3x = \ldots$ OR rearrange $3y = 3x + 12$ to get $3x = \ldots$

9 Solve each pair of simultaneous equations. Use your favourite algebraic method.

a $x + y = 7$, $y = 2x - 8$

b $y + x = 19$, $x = 5y + 1$

c $2x + y = 18$, $y = 2x - 10$

d $y = 2x$, $x = 2y - 9$

10 Sofia and Zara solve the simultaneous equations $y = 3(x + 5)$ and $2x + y = 0$.

Read what they say.

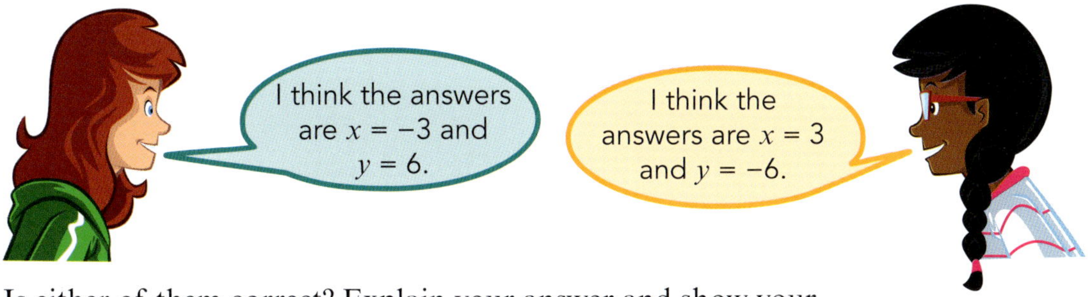

Is either of them correct? Explain your answer and show your working.

11 Afua uses the **method of elimination** to solve the simultaneous equations

$x + y = 37$ and $x - y = 13$.

This is what she writes.

Step 1: Add the two equations.

$$\begin{array}{r} x + \ y = 37 \\ + \ x - \ y = 13 \\ \hline 2x + 0y = 50 \end{array}$$

$$2x = 50, \ x = \frac{50}{2} = 25$$

Step 2: Substitute $x = 25$ into the first equation:

$$25 + y = 37$$
$$y = 37 - 25$$
$$= 12$$

Step 3: Check in second equation

$$25 - 12 = 13 \ ✓$$

Step 4: State answers

$$x = 25 \text{ and } y = 12$$

Tip

When Afua adds the two equations, she eliminates the ys as one is positive and one is negative: $y + -y = 0y = 0$

Use the method of elimination to copy and complete the workings to solve these simultaneous equations.

a $2x + y = 50$ and $x - y = 4$

Step 1: Add the two equations.

$$\begin{array}{r} 2x + y = 50 \\ + \quad x - y = 4 \\ \hline 3x + 0y = \square \end{array}$$

$3x = \square$, $x = \frac{\square}{3} = \square$

Step 2: Substitute $x = \square$ into the first equation:

$2 \times \square + y = 50$

$y = 50 - \square$

$= \square$

Step 3: Check in second equation.

$\square - \square = \square$

Step 4: State answers.

$x = \square$ and $y = \square$

b $x + 4y = 41$ and $x + 2y = 23$

Step 1: Subtract the two equations.

$$\begin{array}{r} x + 4y = 41 \\ - \quad x + 2y = 23 \\ \hline 0x + 2y = \square \end{array}$$

$2y = \square$, $y = \frac{\square}{2} = \square$

Step 2: Substitute $y = \square$ into the first equation:

$x + 4 \times \square = 41$

$x = 41 - \square$

$= \square$

Step 3: Check in second equation.

$\square + 2 \times \square = \square$

Step 4: State answers.

$x = \square$ and $y = \square$

c $3x + 2y = 38$ and $3x - y = 26$

Step 1: Subtract the two equations.

$$\begin{array}{r} 3x + 2y = 38 \\ - \quad 3x - y = 26 \\ \hline 0x + 3y = \square \end{array}$$

$3y = \square$, $y = \frac{\square}{3} = \square$

Step 2: Substitute $y = \square$ into the first equation:

$3x + 2 \times \square = 38$

$3x = 38 - \square$

$3x = \square$, $x = \frac{\square}{3} = \square$

Step 3: Check in second equation.

$3 \times \square - \square = \square$

Step 4: State answers.

$x = \square$ and $y = \square$

Tip

Be careful with the double negative in part **c**: $2y - -y = 2y + y$.

Think like a mathematician

12 **a** Look at the following simultaneous equations.

Discuss with a partner how you can decide whether you need to add or subtract the equations in each part when you solve them using elimination.

In one part you can do either. Which part is it?

i $x + y = 15$ $x - y = 3$ **ii** $x + 6y = 9$ $x + 2y = 1$ **iii** $2x + y = 19$ $3x - y = 21$ **iv** $3x + 2y = 37$ $x + 2y = 19$

b Discuss your answers to part **a** with other learners in the class.

c Describe a general rule you can follow to help you to decide when you should add or subtract simultaneous equations when you solve them using elimination.

d On your own, solve the simultaneous equations in part **a** using elimination.

Check your workings and answers with your partner.

Activity 4.2

Work with a partner for this activity.

Here are five equation cards.

A	$y = 3x$	B	$5x + y = 48$	C	$x + y = 24$
D	$y = 4x - 6$	E	$x = 3y - 48$		

a Choose two cards. Ask your partner to solve the simultaneous equations you have chosen.

Make sure you give your partner a different pair of equations to the pair they choose for you.

Use your favourite method to solve the equations, then ask your partner to check your working and answers.

b Compare your answers with your partner's answers. Did you get the same answers? If you got different answers, check each other's working again, as your answers should be the same.

13 Solve these simultaneous equations. Use any method.

a $2x + y = 22$, $x - y = 5$ **b** $y = 2x - 12$, $x + y = 3$

c $y = 2x$, $x + 3y = 14$ **d** $6x + 7y = 49$, $3x - 7y = 14$

14 a Solve these simultaneous equations using a graphical method.

$3x + y = 8$

$4x + 2y = 12$

b Show that your values for x and y are correct by substituting them into both equations.

Tip

Rearrange both equations to make y the subject, then draw tables of values for $x = 0$, 2 and 4.

Tip

When you are told to use a graphical method you must not use an algebraic method.

In this section, you have learned to solve simultaneous equations using three different methods:

1 Drawing a graph **2** Using substitution **3** Using elimination

Write down the method numbers, 1, 2, and 3, in order from your favourite method to your least favourite method.

What do you like about your favourite method?

What do you dislike about your least favourite method?

Imagine your partner has never solved simultaneous equations. Describe to your partner how to solve simultaneous equations using your favourite method.

Summary checklist

☐ I can solve simultaneous equations.

4.3 Inequalities

In this section you will …

- solve inequalities.

Key words

inequality

solution set

Here is an equation: $2x + 3 = 10$

To solve it, first subtract 3. $2x = 7$

Then divide by 2. $x = 3.5$

Now here is an **inequality**: $2x + 3 < 10$. You can solve an inequality in the same way as an equation.

First subtract 3. $2x < 7$

Then divide by 2. $x < 3.5$

The **solution set** is any value of x less than 3.5.

You can show this on a number line:

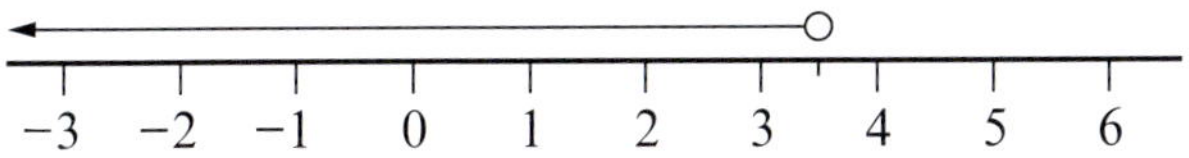

The open circle (○) shows that 3.5 is **not** included.

Tip

The solution to an equation is a single value.

Tip

The solution to an inequality is a range of values.

Tip

Remember the inequality signs:

$<$ means 'is less than'

$\leqslant$ means 'is less than or equal to'

$>$ means 'is greater than'

$\geqslant$ means 'is greater than or equal to'

Tip

For the solution $x \leqslant 3.5$, 3.5 **is** included and you would use a closed circle (●) on your number line.

Worked example 4.3

The perimeter of this triangle is at least 50 cm.

a Write an inequality to show this.

b Solve the inequality.

c Show the solution set on a number line.

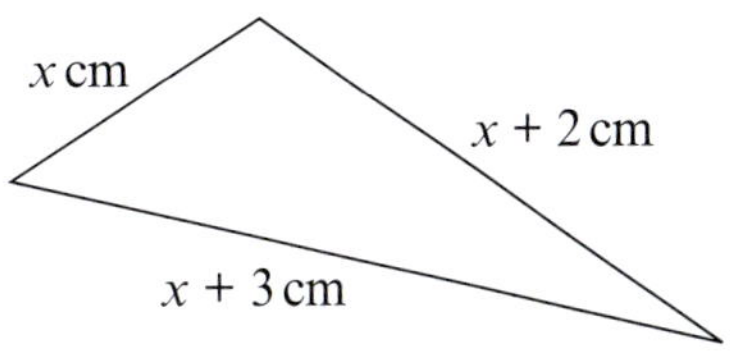

Continued

Answer

a Perimeter $= x + x + 2 + x + 3$ $= 3x + 5$	Write an expression for the perimeter of the triangle and simplify.
$3x + 5 \geqslant 50$	Write the inequality using $\geqslant$. 'At least 50' means '50 or more'.
b $3x \geqslant 45$	Subtract 5 from both sides.
$x \geqslant 15$	Divide both sides by 3.
c 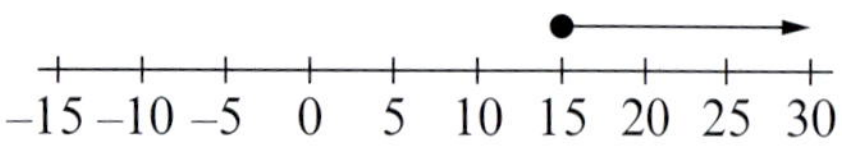	The closed circle (●) shows that 15 is in the solution set.

Exercise 4.3

1 Write an inequality to describe each of these solution sets.

a 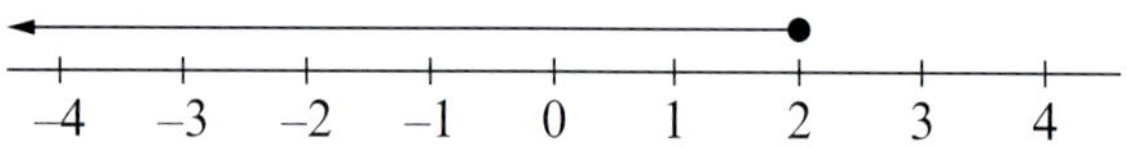

b 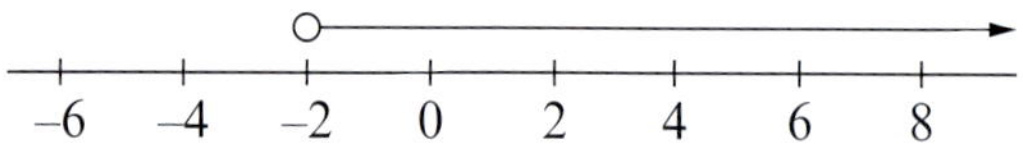

c 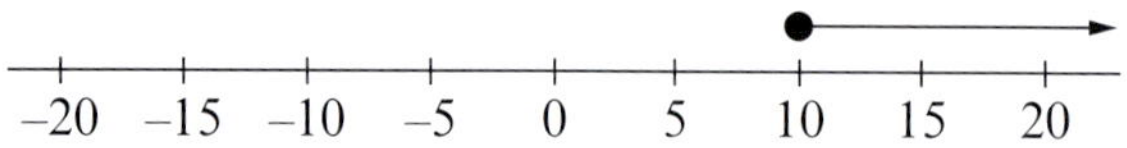

d 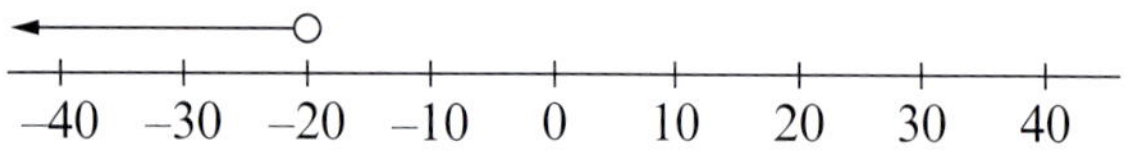

e 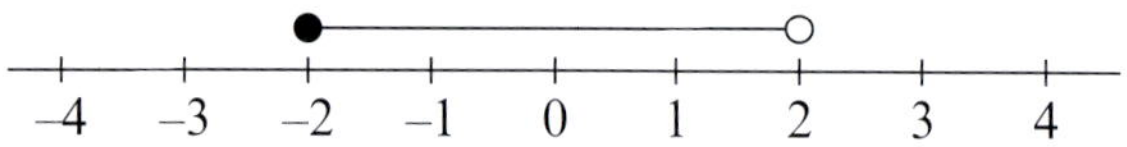

f 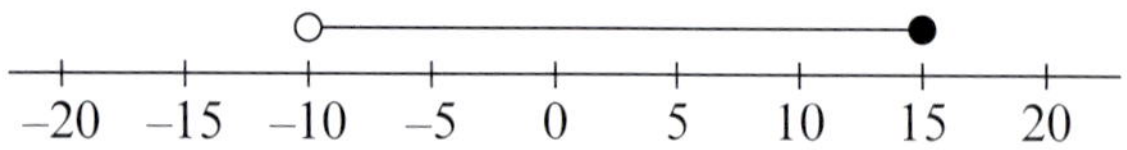

2 Show each of these solution sets on a number line.

a $x > 3$ **b** $x \leqslant -3$ **c** $x < 0$

d $x \geqslant -20$ **e** $0 < x \leqslant 7$ **f** $-2 \leqslant x < 5$

3 N is an integer. Work out

a the smallest possible value of N when $N \geqslant 6.5$

b the largest possible value of N when $N < -3$

c the possible values of N when $-2 \leqslant N < 2$

4 Solve these inequalities.

a $5x > 10$ b $4x + 1 \leqslant 17$

c $3x + 1 < -8$ d $3(x + 1) \geqslant -6$

5 Show each solution set in Question **4** on a number line.

Think like a mathematician

6 Work with a partner to answer this question.

a Solve the inequality $4x + 5 < 17$

b What methods can you use to check that your solution set is correct?

c Discuss your answers to part **b** with other learners in your class.
Critique and improve the different methods to decide which method is best.

7 This is part of Franco's homework.

<u>Question</u>

a Solve the inequality $3(x + 2) \leqslant 2x - 5$

b Check your solution set is correct.

<u>Answer</u>

a Expand brackets: $3x + 2 \leqslant 2x - 5$

Collect like terms: $3x - 2x \leqslant -5 - 2$

Simplify: $x \leqslant -7$

b When $x = -7$ $3(-7 + 2) \leqslant 2 \times -7 - 5$

$-15 \leqslant -19$ (false)

When Franco checks his solution set in part **b**, he gets an incorrect inequality. This shows he has made a mistake.

a Look back at Franco's working and find the mistake he has made.

Show that the correct solution set is $x \leqslant -11$

b Substitute **i** $x = -12$, **ii** $x = -11$ and **iii** $x = -10$ into $3(x + 2) \leqslant 2x - 5$

Explain how this shows that the correct solution set is $x \leqslant -11$

8 a Show that the solution set to the inequality $4(2y + 3) - 5y < 18 - y$ is $y < 1.5$

b Substitute **i** $y = 1$, **ii** $y = 1.5$ and **iii** $y = 2$ into $4(2y + 3) - 5y < 18 - y$ to show that the solution set is correct.

9 Solve these inequalities. Check each solution set.

a $2(a + 4) < 15$
b $3b - 4 \geqslant b + 18$
c $c + 18 \leqslant 30 - c$
d $3(d + 5) > 2(d - 6)$

10 The perimeter of this triangle is not more than 30 cm.

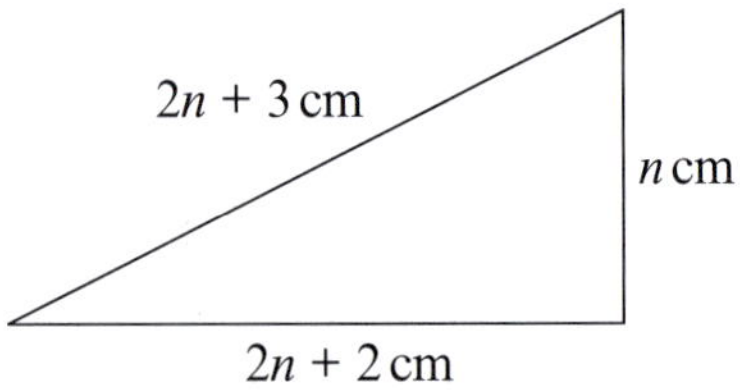

a Write an inequality to show this.
b Solve the inequality.
c What are the largest possible lengths of the sides?

Think like a mathematician

11 Work with a partner to answer this question.
Look at the methods Sergey and Natalia use to solve the inequality, $2x + 1 < 3x + 7$

Sergey

$$2x + 1 < 3x + 7$$
$$2x - 3x < 7 - 1$$
$$-x < 6$$
$$-x - 6 < 0$$
$$-6 < x$$
$$x > -6$$

Natalia

$$2x + 1 < 3x + 7$$
$$2x - 3x < 7 - 1$$
$$-x < 6$$
$$\frac{-x}{-1} > \frac{6}{-1}$$
$$x > -6$$

a Discuss the differences in their methods at the fourth line of each solution.
Do you understand how each method works?
Whose method do you prefer, Sergey's or Natalia's? Explain why.
b Discuss your answers to part **a** with other learners in your class.
c Show that the solution to the inequality $2(x - 8) \geqslant 4x - 26$ is $x \leqslant 5$

12 Solve these inequalities. Check each solution set.

a $-3x < 12$
b $-4x \leqslant -20$
c $-42 > -7x$
d $6 - x \geqslant 19$
e $21 - 3x > x + 5$
f $4 - 10x \leqslant 20 - 2x$

13 The diagram shows triangle ABC.
Side length AB is less than side length AC.

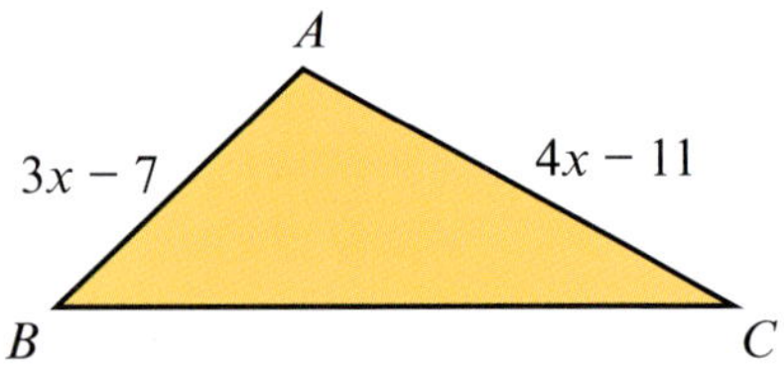

a Write an inequality to show this information.
b Solve your inequality.
c Check your solution is correct.

14 This is how Filipe solves $-1 < x + 5 \leqslant 4$ and represents his answer on a number line.

$$-1 < x + 5 \leqslant 4$$
$$-1 - 5 < x + 5 - 5 \leqslant 4 - 5$$
$$-6 < x \leqslant -1$$

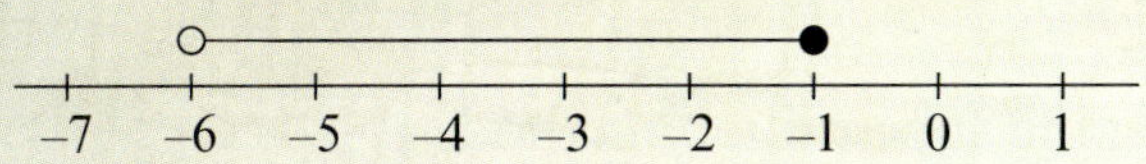

Solve these inequalities. Represent each answer on a number line.

a $4 < x + 2 \leqslant 7$

b $-1 \leqslant y - 6 \leqslant 14$

c $6 < 2n < 18$

d $-15 < 5m < 30$

> **Tip**
>
> To leave x in the central section of the inequality, Filipe subtracts 5 from all three sections of the inequality. This keeps the inequality balanced.

Summary checklist

☐ I can solve inequalities.

Check your progress

1 Solve these equations. Check each of your answers by substituting the answer back into the equation.

a $5x + 14 = -6$ **b** $a - 12 = 5a - 2$ **c** $6(x + 2) = 4(9 - x)$

d $0 = 12 - 2(y - 3)$ **e** $\frac{64}{m} = 4$ **f** $\frac{75}{n + 5} = 5$

2 Solve these simultaneous equations using the substitution method.
$y = 4x - 1$ $y = 2x + 9$

3 Solve these simultaneous equations using the elimination method.
$x + y = 26$ $x - y = 12$

4 Solve these inequalities. Check each solution set.

a $2a + 6 < 10$ **b** $5b - 1 \geqslant b + 19$

c $3(c + 5) > 2(5 - c)$ **d** $4d \leqslant 7d + 15$

5 Solve these inequalities. Represent each answer on a number line.

a $3 < x + 4 \leqslant 6$ **b** $-12 < 3n < 3$

5 Angles

Getting started

1 Two angles of a quadrilateral are 70° and one angle is 80°. Work out the fourth angle.

2

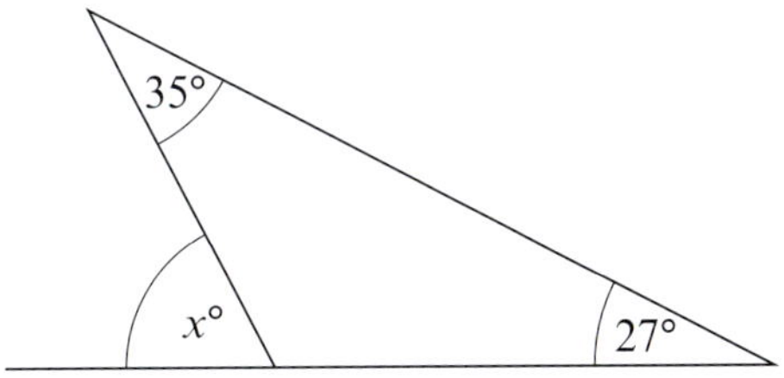

Work out the value of x.

3 From this diagram, give an example of

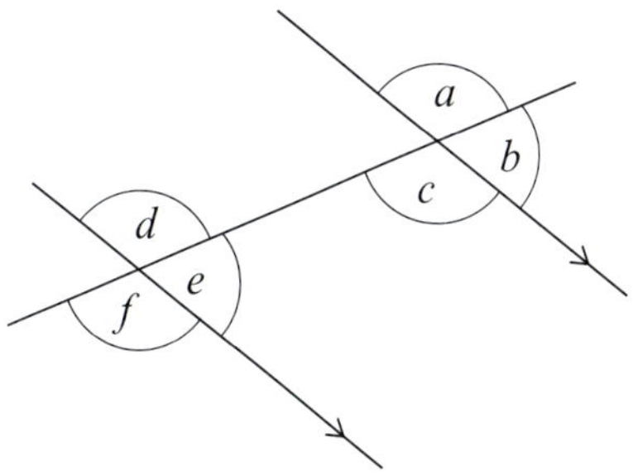

- a two corresponding angles
- b two alternate angles
- c two vertically opposite angles.

4 Use this diagram to explain why $a + b + c = 180°$.

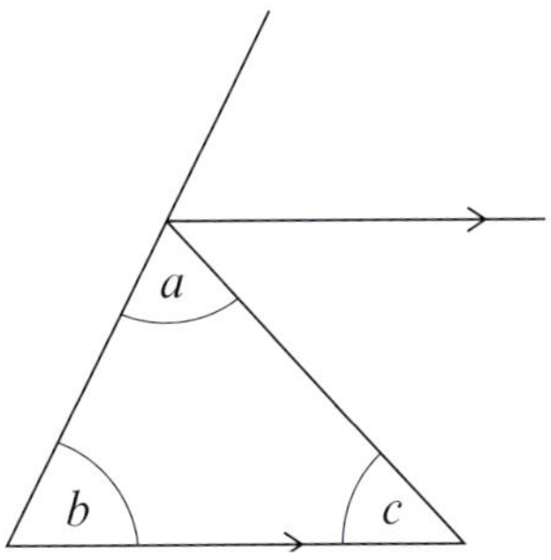

5 a Use a protractor to draw an angle of 75°.
- b Use a ruler and compasses to bisect the angle in part **a**.
- c Ask a partner to check that your bisection is accurate.

Islamic patterns are made from polygons. Here are two examples.

The second pattern is simpler. What polygons can you see in the second pattern?

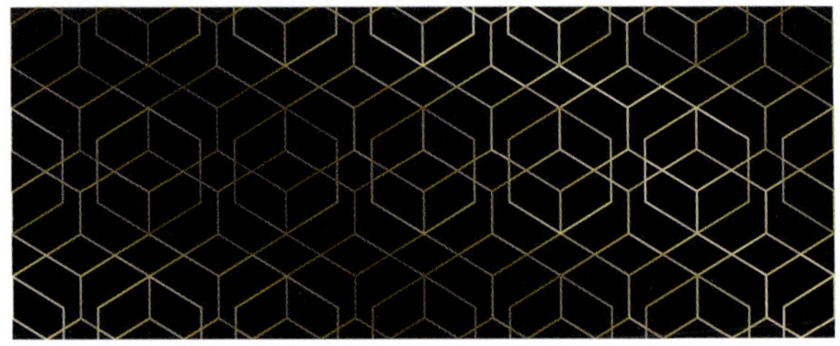

5.1 Calculating angles

In this section you will …

- use the properties of parallel lines to calculate angles
- use the properties of triangles and quadrilaterals to calculate angles
- use several different angle properties together.

In earlier stages, you have learned about angle properties of triangles, quadrilaterals and parallel lines. In this section, you will need to decide which properties to use to work out missing angles.

Worked example 5.1

Calculate the values of x and y.

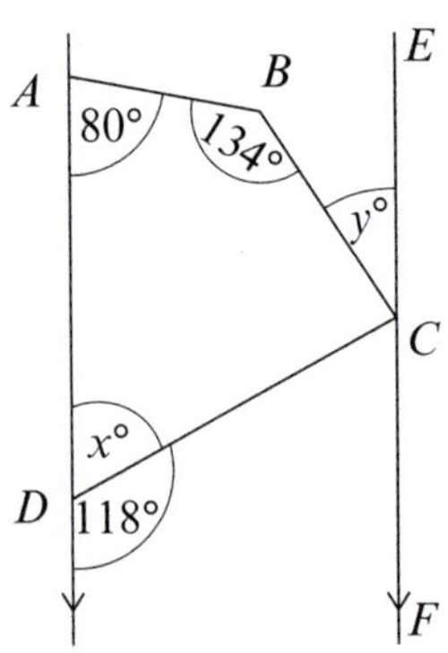

Continued

Answer

The sum of angles on a straight line is 180° and so $x = 180° - 118° = 62°$

Angle C of the quadrilateral is $360° - (62° + 80° + 134°) = 84°$

Angles DCF and ADC are alternate angles so angle $DCF = x° = 62°$

Then $y = 180 - (84 + 62) = 34$

Exercise 5.1

1 Work out the angles of this triangle.

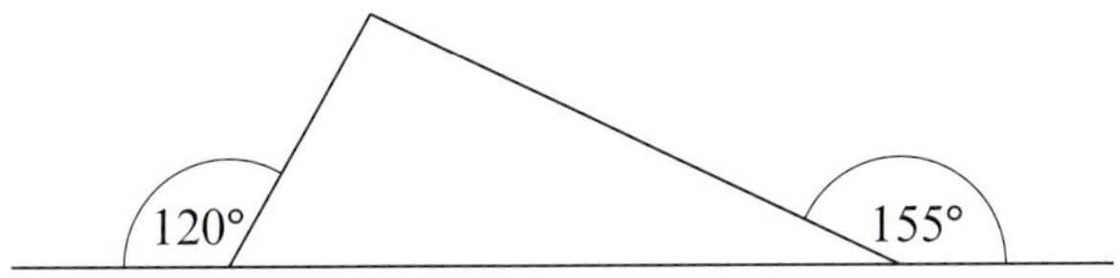

2 In this diagram, $AB = AC = AD$

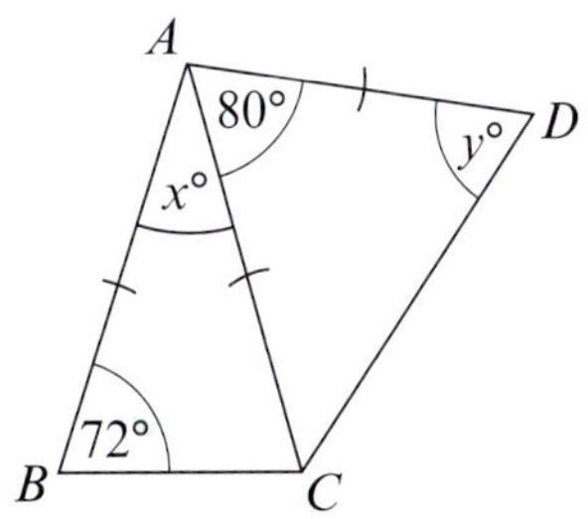

a Calculate x and y.

b Work out angle C of quadrilateral $ABCD$.

c Show that the sum of the four angles of the quadrilateral is 360°.

3 Calculate angles a, b, c and d.

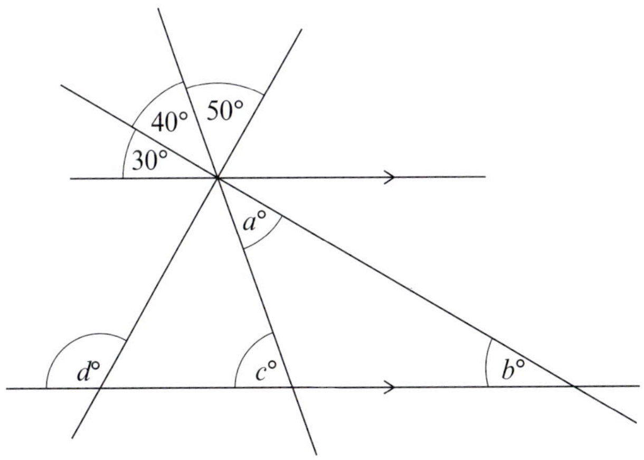

4 The angles of a quadrilateral are $x°$, $(x + 10)°$, $(x + 20)°$ and $(x + 30)°$.
Work out the value of x.

5 **a** What type of quadrilateral is $ABCD$?
Give a reason for your answer.

b Work out the angles of $ABCD$.

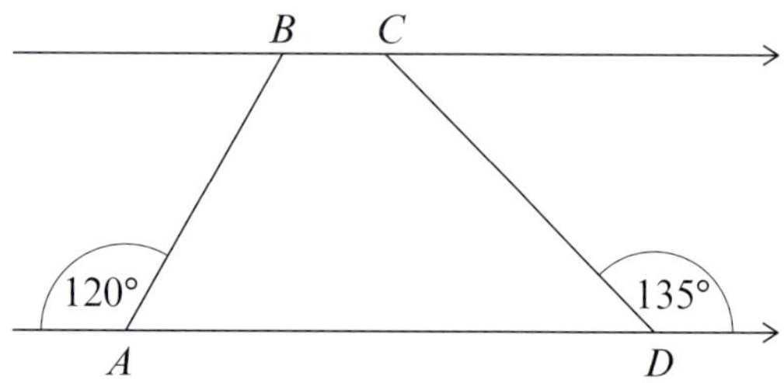

6 $ABCD$ is a kite.

Work out the angles of $ABCD$.

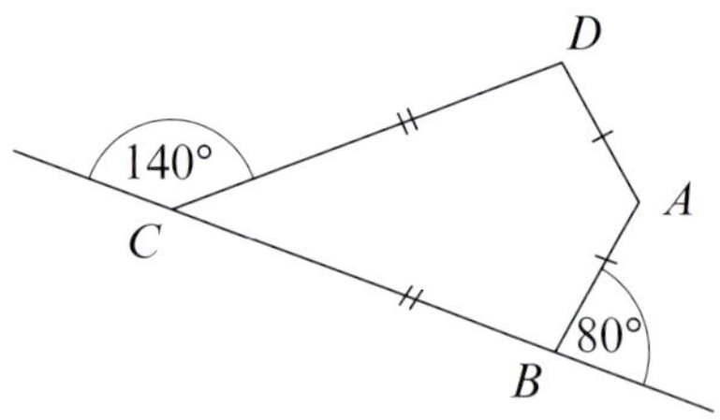

7 O is the centre of the circle. OA, OB and OC are radii.

Angle $AOB = 72°$.

Work out

a angle OAB **b** angle OCB **c** angle ABC.

Give reasons for your answers.

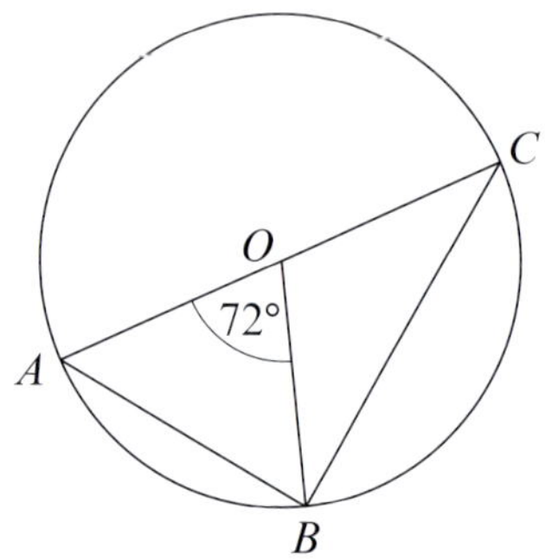

8 Work out the values of x and y. Justify your answers.

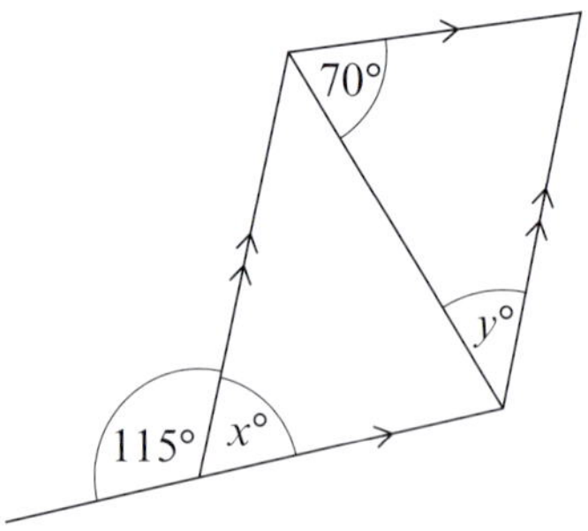

9 Work out the value of x.

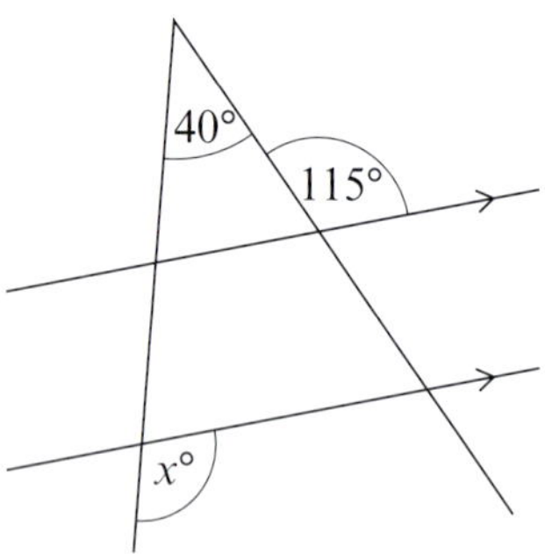

Discuss with a partner how you each solved the problem in Question 9. Did you use the same method or different methods?

10 *ACE* is a straight line.

a Calculate angle *BAD*.

b Show that the sum of the angles of *ABCD* is 360°.

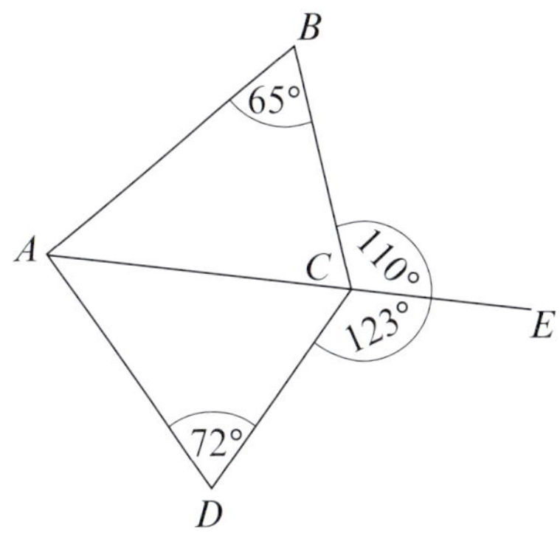

Summary checklist

- [ ] I can solve problems using the angle properties of triangles, quadrilaterals and parallel lines.
- [ ] I can use several different angle properties together.

5.2 Interior angles of polygons

In this section you will …

- derive and use a formula for the sum of the interior angles of a polygon
- work out the interior angles of regular polygons.

Key word

regular polygon

This is a pentagon. It has five sides and five angles. By joining vertices, you can split the pentagon into three triangles as shown. You can see that the angles of the triangles make the interior angles of the pentagon.

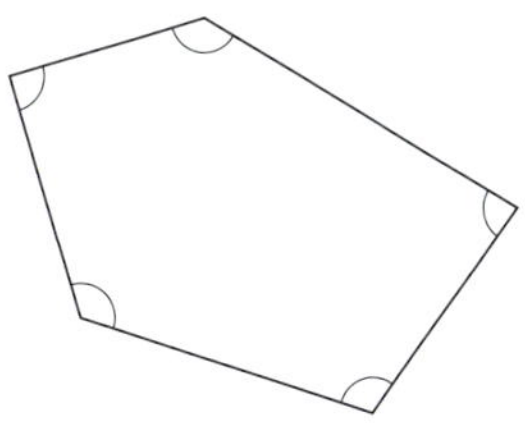

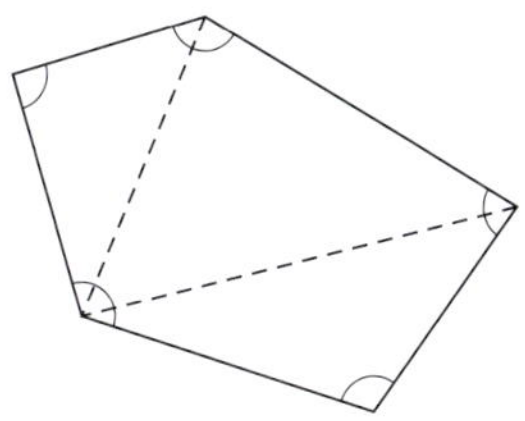

The sum of the interior angles of the pentagon = the sum of the angles of the three triangles

= 3 × 180° = 540°

The sum of the interior angles of **any** pentagon is 540°.

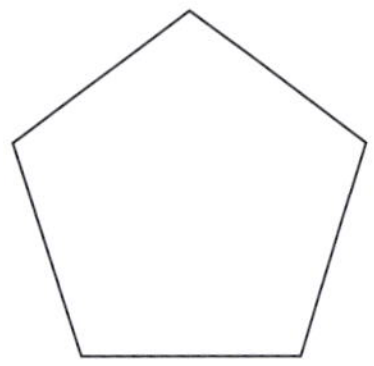

In a **regular polygon**, all the sides are the same length and all the angles are the same size. This is a regular pentagon. The sum of the five angles is 540°, so each angle of a regular pentagon is 540° ÷ 5 = 108°.

Exercise 5.2

1 Work out the missing interior angle of this pentagon.

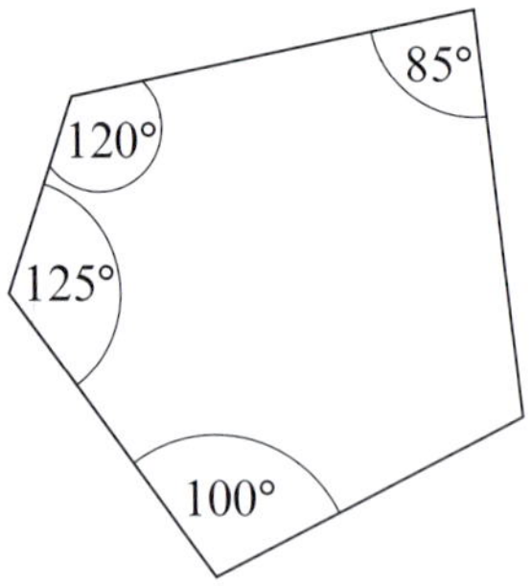

2 Four angles of a pentagon are 125° each. Work out the size of the fifth angle.

3 Two angles of a pentagon are 112° each and two angles are 90° each. Calculate the fifth angle.

4 a Work out the value of x.

  b Work out the largest angle of the pentagon.

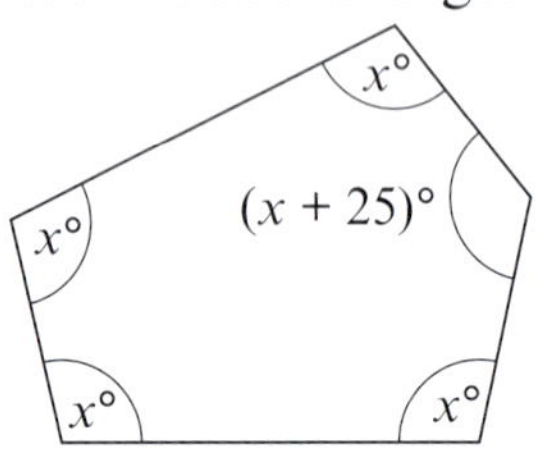

5 The angles of a pentagon are $y°$, $(y + 10)°$, $(y + 20)°$, $(y + 30)°$ and $(y + 40)°$.

  a Work out the value of y.

  b Work out the largest angle of the pentagon.

6 a A hexagon has 6 sides. Draw a hexagon.

  b By joining vertices, split the hexagon into triangles.

  c Show that the sum of the interior angles of a hexagon is 720°.

  d How big is each angle of a regular hexagon?

7 a Calculate the missing angle of this hexagon.

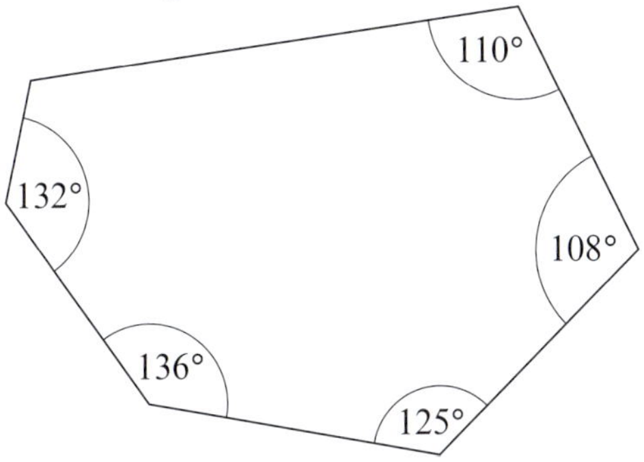

b Calculate the value of x.

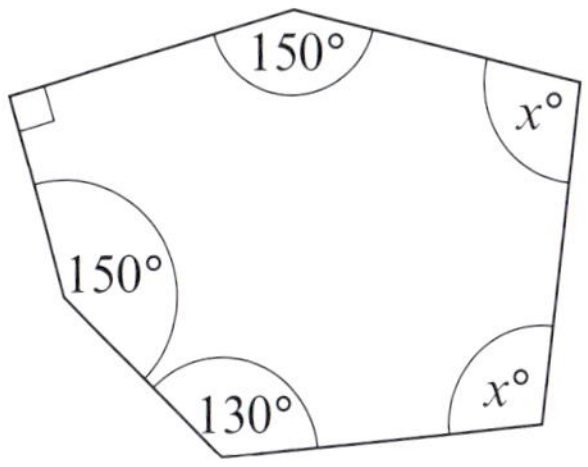

8 Work out the sum of the interior angles of

a an octagon
b a decagon.

Justify your answer in each case.

Tip

An octagon has 8 sides. A decagon has 10 sides.

9 a Copy and complete this table.

Polygon	Number of sides	Sum of interior angles
triangle	3	
quadrilateral	4	360°
pentagon		
hexagon		
octagon		
decagon	10	

b Derive a formula for the sum of the interior angles of a polygon with n sides.

c A nonagon is a polygon with 9 sides. Show that your formula from part **b** gives the correct answer for the sum of the angles of a nonagon.

10 a 7 of the interior angles of an octagon are 140° each. Work out the eighth angle.

b Work out the interior angle of a regular octagon.

11 This is a regular decagon.
How big is each interior angle?

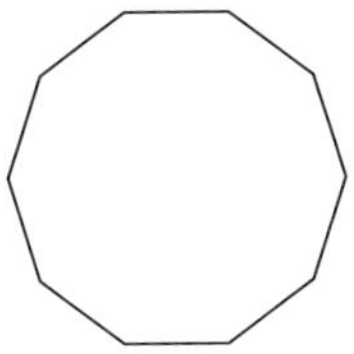

12 a Show that it is possible for 2 squares and 3 equilateral triangles to meet at one point.

b Draw a different way for 2 squares and 3 equilateral triangles with sides the same length to meet at one point.

c Can you work out a third way for 2 squares and 3 equilateral triangles to meet at one point? Give a reason for your answer.

Think like a mathematician

13 A tessellation is an arrangement of shapes that completely covers a space. Squared paper is a tessellation of squares.

a Draw a tessellation of equilateral triangles.

b Draw a tessellation of regular hexagons.

c Explain why it is not possible to draw a tessellation of regular pentagons.

d Draw a tessellation of squares and equilateral triangles. Is there more than one way to do this?

e Draw a tessellation using regular octagons and squares.

f What other tessellations can you draw using regular polygons?

Tip

For part **d**, look at your answer to Question 12.

Here is a different way to split a pentagon into triangles, using a point inside the shape.

Can you use the diagram to work out the sum of the angles of the pentagon?

Does it give the same answer as the previous method?

Summary checklist

- [ ] I can use the formula $(n - 2) \times 180^\circ$ to work out the sum of the interior angles of a polygon with n sides.
- [ ] I can calculate the interior angles of a regular polygon.

5.3 Exterior angles of polygons

In this section you will …

- learn about the sum of the exterior angles of a polygon
- work out and use the exterior angles of regular polygons.

Key word

exterior angle of a polygon

Here is a pentagon $ABCDE$. The exterior angles are shown. Imagine you are walking round the pentagon in an anticlockwise direction, starting and finishing at P. At A you turn through $a°$. At B you turn through $b°$, and so on. When you get back to P, you have turned through one whole turn or 360°. This shows that $a° + b° + c° + d° + e° = 360°$ and so the sum of the exterior angles of a pentagon is 360°.

There is nothing special about a pentagon. You can do the same for **any** polygon.

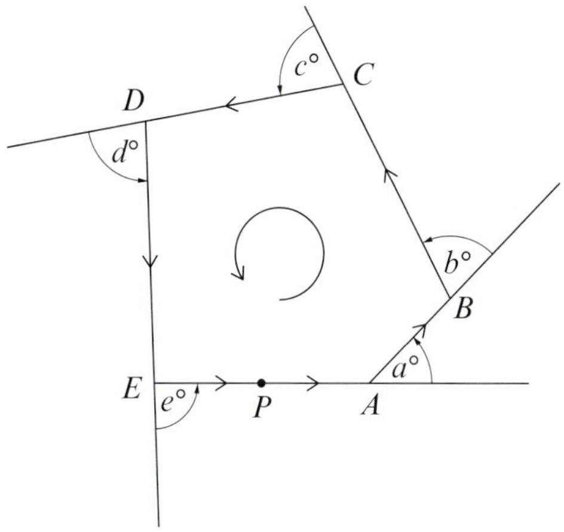

The sum of the exterior angles of any polygon is 360°.

Worked example 5.2

The exterior angle of a regular polygon is 36°. How many sides does it have?

Answer

All the exterior angles are 36° and the sum of the exterior angles is 360°.

The number of sides is $360 \div 36 = 10$ sides.

Exercise 5.3

1 a Draw a hexagon.
  b Draw the exterior angles on your hexagon.
  c Explain why the sum of the exterior angles is 360°.

2 Work out the lettered angles in these diagrams.

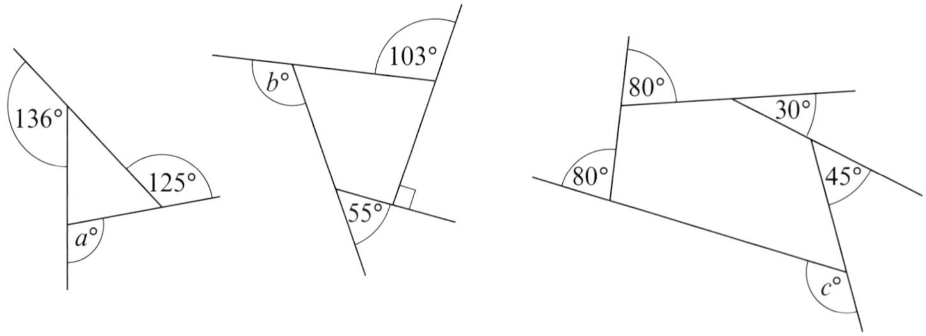

3 **a** There are two exterior angles at one vertex in this diagram.

Are these two angles equal? Give a reason for your answer.

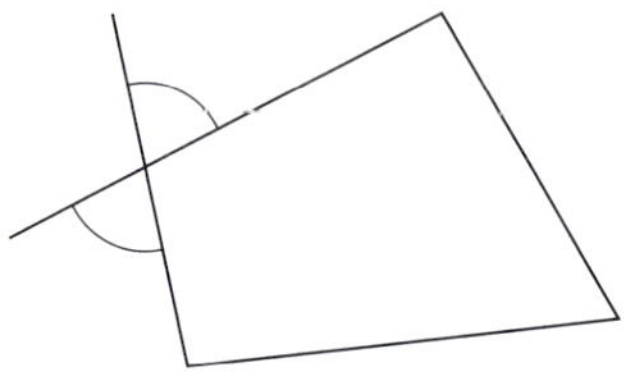

b Do these four angles add up to 360°? Give a reason for your answer.

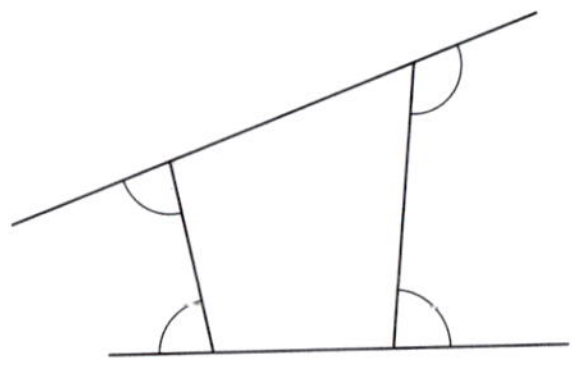

4 What are the exterior angles of

a an equilateral triangle **b** a square **c** a regular pentagon?

5 **a** What is the sum of the exterior angles of an octagon?

b Work out the exterior angle of a regular octagon.

6 **a** Copy and complete this table of regular polygons.

Regular polygon	Number of sides	Exterior angle
equilateral triangle	3	120°
square	4	
regular pentagon	5	72°
regular hexagon		
regular octagon	8	
regular decagon		

b Derive a formula for the exterior angle of a regular polygon with n sides.

c Use your formula from part **b** to work out the exterior angle of a regular polygon with

i 12 sides **ii** 20 sides.

7 The exterior angle of a regular polygon is 40°.

a Work out the number of sides.

b Write the interior angle.

8 a Work out the interior angle of a regular polygon when the exterior angle is

i 30° ii 20° iii 10°.

b Work out the number of sides of each of the regular polygons in part **a**.

9 Here is part of a regular polygon.

How many sides does the polygon have?

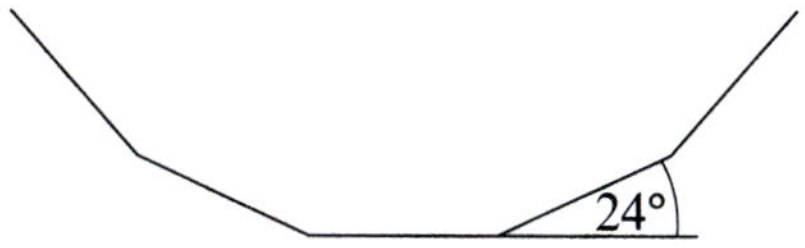

10 Work out the number of sides in a regular polygon when the exterior angle is

a 45° b 30° c 18° d 15°.

11 Here are two regular octagons.

a Show that the angle *ABC* is a right angle.

b Draw a diagram to show how four regular octagons can be arranged around a square.

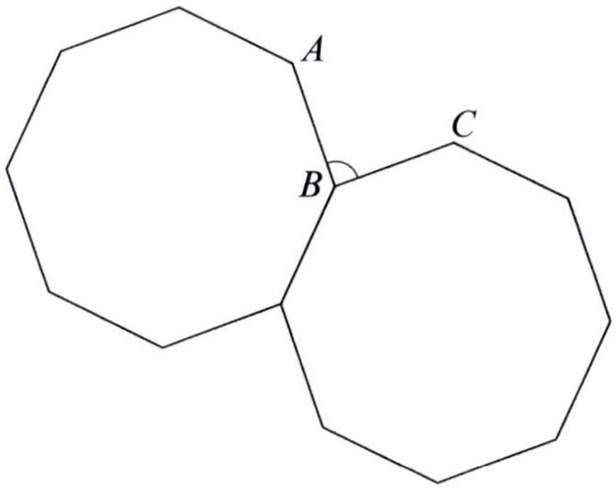

12 This diagram shows part of three identical regular polygons joined together around an equilateral triangle.

Work out the number of sides of each regular polygon.

Show how you get your answer.

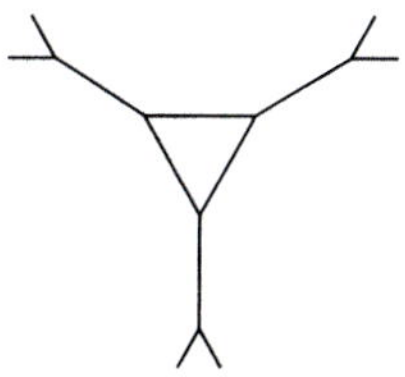

13 Show that it is possible for the interior angle of a regular polygon to be 168° or 170° but it is not possible for the interior angle of a regular polygon to be 169°.

If a regular polygon has n sides, each interior angle, in degrees, is

$$180 - \frac{360}{n} \qquad (1)$$

However, the sum of the interior angles is $(n-2) \times 180$ degrees

Therefore, each interior angle, in degrees, is

$$(n-2) \times 180 \div n \qquad (2)$$

Do the formulae (1) and (2) give the same answers?

Summary checklist

- [ ] I can show that the sum of the exterior angles of a polygon is 360°.
- [ ] I can work out the exterior angle of a regular polygon.

5.4 Constructions

In this section you will ...

- learn to construct angles of 60°, 45° and 30°
- learn to use a circle to draw a regular polygon.

Key word

inscribe

construct (geometry)

You know how to construct a perpendicular or bisect an angle using a ruler and compasses. In this section, you will learn to do more constructions with a ruler and compasses. Here are three examples.

Worked example 5.3

Inscribe a square in a circle.

Answer

a Draw a circle and a diameter.

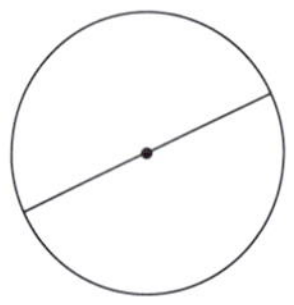

b **Construct** the perpendicular bisector of the diameter.

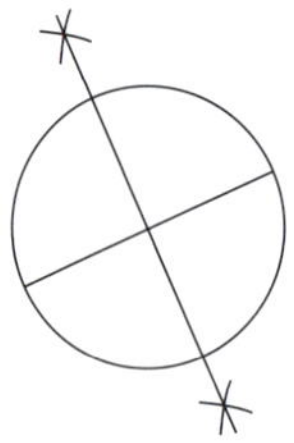

Tip

Put the point of the compasses on the end of the diameter.

c The points where the diameters meet the circle are the vertices of a square.

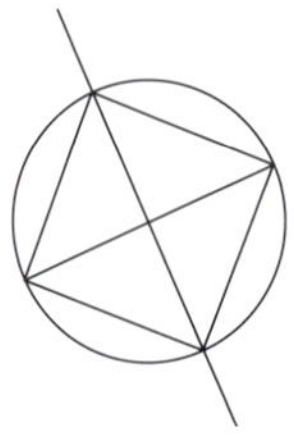

Worked example 5.4

Construct an angle of 45°.

Answer

Draw a line segment and its perpendicular bisector.

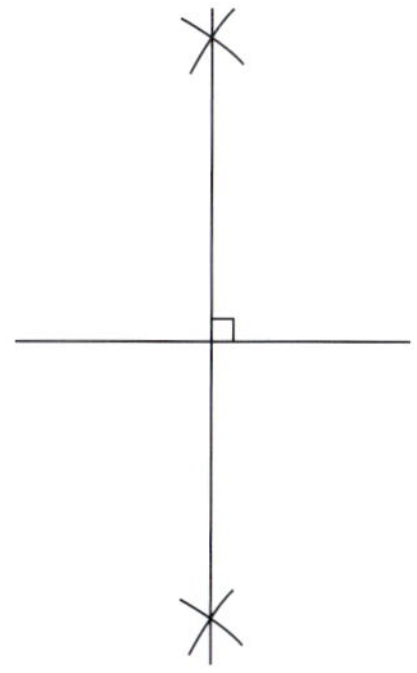

Bisect one of the right angles. This gives two angles of 45°.

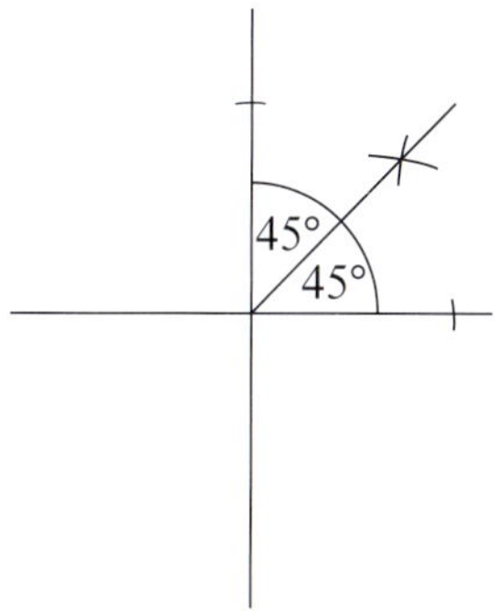

Worked example 5.5

Construct an angle of 60°.

Answer

Draw a line segment AB.

Open the compasses to the length of AB.

Draw arcs from A and B.

The point where the arcs cross is C.

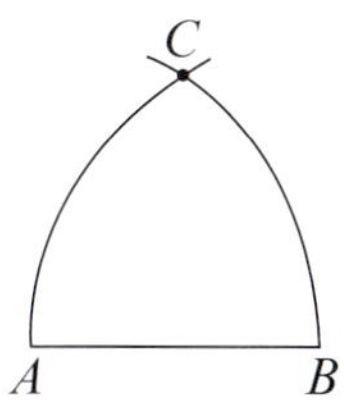

Continued

Join A to C. Angle CAB is 60°.

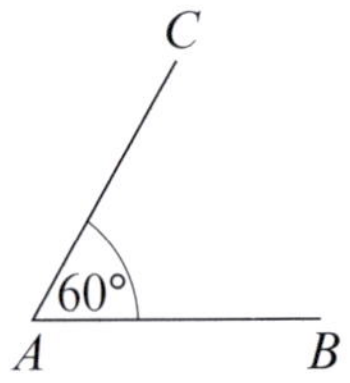

Join B to C. Angle CBA is 60°.

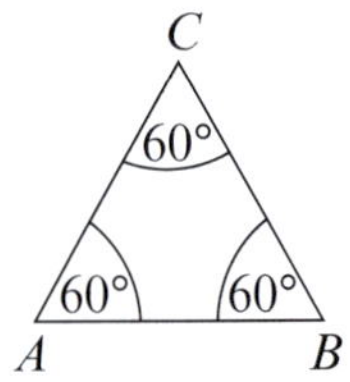

Exercise 5.4

Use plain paper for your constructions in this exercise. Only use a ruler and compasses for the constructions.

1 **a** Construct an angle of 60°.

b Bisect your angle in part **a** to make an angle of 30°.

c Use a protractor to check the accuracy of your angles.

2 **a** Draw an equilateral triangle with each side 6 cm long.

b Use a ruler and protractor to check the accuracy of your drawing.

3 **a** Draw a circle with a radius of 4 cm.

b Inscribe a square in the circle.

c Measure the length of each side of your square.

4 **a** Construct two perpendicular diameters in a circle.

b Construct a diameter bisecting each of the diameters in part **a**. Your diagram should look like this:

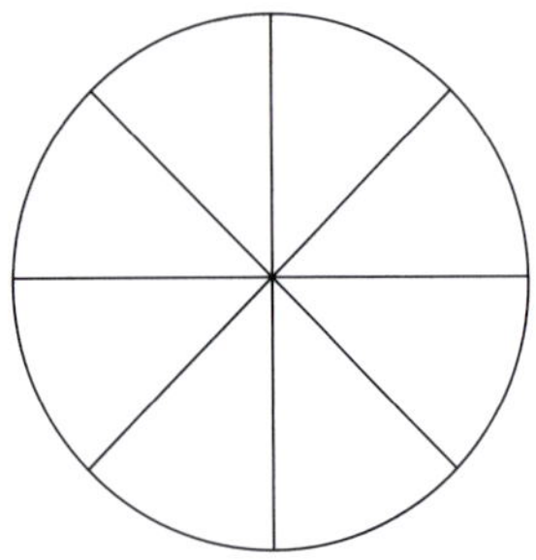

c Join the ends of the diameters to form a regular octagon.

d What is the interior angle of a regular octagon?

e Ask a partner to check that your octagon is regular by measuring the sides and angles.

5 **a** Construct a triangle with angles 30°, 60° and 90°.

b The longest side of your triangle should be double the length of the shortest side. Use this fact to check the accuracy of your drawing.

6 a Construct an equilateral triangle.

b Use your equilateral triangle to construct a triangle with angles 30°, 30° and 120°.

7 O is the centre of a circle. OAB and OCB are equilateral triangles.

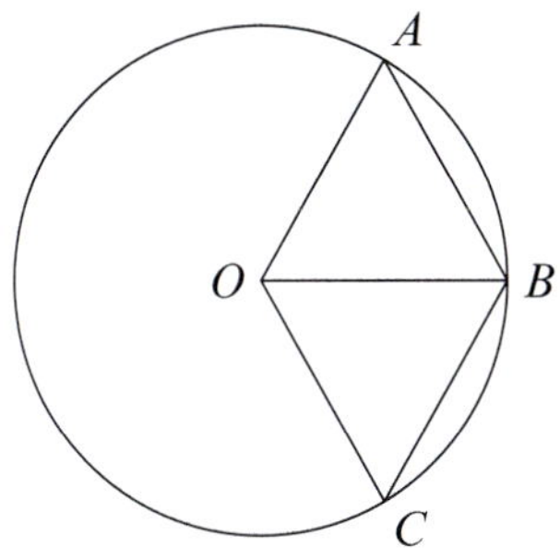

a Construct a copy of the diagram.

b Extend the diagram to inscribe a regular hexagon in the circle.

c What size are the angles of a regular hexagon?

d Ask a partner to check the accuracy of your construction.

8 Use a ruler and compasses to construct angles of

a 120° b 15°.

9 a Draw a circle with a radius of 6 cm.

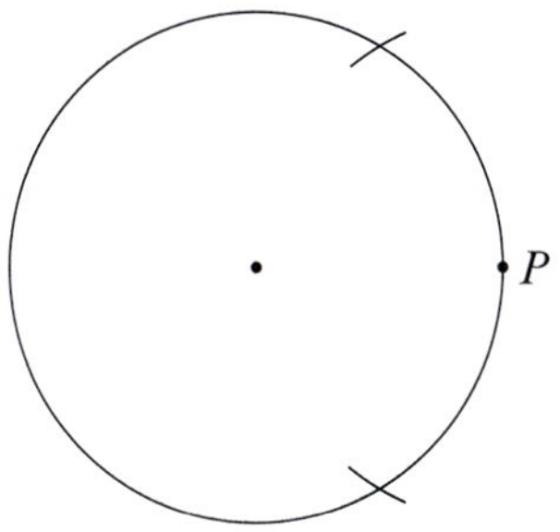

b Mark point P on the circumference. Put your compass point on P. Draw two arcs on the circumference of radius 6 cm.

c Draw more arcs on the circumference from these two points. Do not change the angle between the arms of your compasses when you do this.

d Keep your compasses the same and draw one more arc so you have six points on the circumference.

e Join the six points to make a hexagon.

f Check that your hexagon is regular and that the length of each side is 6 cm.

10 a This diagram shows four identical equilateral triangles.

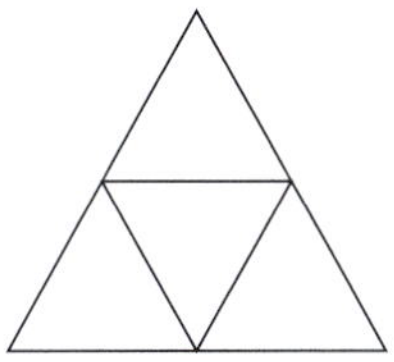

Construct a copy of the diagram.

b This diagram shows four identical triangles with angles 30°, 60° and 90°.

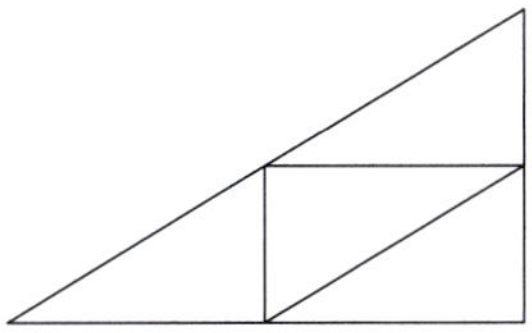

Construct a copy of the diagram.

11 a Draw a large circle. Inscribe a regular dodecagon inside the circle.

b What is the size of each angle of a regular dodecagon? Use this fact to check the accuracy of your drawing.

Tip

A dodecagon has 12 sides.

12 This pattern has rotational symmetry of order 6.

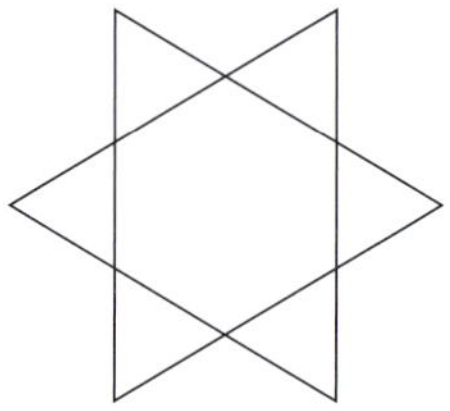

a **i** Construct a copy of the pattern.

ii How did you do the construction? Is there a different way? Which way is better?

This pattern has rotational symmetry of order 4.

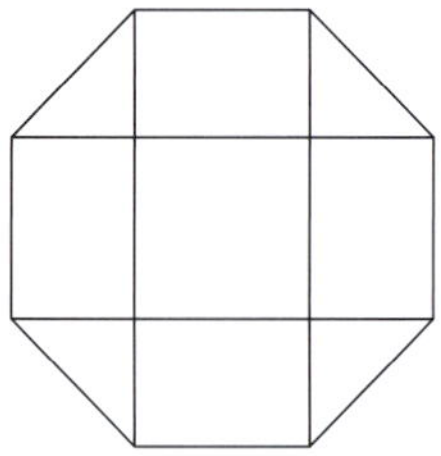

b **i** Construct a copy of the pattern.

ii How did you do the construction? Is there a different way? Which way is better?

13 Here are two rhombuses.

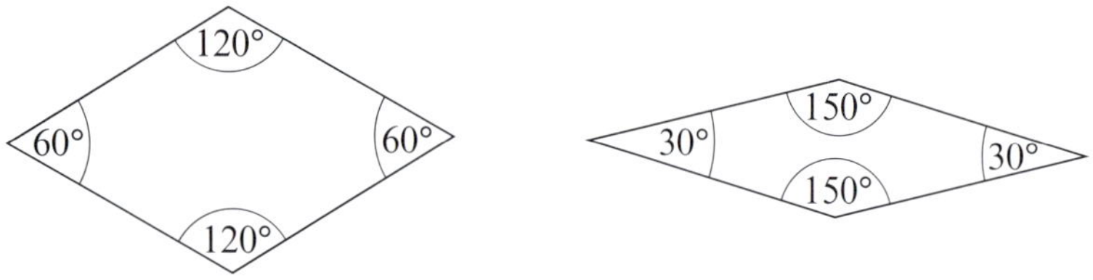

a Construct a copy of each rhombus.

b Ask a partner to check the accuracy of your drawings.

Summary checklist

- [ ] I can construct angles of 30°, 60° and 90° using a ruler and compasses.
- [ ] I can inscribe regular polygons in a circle.

5.5 Pythagoras' theorem

In this section you will ...

- learn the relationship between the three sides of a right-angled triangle
- use two sides of a right-angled triangle to calculate the third side.

Key words

hypotenuse

Pythagoras' theorem

A builder has built a wall. He wants to build a second wall at right angles to the first wall. How can he do this? One way is to use the 3-4-5 rule.

The builder measures out lengths of 3 metres, 4 metres and 5 metres on the ground in a triangle with the 3-metre side along the first wall as shown.

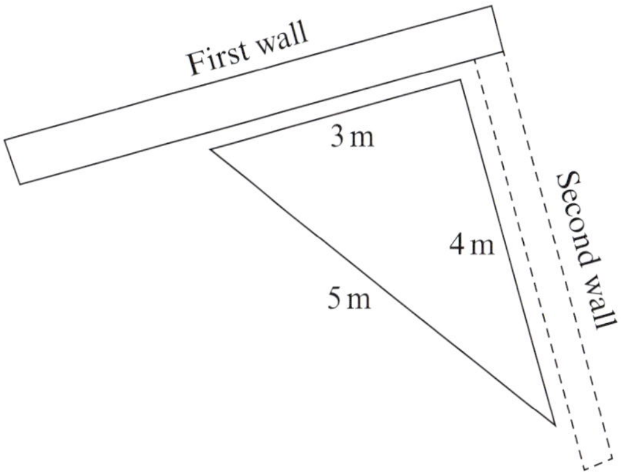

They build the second wall along the 4-metre side. The triangle is right-angled. The right angle is between the 3 m and 4 m sides. The longest side of a right-angled triangle is called the **hypotenuse**. In this example, the hypotenuse is 5 m long.

$3^2 = 9$, $4^2 = 16$ and $5^2 = 25$.
Hence $3^2 + 4^2 = 5^2$.

Tip

9 + 16 = 25

> The square of the hypotenuse is equal to the sum of the squares of the other two sides.

This result is true for **any** right-angled triangle: $a^2 + b^2 = c^2$

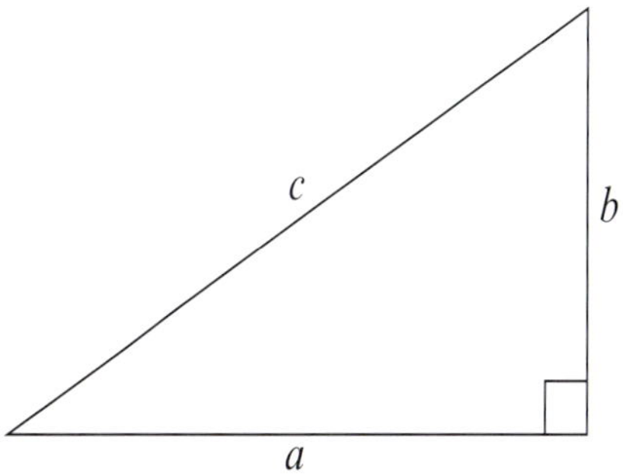

This result is called **Pythagoras' theorem**.
Pythagoras was born on the Greek island of Samos and wrote a proof of this theorem over 2500 years ago.

Worked example 5.6

$ABCD$ is a rectangle. Calculate the length of the diagonal AC.

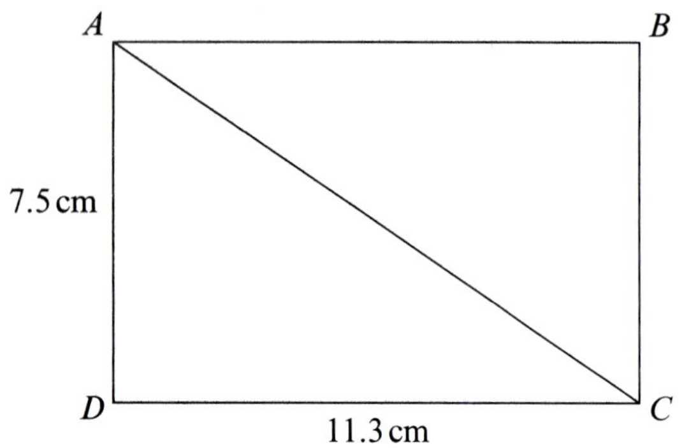

Answer

ADC is a right-angled triangle. AC is the hypotenuse.

If AC is x cm, then by Pythagoras' theorem:

$x^2 = 7.5^2 + 11.3^2 = 183.94$

So $x = \sqrt{183.94} = 13.6$ to 1 d.p.

> The square root of 183.94 is an irrational number. Round to 1 decimal place.

Worked example 5.7

Ari says: $a^2 = 6.0^2 + 3.5^2 = 48.25$, and so $a = \sqrt{48.25} = 6.9$

a Show that Ari is incorrect.

b Work out the correct value of a.

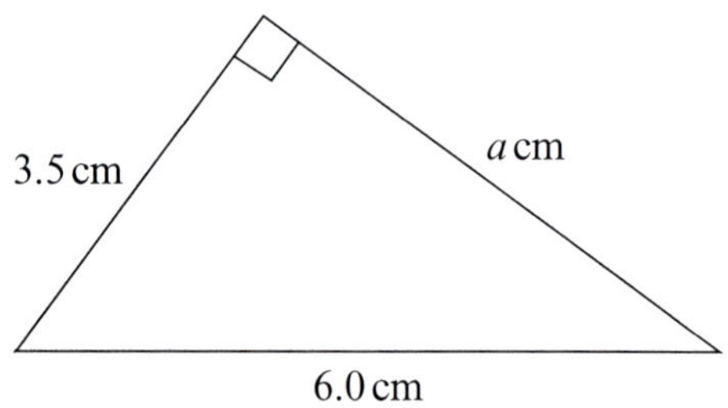

Answer

a Ari is incorrect because the hypotenuse is the 6.0 cm side, not the a cm side.

> The hypotenuse is the side opposite the right angle.

b Using Pythagoras' theorem: $a^2 + 3.5^2 = 6.0^2$

So $a^2 = 6.0^2 - 3.5^2 = 23.75$

and $a = \sqrt{23.75} = 4.9$ to 1 d.p.

Exercise 5.5

1 Calculate the length of the hypotenuse in each of these triangles.

a
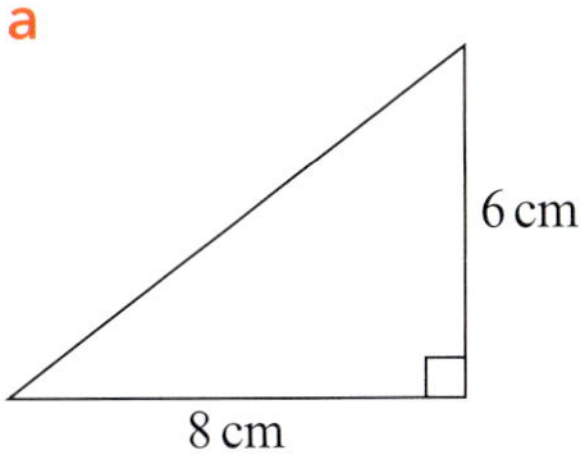

b
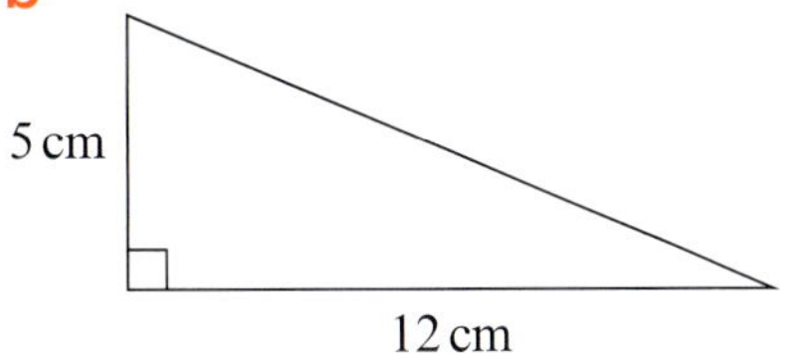

c
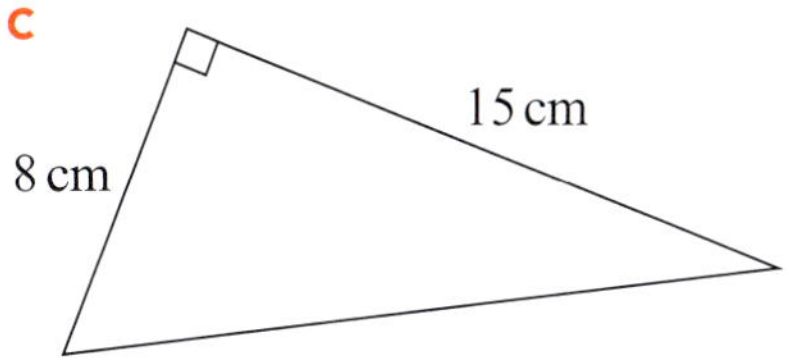

2 Calculate the length of the hypotenuse in each of these triangles.
Round your answers to 1 decimal place.

a
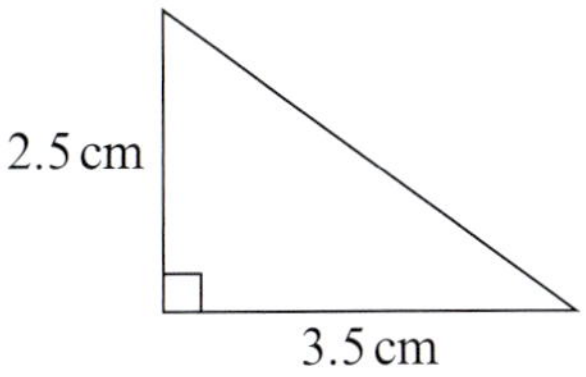

b
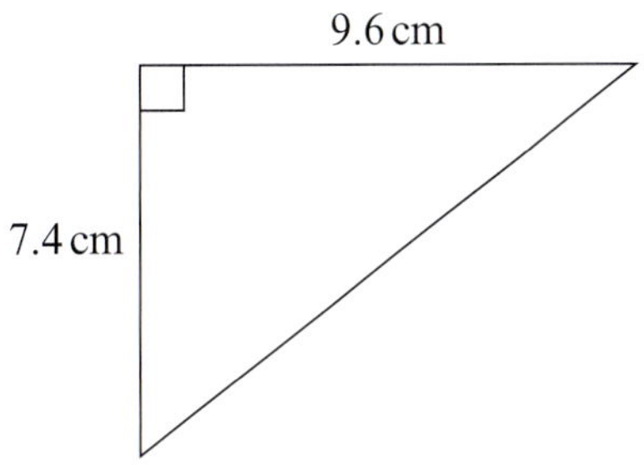

c
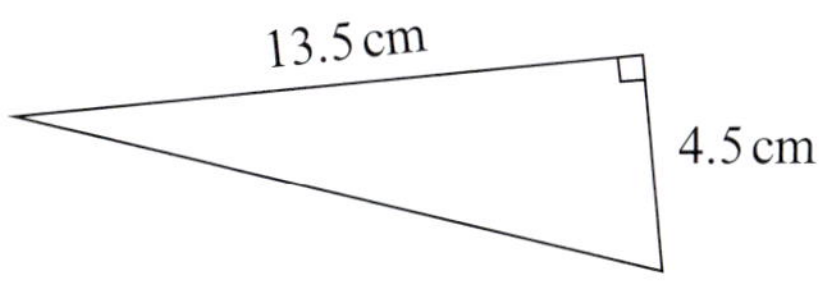

3 Calculate the length of the missing side in each of these triangles.

a
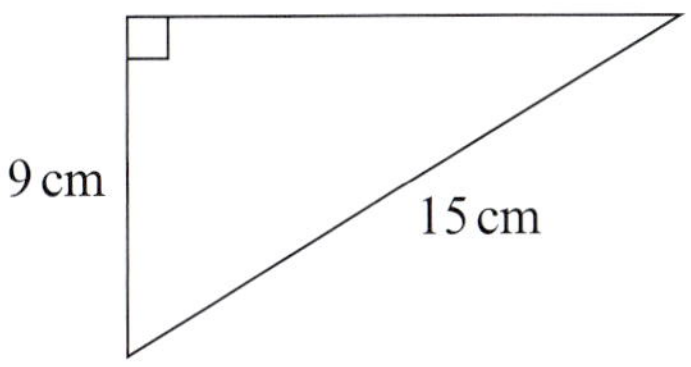

b
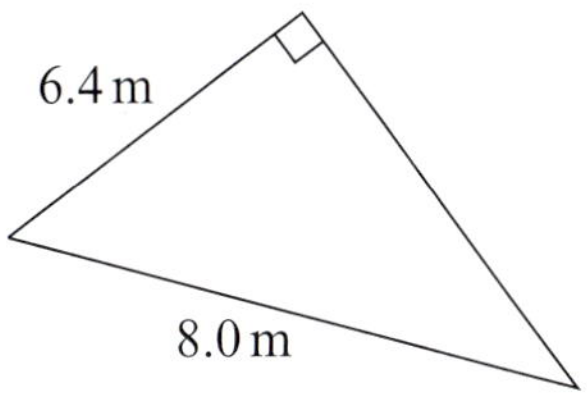

c
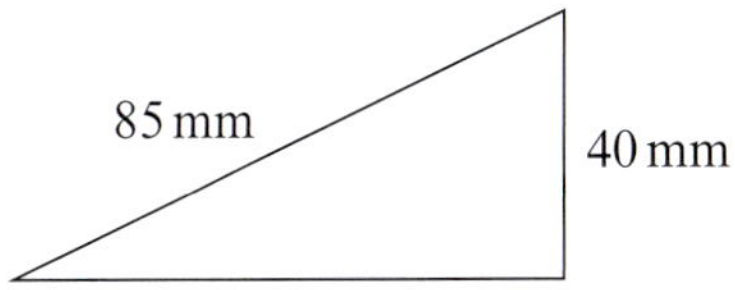

4 Calculate the length of the missing side in each of these triangles.
Round your answers to 1 decimal place.

a
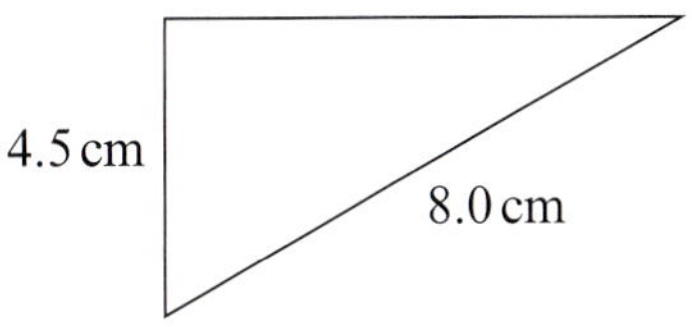

b
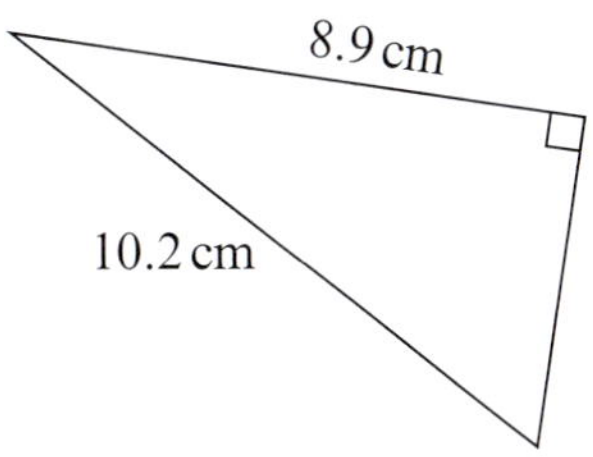

c
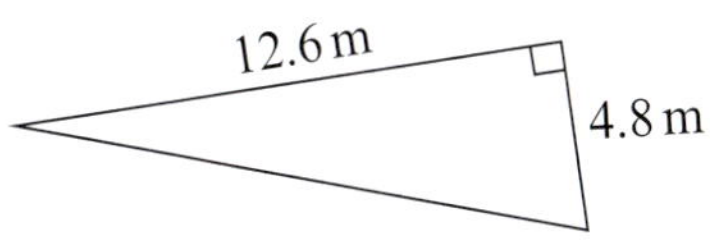

5 In this question, you can leave your answers as square roots.

$AB = BC = CD = DE = 1$ unit

a Calculate the length of AC.

b Calculate the length of AD.

c Calculate the length of AE.

d Show how the pattern continues.

e If you continue the pattern, will there be a line with length 3? Or with length 4? Explain your answer.

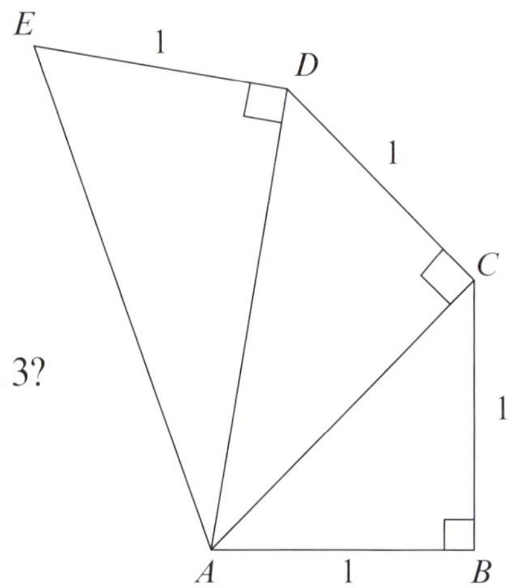

6 The size of a TV screen is the length of the diagonal.

a A TV screen is 70 cm wide and 39 cm high.

Show that this is an 80 cm screen.

b Another TV screen is 105 cm wide and 58 cm high. Calculate the size of this screen.

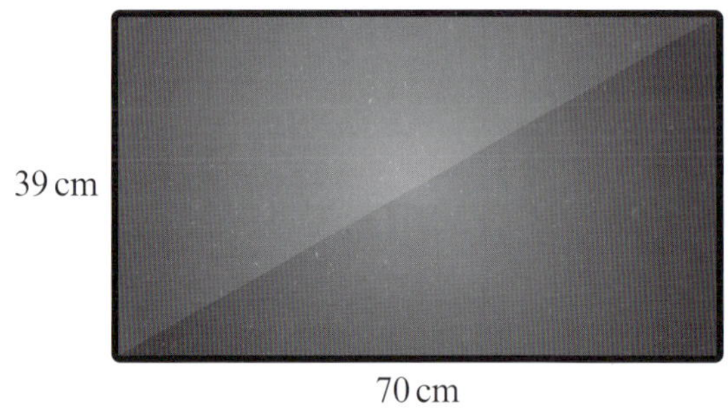

7 A ladder is leaning against a wall. The length of the ladder is 3.50 m.

The foot of the ladder is 0.91 m from the foot of the wall.

How far up the wall is the top of the ladder? Round your answer to the nearest centimetre.

8 a Construct a triangle with sides 5.1 cm, 6.8 cm and 8.5 cm.

b Use a calculation to show that one of the angles must be a right angle.

c Check that the triangle you have drawn is right-angled.

9 Two sides of a right-angled triangle are 15 cm and 20 cm.

Work out the possible lengths of the third side. Give reasons for your answers.

10 A soccer pitch is 90 m long and 40 m wide.

Zena walks from A to B round the edge of the pitch.

a How far does Zena walk?

b How much shorter is the distance if Zena walks from A to B in a straight line?

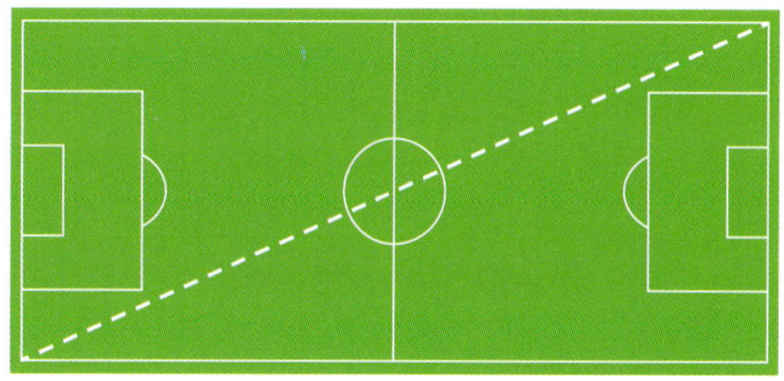

11 Here are a square and a rectangle.

a Show that the square and rectangle have the same perimeter.

b Calculate the length of the diagonal of each shape.

c Sketch another rectangle with the same perimeter. Calculate its diagonal.

d Sofia says:

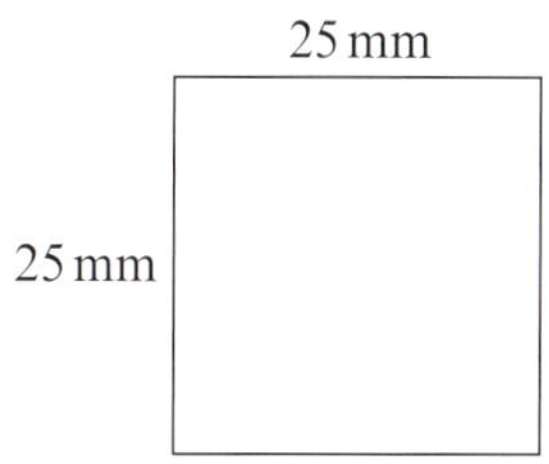

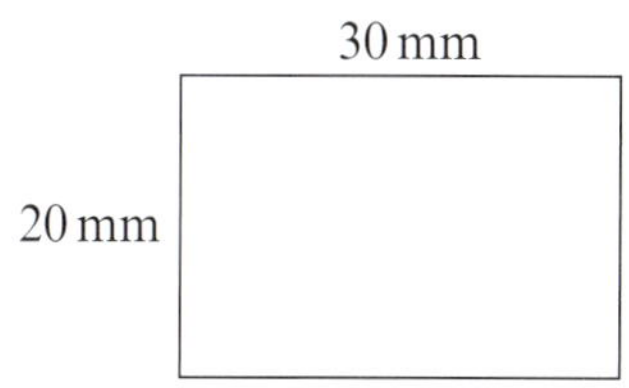

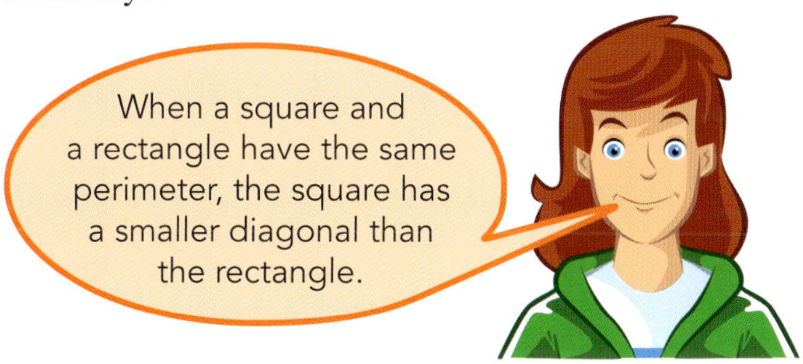

What evidence can you find to support Sofia's conjecture?

12 One side of a right-angled triangle is $\sqrt{17}$ units. The other two sides are integers.

How long are the other two sides? Is there more than one possible answer?

Think like a mathematician

13 a Here is a rectangle.

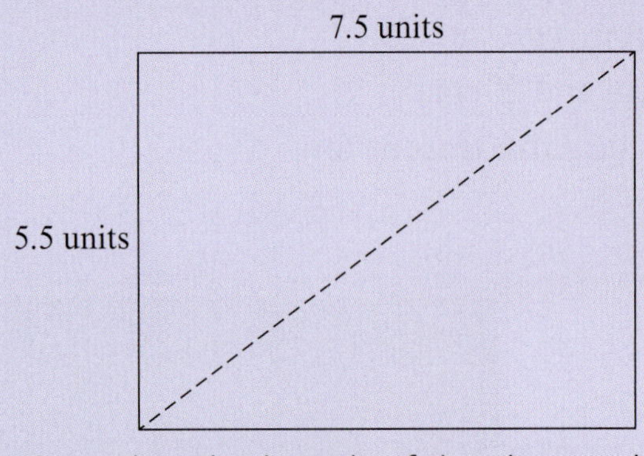

Show that the length of the diagonal is $\sqrt{86.5}$ units.

b Here is a rectangle.

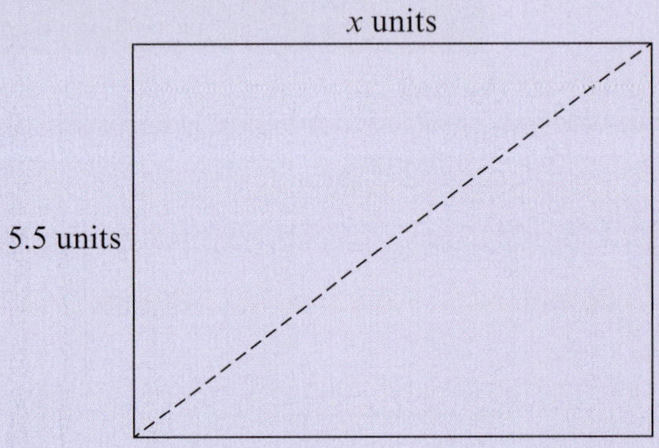

Show that the length of the diagonal is $\sqrt{x^2 + 30.25}$ units.

c Here is a rectangle.

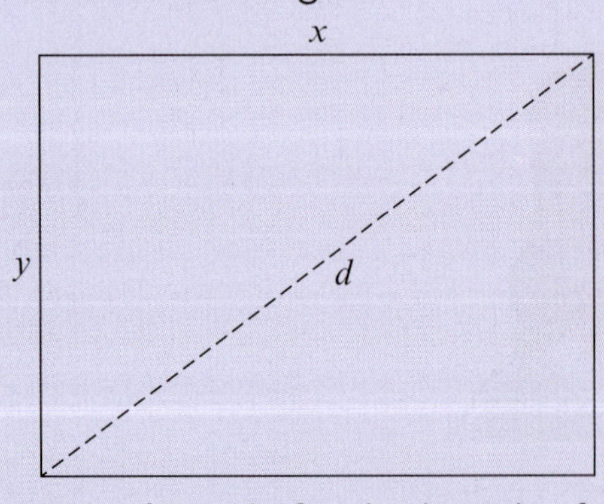

Find a formula for the length of the diagonal, d, in terms of x and y.

14 **a** Each side of this square is 7 units.

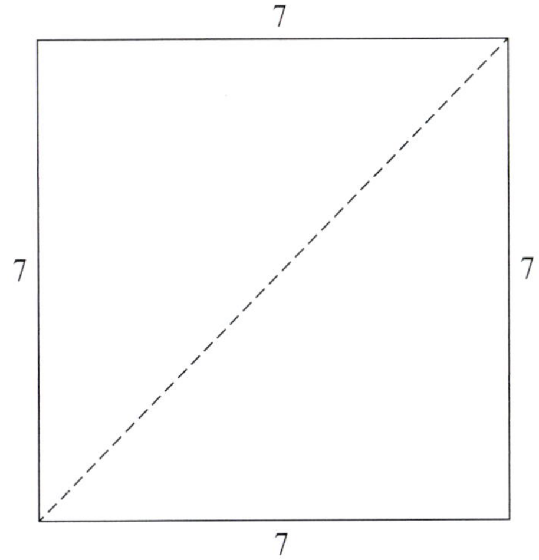

Show that:

i the length of the diagonal is $\sqrt{98}$ **ii** $\sqrt{98} = 7\sqrt{2}$

b Each side of this square is x.

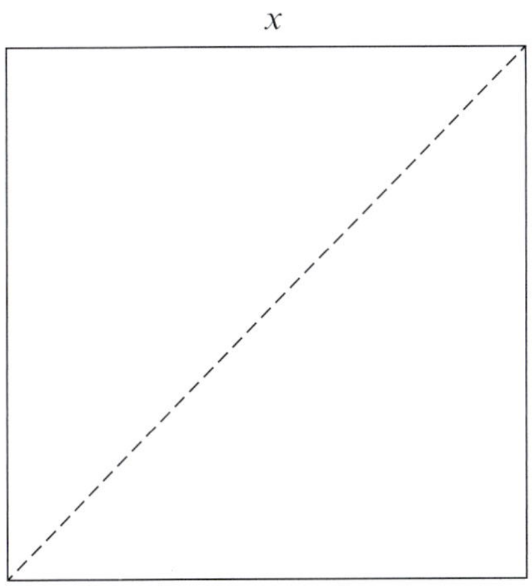

Show that the length of the diagonal is $x\sqrt{2}$.

Summary checklist

- [ ] I can use Pythagoras' theorem to calculate the third side of a right-angled triangle.

Check your progress

1 Work out the value of a. Justify your answer.

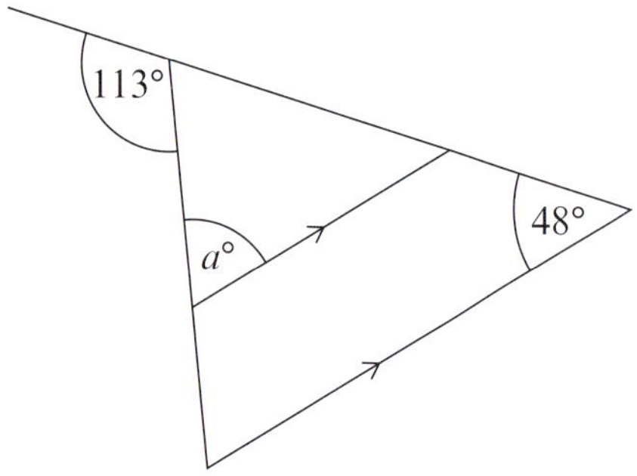

2 The angles of a pentagon are x°, x°, x°, x° and $(x + 10)$°. Work out the size of the largest angle.

3 AB, BC and CD are three sides of a regular polygon.

How many sides does the polygon have?

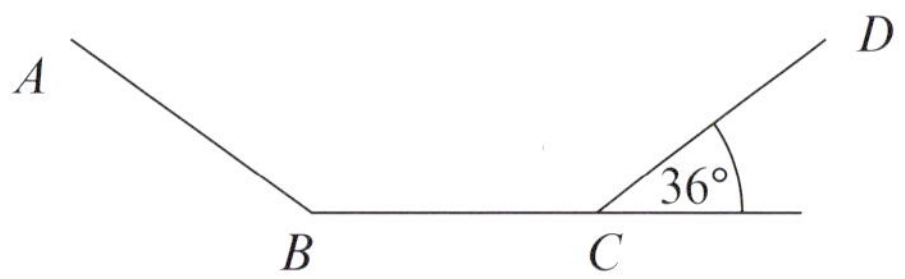

4 a Construct a square inside a circle with radius 6 cm. Use only a ruler and compasses.

b Measure the side of the square.

5 The side of a square is 25 m. How long is the diagonal?

6 Calculate the lengths x and y.

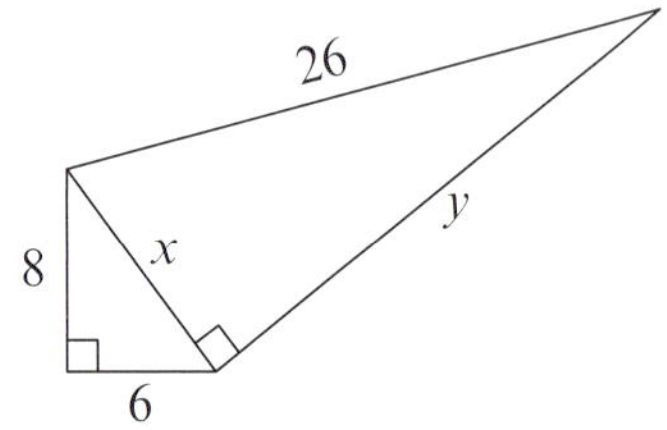

Project 2

Angle tangle

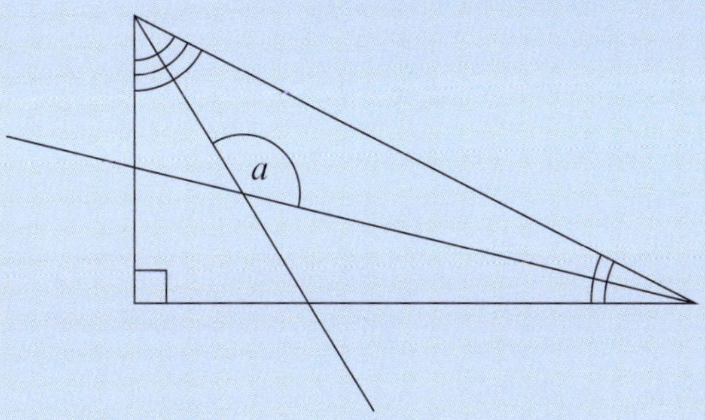

Construct a right-angled triangle, and bisect the two angles that are not 90°.

Now measure the angle *a*, where the two bisectors cross each other.

Do this a few times, starting with different right-angled triangles.

What do you notice?

Can you explain what is happening?

Next, construct a triangle where one of the angles is 60° and bisect the other two angles.

Again, measure the angle *a*, where the two bisectors cross each other.

Do this a few times, starting with different triangles with a 60° angle.

What do you notice?

Can you explain what is happening?

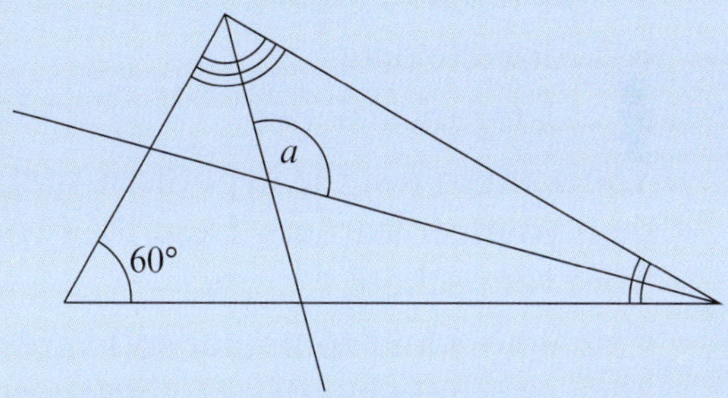

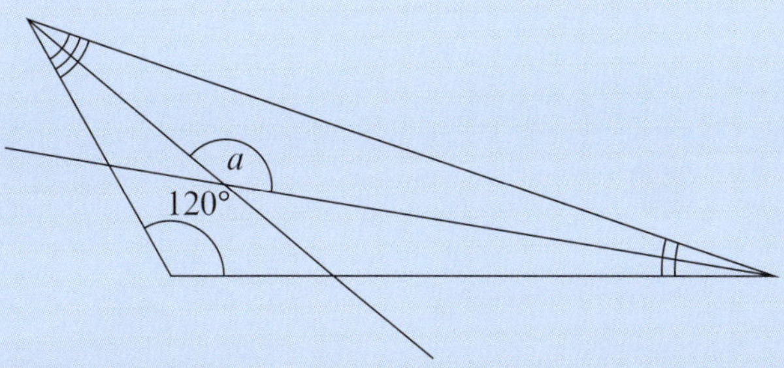

Next, construct a triangle where one of the angles is 120° and bisect the other two angles.

Again, measure the angle *a*, where the two bisectors cross each other.

What do you notice this time?

If you draw a triangle with an angle of x° and bisect the other two angles, is there a formula to work out the angle *a*, where the two bisectors cross, in terms of x?

6 Statistical investigations

Getting started

1 You are doing a statistical survey of cars in a car park.

Give two examples of

a continuous data

b discrete data

c categorical data.

2 You want to test the hypothesis that older learners in your school do more homework than younger learners. Describe two ways to choose a representative sample of 20 learners from your school.

3 Calculators and computer software can be used to generate random numbers. Explain how you could use these to pick a random sample of 50 people from a population of 632 people.

Here are some survey results found on the internet.

1 in 4 US citizens think the Sun goes round the Earth.

The average reading age in Britain is 9 years.

A third of employees are annoyed by colleagues who do not read their emails.

92% of people taking vitamin pills said the pills gave them more energy.

38% of UK shoppers buy online at least once a week.

60% of people think data collection by smart devices invades their privacy.

When you see a survey result, before you believe the information, you should check its reliability. Ask yourself:

- Who did the survey?
- How was the survey carried out?
- How big was the sample?
- How was the sample chosen?
- Was it a representative sample?

Check that the people doing the survey are not prejudiced and are not trying to influence you in a particular way. For example, someone selling a particular product might want to persuade you to buy it. Do not trust results that are based on a small unrepresentative sample. You must also make sure the subject is clearly defined. For example, what exactly is 'reading age'? How do people decide they have 'more energy'?

6.1 Data collection and sampling

In this section you will …

- plan how to collect statistical data to test a set of predictions
- use data to make inferences and generalisations
- look at alternative ways to choose a sample and decide which is the best method to use.

How is height related to other body measurements? This is something you can investigate by collecting data. First you need to ask some statistical questions, for example:

- Are height and shoe size connected?
- Are height and hand span connected?
- Do boys and girls of the same height have the same size hands?
- Do people with large hands also have large feet?
- Are arm length and leg length connected?

When you have some questions, you can make predictions to test, for example:

1. Taller boys have a larger shoe size than shorter boys.
2. Girls with large hands also have large feet.
3. People with long arms also have long legs.

To test your predictions, you need to think about the data you want to collect. For prediction 1, height could be continuous data if you use a tape measure, or it could be categorical data if you decide to classify people as short, average or tall. Shoe sizes are discrete numerical data. For prediction 3, you will need to decide how to collect the measurements. To measure the length of an arm or a leg might make people uncomfortable.

You will need a sample. You must think about different ways to choose a sample and the best method to use. It is a good idea to test your data collection method in a small trial. You might want to change your design after you have done this.

Worked example 6.1

You want to investigate the prediction that, in your school, teenagers with small feet also have small hands and teenagers with large feet also have large hands.

What data could you collect to do this investigation? Decide which data you would collect and give a reason for your answer.

Answer

To measure the size of feet, I could measure the length of the foot or I could use shoe size. Foot lengths are continuous data and more accurate. However, it might be embarrassing to measure someone's feet and so it might be more appropriate to use shoe size instead. This is easy to collect.

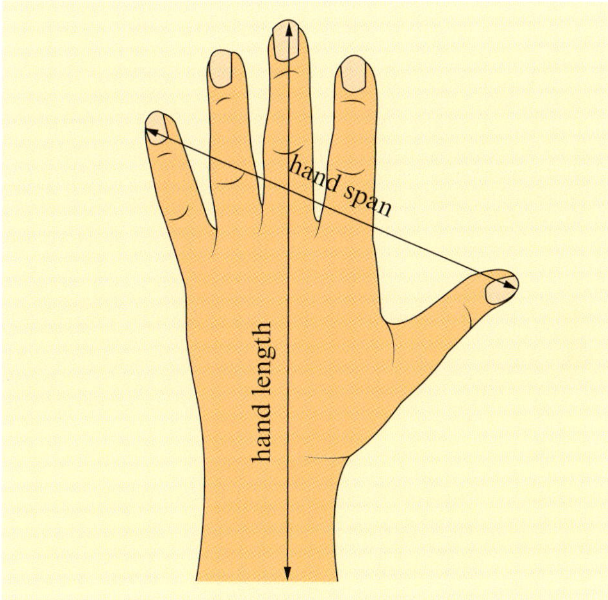

To measure hand size, I could ask each person to put their hand on a sheet of squared paper, draw round it and work out the area by counting squares. A second way would be to measure the hand span or the length (for example, from the wrist to the end of the middle finger).

Measuring a length will be easier than trying to count squares. I can do a trial where I measure both hand span and length to see which I prefer.

Exercise 6.1

Each question in this exercise is about planning a statistical investigation. It is a good idea to work on each question in pairs.

1 You are going to investigate the ability of learners in your school to estimate. This could be the ability to estimate the length of a line, the size of an angle, the number of items in a jar, a particular length of time, or something else.

- **a** Write some questions you could ask about estimation.
- **b** Write some predictions you could test.
- **c** Describe some different ways of choosing a sample to test one or more of your predictions.
- **d** Which sample method is best? Give a reason for your answer.
- **e** Carry out a small trial of your investigation. Can you think of ways to improve your investigation?
- **f** Use the results of your trial to make a generalisation about learners' ability to estimate.

> **Tip**
>
> Example generalisations: 'Older learners are better at estimating.' or 'Girls are better at estimating than boys.'

2 You are going to investigate the attitudes of learners to the structure of the school day. Here are some things you could think about: the length of lessons; the number of lessons in a day; breaks; start and finish times. You might think of other areas of interest.

a Write some questions you could ask about the structure of the school day.

b Write some predictions you can test.

c Describe some different ways of choosing a sample to test one or more of your predictions.

d Which sample method is best? Give a reason for your answer.

e Carry out a small trial of your investigation. Can you think of ways to improve your investigation?

f Use the results of your trial to make a generalisation about learners' attitudes to the structure of the school day.

> **Tip**
>
> Example generalisation: 'Learners think lessons should be longer.'

3 You are going to investigate news articles. The articles could be in newspapers or online. You could investigate readability, length, vocabulary or other aspects.

a Write some questions you could ask about news articles.

b Write some predictions you can test.

c Describe some different ways of choosing a sample to test one or more of your predictions.

d Which sample method is best? Give a reason for your answer.

e Carry out a small trial of your investigation. Can you think of ways to improve your investigation?

f Use the results of your trial to make a generalisation about news articles.

In this exercise, you have carried out several statistical investigations. What advice would you give to someone who is going to plan a statistical investigation? Suggest three pieces of advice.

Summary checklist

- [ ] I can make related predictions and plan a statistical investigation to test the predictions.
- [ ] I can use data to make inferences and generalisations.
- [ ] I can describe several ways to select a sample and choose the best method, with a reason.

6.2 Bias

In this section you will ...

- learn about sources of bias
- learn about ways to choose an unbiased sample
- learn how to identify wrong or misleading information.

Key words

bias
misleading

The reliability of the results of a statistical investigation depend on the quality of the data collected. Data from a sample that is not representative of the whole population might not give a valid outcome. A sample that does not represent the whole population is **biased**. There are different possible sources of bias.

Worked example 6.2

An investigation is carried out to test the prediction that people in a town are in favour of building a new library.

A survey is carried out on people using a supermarket between 09:00 and 12:00 one Wednesday and Thursday.

a Explain why this will give a biased sample.
b Suggest a way to improve the investigation.

Answer

a A survey at that time and in that place will include few people who are at work during the day. The sample will be biased if people who work during the day are underrepresented. It could include people who do not use the present library and who will not have an opinion.

b It would be better to do the survey in different places and at different times. The survey could be carried out at the present library. This will give a variety of people who actually use the library, especially if you speak to people at different times of day and on different days.

Worked example 6.3

A company employs 187 men and 362 women.

You want to choose a representative sample of 40 men and women.

a How many men and women should you choose?

b List three other factors to consider when choosing a representative sample.

Answer

a The company has $187 + 362 = 549$ employees.

The percentage who are men $= \frac{187}{549} \times 100\% = 34.1\%$

34.1% of the sample should be men.

34.1% of $40 = 0.341 \times 40 = 14$ to the nearest whole number.

The sample should have 14 men and 26 women.

b Other possible factors are, for example, age, job and salary.

Exercise 6.2

1 In a college there are 200 girls and 150 boys.
You want to choose a representative sample of 30 students.
How many girls and boys should you choose?

2 Look at this advert.

In a survey of 142 customers, 85% said Supremo Shampoo made their hair feel softer.

a What is the purpose of the advert?

b List two possible sources of bias.

3 You are doing a statistical investigation. You need to find the opinions of a large sample of people.

a Give two advantages of using social media.

b Give two disadvantages of using social media.

4 This table shows the numbers of students in a college.

	Male	Female	Total
Age 16	50	75	125
Age 17	42	92	134
Total	92	167	259

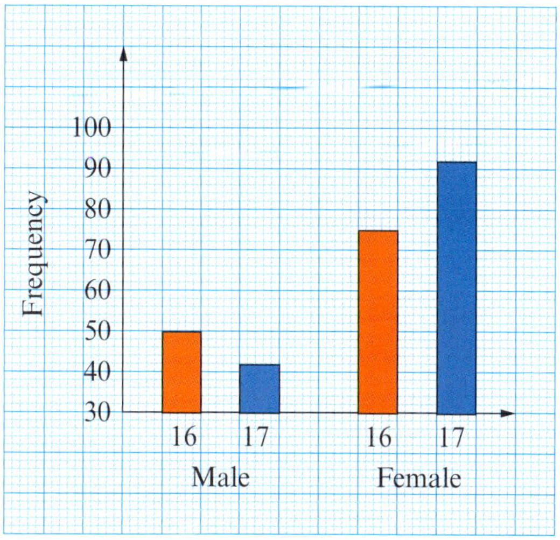

You want a representative sample of 40 students.

a How many students in your sample should be 16-year-old males?

b How many students in your sample should be females?

The graph shows the data in the table.

c Explain why the graph is **misleading**.

d Draw an improved version of the graph.

5 A statistician wants to investigate people's attitudes towards a plan for a new housing development.

The statistician gives out 350 questionnaires and receives 105 replies.

a Work out the percentage of replies.

b How might the low percentage of replies cause bias?

6 A sample of people were given two versions of a drink, the original recipe and a new recipe.

They were asked, 'Do you prefer the new recipe?'

85% said, 'yes'.

a Why might this result be biased?

b How could you arrange the tasting and questioning to avoid bias?

7 Here are questions from surveys that will give biased results. For each question

i explain why it will give a biased result

ii rewrite the question in a better way.

a Do you agree that global warming is caused by humans?

b Do you think entry to this exhibition should be free?

c Are you overweight?

d Do you think you take enough exercise?

8 Customers who have stayed at a hotel are asked to complete an online survey. The hotel wants to know if the customers felt they received good service and value for money.

How could the results from this survey be biased?

9 You are planning to do a survey of customers in a supermarket or shopping mall. You will do the survey on a Sunday. You will ask a sample of customers a small number of questions. You want equal numbers of men and women. You want 25% of your sample to be under 30 and the rest to be aged 30 or over. You want to ask 120 people altogether.

Describe how you could carry out this survey. In particular, describe how you will choose your sample and when you will do your survey.

10 Marcus wants to know if more men or women use a gym on Monday evening and on Friday evening.

He looks at the first 30 visitors on a Monday evening and on a Friday evening. He records the results in a table and draws a diagram to illustrate the data as shown.

	Men	Women	Total
Monday	18	12	30
Friday	13	17	30

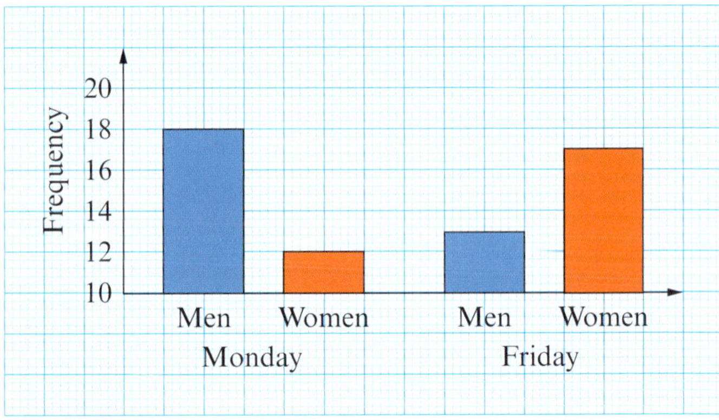

Marcus says:

a Are Marcus' conclusions valid? Give a reason for your answer.

b Explain why Marcus' diagram is misleading.

c Draw an improved version of the diagram.

Summary checklist

- ☐ I can explain sources of bias when collecting data.
- ☐ I can ask questions about the validity of a statistical investigation.
- ☐ I can identify wrong or misleading information.

Check your progress

1 You have been asked to find out the opinions of people about different types of cake.

  a Give three examples of questions you could ask.

  b Write a prediction for each of your questions.

2 You want to do a survey of the parents of learners in your school. Describe what you think is a good way to select a sample of 20 parents. Give a reason for your method.

3 A train company wants to do a survey of customers travelling on a particular line.

  They decide to give a questionnaire to 100 customers on the train leaving the station at 08:00 on a Monday morning.

  a Describe ways this sample will be biased.

  b Suggest how to choose a less biased sample of customers.

7 Shapes and measurements

Getting started

1 Work out the circumference of these circles. Use the π button on your calculator.

Round your answers correct to 2 decimal places (2 d.p.).

a diameter = 12 cm

b radius = 3.5 m

2 The circumference of a circle is 15 cm.

Work out the diameter of the circle. Give your answer correct to the nearest millimetre.

Tip

If you cannot remember the formula you need to use, look at the introduction text.

3 Work out the area of each compound shape.

a

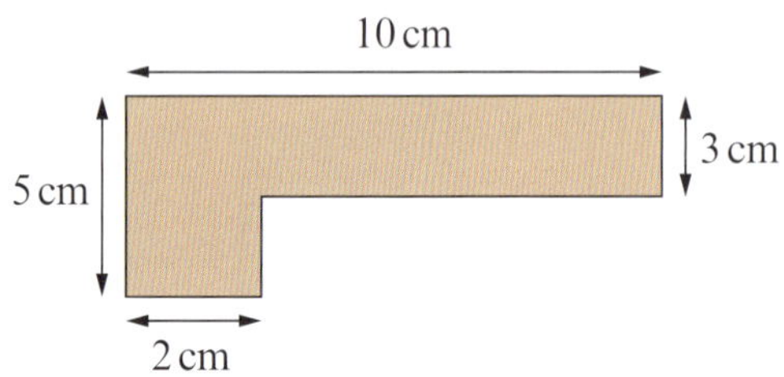

b

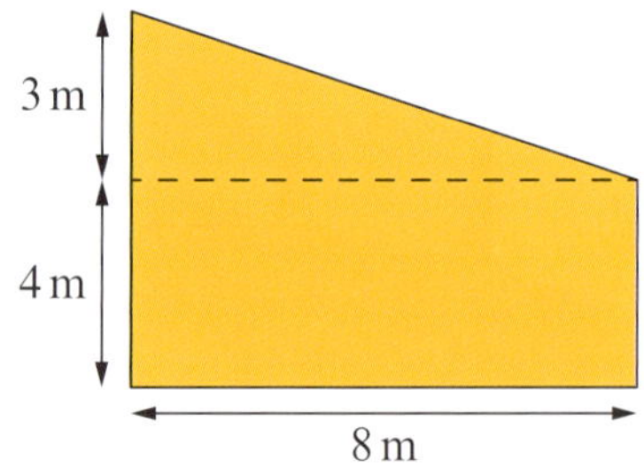

4 Sort these cards into three groups.

Group 1: units of length. **Group 2:** units of mass. **Group 3:** units of capacity.

A	metres	B	grams	C	litres
D	centimetres	E	millilitres	F	kilograms
G	millimetres	H	kilometres		

5 Work out these calculations.

a $3.2 \times 100\,000$

b $0.56 \times 1\,000\,000\,000$

c $6820 \div 1000$

d $4\,500\,000 \div 1\,000\,000$

Here are some algebraic formulae that you have already used.
The formulae are written in words and also using letters.

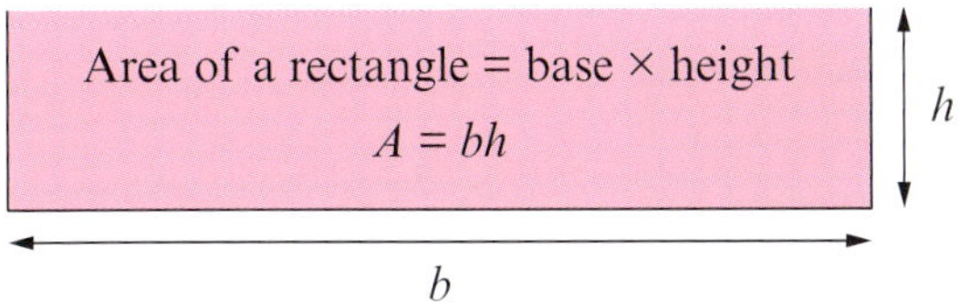

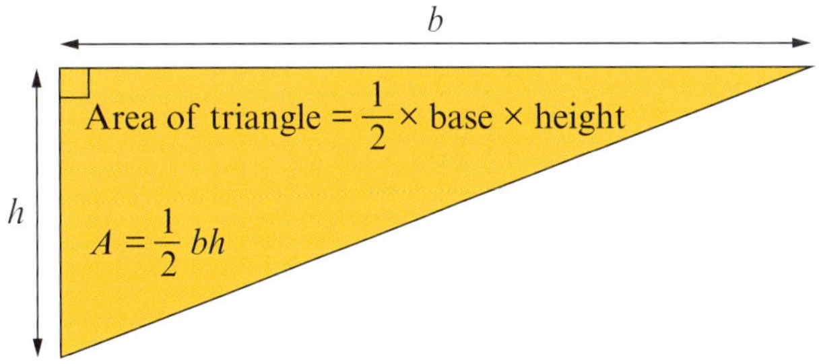

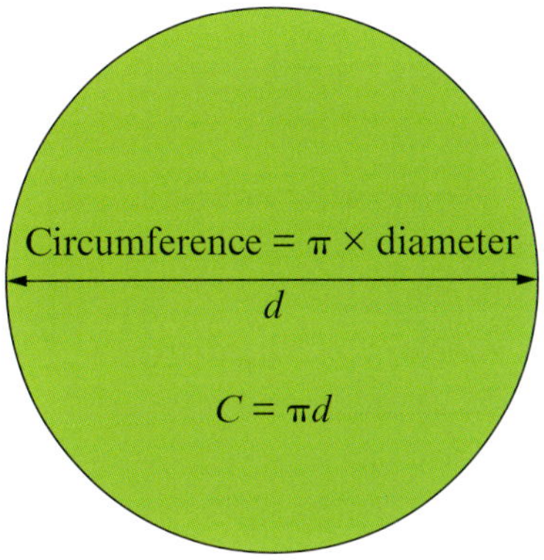

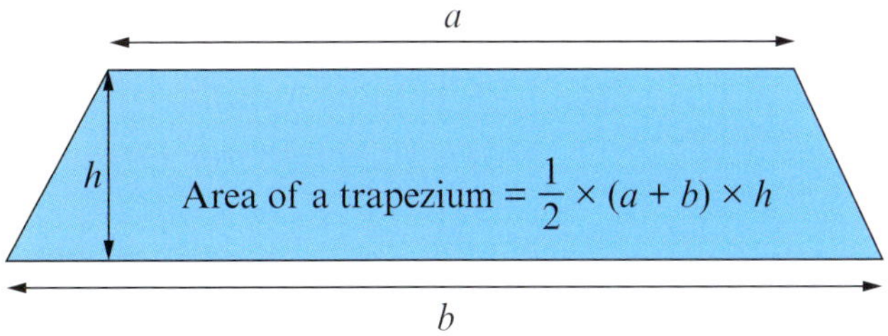

Here is a square puzzle, which is divided into four parts. All lengths are given in centimetres. Work out the area of each part. (There are two triangles and two trapezia). Then show that the total area of the parts is 64 cm². Notice that the area of the square is $8 \times 8 = 64$ cm².

Tip

Trapezia is the plural of trapezium.

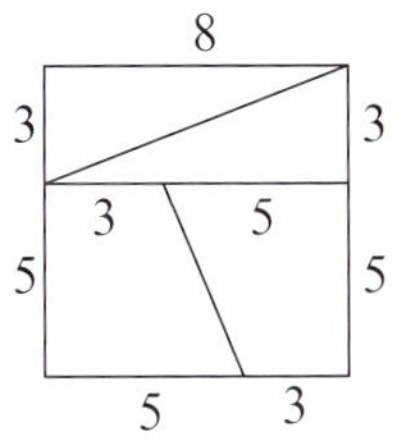

The parts of the square can be rearranged to make a rectangle as shown. The area of the rectangle is $5 \times 13 = 65$ cm². The area should be 64 cm²! Can you work out where the extra 1 cm² has come from?

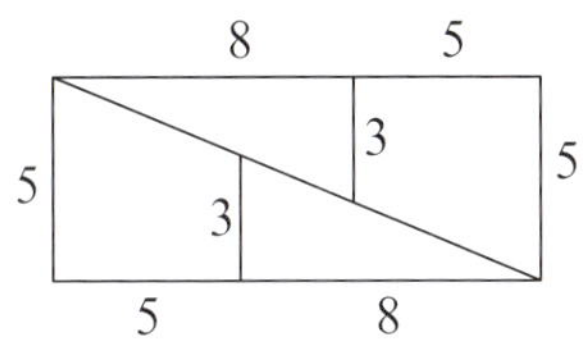

7.1 Circumference and area of a circle

In this section you will ...

- know and use the formulae for the circumference and area of a circle.

You already know how to work out the circumference of a circle using this formula:

$C = \pi d$ where: C is the circumference of the circle
d is the diameter of the circle

You can work out the area of a circle using this formula:

$A = \pi r^2$ where: A is the area of the circle
r is the radius of the circle

Notice that the formula for the **circumference** uses the **diameter** while the formula for the **area** uses the **radius**.

Tip

Remember that:

diameter = radius × 2

radius = diameter ÷ 2

Worked example 7.1

Work out the area of a circle with

a radius 4 cm

b diameter 7 m.

Use the π button on your calculator. Give your answers correct to 3 significant figures (3 s.f.).

Answer

a $A = \pi r^2$	Write the formula you are going to use.
$= \pi \times 4^2$	Substitute $r = 4$ into the formula.
$= \pi \times 16$	Work out 4^2, then multiply by π.
$= 50.3\ \text{cm}^2$	Round your answer correct to 3 s.f. and remember the units, cm^2.
b $r = d \div 2 = 7 \div 2 = 3.5\ \text{m}$	You are given the diameter, so work out the radius first.
$A = \pi r^2$	Write the formula you are going to use.
$= \pi \times 3.5^2$	Substitute $r = 3.5$ into the formula.
$= \pi \times 12.25$	Work out 3.5^2, then multiply by π.
$= 38.5\ \text{m}^2$	Round your answer correct to 3 s.f. and remember the units, m^2.

Exercise 7.1

1 Copy and complete the workings to work out the area of each circle.
Use $\pi = 3.14$. Round your answers correct to 1 decimal place (1 d.p.).

a radius = 2 cm

$A = \pi r^2$
$= 3.14 \times 2^2$
$= 3.14 \times \square$
$= \square\ \text{cm}^2$ (1 d.p.)

b radius = 9 cm

$A = \pi r^2$
$= 3.14 \times 9^2$
$= 3.14 \times \square$
$= \square\ \text{cm}^2$ (1 d.p.)

c radius = 4.2 m

$A = \pi r^2$
$= 3.14 \times 4.2^2$
$= 3.14 \times \square$
$= \square\ \text{m}^2$ (1 d.p.)

2 Copy and complete the workings to work out the area of each circle.
Use $\pi = 3.142$. Round your answers correct to 2 decimal places (2 d.p.).

a diameter = 16 cm

$r = d \div 2$
$= 16 \div 2$
$= 8$ cm
$A = \pi r^2$
$= 3.142 \times 8^2$
$= 3.142 \times \square$
$= \square\ \text{cm}^2$ (2 d.p.)

b diameter = 9 cm

$r = d \div 2$
$= 9 \div 2$
$= \square$ cm
$A = \pi r^2$
$= 3.142 \times \square^2$
$= 3.142 \times \square$
$= \square\ \text{cm}^2$ (2 d.p.)

c diameter = 2.6 m

$r = d \div 2$
$= 2.6 \div 2$
$= \square$ m
$A = \pi r^2$
$= 3.142 \times \square^2$
$= 3.142 \times \square$
$= \square\ \text{m}^2$ (2 d.p.)

Think like a mathematician

3 Work with a partner to answer this question.

a Use the π button on your calculator to work out the accurate area of a circle with radius 7 cm.
Write your answer correct to three decimal places (3 d.p.).

b Now work out the area of the same circle using approximate values for π of

i 3.14 **ii** 3.142 **iii** $\frac{22}{7}$

Continued

c Use this formula to work out the percentage difference between the accurate answer (part **a**) and each of the approximate answers in part **b**. Give your percentages correct to two decimal places (2 d.p.).

$$\text{percentage difference} = \frac{\text{difference between accurate and approximate answers}}{\text{accurate answer}} \times 100$$

Tip

In the formula for percentage difference, the difference between accurate and approximate answers is:

accurate answer – approximate answer **or** approximate answer – accurate answer

Choose the subtraction which gives you a positive difference.

d Which approximate value for π gives the smallest percentage difference?

e When you answer questions and you need to use π, which value of π do you think it is best to use? Explain why.

4 Work out the area of each circle. Use the π button on your calculator. Round your answers correct to 3 significant figures (3 s.f.).

a radius = 6 cm
b radius = 4.25 m
c diameter = 23 cm
d diameter = 4.8 m

5 Ellie and Hans work out the answer to this question.

Question
Work out the area of a circle with radius 1.7 m. Use π = 3.14

This is what they write.

Ellie
$3.14 \times 1.7 = 5.338$
$5.338^2 = 28.494244$
Area = $28.5\ m^2$ (3 s.f.)

Hans
$1.7^2 = 3.4$
$3.14 \times 3.4 = 10.676$
Area = $10.7\ m^2$ (3 s.f.)

a Critique their solutions. Explain any mistakes they have made.

b Write a full worked solution to show them the correct way of answering the question.

Think like a mathematician

6 Work with a partner to answer this question.

So far in this unit you have used the formula $A = \pi r^2$

In questions **1**, **4a** and **4b**, you found the area when you were given the radius.

In questions **2**, **4c** and **4d**, you found the area when you were given the diameter.

Can you write a formula to work out the area which uses d (diameter) instead of r (radius)?

Write your formula in its simplest form.

Test your formula on questions **4c** and **4d**. Does it work?

Compare your formula with other pairs in the class.

Tip

When you write an algebraic formula, try to use letters not words.

For the rest of the questions in this exercise, use the π button on your calculator.

7 Work out **i** the area and **ii** the circumference of each circle.

Give your answers correct to one decimal place (1 d.p.).

a radius = 5.6 cm **b** diameter = 32 mm

8 This is part of Pria's homework.

Question

Work out the area of this semicircle.

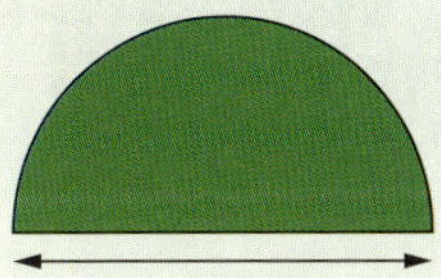

Answer

Area of semicircle = half of area of circle

Estimate: $d \approx 12$, so $r \approx 6$ and $\pi \approx 3$

$A \approx \frac{1}{2} \times 3 \times 6^2 = \frac{1}{2} \times 3 \times 36 = 54\ \text{cm}^2$

Accurate: $r = 11.85 \div 2 = 5.925$

$A \approx \frac{1}{2} \times \pi \times 5.925^2 = 55.14\ \text{cm}^2$

Check: $55.14\ \text{cm}^2$ *is close to* $54\ \text{cm}^2$ ✓

Use Pria's method to work out an estimate of the area and calculate the accurate area of a semicircle with

a radius = 6.2 cm **b** radius = 14.85 m

c diameter = 14.7 cm **d** diameter = 19.28 m

Round your answers correct to 2 d.p.

9 Work out **i** the area and **ii** the perimeter of each semicircle.
Give your answers correct to one decimal place (1 d.p.).

a radius = 12.5 m **b** diameter = 46 mm

Tip

Remember, the perimeter of a semicircle is half the circumference plus the diameter.

Activity 7.1

Work with a partner for this activity.

On a piece of paper, write two different questions for your partner to answer. You can ask them to work out the area or the circumference of a circle, or the area or the perimeter of a semicircle. You must give them either the radius or the diameter for each question. You must state the accuracy required for the answers.

Work out the answers to your questions, then swap papers and work out the answers to your partner's questions.

Swap back and mark each other's work. Discuss any mistakes that have been made.

10 The diagram shows a semicircle and a quarter of a circle.
Marcus makes this conjecture.

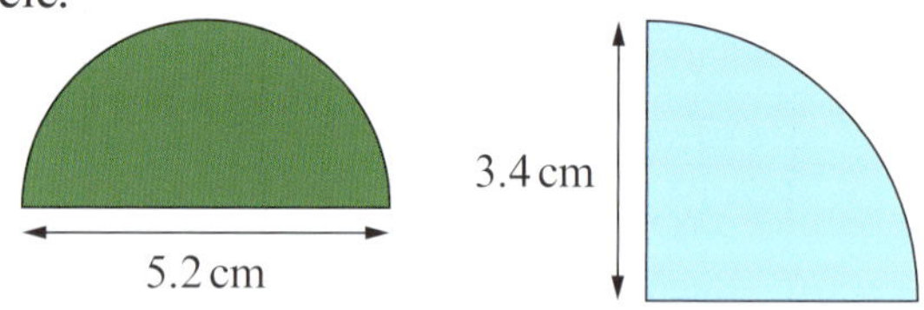

Is Marcus correct? Show working to support your answer.

11 Dan and Abi use different methods to work out the answer to this question.

> *Question*
> *Work out the radius of a circle with an area of 12.6 cm².*
> *Give your answer correct to 2 significant figures.*

This is what they write.

Dan		Abi	
Step 1: Make r the subject of the formula. $A = \pi \times r^2$ $\frac{A}{\pi} = r^2$ $r = \sqrt{\frac{A}{\pi}}$	Step 2: Substitute in the numbers. $r = \sqrt{\frac{12.6}{\pi}}$ $= 2.00267...$ $= 2.0$ cm (2 s.f.)	Step 1: Substitute in the numbers $A = \pi \times r^2$ $12.6 = \pi \times r^2$	Step 2: Solve the equation $\pi \times r^2 = 12.6$ $r^2 = \frac{12.6}{\pi} = 4.0107...$ $r = \sqrt{4.0107...}$ $= 2.00267...$ $r = 2.0$ cm (2 s.f.)

a Critique Dan and Abi's methods.

b Which method do you think is better? Explain why.

c Use your favourite method to work out the radius of these circles. Give your answers correct to one decimal place (1 d.p.).

i area = $35\,\text{cm}^2$ ii area = $18.25\,\text{m}^2$

iii area = $254\,\text{mm}^2$

12 Here are six question cards and six answer cards.

A Work out C when $d = 15.21$

B Work out A when $d = 11.85$

C Work out C when $r = 9.5$

D Work out A when $r = 7.28$

E Work out d when $C = 87.2$

F Work out r when $A = 304.09$

i 110.29 ii 9.84 iii 166.50

iv 27.8 v 47.78 vi 59.7

a Using **estimation**, match each question card with the correct answer card. **Do not use** a calculator.

b Use a calculator to check you have matched the cards correctly.

13 The area of a circular pond is $21.5\,\text{m}^2$.

Work out the circumference of the pond.

Give your answer correct to the nearest centimetre.

14 The circumference of a circular lawn is 32.56 m.
Work out the area of the lawn.
Give your answer correct to the nearest square metre.

15 This is part of Dirk's classwork.

> <u>Question</u>
> Work out the circumference and the area of a circle with diameter 18 cm.
> Write your answers in terms of π.
> <u>Answer</u>
> $C = \pi d = \pi \times 18 = 18\pi$ cm
> $A = \pi r^2 = \pi \times 9^2 = \pi \times 81 = 81\pi$ cm^2

Tip

'Write your answers in terms of π' means you can leave the answers as 18π cm and 81π cm^2. You do not have to work out the value of $18 \times \pi$ and $81 \times \pi$ and write a rounded answer.

a Critique this method of writing the answers. Does it have any advantages or disadvantages?

b Answer these questions. Write your answers in terms of π.

- **i** Work out the circumference of a circle with diameter 25 mm.
- **ii** Work out the area of a circle with radius 12 mm.
- **iii** Work out the circumference of a circle with radius 22.5 cm.
- **iv** Work out the area of a circle with diameter 40 cm.

c The diagram shows a semicircle.
Show that

- **i** the area of the semicircle is 72π m^2
- **ii** the perimeter of the semicircle is $12\pi + 24$ m.

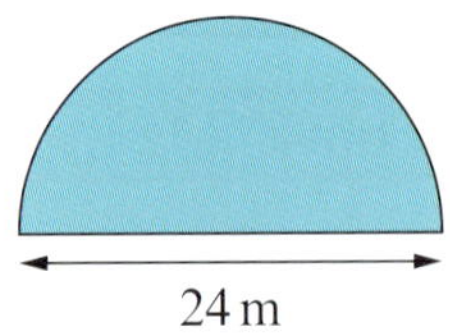

Look back at this exercise.

a How confident do you feel in your understanding of this section?

b What can you do to increase your level of confidence?

Summary checklist

☐ I can use the formulae for the circumference and area of a circle.

7.2 Areas of compound shapes

In this section you will …

- estimate and calculate areas of compound 2D shapes.

You can already work out the areas of compound shapes that are made from rectangles and triangles. You can also use other simple shapes, such as circles, in a compound shape. The method to work out the area is the same:

1. Divide the compound shape into simple shapes.
2. Work out the area of each simple shape.
3. Add or subtract the areas of the simple shapes to find the required area.

Worked example 7.2

Work out the shaded area of each compound shape. Give your answers correct to 3 s.f.

a

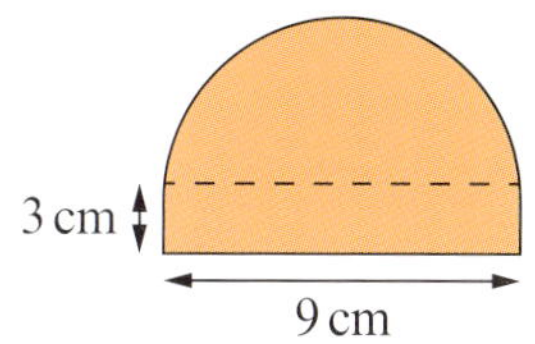

b

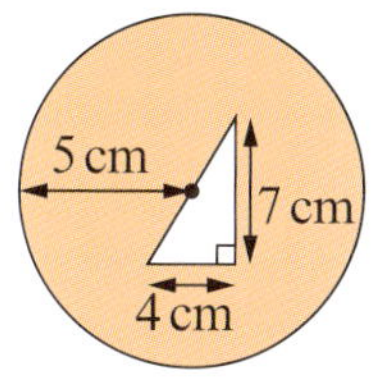

Answer

a

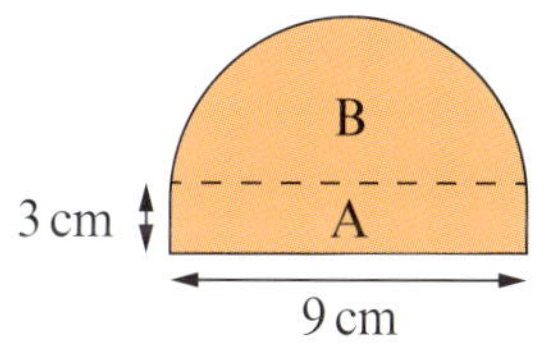

Divide the compound shape into two simple shapes, A and B.

You know the length and width of rectangle A.

B is a semicircle with radius = 9 ÷ 2 = 4.5 cm

Area A = $l \times w = 3 \times 9 = 27\,\text{cm}^2$

Work out the area of rectangle A.

Area B = $\frac{1}{2}\pi r^2 = \frac{1}{2} \times \pi \times 4.5^2 = 31.8\,\text{cm}^2$

Work out the area of semicircle B.

Total area = 27 + 31.8
= $58.8\,\text{cm}^2$

Add together the areas of the rectangle and the semicircle to find the area of the compound shape.

b Area of circle = $\pi r^2 = \pi \times 5^2$
= $78.5\,\text{cm}^2$

Work out the area of the circle.

Area of triangle = $\frac{1}{2}bh = \frac{1}{2} \times 4 \times 7$
= $14\,\text{cm}^2$

Work out the area of the triangle.

Shaded area = 78.5 − 14
= $64.5\,\text{cm}^2$

The orange-shaded area is the area of the circle **minus** the area of the triangle.

Exercise 7.2

1 Copy and complete the workings to calculate the areas of these compound shapes.

a

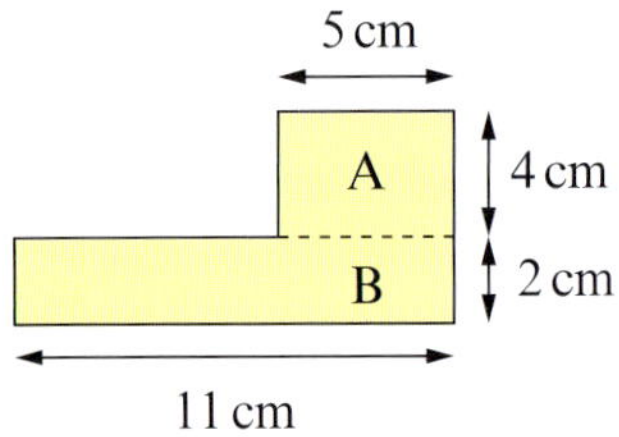

Area A $= l \times w = 5 \times \square = \square$

Area B $= l \times w = 11 \times \square = \square$

Total area $= \square + \square = \square\,\text{cm}^2$

b

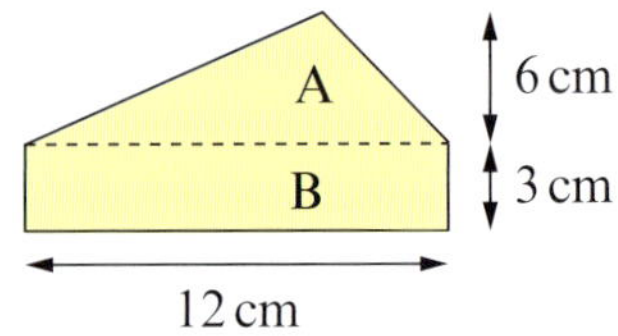

Area A $= \frac{1}{2} \times b \times h = \frac{1}{2} \times 12 \times 6 = \square$

Area B $= l \times w = \square \times \square = \square$

Total area $= \square + \square = \square\,\text{cm}^2$

c

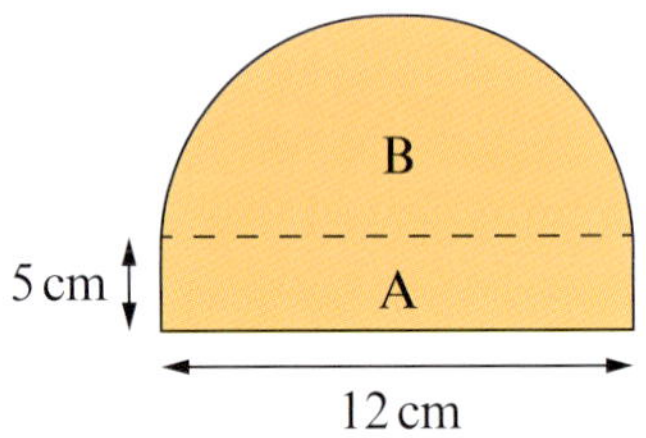

Area A $= l \times w = \square \times \square = \square$

Area B $= \frac{1}{2}\pi r^2 = \frac{1}{2} \times \pi \times \square^2 = \square$

Total area $= \square + \square = \square\,\text{cm}^2$

d

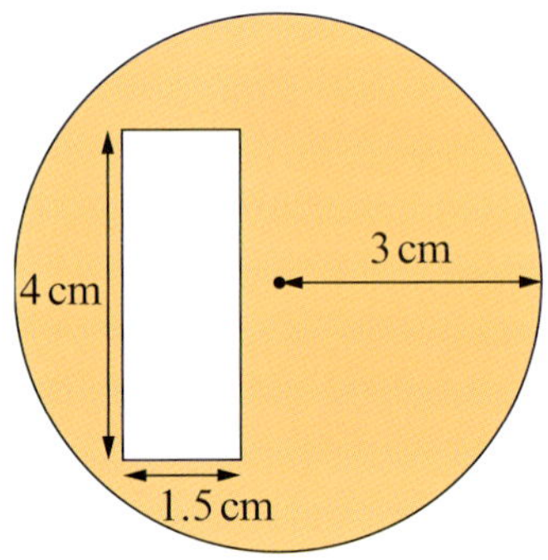

Area rectangle $= l \times w = \square \times \square = \square$

Area circle $= \pi r^2 = \pi \times \square^2 = \square$

Shaded area $= \square - \square = \square\,\text{cm}^2$

2 For each of these compound shapes, work out

i the missing lengths shown by $\square$

ii the area of the compound shape.

a

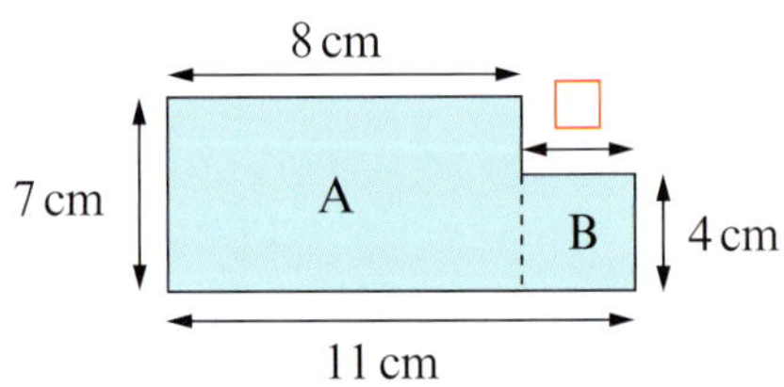

b

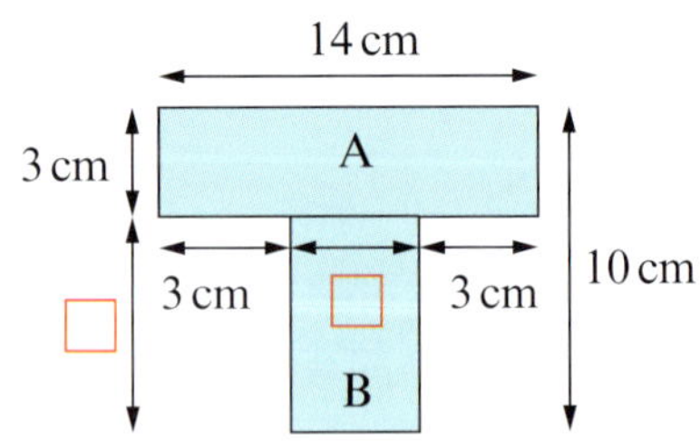

c

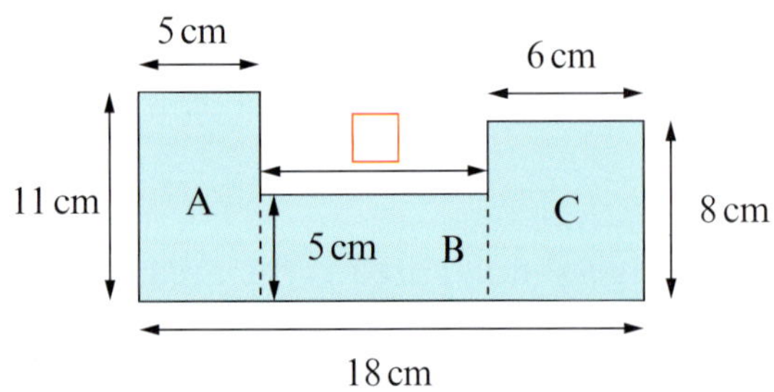

3 For each of these compound shapes, work out

i an estimate of the area of the shape

ii the area of the shape correct to one decimal place (1 d.p.).

> **Tip**
>
> Remember: to work out an estimate, round all the numbers to one significant figure.

a 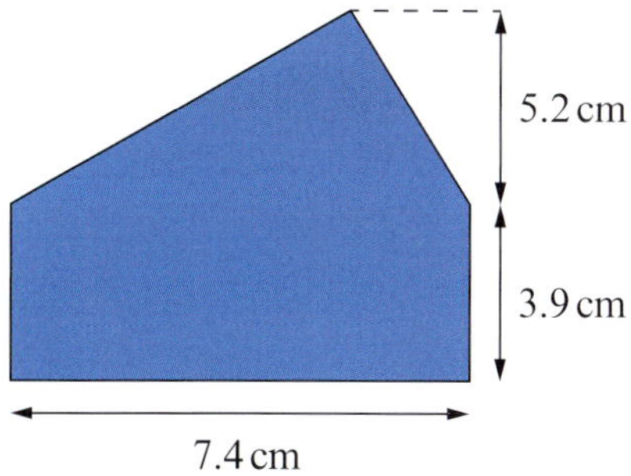

b 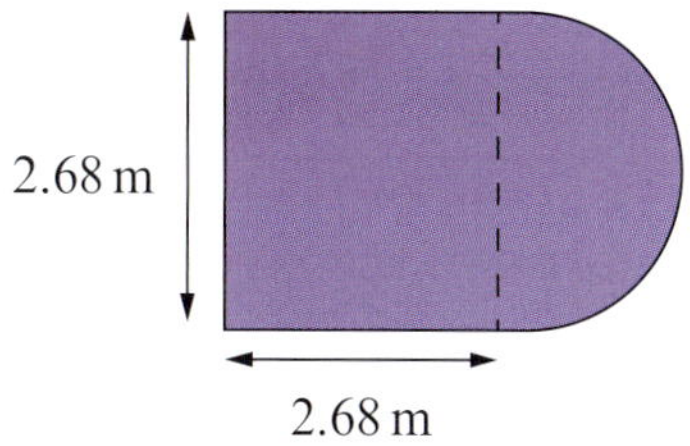

c 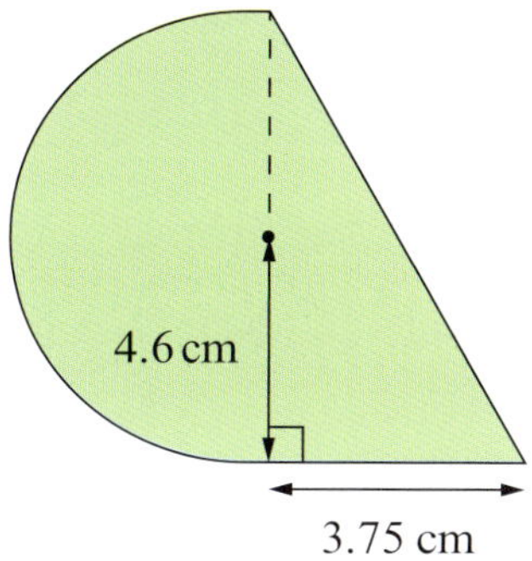

d 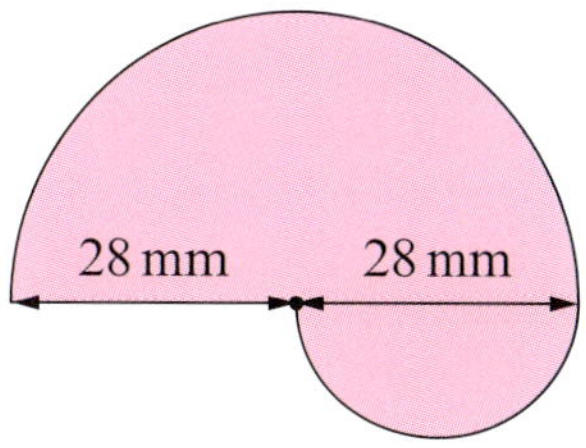

Think like a mathematician

4 This is part of Kira's homework.

<u>Question</u>

A compound shape is made of two semicircles and a square.

The square has side length 12 cm.

Work out the area of the shape.

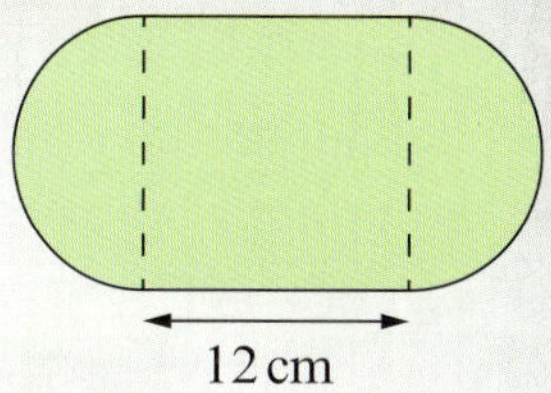

<u>Answer</u>

diameter = 12 cm, so radius = 6 cm

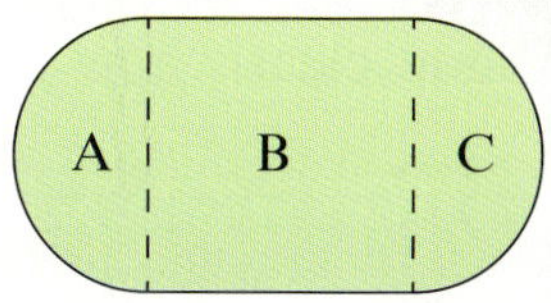

Area A $= \frac{1}{2}\pi r^2 = \frac{1}{2}\pi \times 6^2 = 56.5$

Area B $= 12 \times 12 = 144$

Area C $= \frac{1}{2}\pi r^2 = \frac{1}{2} \times \pi \times 6^2 = 56.5$

Total area $= 56.5 + 144 + 56.5 = 257\ \text{cm}^2$

Continued

a Critique Kira's method.

b Can you improve her method? Explain your answer.

c Discuss your answers to parts **a** and **b** with other learners in your class.

5 Work out the area of each shaded compound shape.

a

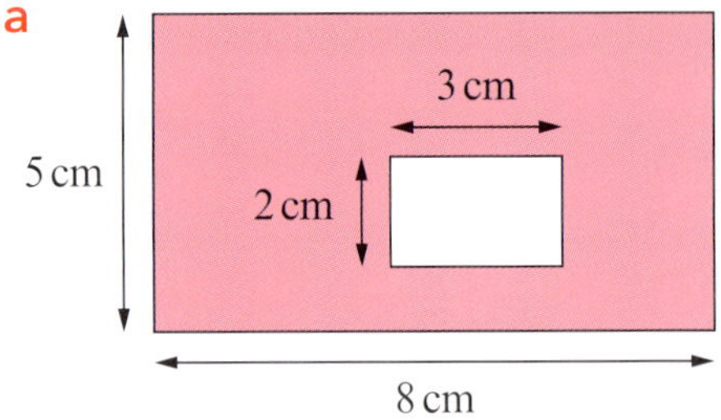

b

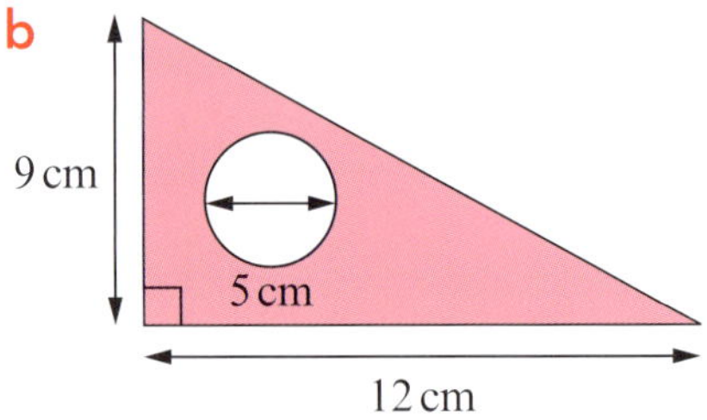

c

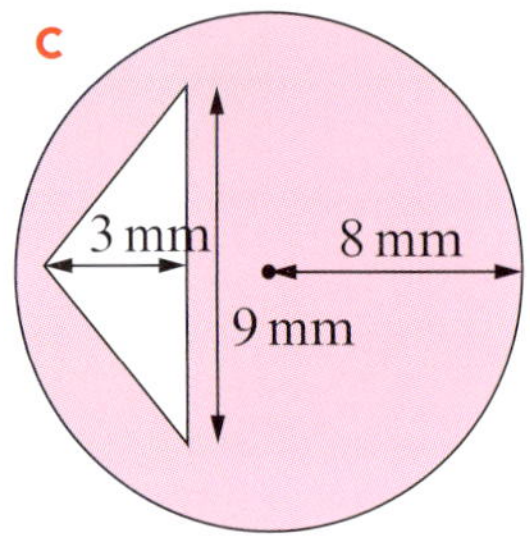

6 Sofia draws these two shapes.

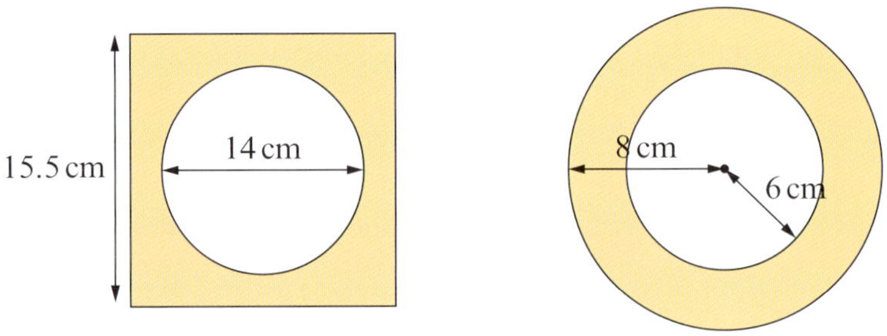

Sofia makes this conjecture:

Is Sofia correct? Show clearly how you worked out your answer.

Activity 7.2

Work with a partner for this activity.

Here are five compound shapes.

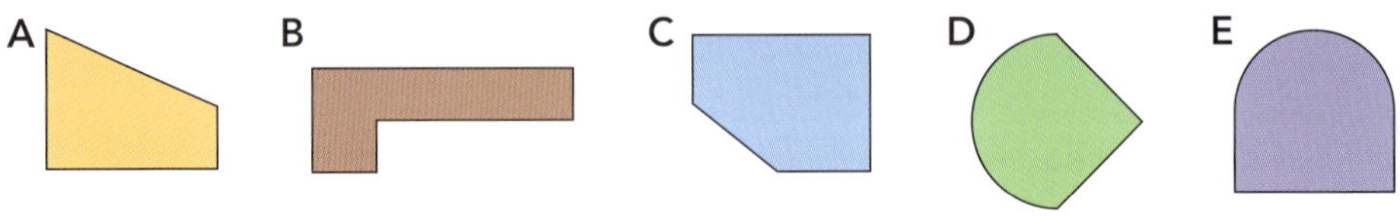

Continued

Take it in turns to choose a shape. You must choose a different shape each time.

Draw the shape on a piece of paper and write on some dimensions (e.g. some lengths, widths, etc.).

You must write just enough dimensions so that your partner can work out the area of the compound shape.

Ask your partner to work out the area of your shape, then mark their work.

Discuss any mistakes that have been made.

Do this twice each, so you use four out of the five shapes.

> **Tip**
>
> Remember to include units and to check that your measurements make sense.

Think like a mathematician

7 Work with a partner to answer this question.

The diagram shows an isosceles triangle inside a semicircle.

The base of the triangle is the diameter of the semicircle.

The height of the triangle is the radius of the semicircle.

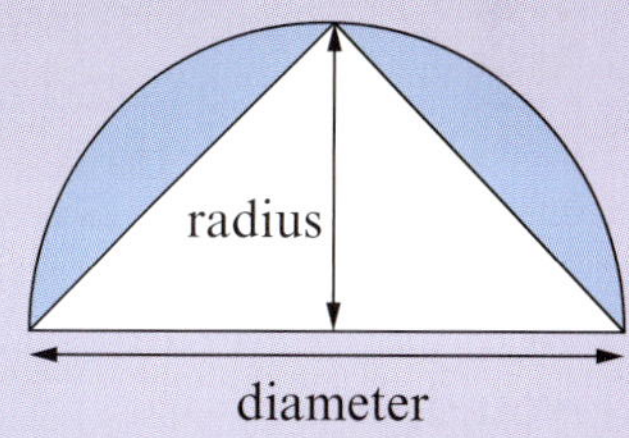

When the radius = 8 cm, you can work out an expression for the shaded area as shown:

Area of semicircle $= \frac{1}{2}\pi r^2 = \frac{1}{2} \times \pi \times 8^2$

$= \frac{1}{2} \times \pi \times 64 = 32\pi$ ← *Leave your answer in terms of π.*

Area of triangle $= \frac{1}{2}bh = \frac{1}{2} \times 16 \times 8 = 64$

Shaded area $= 32\pi - 64 = 32(\pi - 2)\,\text{cm}^2$ ← *Factorise the expression.*

a Use the method shown to work out an expression for the shaded area when the radius is

i 6 cm **ii** 10 cm **iii** 12 cm **iv** 3 cm

b What do you notice about your answers to part **a**?

c Use the method shown to write a general expression, using algebra, for the shaded area when the radius is *r*.

d Discuss your answers to parts **a**, **b** and **c** with other learners in your class.

8 Arun draws these two shapes.

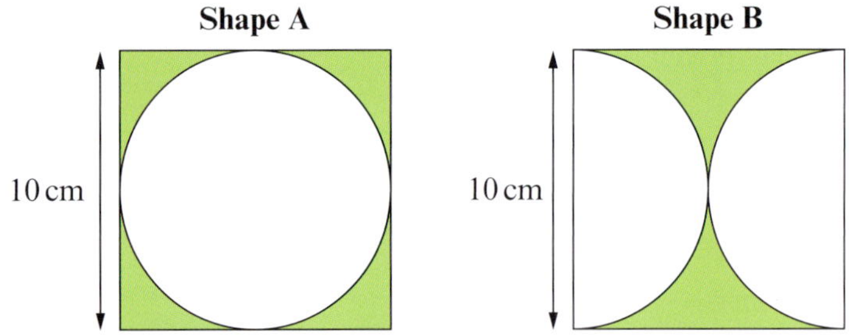

The side lengths of the squares are the diameters of the circle and semicircles.

Arun makes this conjecture:

What do you think? Explain your answer. Show any working that you do.

9 The diagram shows a circle inside a square.

The side length of the square is the diameter of the circle.

a Show that when the radius of the circle is 4 cm, you can write the shaded area as $16(4 - \pi)\,\text{cm}^2$.

b Work out an expression for the shaded area when the radius is

i 5 cm　　ii 3 cm

iii 6 cm　　iv 10 cm

c What do you notice about your answers to parts **a** and **b**?

d Write a general expression, using algebra, for the shaded area when the radius is r.

Summary checklist

- [ ] I can estimate and calculate areas of compound 2D shapes.

› 7.3 Large and small units

In this section you will ...

- know and recognise very small or very large units of length, capacity and mass.

Key words

prefix

tonne

You already know some of the units used for length, capacity and mass. Here is a reminder of the units you have used so far:

Length
kilometre (km)
metre (m)
centimetre (cm)
millimetre (mm)
1000 m = 1 km 100 cm = 1 m 10 mm = 1 cm

Capacity
litre (L)
millilitre (mL)
1000 ml = 1 L

Mass
kilogram (kg)
gram (g)
1000 g = 1 kg

There are other units you can use to measure very large or very small lengths, capacities and masses. This table shows some of the **prefixes** you can use.

Prefix	Letter	Multiply by:	Multiply by:
tera	T	1 000 000 000 000	10^{12}
giga	G	1 000 000 000	10^{9}
mega	M	1 000 000	10^{6}
kilo	k	1000	10^{3}
hecto	h	100	10^{2}
centi	c	0.01	10^{-2}
milli	m	0.001	10^{-3}
micro	μ	0.000 001	10^{-6}
nano	n	0.000 000 001	10^{-9}

Tip

The letter used for the prefix 'micro' is the Greek letter μ, which you read as 'mew'.

Tip

Remember: $0.01 = \frac{1}{100}$

Tip

Remember: $0.001 = \frac{1}{1000}$

You have already met these prefixes:

- 'kilo' as in kilogram or kilometre (you know that: 1 kilogram = 1000 × 1 gram and 1 kilometre = 1000 × 1 metre)
- 'centi' as in centimetre (you know that: 1 centimetre = 0.01 × 1 metre)
- 'milli' as in millilitre or millimetre (you know that: 1 millilitre = 0.001 × 1 litre and 1 millimetre = 0.001 × 1 metre)

Another unit of mass with a special name is the **tonne**.
1 tonne (t) = 1000 kilograms (kg)

Worked example 7.3

Describe a microlitre.

Answer

A microlitre is a very small measure of capacity. It is represented by the letters μL.

1 microlitre = 0.000 001 litres which is the same as $1\,\mu L = 1 \times 10^{-6}\,L$.

You can also say that there are one million microlitres in a litre or that 1 microlitre is one millionth of a litre.

Exercise 7.3

1 Copy and complete these descriptions. Use all the words and letters in the box.

length	one thousandth	mg	mass	one billionth	nm
metres	one thousand	g	m	one billion	grams

a A milligram is a very small measure of ....
It is represented by the letters ......
1 milligram = 0.001 ...... which is the same as
$1\,mg = 1 \times 10^{-3}$ ......
You can also say that there are .... milligrams in a gram or that 1 milligram is .... of a gram.

b A nanometre is a very small measure of ....
It is represented by the letters ......
1 nanometre = 0.000 000 001 ...... which is the same as
$1\,nm = 1 \times 10^{-9}$ ......
You can also say that there are .... nanometres in a metre or that 1 nanometre is .... of a metre.

Tip

Look at Worked example 7.3 to help you.

2 Copy and complete these descriptions. Use all the words, letters and numbers in the box.

kL	one thousandth	large	Gm	litres	one billionth
metres	capacity	3	one billion	9	kilolitre

a A kilolitre is a very large measure of ....
It is represented by the letters ......

1 ...... = 1000 litres which is the same as 1 kL = $1 \times 10^{\cdots}$ L.

You can also say that there are one thousand ...... in a kilolitre or that 1 litre is .... of a kilolitre.

b A gigametre is a very ...... measure of length.
It is represented by the letters ......

1 gigametre = 1 000 000 000 ...... which is the same as 1 Gm = $1 \times 10^{\cdots}$ metres.

You can also say that there are .... metres in a gigametre or 1 metre is .... of a gigametre.

3 **a** Write these lengths in order of size, starting with the smallest.

8 centimetres	8 gigametres	8 micrometres
8 millimetres	8 metres	8 kilometres

b Underneath each of the lengths in part **a**, write the length using the correct letters for the units, not words. For example, underneath 8 millimetres you write 8 mm.

Think like a mathematician

4 **a** Marcus and Arun make these conjectures:

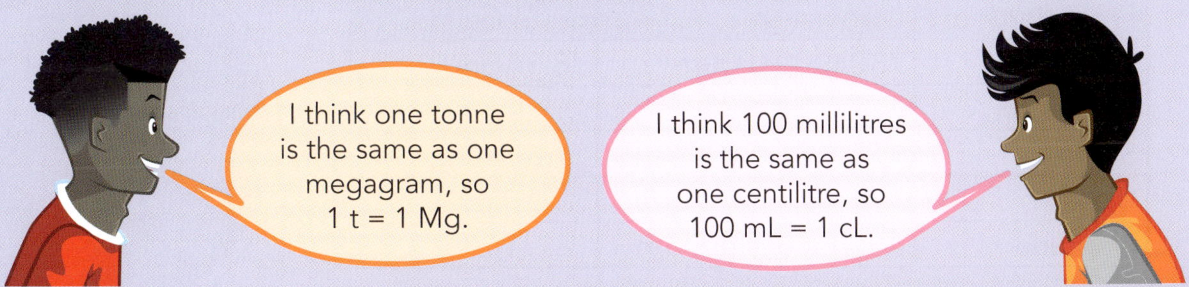

Are Marcus and Arun's conjectures correct? Show working to support your decisions.

b Discuss your answers to part **a** with other learners in your class.

c Make a conjecture different to those of Marcus and Arun.
For example, you could say, 'I think there are 1000 nanograms in a microgram.'
Ask a partner to decide if your conjecture is true or false, and to explain why.

d Discuss your answers to part **c** with other learners in your class.

5 Copy and complete these conversions.

a 2.5 Mm to m ⟶ 1 Mm = 1 000 000 m, so
2.5 Mm = 2.5 × 1 000 000 = ... m

b 0.75 GL to L ⟶ 1 GL = 1 000 000 000 L, so
0.75 GL = 0.75 × 1 000 000 000 = ... L

c 13.2 hg to g ⟶ 1 hg = ... g, so
13.2 hg = 13.2 × ...... = ... g

Tip

Use the table of prefixes in the introduction.

6 This is how Hania converts 225 000 000 nanograms into grams.

1 ng = 0.000 000 001 g, so 1 000 000 000 ng = 1 g
225 000 000 ng = 225 000 000 ÷ 1 000 000 000

$$= \frac{225\,\not{000}\,\not{000}}{1000\,\not{000}\,\not{000}}$$

= 225 ÷ 1000 = 0.225 g

Tip

Hania changes the conversion so that instead of multiplying by 0.000 000 001 she divides by 1 000 000 000.

Use Hania's method to copy and complete these conversions.

a 364 cL to L ⟶ 100 cL = 1 L, so
364 cL = 364 ÷ 100 = ... L

b 12 000 mg to g ⟶ 1000 mg = 1 g, so
12 000 mg = 12 000 ÷ 1000 = ... g

c 620 000 μm to m ⟶ ...... μm = 1 m, so
620 000 μm = 620 000 ÷ ...... = ... m

Tip

Use the table of prefixes in the introduction.

7 The table shows the approximate distances from Earth to some other planets.

Copy and complete the table.

From Earth to:	Distance in ...	Distance in ...
Mars	78 340 000 000 m	78.34 Gm
Jupiter	628 700 000 000 m	...... Gm
Saturn	1 280 000 000 000 m	...... Tm
Uranus	2 724 000 000 000 m	...... Tm
Neptune	4 350 000 000 000 m	...... Tm

8 The yellow cards show the approximate mass, in grams, of some very small objects.

A Grain of sugar 0.0006 g

B Poppy seed 0.0003 g

C Dust particle 0.000 000 6 g

D Grain of rice 0.03 g

E Grain of salt 0.000 06 g

The blue cards show the masses of the objects measured in milligrams, micrograms or nanograms.

i	600 ng	ii	60 µg	iii	30 mg	iv	300 µg	v	600 µg

Match each yellow card with the correct blue card.

Think like a mathematician

9 Work with a partner to answer this question.

Here is some information.

A light year is the **distance** light travels in one year. It is a unit of measurement used to measure distances in space.

Light travels at a **speed** of approximately 300 000 000 metres in one second.

You can use the formula:

distance = speed × time

to work out the distance something travels when you know its speed and the time it takes.

There are:

- 60 seconds in one minute
- 60 minutes in one hour
- 24 hours in one day
- 365.25 days in one year.

Sofia says:

a Is Sofia correct? Show working to support your answer.

b The speed of light is actually 299 792 458 metres per second.
Use this value to calculate a more accurate value for a light year.

c The letters ly are used to represent a light year.
1 ly = 9 460 730 472 580 800 m
Write the number 9 460 730 472 580 800 correct to three significant figures.

d The distance of Barnard's Star from the Earth is approximately 6 ly.
Use your answer to part **c** to work out the distance of Barnard's Star from the Earth in metres.

e Discuss and compare your answers to parts **a** to **d** with other learners in your class.

10 Bytes are units of memory in a computer.

Some of the larger amounts of memory are called kilobytes (KB), megabytes (MB), gigabytes (GB) and terabytes (TB).

The table shows the conversions between these units of memory.

Unit of memory	Number of bytes as a power of 2	Number of bytes as a number
1 KB	2^{10}	1024
1 MB	2^{20}	1 048 576
1 GB	2^{30}	1 073 741 824
1 TB	2^{40}	1 099 511 627 776

This shows that 1 kilobyte = 2^{10} bytes which is the same as 1 KB = 1024 bytes

This shows that 1 gigabyte = 2^{30} bytes which is the same as 1 GB = 1 073 741 824 bytes

a A shop sells these items.

A

Memory: 1 TB

B

Memory: 64 GB

C

Memory: 128 GB

D

Memory: 512 MB

Write the items in order of memory size, from the smallest to the largest.

b Ela buys a computer with 2 GB of RAM memory. How many bytes is 2 GB?

c Anoop buys a 32 GB memory card for his camera.
It is possible to store approximately 340 photographs on 1 GB of memory.
Approximately how many photographs can Anoop store on his memory card?

d Doroata buys an external hard drive for her computer which has 8 TB of memory.
It is possible to store approximately 233 films on 1 TB of memory.
Approximately how many films can Doroata store on her external hard drive?

11 Magnar wants to buy a new computer. He looks at three different models, **A**, **B** and **C**.
He looks at the speed, in nanoseconds, at which each computer can access the memory.

Model A	Model B	Model C
Speed: 40 ns	Speed: 10 ns	Speed: 60 ns

Magnar thinks Model **C** is the fastest. Is he correct? Explain your answer.

Without looking back at the introduction and exercise questions in this section, answer these questions to see what you can remember.

a Write these prefixes in order of size, starting with the smallest.

milli | tera | micro | mega | hecto
giga | nano | kilo | centi

b Underneath each prefix in your list for part **a**, write the letter that represents this prefix.

c Check your answers against the table in the introduction.
How many prefixes and their letters did you get correct? Which prefixes did you find easy to remember?
Which prefixes did you find difficult to remember? Can you explain why?

Summary checklist

☐ I know and can recognise very small or very large units of length, capacity and mass.

Check your progress

1 Work out the circumference of these circles. Use the π button on your calculator. Give your answers correct to two decimal places (2 d.p.).

a diameter = 12.5 cm
b radius = 3.4 m

2 Work out the area of these circles. Use the π button on your calculator. Give your answers correct to three significant figures (3 s.f.).

a diameter = 12.5 cm
b radius = 3.4 m

3 Work out the area of this compound shape.
Use the π button on your calculator.
Give your answer correct to one decimal place (1 d.p.).

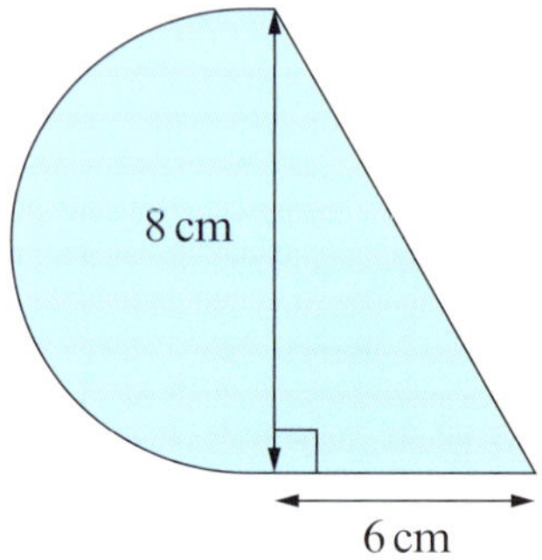

4 Work out the shaded area in this diagram.
Use the π button on your calculator.
Give your answer correct to two significant figures (2 s.f.).

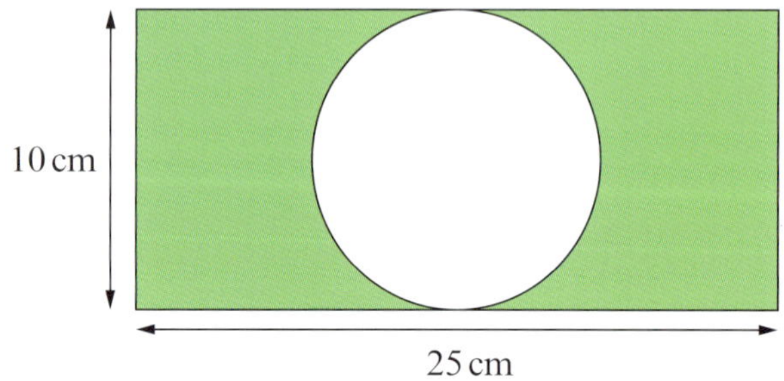

5 a Write these masses in order of size, starting with the smallest.

5 tonnes	5 milligrams	5 nanograms
5 grams	5 micrograms	5 kilograms

b Underneath each mass in part **a**, write the mass using the correct letters for the units, not words. For example, underneath 5 grams you write 5 g.

8 Fractions

Getting started

1 Use a written method to convert these fractions into decimals.
Write if the fraction is a terminating or recurring decimal.

a $\frac{5}{8}$ b $\frac{5}{6}$

2 Work out these calculations. Give each answer as a mixed number in its simplest form.

a $3\frac{1}{9} + 2\frac{2}{9}$ b $4\frac{4}{5} + 1\frac{7}{10}$ c $8\frac{3}{4} - 2\frac{1}{3}$

3 Work out

a $5\frac{2}{3} \times 12$ b $6 \div \frac{3}{5}$

4 Work out these calculations. Give each answer in its simplest form.

a $\frac{3}{7} \times \frac{7}{9}$ b $\frac{4}{5} \div \frac{6}{11}$

5 Work out mentally

a $\frac{2}{7} + \frac{3}{14}$ b $\frac{3}{4} - \frac{2}{5}$

c $4 \div \frac{2}{5}$ d $5 \times \left(\frac{3}{5} - \frac{1}{2}\right)$

This is a well-known puzzle, called a tangram. There are seven parts, called tans. These parts can be used to make different shapes. The idea of the puzzle is to form a specific shape, given only an outline, using all seven pieces. The pieces are not allowed to overlap.

For example:

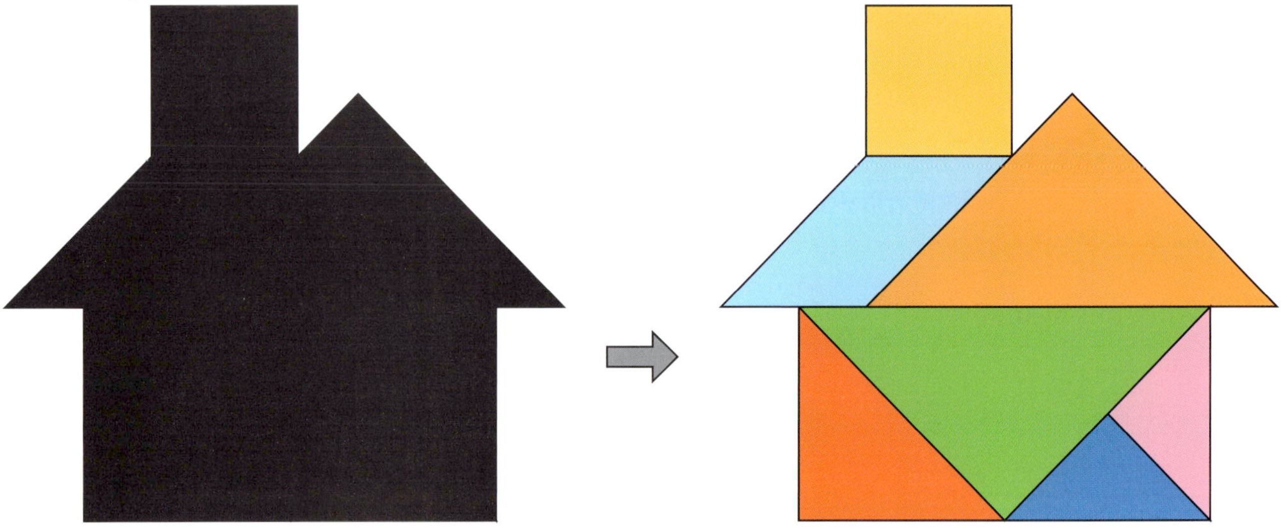

Which tans have the same area?

Suppose the whole shape has area 1. If you find the area of each tan as a fraction, you should find that each area is $\frac{1}{4}$, $\frac{1}{8}$ or $\frac{1}{16}$.

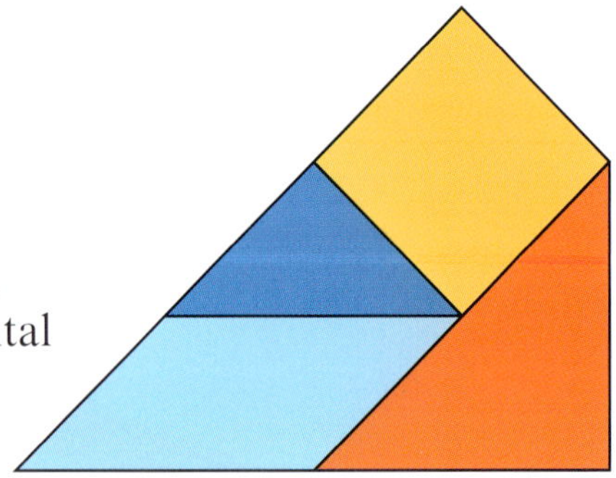

Work out the area of this shape. Can you work out your answer in different ways? For example, by addition or by subtraction?

In this unit you will continue working with fractions. You will add, subtract, multiply and divide fractions using both written and mental methods. You will also learn how to make calculations with fractions and decimals easier.

8.1 Fractions and recurring decimals

In this section you will …

- deduce whether fractions have recurring or terminating decimal equivalents.

Key words

equivalent decimal

recurring decimal

terminating decimal

You already know how to use equivalent fractions to convert a fraction to an **equivalent decimal**. For example: $\frac{1}{5} = \frac{2}{10} = 0.2$
You also know how to use division to convert a fraction to an equivalent decimal. For example: $\frac{13}{25} = 13 \div 25 = 0.52$

The decimals 0.2 and 0.52 are **terminating decimals** because they come to an end. You also know that you can write the fraction $\frac{1}{3}$ as $0.\dot{3}$ and that this is a **recurring decimal** because the digit 3 is repeated forever. You can use what you already know about terminating and recurring decimals to deduce whether other fractions are terminating or recurring.

Tip

You can use a written method or a calculator to use division to convert a fraction to an equivalent decimal.

Worked example 8.1

a $\frac{1}{5}$ is equivalent to a terminating decimal. Use this information to deduce if $\frac{3}{5}$ is a terminating or recurring decimal.

b $\frac{1}{3}$ is equivalent to a recurring decimal. Use this information to deduce if $\frac{2}{3}$ is a terminating or recurring decimal.

Answer

a $\frac{1}{5} = 0.2$ $\frac{3}{5} = 3 \times \frac{1}{5}$ $= 3 \times 0.2$ $= 0.6$, so terminating	You know that $\frac{1}{5} = 0.2$, which is a terminating decimal. $\frac{3}{5}$ is three times $\frac{1}{5}$ The whole number 3 multiplied by the terminating decimal 0.2 will give the terminating decimal 0.6
b $\frac{1}{3} = 0.\dot{3}$ $\frac{2}{3} = 2 \times \frac{1}{3}$ $= 2 \times 0.\dot{3}$ $= 0.\dot{6}$, so recurring	You know that $\frac{1}{3} = 0.\dot{3}$, which is a recurring decimal. $\frac{2}{3}$ is two times $\frac{1}{3}$ The whole number 2 multiplied by the recurring decimal $0.\dot{3}$ will give the recurring decimal $0.\dot{6}$.

Exercise 8.1

1 **a** Copy and complete:

$\frac{1}{4} = 0.25$ which is a terminating decimal

$\frac{2}{4} = 2 \times \frac{1}{4} = 2 \times 0.25 = \square$ which is a .... decimal

$\frac{3}{4} = 3 \times \frac{1}{4} = 3 \times 0.25 = \square$ which is a .... decimal

b Copy and complete:

$\frac{1}{5} = 0.2$ which is a terminating decimal

$\frac{2}{5} = 2 \times \frac{1}{5} = 2 \times 0.2 = \square$ which is a .... decimal

$\frac{4}{5} = 4 \times \frac{1}{5} = 4 \times 0.2 = \square$ which is a .... decimal

2 **a** Work out the decimal equivalent of $\frac{1}{9}$

b Is $\frac{1}{9}$ a terminating or recurring decimal?

c Use your answers to parts **a** and **b** to write the decimal equivalents of these fractions. Write if each decimal is terminating or recurring.

i $\frac{2}{9}$ **ii** $\frac{3}{9}$ **iii** $\frac{4}{9}$ **iv** $\frac{5}{9}$

v $\frac{6}{9}$ **vi** $\frac{7}{9}$ **vii** $\frac{8}{9}$

Think like a mathematician

3 Work with a partner to answer this question.

a Look back at your answers to Question **2**, parts **c ii** and **v**. You have met these recurring decimals before, but for different fractions. Which fractions? Explain the connection between these fractions and the fractions $\frac{3}{9}$ and $\frac{6}{9}$

b Read what Marcus and Zara say:

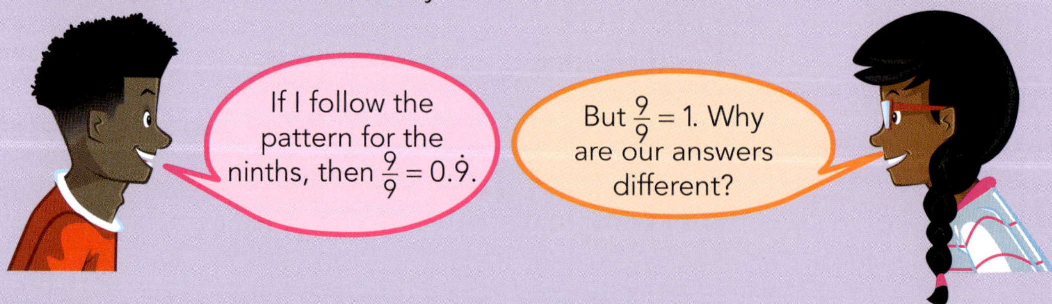

Discuss Marcus' and Zara's statements. Are their answers different? Explain your answer.

4 a Work out the decimal equivalent of $\frac{1}{8}$.

b Is $\frac{1}{8}$ a terminating or recurring decimal?

c Use your answers to parts **a** and **b** to write down the decimal equivalents of these fractions. Write if each decimal is terminating or recurring.

i $\frac{2}{8}$ ii $\frac{3}{8}$ iii $\frac{4}{8}$ iv $\frac{5}{8}$ v $\frac{6}{8}$ vi $\frac{7}{8}$

d Look at your answers to part **c i, iii** and **v**. Did you write these fractions in their simplest form before you changed them into decimals? If you did, explain why. If you did not, do you think it would have been easier if you had?

Think like a mathematician

5 Work with a partner to answer this question.

You have seen from Question **2** that $\frac{1}{9}$ is a recurring decimal and that all proper fractions with the denominator 9 are recurring decimals.

a $\frac{1}{6}$ is a recurring decimal. Are all proper fractions with the denominator 6 recurring decimals?

b $\frac{1}{7}$ is a recurring decimal. Are all proper fractions with the denominator 7 recurring decimals?

c Why are your answers to parts **a** and **b** different?

d Investigate other unit fractions that are recurring decimals, such as $\frac{1}{11}$ and $\frac{1}{12}$. Are all the fractions with the same denominator (e.g. 11 or 12) recurring decimals? Can you find a general rule to help you to decide if all the fractions with the same denominator as such unit fractions will be recurring decimals as well?

6 Here are five fraction cards.

A $\frac{1}{3}$ B $\frac{1}{6}$ C $\frac{1}{9}$ D $\frac{1}{12}$ E $\frac{1}{15}$

a Without doing any calculations, answer this question.

Are these fractions terminating or recurring decimals? Explain how you know.

b All the numerators are changed from 1 to 2, so the cards now look like this:

A $\frac{2}{3}$ B $\frac{2}{6}$ C $\frac{2}{9}$ D $\frac{2}{12}$ E $\frac{2}{15}$

Are these fractions terminating or recurring decimals? Explain your answer.

c If all the numerators in part **b** are changed from 2 to 3, are the fractions terminating or recurring decimals? Explain your answer.

d Look back at your answers to parts **b** and **c** and answer this question.

When a fraction has a denominator which has a factor of 3, is the fraction always equivalent to a recurring decimal? Discuss your answer with other learners in your class.

7 Decide if these statements about proper fractions are 'Always true', 'Sometimes true' or 'Never true'.

Justify your answers.

a A fraction with a denominator of 7 is a recurring decimal.

b A fraction with a denominator which is a multiple of 2 is a recurring decimal.

c A fraction with a denominator which is a multiple of 10 is a terminating decimal.

d A fraction with a denominator which is a power of 2 is a recurring decimal.

Tip

7d The numbers which are powers of 2 are $2^1 = 2$, $2^2 = 4$, $2^3 = 8$ etc.

8 Here are five fraction cards.

A $\frac{5}{7}$ B $\frac{3}{14}$ C $\frac{11}{21}$ D $\frac{9}{35}$ E $\frac{3}{42}$

a Without doing any calculations, answer this question.

Do you think these fractions are terminating or recurring decimals? Explain why.

b Which fraction is different from the others? Explain this difference.

Does this change your answer to part **a**? Explain why.

c Read what Sofia and Arun say.

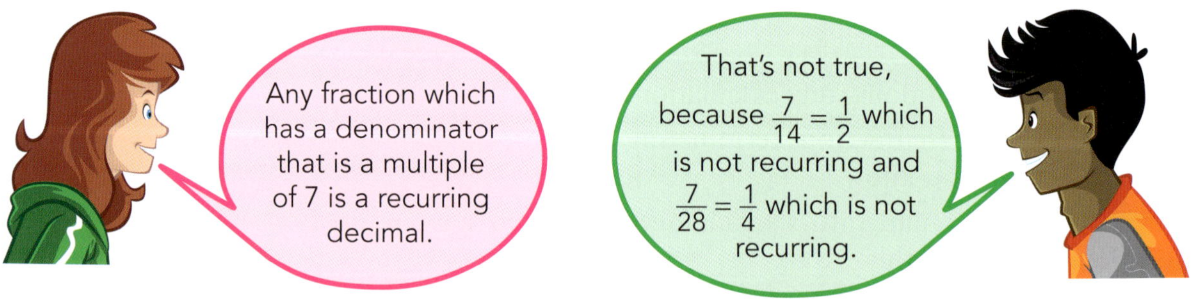

What must Sofia add to her statement to make her statement true?

9 This is part of Ed's homework.

Question
Write 12 minutes as a fraction of an hour.
Is your answer a terminating or recurring decimal?
Answer
12 minutes is the same as $\frac{12}{60} = \frac{1}{5}$ *of an hour and* $\frac{1}{5} = 0.2$, *so terminating.*

Use Ed's method to decide if these lengths of time, as a fraction of an hour, are terminating or recurring decimals.

a 20 minutes
b 36 minutes
c 45 minutes
d 55 minutes
e 1 hour 8 minutes
f 3 hours 21 minutes

Tip
Think about the number of minutes in an hour.

10 Without using a calculator, decide if these fractions are terminating or recurring decimals.

a $\frac{8}{3}$
b $\frac{21}{5}$
c $\frac{28}{9}$
d $\frac{39}{12}$

Tip
Change the improper fractions into mixed numbers first.

11 The table shows the number of hours that six friends work each week.
There are 168 hours in one week.

Number of hours worked in one week.					
Abi	21	Bim	28	Caz	32
Dave	35	Enid	40	Fin	42

a Sort the friends into two groups according to the number of hours they work, as a fraction of one week. Explain the criteria you used to group them.
b Sort the friends into two different groups according to the number of hours they work, as a fraction of one week. Explain the criteria you used to group them this time.

Activity 8.1

Work with a partner for this activity.
Here are 10 fraction cards.

$\frac{21}{35}$ $\frac{16}{72}$ $\frac{17}{20}$ $\frac{14}{16}$ $\frac{24}{45}$ $\frac{12}{18}$ $\frac{9}{12}$ $\frac{15}{21}$ $\frac{30}{36}$ $\frac{13}{25}$

Continued

Decide who is going to go first, you or your partner.

The first person chooses a card. The other person must decide if the fraction is a terminating or recurring decimal, and then choose a card that is the same (a terminating or recurring decimal). Check the cards match, then swap over.

Do this twice each; when a card has been used, it cannot be used again.

In this section, you have learned to deduce whether fractions have recurring or terminating decimal equivalents.

Explain to a partner one important thing you have learned from this section that will help you to decide whether fractions have recurring or terminating decimal equivalents.

Summary checklist

- [ ] I can deduce whether fractions have recurring or terminating decimal equivalents.

8.2 Fractions and the correct order of operations

In this section you will …

- carry out calculations involving fractions and mixed numbers using the correct order of operations
- estimate the answers to calculations.

You already know how to carry out a variety of calculations involving fractions and mixed numbers. In this section you will develop these skills, making sure you use the correct order of operations.

Worked example 8.2

Work out

a $3\frac{1}{2}-\left(\frac{3}{4}+\frac{4}{5}\right)$ b $2\frac{1}{3}+\frac{4}{9}\times\frac{1}{2}$

Answer

a $\frac{3}{4}+\frac{4}{5}=\frac{15}{20}+\frac{16}{20}=\frac{31}{20}$ Work out the brackets first.

$3\frac{1}{2}=\frac{7}{2}=\frac{70}{20}$ Write $3\frac{1}{2}$ as an improper fraction with a denominator of 20.

$\frac{70}{20}-\frac{31}{20}=\frac{39}{20}=1\frac{19}{20}$ Finally do the subtraction. Write the answer as a mixed number in its simplest form.

b $\frac{4}{9}\times\frac{1}{2}=\frac{4\times1}{9\times2}=\frac{4}{18}=\frac{2}{9}$ Work out the multiplication first. Write the answer in its simplest form.

$2\frac{1}{3}=2\frac{3}{9}$ Write $2\frac{1}{3}$ as a mixed number with a denominator of 9.

$2\frac{3}{9}+\frac{2}{9}=2\frac{5}{9}$ Finally do the addition. Write the answer as a mixed number in its simplest form.

Exercise 8.2

1 Copy and complete these calculations.

a $5\frac{2}{3}+\left(\frac{3}{5}-\frac{1}{2}\right)$

Brackets: $\frac{3}{5}-\frac{1}{2}=\frac{\square}{10}-\frac{\square}{10}=\frac{\square}{10}$

Addition: $5\frac{2}{3}+\frac{\square}{10}=5\frac{\square}{30}+\frac{\square}{30}=5\frac{\square}{30}$

b $10-\frac{5}{6}\times\frac{7}{10}$

Multiplication: $\frac{5}{6}\times\frac{7}{10}=\frac{5\times7}{6\times10}=\frac{\square}{60}=\frac{\square}{12}$

Rewrite 10: $10=9\frac{12}{12}$

Subtraction: $9\frac{12}{12}-\frac{\square}{12}=9\frac{\square}{12}$

c $5\div\frac{3}{4}+\left(\frac{2}{3}\right)^2$

Brackets: $\left(\frac{2}{3}\right)^2=\frac{2}{3}\times\frac{2}{3}=\frac{2\times2}{3\times3}=\frac{\square}{\square}$

Division: $5\div\frac{3}{4}=5\times\frac{4}{3}=\frac{\square}{3}$

Addition: $\frac{\square}{3}+\frac{\square}{9}=\frac{\square}{9}+\frac{\square}{9}=\frac{\square}{9}=\square\frac{\square}{9}$

Tip

Make sure you write your answer in its simplest form.

2 Work out these calculations. Write each answer as a mixed number in its simplest form.

Show all the steps in your working.

a $2\frac{1}{8}+\frac{1}{4}\times\frac{3}{4}$ **b** $\frac{9}{10}\times\frac{1}{2}+2\frac{4}{5}$ **c** $4\frac{1}{3}-\left(5\frac{1}{2}-3\frac{1}{6}\right)$ **d** $\frac{2}{3}\div\frac{4}{9}+2\frac{1}{4}$

Think like a mathematician

3 Work with a partner or in a small group to discuss this question.

a Estimate an answer to this calculation. $6\frac{4}{5}+3\frac{1}{4}-\left(5\frac{2}{3}-2\frac{7}{10}\right)$
Write how you worked out your estimate.

b Work out the accurate answer to the calculation.

c Do you think your estimate was a good estimate of the accurate answer? Critique the method you used and explain how you could improve it.

d Discuss your answers to parts **a** and **c** with other learners in the class, and decide on the best method to use to estimate the answers to fraction calculations.

4 Work out **i** an estimate **ii** the accurate answer to these calculations.

Show all the steps in your working.

a $8\frac{9}{10}-\left(2\frac{1}{5}+3\frac{5}{8}\right)$ **b** $7\frac{2}{3}+\left(2\frac{5}{12}-\frac{7}{8}\right)$ **c** $5\frac{1}{9}+2\frac{1}{3}\times16$ **d** $15\frac{3}{4}-\frac{7}{12}\times\frac{1}{2}$

5 This is part of Fiona's homework. Her method is to change all the mixed numbers into improper fractions, then work through the solution and change back to a mixed number at the very end.

<u>Question</u>

Work out $5\frac{2}{3}-\left(1\frac{3}{5}+2\frac{5}{6}\right)$

<u>Answer</u>

Change to improper fractions: $\frac{17}{3}-\left(\frac{8}{5}+\frac{17}{6}\right)$

Work out brackets: $\frac{8}{5}+\frac{17}{6}=\frac{48}{30}+\frac{85}{30}=\frac{133}{30}$

Work out subtraction: $\frac{17}{3}-\frac{133}{30}=\frac{170}{30}-\frac{133}{30}=\frac{37}{30}$

Simplify: $\frac{37}{30}=1\frac{7}{30}$

a Critique Fiona's method.

b Can you think of a better/easier method to use to answer this type of question?

6 The diagram shows the lengths of two sides of a triangle.
The triangle has a perimeter of 25 m.

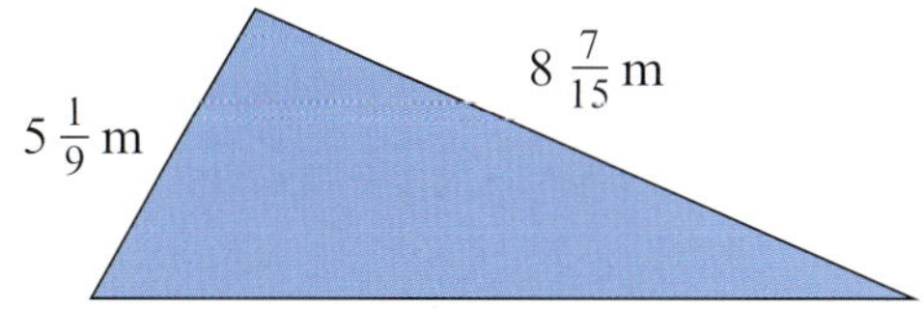

a Write the calculation you must do to work out the length of the third side of the triangle.

b Read what Zara says:

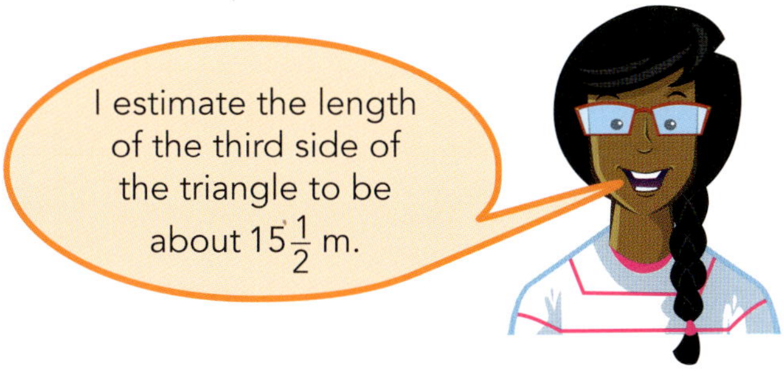

What do you think of Zara's estimate? Explain your answer.

c Work out the length of the third side of the triangle. Was your answer to part **b** correct? Explain your answer.

7 Holly has three bags of apples.

The first bag has a mass of $2\frac{4}{5}$ kg.

The mass of the second bag is twice the mass of the first bag.

The total mass of the three bags is $11\frac{13}{20}$ kg.

Work out the mass of the third bag.

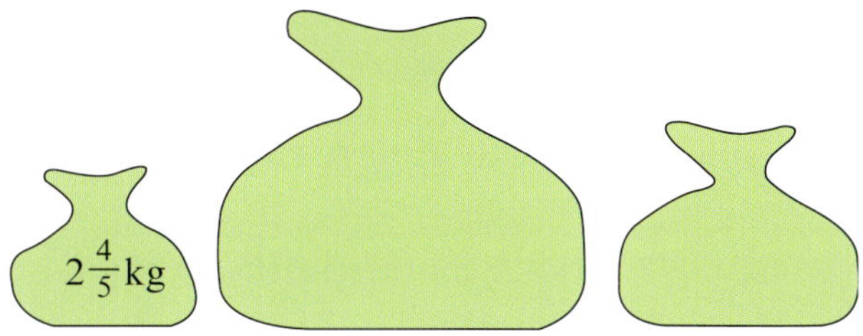

8 Copy and complete the workings to calculate the answer to

$6 \div \frac{4}{5} + 3\frac{1}{4} \times 5$

Division: $6 \div \frac{4}{5} = 6 \times \frac{5}{4} = \frac{\square}{4}$

Multiplication: $3\frac{1}{4} \times 5 = \frac{\square}{4} \times 5 = \frac{\square}{4}$

Addition: $\frac{\square}{4} + \frac{\square}{4} = \frac{\square}{4} = \square\frac{\square}{4}$

9 Work out the area of each shape. Show all your working.

a

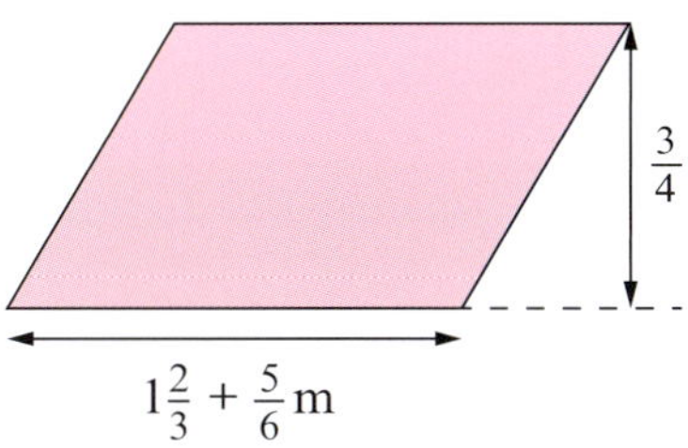

b

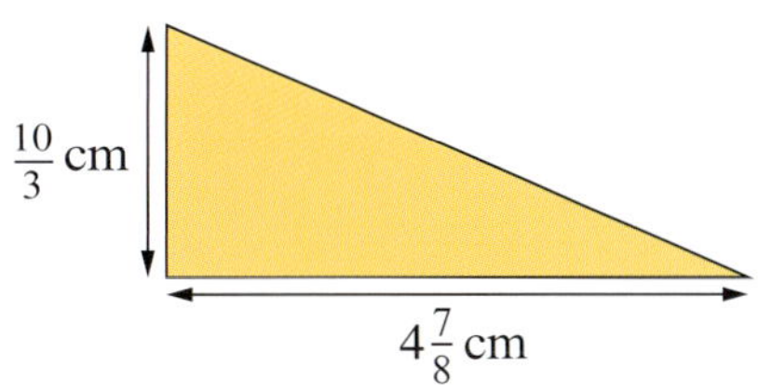

c

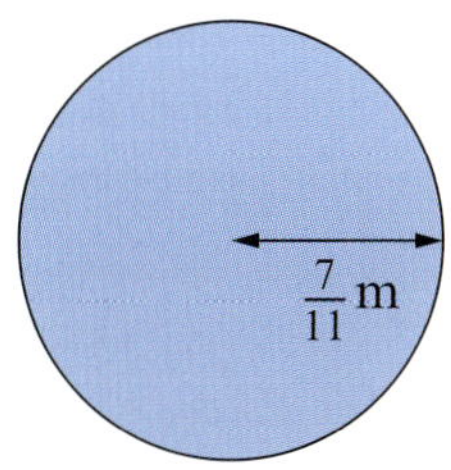

Use $\pi = \frac{22}{7}$

Think like a mathematician

10 Work with a partner to answer these questions.

Marcus and Arun are discussing how to square a mixed number.

Read what they say.

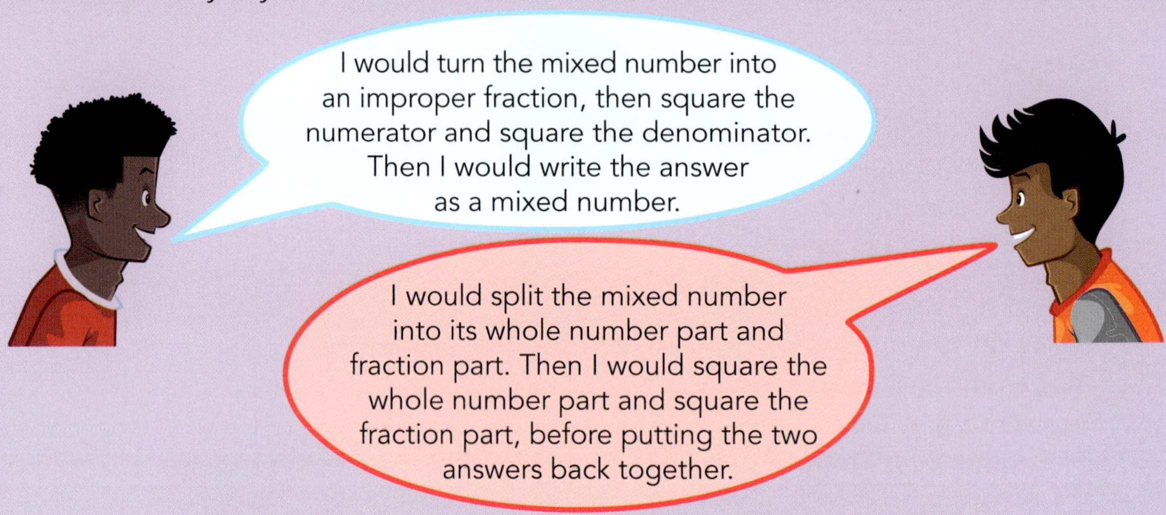

a Try both their methods to square the mixed number $1\frac{1}{2}$. Do you get the same answers?

Whose method do you think is correct? Explain why.

Check the answer by using a calculator to work out $\left(1\frac{1}{2}\right)^2$

b Discuss your answers to part **a** with other learners in your class.

Write a general rule that you must use when you square a mixed number.

11 Work out the answers to these calculations.

a $\left(2\frac{1}{2}\right)^2 - 2\frac{1}{2}$ **b** $9 \times 3\frac{1}{3} - \left(\frac{2}{3}\right)^2$ **c** $4\frac{1}{5} + 10 \times \left(1\frac{1}{5}\right)^2$

12 The diagram shows a compound shape made of a square joined to a rectangle.

a Write the calculation you must do to work out the total area of the shape.

b Work out the area of the shape.

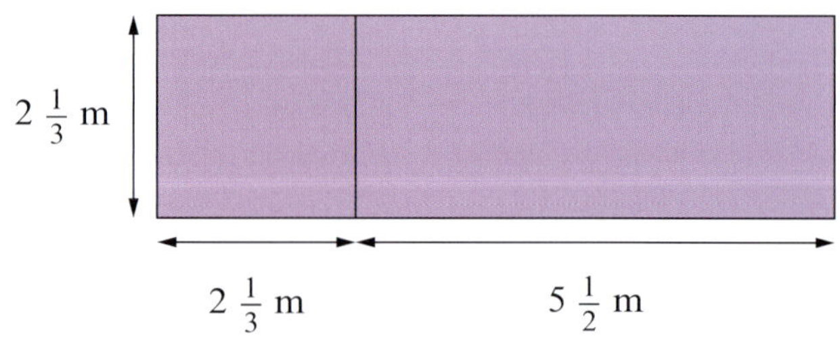

Summary checklist

- [ ] I can carry out calculations involving fractions and mixed numbers using the correct order of operations.
- [ ] I can estimate the answers to calculations.

〉 8.3 Multiplying fractions

In this section you will …

- cancel common factors before multiplying fractions
- estimate the answers to calculations.

Key word

cancelling common factors

You already know how to multiply an integer by a fraction and a fraction by a fraction. You can complete multiplications more easily by **cancelling common factors** before you multiply.

Worked example 8.3

Work out

a $\frac{2}{3} \times 18$ **b** $\frac{3}{4} \times 26$ **c** $\frac{5}{7} \times \frac{4}{9}$ **d** $\frac{2}{7} \times \frac{14}{15}$ **e** $2\frac{1}{5} \times \frac{15}{22}$

Answer

a $\frac{2}{\cancel{3}^1} \times \cancel{18}^6$

$= 2 \times 6 = 12$

Divide 3 and 18 by 3. The 3 cancels to 1 and the 18 cancels to 6.

$\frac{2}{1}$ is the same as 2, so just work out $2 \times 6 = 12$.

b $\frac{3}{\cancel{4}^2} \times \cancel{26}^{13}$

$= \frac{3}{2} \times 13 = \frac{39}{2}$

$= 19\frac{1}{2}$

4 does not divide into 26, but 4 and 26 can both be divided by 2 to give 2 and 13.

$3 \times 13 = 39$, so the answer is $\frac{39}{2}$.

This is an improper fraction, so change it to a mixed number.

c $\frac{5}{7} \times \frac{4}{9} = \frac{5 \times 4}{7 \times 9}$

$= \frac{20}{63}$

There are no common factors between the numbers in the numerators and denominators, so simply multiply 5 by 4 and multiply 7 by 9.

$\frac{20}{63}$ cannot be cancelled further and is a proper fraction.

d $\frac{2}{\cancel{7}^1} \times \frac{\cancel{14}^2}{15}$

$\frac{2}{1} \times \frac{2}{15} = \frac{2 \times 2}{1 \times 15}$

$= \frac{4}{15}$

7 divides into 7 and into 14 to give 1 and 2. There are no other common factors.

Now multiply 2 by 2 and multiply 1 by 15.

$\frac{4}{15}$ cannot be cancelled further and is a proper fraction.

Continued

e $2\frac{1}{5} = \frac{11}{5}$

$\frac{{}^{1}\cancel{11}}{{}_{1}\cancel{5}} \times \frac{\cancel{15}^{3}}{\cancel{22}_{2}}$

$\frac{1}{1} \times \frac{3}{2} = \frac{1 \times 3}{1 \times 2}$

$= \frac{3}{2} = 1\frac{1}{2}$

Write $2\frac{1}{5}$ as an improper fraction first.

5 divides into 5 and into 15 to give 1 and 3. 11 divides into 11 and into 22 to give 1 and 2.

Now multiply 1 by 3 and multiply 1 by 2.

$\frac{3}{2}$ is an improper fraction, so change it to a mixed number.

Exercise 8.3

1 Copy and complete these multiplications. Cancel common factors before multiplying.

a $\frac{3}{4} \times 12 = \frac{3}{\cancel{4}^{1}} \times \cancel{12}^{\square} = 3 \times \square = \square$

b $\frac{5}{7} \times 28 = \frac{5}{\cancel{7}^{1}} \times \cancel{28}^{\square} = 5 \times \square = \square$

c $\frac{4}{5} \times 45 = \frac{4}{\cancel{5}^{1}} \times \cancel{45}^{\square} = 4 \times \square = \square$

d $\frac{3}{8} \times 72 = \frac{3}{\cancel{8}^{\square}} \times \cancel{72}^{\square} = 3 \times \square = \square$

2 Copy and complete these multiplications. Cancel common factors before multiplying.

Write each answer as a mixed number in its simplest form.

a $\frac{3}{8} \times 36 = \frac{3}{\cancel{8}^{2}} \times \cancel{36}^{9} = \frac{3}{2} \times 9 = \frac{\square}{2} = \square\frac{\square}{2}$

b $\frac{4}{9} \times 39 = \frac{4}{\cancel{9}^{3}} \times \cancel{39}^{13} = \frac{4}{3} \times 13 = \frac{\square}{3} = \square\frac{\square}{3}$

c $\frac{5}{6} \times 8 = \frac{5}{\cancel{6}^{3}} \times \cancel{8}^{\square} = \frac{5}{3} \times \square = \frac{\square}{3} = \square\frac{\square}{3}$

d $\frac{7}{10} \times 45 = \frac{7}{\cancel{10}^{\square}} \times \cancel{45}^{9} = \frac{7}{\square} \times 9 = \frac{63}{\square} = \square\frac{\square}{\square}$

Think like a mathematician

3 Work with a partner to answer this question.
This is part of Sofia's homework.

Question
Work out $16 \times \frac{11}{24}$
Answer

$16 \times \frac{11}{24} = \cancel{16}^4 \times \frac{11}{\cancel{24}^6} = 4 \times \frac{11}{6}$
$= \frac{44}{6} = 7\frac{2}{6} = 7\frac{1}{3}$

Read what Sofia says:

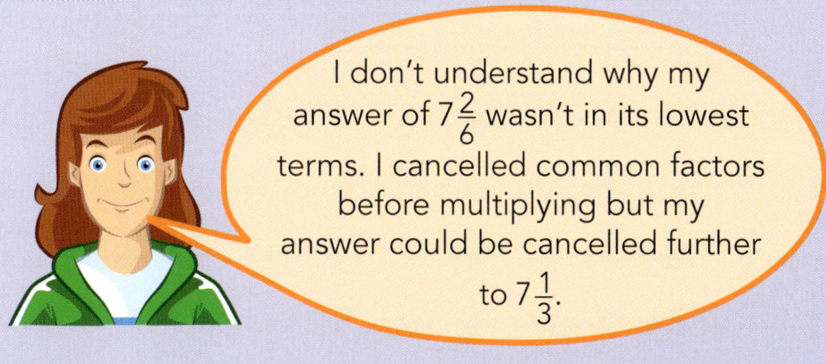

a Look at Sofia's solution. Discuss why she had to cancel her answer at the end, even though she had cancelled common factors before she multiplied.

b Write a solution for Sofia where she would not have to cancel her answer at the end.

c What words are missing from this general statement?
When you cancel common factors before multiplying, if you cancel using the ...., your answer will always be in its simplest form.

d Discuss your answers to parts **a**, **b** and **c** with other learners in your class.

4 Work out these multiplications. Cancel common factors before multiplying.

a $\frac{7}{11} \times 132$ b $\frac{7}{9} \times 180$ c $\frac{1}{12} \times 30$ d $\frac{9}{14} \times 35$

5 Work out these multiplications. Cancel common factors before multiplying.
Write each answer in its lowest terms. Two of them have been started for you.

a $\frac{6}{7} \times \frac{5}{9} = \frac{\cancel{6}^2}{7} \times \frac{5}{\cancel{9}^3} = \frac{2 \times 5}{7 \times 3} = \frac{\square}{\square}$ b $\frac{3}{8} \times \frac{5}{6}$ c $\frac{8}{9} \times \frac{3}{13}$

d $\frac{8}{5} \times \frac{5}{12} = \frac{\cancel{8}^2}{\cancel{5}^1} \times \frac{\cancel{5}^1}{\cancel{12}^3} = \frac{2 \times 1}{1 \times 3} = \frac{\square}{\square}$ e $\frac{8}{21} \times \frac{9}{20}$ f $\frac{2}{5} \times \frac{15}{16}$

6 This is part of Razi's homework.
Razi works out the answer to the question by cancelling common factors **before** multiplying.
He checks his answer is correct by cancelling common factors **after** multiplying.

Question

I eat $\frac{1}{4}$ of a pizza. My brother eats $\frac{2}{3}$ of what is left.
What fraction of the pizza does my brother eat?

Answer

$\frac{3}{4}$ *is left, so* $\frac{3}{4} \times \frac{2}{3} = \frac{\cancel{3}^1}{\cancel{4}^2} \times \frac{\cancel{2}^1}{\cancel{3}^1}$

$= \frac{1}{2} \times \frac{1}{1}$

$= \frac{1}{2}$

Check

$\frac{3}{4} \times \frac{2}{3} = \frac{\cancel{6}^1}{\cancel{12}^2} = \frac{1}{2}$

Use Razi's method to work out and check the answers to these questions.

a The guests at a party eat $\frac{5}{8}$ of a cake. Sam eats $\frac{1}{3}$ of what is left. What fraction of the cake does Sam eat?

b The guests at a party eat $\frac{7}{10}$ of the rolls. Ed eats $\frac{5}{6}$ of what is left. What fraction of the rolls does Ed eat?

7 Lewis uses this formula to work out the distance, in kilometres, his car will travel when he knows the average speed, in kilometres per hour, and the time in hours.

distance = average speed × time

Lewis thinks that if he drives for 50 minutes at an average speed of 220 kilometres per hour he will travel more than 180 km.

Is Lewis correct? Explain your answer.

Show all your working.

Tip

Start by changing 50 minutes into a fraction of an hour, so you can use this fraction in the formula.

8 This is part of Mia's classwork.

Question

Work out $2\frac{1}{2} \times 2\frac{4}{15}$

Estimate

$2\frac{1}{2} \times 2 = 5$

Answer

① Change to improper fractions: $\frac{5}{2} \times \frac{34}{15}$

② Cancel common factors: $\frac{\cancel{5}^{1}}{\cancel{2}^{1}} \times \frac{\cancel{34}^{17}}{\cancel{15}^{3}}$

③ Multiply: $\frac{1}{1} \times \frac{17}{3} = \frac{17}{3}$

④ Change to a mixed number: $\frac{17}{3} = 5\frac{2}{3}$

⑤ Check with estimate: $5\frac{2}{3} \approx 5$ ✓

Mia's method to estimate the answer is to round one of the fractions to the nearest half and to round the other fraction to the nearest whole number.

Use Mia's method to estimate and to work out these multiplications. Write each answer as a mixed number in its simplest form.

a $1\frac{1}{2} \times 3\frac{3}{5}$ b $2\frac{1}{4} \times 3\frac{2}{3}$ c $1\frac{1}{8} \times 3\frac{1}{6}$

d $3\frac{2}{3} \times 1\frac{5}{22}$ e $3\frac{3}{4} \times 4\frac{3}{5}$ f $4\frac{4}{7} \times 2\frac{5}{16}$

Think like a mathematician

9 Work with a partner to answer this question.

a Read what Marcus says.

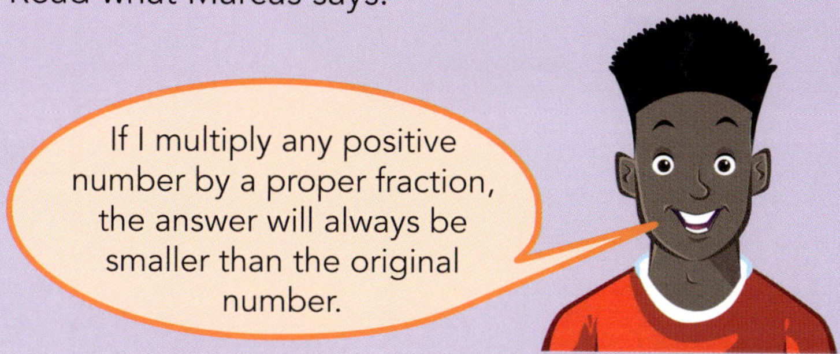

Use specialising to show that Marcus is correct.

b Use specialising to complete these general statements.

i When you multiply any positive number by an improper fraction, the answer will always be .... than the original number.

ii When you multiply any positive number by a mixed number, the answer will always be .... than the original number.

c Discuss your answers to parts **a** and **b** with other learners in your class.

Tip

You can specialise by testing examples such as $8 \times \frac{1}{2}$, $4\frac{1}{2} \times \frac{2}{3}$, $\frac{5}{9} \times \frac{3}{10}$, etc.

10 Work out these calculations. Before you do each calculation, write down if the answer should be bigger or smaller than the first number in the calculation.

a $3 \times \frac{3}{4}$ b $6\frac{2}{3} \times 1\frac{1}{4}$ c $\frac{4}{3} \times \frac{9}{8}$

11 Here are six calculation cards.

A	$\left(\frac{2}{3}+\frac{3}{4}\right)\times\frac{4}{11}$	B	$\left(1\frac{1}{2}-\frac{7}{8}\right)\times\frac{26}{15}$	C	$3\frac{1}{2}\times\frac{4}{5}\times\frac{10}{3}$
D	$\left(2-\frac{1}{3}\right)\times\left(1-\frac{4}{5}\right)$	E	$\left(\frac{5}{4}\right)^2-1\frac{3}{8}\times\frac{2}{11}$	F	$5\frac{1}{3}-5\frac{3}{4}\times\frac{8}{9}$

a Work out the answers to the calculations.

b Sort the cards into groups.
Describe the characteristics of the groups you have chosen.

c Sort the cards again but this time into different groups.
Describe the characteristics of the new groups you have chosen.

Tip

'Describe the characteristics of the groups' is the same as explaining the reasons why you put the calculations into the groups you did.

Look back at this section on cancelling common factors before multiplying fractions.

a What did you find easy?

b What did you find difficult?

c Are there any parts you think you need to practise more?

Summary checklist

☐ I can cancel common factors before multiplying fractions.

☐ I can estimate the answers to calculations.

8.4 Dividing fractions

In this section you will …

- cancel common factors before dividing fractions
- estimate the answers to calculations.

You already know how to divide an integer by a fraction and also a fraction by a fraction. In both cases, you turn the fraction you are dividing by upside down, and then multiply instead. This is called multiplying by the reciprocal of the fraction. Just as you did in Section 8.3, you can cancel common factors before you multiply, to make the calculations easier.

Worked example 8.4

Work out

a $18 \div \frac{2}{3}$ **b** $26 \div \frac{3}{4}$ **c** $\frac{1}{7} \div \frac{5}{21}$ **d** $2\frac{4}{5} \div 1\frac{3}{25}$

Answer

a $18 \div \frac{2}{3} = 18 \times \frac{3}{2}$

Start by turning the fraction you are dividing by upside down and multiplying.

$\cancel{18}^{9} \times \frac{3}{\cancel{2}^{1}} = 9 \times \frac{3}{1}$

2 divides into 2 and into 18, so the 2 cancels to 1 and the 18 cancels to 9.

$= 9 \times 3 = 27$

$\frac{3}{1}$ is the same as 3, so work out 9 × 3.

b $26 \div \frac{3}{4} = 26 \times \frac{4}{3}$

Start by turning the fraction you are dividing by upside down and multiplying.

$= \frac{26 \times 4}{3} = \frac{104}{3}$

There are no common factors to cancel, so multiply 26 by 4.

$= 34\frac{2}{3}$

Change $\frac{104}{3}$ to a mixed number.

c $\frac{1}{7} \div \frac{5}{21} = \frac{1}{7} \times \frac{21}{5}$

Start by turning $\frac{5}{21}$ upside down and multiplying.

$\frac{1}{\cancel{7}^{1}} \times \frac{\cancel{21}^{3}}{5} = \frac{1}{1} \times \frac{3}{5}$

7 divides into 7 and into 21, so the 7 cancels to 1 and the 21 cancels to 3.

$= \frac{1 \times 3}{1 \times 5} = \frac{3}{5}$

Multiply 1 by 3 and multiply 1 by 5. The answer is a proper fraction, so leave it as it is.

Continued

d $2\frac{4}{5} \div 1\frac{3}{25} = \frac{14}{5} \div \frac{28}{25}$

Start by changing the mixed numbers into improper fractions.

$\frac{\cancel{14}^{1}}{\cancel{5}^{1}} \times \frac{\cancel{25}^{5}}{\cancel{28}^{2}} = \frac{1}{1} \times \frac{5}{2}$

Turn $\frac{28}{25}$ upside down and multiply. Cancel any common factors.

$= \frac{1 \times 5}{1 \times 2} = \frac{5}{2}$

Multiply 1 by 5 and multiply 1 by 2.

$= 2\frac{1}{2}$

Change $\frac{5}{2}$ to a mixed number.

Exercise 8.4

1 Copy and complete these divisions.
Write each answer in its simplest form and as a mixed number when appropriate.

a $16 \div \frac{4}{7} = \cancel{16}^{4} \times \frac{7}{\cancel{4}^{1}} = 4 \times 7 = \square$

b $21 \div \frac{3}{5} = \cancel{21}^{7} \times \frac{5}{\cancel{3}^{1}} = 7 \times 5 = \square$

c $14 \div \frac{2}{9} = 14 \times \frac{9}{2} = \square \times 9 = \square$

d $8 \div \frac{4}{11} = 8 \times \frac{\square}{\square} = \square \times \square = \square$

2 Match each question card (**A** to **E**) with the correct answer card (**i** to **v**).

A	$25 \div \frac{5}{8}$	B	$22 \div \frac{2}{3}$	C	$6 \div \frac{4}{9}$	D	$32 \div \frac{6}{13}$	E	$42 \div \frac{4}{7}$
i	33	ii	$73\frac{1}{2}$	iii	40	iv	$13\frac{1}{2}$	v	$69\frac{1}{3}$

3 Copy and complete these divisions.
Write each answer in its lowest terms and as a mixed number when appropriate.

a $\frac{8}{9} \div \frac{4}{7} = \frac{\cancel{8}^{2}}{9} \times \frac{7}{\cancel{4}^{1}} = \frac{2 \times 7}{9 \times 1} = \frac{\square}{\square} = \square\frac{\square}{\square}$

b $\frac{7}{9} \div \frac{2}{5} = \frac{7}{9} \times \frac{5}{2} = \frac{7 \times 5}{9 \times 2} = \frac{\square}{\square} = \square\frac{\square}{\square}$

c $\frac{6}{7} \div \frac{3}{14} = \frac{\cancel{6}^{2}}{\cancel{7}^{1}} \times \frac{\cancel{14}^{2}}{\cancel{3}^{1}} = \frac{2 \times 2}{1 \times 1} = \square$

d $\frac{5}{6} \div \frac{15}{24} = \frac{5}{6} \times \frac{24}{15} = \frac{\square \times \square}{\square \times \square} = \frac{\square}{\square} = \square\frac{\square}{\square}$

4 Write these cards in order of answer size, starting with the smallest.

A $\frac{25}{31} \div \frac{5}{8}$ **B** $\frac{8}{15} \div \frac{12}{25}$ **C** $\frac{9}{28} \div \frac{15}{42}$ **D** $\frac{6}{7} \div \frac{9}{10}$

5 This is part of Jake's homework.

Question

Work out $2\frac{1}{2} \div 3\frac{4}{7}$

Estimate

$3 \div 4 = \frac{3}{4}$

Answer

① *Change to improper fractions:* $\frac{5}{2} \div \frac{25}{7}$

② *Invert and multiply:* $\frac{5}{2} \times \frac{7}{25}$

③ *Cancel common factors:* $\frac{\cancel{5}^{1}}{2} \times \frac{7}{\cancel{25}^{5}}$

④ *Multiply:* $\frac{1}{2} \times \frac{7}{5} = \frac{7}{10}$

⑤ *Check with estimate:* $\frac{7}{10}\left(=\frac{28}{40}\right) \approx \frac{3}{4}\left(=\frac{30}{40}\right)$ ✓

Jake's method to estimate the answer is to round each fraction to the nearest whole number.

Use Jake's method to estimate and work out these divisions.

Write each answer in its simplest form and as a mixed number where appropriate.

a $1\frac{1}{2} \div 1\frac{4}{5}$ **b** $2\frac{1}{4} \div 1\frac{2}{3}$ **c** $4\frac{1}{8} \div 5\frac{1}{6}$

d $2\frac{2}{3} \div 3\frac{1}{4}$ **e** $5\frac{1}{2} \div 2\frac{3}{4}$ **f** $4\frac{4}{5} \div 2\frac{2}{3}$

g $1\frac{1}{4} \div \frac{10}{11}$ **h** $\frac{3}{5} \div 2\frac{1}{10}$

Think like a mathematician

6 Work with a partner to answer this question.

a Read what Zara says.

> **Tip**
>
> You can specialise by testing examples such as $3 \div \frac{1}{2}$, $1\frac{1}{2} \div \frac{2}{3}$, $\frac{5}{8} \div \frac{1}{6}$, etc.

Use specialising to show that Zara is correct.

b Use specialising to complete these general statements.

i When you divide any positive number by an improper fraction, the answer will always be …….. than the original number.

ii When you divide any positive number by a mixed number, the answer will always be …….. than the original number.

c Discuss your answers to parts **a** and **b** with other learners in your class.

7 Work out these calculations. Before you do each calculation, write down if the answer to the division should be bigger or smaller than the first number in the calculation.

a $7 \div \frac{3}{4}$ **b** $4\frac{2}{5} \div 1\frac{1}{10}$ **c** $3\frac{2}{3} \div \frac{7}{4}$

Think like a mathematician

8 Work with a partner to answer this question.

Arun makes this conjecture.

Do you think Arun's conjecture is true? Show working to support your decision.

9 This is part of Helen's homework.

Question

Work out $\frac{3}{4} \div \frac{2}{3}$

Answer

$\frac{3}{4} \div \frac{2}{3} = \frac{3}{4} \times \frac{3}{2}$

$= \frac{9}{8}$

$= 1\frac{1}{8}$

Check

$1\frac{1}{8} = \frac{9}{8}, \frac{9}{8} \times \frac{2}{3} = \frac{18}{24}$

$\frac{18}{24} = \frac{18 \div 6}{24 \div 6}$

$= \frac{3}{4}$ ✓

Helen uses inverse operations to check her answer is correct.

Work out the answers to these divisions.

Use Helen's method to check your answers are correct.

a $\frac{2}{5} \div \frac{3}{7}$ **b** $\frac{4}{7} \div \frac{1}{5}$ **c** $\frac{6}{7} \div \frac{3}{4}$

d $\frac{8}{9} \div \frac{4}{5}$ **e** $\frac{2}{9} \div \frac{6}{11}$ **f** $\frac{10}{11} \div \frac{5}{6}$

10 The circumference of a circle is $14\frac{1}{7}$ cm.
Sofia makes this conjecture.

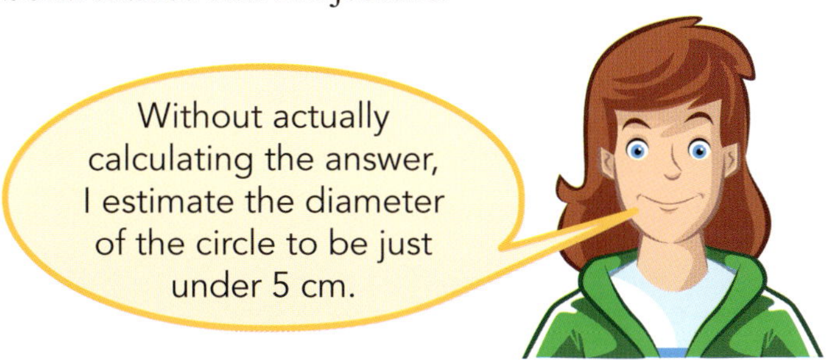

a Explain how Sofia estimated this value for the diameter.

b Show that Sofia's estimate is a good estimate of the accurate answer. Use $\pi = \frac{22}{7}$

11 Work out

a $\left(1-\frac{1}{3}\right)\div\left(1-\frac{3}{5}\right)$ **b** $\left(\frac{2}{5}+\frac{3}{10}\right)\div\frac{7}{15}$ **c** $5\frac{1}{3}-1\frac{3}{7}\div\frac{5}{14}$

12 Sebastian uses this formula to work out the average speed of his car, in kilometres per hour, when he knows the distance, in kilometres, and the time in hours.

$$\text{average speed} = \frac{\text{distance}}{\text{time}}$$

Sebastian travels $115\frac{5}{8}$ km in $1\frac{1}{4}$ hours.

What is Sebastian's average speed?

13 Which is greater: $\left(2\frac{1}{2}-\frac{4}{5}\right)\div\frac{34}{15}$ or $\left(\frac{2}{3}\right)^2+1\frac{5}{6}\div5\frac{1}{2}$? Show your working.

Summary checklist

- [ ] I can cancel common factors before dividing fractions.
- [ ] I can estimate the answers to calculations.

8.5 Making calculations easier

In this section you will ...

- simplify calculations containing decimals and fractions.

Key word

strategies

When you are calculating using fractions and decimals, you can often make a calculation easier by using different **strategies**. This section will help you to practise the skills you need to choose the best strategy to use. You will be able to do some of the calculations mentally. For other calculations you will need to write your working. Whatever calculation you do, you must remember to use the correct order of operations.

Worked example 8.5

Work out

a $\left(\frac{1}{4}+2.75\right)^2+2$ **b** $1.5\times1.5\times16$ **c** 0.32×5^2

Continued

Answer

a $\frac{1}{4} + 2.75 = 3$	Brackets first: you can think of $\frac{1}{4}$ as 0.25 or you can think of 2.75 as $2\frac{3}{4}$. The total is 3.
$(3)^2 + 2 = 9 + 2$ $= 11$	Indices second, then finally the addition.
b $\frac{3}{2} \times \frac{3}{2} \times 16 = \frac{9}{\cancel{4}^1} \times \cancel{16}^4$	Write 1.5 as $\frac{3}{2}$ so you can cancel the 2s into the 16. Multiply the fractions, then divide the 4 into the 16.
$= 9 \times 4 = 36$	The answer is now easy to calculate: $\frac{9}{1} = 9$ and $9 \times 4 = 36$
c $\frac{32}{100} \times 25 = \frac{32}{\cancel{100}^4} \times \cancel{25}^1$	Indices first: $5^2 = 25$. Write 0.32 as $\frac{32}{100}$ because you know 25 divides into 100 exactly 4 times.
$= \frac{32}{4} = 8$	The answer is now easy to calculate, $32 \div 4 = 8$

Exercise 8.5

1 Work out these calculations.
Some working has been shown to help you.

a $\left(\frac{1}{2} + 5.5\right)^2 - 1 \Rightarrow \left(\frac{1}{2} + 5\frac{1}{2}\right)^2 = (\square)^2 = \square \Rightarrow \square - 1 = \square$

b $\left(3\frac{1}{5} - 0.2\right)^3 + 23 \Rightarrow \left(3\frac{1}{5} - \frac{1}{5}\right)^3 = (\square)^3 = \square \Rightarrow \square + 23 = \square$

c $6^2 - \left(3\frac{3}{10} + 0.7\right) \Rightarrow \left(3\frac{3}{10} + \frac{7}{10}\right) = \square \Rightarrow 6^2 = \square \Rightarrow \square - \square = \square$

2 Work out these calculations. Use the same strategies as in Question **1**.

a $6 \times \left(3.25 + 4\frac{3}{4}\right)$ b $\left(2.1 + 4\frac{9}{10}\right)^2$ c $4 \times 3.2 - \frac{4}{5}$

3 Work out these calculations.
Some working has been shown to help you.

a $1.5 \times 2.5 \times 40 \Rightarrow \frac{3}{2} \times \frac{5}{2} = \frac{\square}{4} \Rightarrow \frac{\square}{\cancel{4}^1} \times \cancel{40}^{10} = \square \times 10 = \square$

b $1.25 \times 3\frac{1}{2} \times 56 \Rightarrow \frac{5}{4} \times \frac{7}{2} = \frac{\square}{8} \Rightarrow \frac{\square}{\cancel{8}^1} \times \cancel{56}^7 = \square \times 7 = \square$

c $2.75 \times 18 \Rightarrow 2\frac{3}{4} \times 18 = \frac{\square}{4} \times 18 \Rightarrow \frac{\square}{\cancel{4}^2} \times \cancel{18}^9 = \frac{\square}{2} = \square\frac{\square}{2}$

4 Work out these calculations. Use the same strategies as in Question **3**.

a $1.5 \times 3.5 \times 24$ b $2.25 \times 1\frac{1}{2} \times 32$ c 3.75×28

5 Akeno and Dae use different methods to work out the volume of this cuboid.

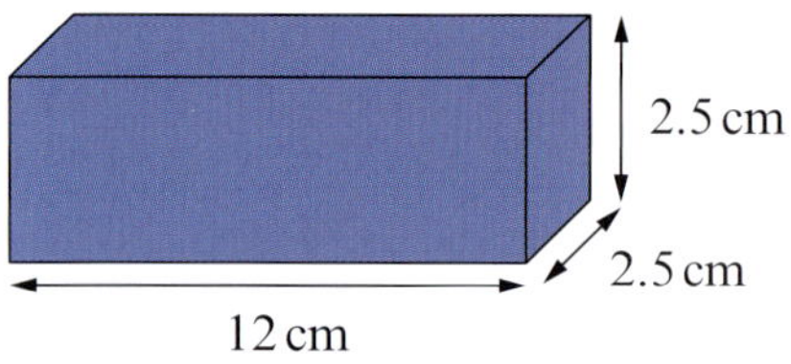

This is what they write.

Akeno	Dae
Volume $= 2.5 \times 2.5 \times 12$	Volume $= 2.5 \times 2.5 \times 12$
$= \frac{5}{2} \times \frac{5}{2} \times 12 = \frac{25}{\cancel{4}^1} \times \cancel{12}^3$	$2.5 \times 12 = 2 \times 12 + \frac{1}{2} \times 12 = 24 + 6 = 30$
$= 25 \times 3 = 75\text{ cm}^3$	$2.5 \times 30 = 2 \times 30 + \frac{1}{2} \times 30 = 60 + 15 = 75\text{ cm}^3$

a Critique their methods.

b Whose method do you prefer? Explain why.

c Whose method would be easier to use when, instead of 12 cm, the length of the cuboid is

i 14 cm ii 15 cm?

Explain your answers.

6 Work out these calculations.

Some working has been shown to help you.

a $0.28 \times 5^2 \Rightarrow 0.28 = \frac{28}{100}, 5^2 = 25 \Rightarrow \frac{28}{\cancel{100}^{\square}} \times \cancel{25}^{\square} = \square$

b $0.7 \times 4\frac{2}{7} \Rightarrow 0.7 = \frac{7}{10}, 4\frac{2}{7} = \frac{30}{7} \Rightarrow \frac{\cancel{7}^{\square}}{\cancel{10}_{\square}} \times \frac{\cancel{30}^{\square}}{\cancel{7}_{\square}} = \square$

c $1.3 \times (4^3 - 4) \Rightarrow 1.3 = \frac{13}{10}, 4^3 - 4 = \square \Rightarrow \frac{13}{\cancel{10}_{\square}} \times \cancel{\square}^{\square} = \square$

7 Work out these calculations. Use the same strategies as in Question **6**.

a $1.6 \times \frac{5}{8}$ b $0.81 \times 1\frac{1}{9}$ c 0.328×5^3

8 The diagram shows a path.
The length of the path is 3.2 m.
The width of the path is $\frac{5}{8}$ m.
What is the area of the path?

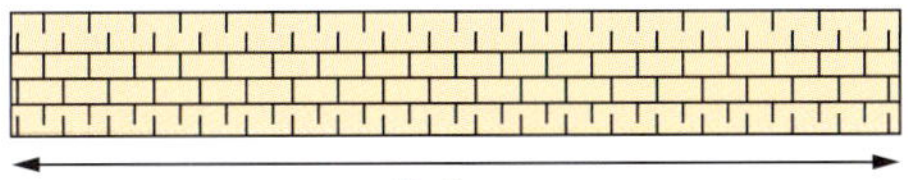

Think like a mathematician

9 Work with a partner to answer these questions.

a What strategy could you use to work out $0.2^2 \times 1\frac{2}{3}$ and $0.75^2 \times 2\frac{4}{9}$?

b Decide if it is best to write each answer as a decimal or a fraction.

c Discuss your strategies with other learners in your class.
Critique and improve on these strategies, and decide on the best strategy.

d Use the best strategy to work out $0.8^2 \times 7\frac{1}{2}$.

10 The area of this triangle is $1\frac{1}{20}$ m^2.
Work out the length of the triangle.

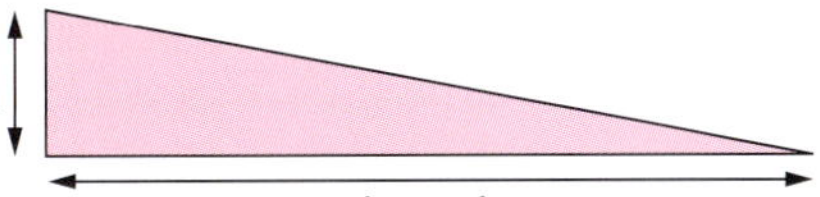

Think like a mathematician

11 Work with a partner to answer these questions.

a What strategy could you use to work out $\sqrt{2.25} + 5\frac{1}{2}$ and $10 - \sqrt{12.25}$?

b Decide if it is best to write each answer as a decimal or a fraction.

c Discuss your strategies with other learners in your class.
Critique and improve on these strategies, and decide on the best strategy.

d Use the best strategy to work out $4.25 \times \sqrt{1\frac{7}{9}}$

12 Hiromi uses this formula in his science lesson.

$$K = \frac{1}{2}mv^2$$

a Use the formula to work out the value of K when $m = 2\frac{1}{4}$ and $v = 1\frac{1}{3}$

b This is how Hiromi rearranges the formula to make v the subject:

$$\frac{1}{2}mv^2 = K \Rightarrow mv^2 = 2K \Rightarrow mv = \sqrt{2K} \Rightarrow v = \frac{\sqrt{2K}}{m}$$

Tip

Remember: $\frac{1}{2}mv^2$ means $\frac{1}{2} \times m \times v^2$

Use your values of K, m and v from part **a** to show that Hiromi has rearranged the formula incorrectly.

c Rearrange the formula correctly to make v the subject.

d Use your formula in part **c** to work out the value of v when $K = 18$ and $m = 25$.

Check your answer is correct by substituting $m = 25$ and your value for v into the original formula.

Activity 8.5

Work with a partner for this activity.

Here are four expression cards and four cards with different values for x.

A	$(0.5+x)^2-1$	B	$1.5\times x\times 8$	C	$10+\sqrt{\frac{1}{2}x}$	D	$(1-0.96)\times x$
i	$x=\frac{1}{2}$	ii	$x=4\frac{1}{2}$	iii	$x=12\frac{1}{2}$	iv	$x=24\frac{1}{2}$

Take it in turns to give your partner one expression card and one x-value card.

Ask them to work out the value of the expression using the x-value card.

While they are working it out, work out the answer yourself. Then compare your answers.

Discuss any mistakes that have been made.

Do this twice each.

In this exercise, you have used different strategies to work out calculations involving fractions and decimals.

Look back at Worked example 8.5 and the types of question shown in parts **a**, **b** and **c**.

a Which type of question have you found

  i the easiest

  ii the most difficult to work out?

b Which types of question are you confident in working out?

c Which types of question do you need more practice in working out?

Summary checklist

☐ I can simplify calculations containing decimals and fractions.

Check your progress

1 Write down if these fractions are terminating or recurring decimals.

a $\frac{4}{9}$ b $\frac{3}{16}$ c $\frac{8}{15}$ d $1\frac{7}{32}$

2 Work out these calculations. Write each answer as a mixed number in its simplest form.

a $4\frac{7}{8}+\frac{1}{2}\times\frac{3}{4}$ b $\frac{2}{5}\div\frac{3}{10}+1\frac{1}{4}$ c $5\frac{1}{2}-\left(2\frac{1}{5}-1\frac{2}{3}\right)$

3 Work out these multiplications. Cancel common factors before multiplying.

a $\frac{5}{8}\times 20$ b $\frac{7}{9}\times\frac{12}{35}$

4 Work out these divisions. Cancel common factors before multiplying.

a $40\div\frac{5}{6}$ b $\frac{9}{52}\div\frac{3}{13}$

5 Work out these calculations.

a $8\times\left(6.25+3\frac{3}{4}\right)$ b $1.25\times 2.5\times 16$ c $1.2\times\frac{5}{18}$

Project 3

Selling apples

Sofia picked 93 apples from the trees in her orchard.

- On the first day, she ate three apples and then sold $\frac{4}{15}$ of the apples that were left.
- On the second day, she ate three apples and then sold $\frac{4}{9}$ of the apples that were left.
- On the third day, she ate three apples and then sold $\frac{1}{8}$ of the apples that were left.
- On the fourth day, she ate three apples and then sold $\frac{2}{5}$ of the apples that were left.
- On the fifth day, she ate three apples and then sold $\frac{3}{4}$ of the apples that were left.

How many apples did Sofia have left at the end of the fifth day?

Zara picked 78 apples.

Every morning, she ate three apples and then sold as many apples as she could. Zara recorded the fraction she sold each day. At the end of the sixth day, she only had three apples left.

Here are the fractions she sold each day. Unfortunately, they are mixed up. Can you work out which is the correct fraction for each of the six days?

$\frac{1}{4}$ $\frac{1}{4}$ $\frac{4}{15}$ $\frac{1}{2}$ $\frac{2}{9}$ $\frac{2}{5}$

Arun picked almost 100 apples, and they lasted for more than two weeks!

Each day, he started by eating three apples. Then he sold a fraction of the apples left. The fraction always had a denominator that was smaller than the number of apples.

- Can you suggest what fraction Arun might have sold each day?
- What is the largest number of days for which the apples could have lasted?

9 Sequences and functions

Getting started

1 For each of these sequences, write

   i the term-to-term rule   ii the next two terms.

   a $4, 4\frac{2}{5}, 4\frac{4}{5}, 5\frac{1}{5}, \ldots, \ldots$ b 8.5, 8.2, 7.9, 7.6, …, …

2 This sequence of patterns is made from dots.

Pattern 1   Pattern 2   Pattern 3

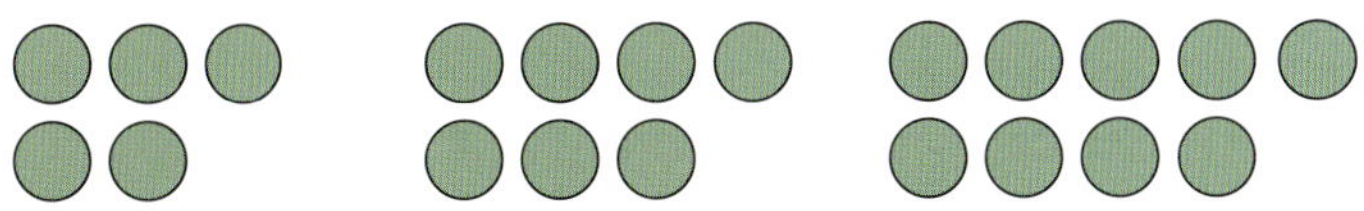

   a Write the sequence of the numbers of dots.
   b Write the term-to-term rule.
   c Draw the next pattern in the sequence.
   d Copy and complete the table to find the position-to-term rule.

position number	1	2	3	4
term	5	7	…	…
… × position number	…	…	…	…
… × position number + …	…	…	…	…

   Position-to-term rule is: term = … × position number + …

3 Work out the first three terms and the 10th term of the sequences with the given nth terms.

   a $\frac{1}{2}n + 12$ b $4n - 3.5$

4 Work out an expression for the nth term of each sequence.

   a 8, 11, 14, 17, …   b 19, 14, 9, 4, …

Continued

5 Work out the missing values in the tables for these function machines.
Copy and complete the tables.

a i

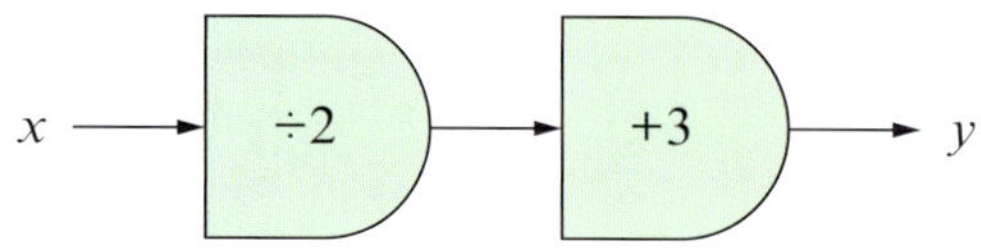

x	6	11		
y			12	$15\frac{1}{2}$

ii

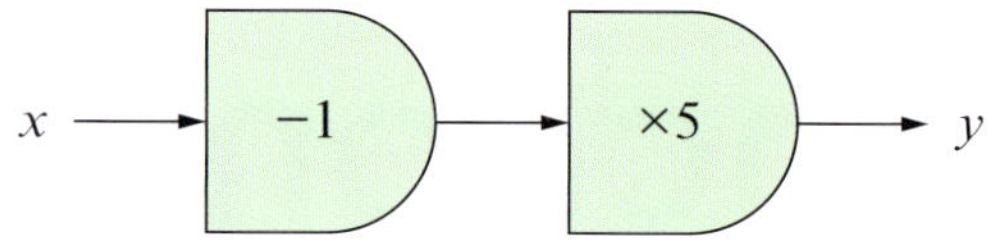

x	−2	$1\frac{1}{2}$		
y			35	$52\frac{1}{2}$

b Copy and complete the equation for each function in part **a**.

i $y = \frac{x}{\square} + \square$

ii $y = \square(x - \square)$

Studying patterns and sequences is one branch of algebra.

The word algebra comes from the title of a book written by the Persian mathematician Muhammad ibn Mūsā al-Khwārizmī in 820 CE (you can see his statue in the image below). The title of the book was *Hisab al-jabr w'al-muqabala*. Can you see a word in the title that looks similar to the word algebra? This was the first book ever written about algebra.

Other branches of algebra include:

- writing and using expressions
- writing and solving equations
- writing and using formulae
- drawing graphs of functions.

What is your favourite branch of algebra? Why do you like it? Compare your answer with a partner.

Tip

You have already done some work on these branches of algebra in stages 7 and 8, and in Unit 2 of this book.

9.1 Generating sequences

In this section you will …

- make sequences of numbers from a given term-to-term rule.

Key words

linear sequence

non-linear sequence

In a **linear sequence**, the terms increase (or decrease) by the **same** amount each time. In a **non-linear sequence**, the terms increase (or decrease) by a **different** amount each time.

This is a linear sequence of numbers: $1 \quad 3\frac{1}{2} \quad 6 \quad 8\frac{1}{2} \quad 11 \quad \ldots \quad \ldots$

You can see that each term is $2\frac{1}{2}$ more than the term before, so the term-to-term rule is 'add $2\frac{1}{2}$'.

This is a non-linear sequence of numbers: $3 \quad 6 \quad 11 \quad 18 \quad 27 \quad \ldots \quad \ldots$

Look at the differences between consecutive terms.

$$3 (+3) = 6,\ 6 (+5) = 11,\ 11 (+7) = 18,\ 18 (+9) = 27, \ldots$$

The differences between the terms are **not** the same. The term-to-term rule is 'add 3, add 5, add 7, add 9, …'.

Tip

This type of sequence is called a quadratic sequence. You will do more work on quadratic sequences in Section 9.2.

You can generate a sequence when you are given the first term and the term-to-term rule.

For example, when the first term is 2 and the term-to-term rule is 'multiply by 2, then add 0.5', you get the non-linear sequence 2, 4.5, 9.5, 19.5, …

Tip

2nd term is	$2 \times 2 + 0.5 = 4.5$
3rd term is	$4.5 \times 2 + 0.5 = 9.5$
4th term is	$9.5 \times 2 + 0.5 = 19.5$

Worked example 9.1

a Are these sequences linear or non-linear?

i 6, 4, 2, 0, −2, … **ii** 8, 5, 1, −4, −10, …

b The first term of a sequence is 4.
The term-to-term rule is: multiply by 2.
Write the first three terms of the sequence.

c The first term of a sequence is 3.
The term-to-term rule of the sequence is: square, then subtract 5.
Write the first three terms of the sequence.

Answer

a **i** The sequence is linear.

The sequence decreases by the same amount (2) each time.

ii The sequence is non-linear.

The sequence decreases by a different amount (3, 4, 5, 6, …) each time.

b First three terms are 4, 8, 16

Write the first term (4), then use the term-to-term rule to work out the second and third terms.

Second term = $4 \times 2 = 8$, third term = $8 \times 2 = 16$

c First three terms are 3, 4, 11

Write the first term (3), then use the term-to-term rule to work out the second and third terms.

Second term = $3^2 - 5 = 4$, third term = $4^2 - 5 = 11$

Exercise 9.1

1 Write whether each sequence is linear or non-linear.
Explain your answers.

- **a** 11, 15, 19, 23, 27, …
- **b** 20, 30, 40, 50, 60, …
- **c** 4, 5, 7, 10, 14, …
- **d** 20, 18, 15, 11, 6, …
- **e** 100, 95, 90, 85, 80, …
- **f** 10, 7, 1, −8, −20, …
- **g** 0.5, 1, 1.5, 2, 2.5, …
- **h** $3\frac{1}{2}, 5\frac{1}{2}, 9\frac{1}{2}, 17\frac{1}{2}, 33\frac{1}{2}, \ldots$
- **i** 20, 12, 4, −4, −12, …

2 Write the first three terms of each of these sequences. Show your working.

	First term	Term-to-term rule
a	3.5	Add 0.7
b	2	Add $\frac{1}{2}$, then multiply by 2
c	$4\frac{1}{3}$	Subtract $\frac{2}{3}$
d	40	Divide by 2, then subtract 2
e	1.25	Multiply by 2, then add 0.75
f	1	Multiply by 3, then subtract $\frac{1}{2}$

Tip

For part **a**, work out $3.5 + 0.7 = 4.2$, then $4.2 + 0.7 = \square$, then $\square + 0.7 = \square$

3 Cards **A** to **D** show term-to-term rules. Cards **i** to **iv** show sequences that all have a first term of 3.

A: square, then add one

B: add one, then square

C: square, then subtract one

D: subtract one, then square

i: 3, 16, 289, …

ii: 3, 4, 9, …

iii: 3, 10, 101, …

iv: 3, 8, 63, …

Match each term-to-term rule (**A** to **D**) with the correct sequence (**i** to **iv**).

4 Work out the first three terms of these sequences.

a first term 4 term-to-term rule is square, then subtract 11

b first term 2 term-to-term rule is square, then add 3

c first term 5 term-to-term rule is subtract 2, then square

d first term 0 term-to-term rule is add 3, then square

Think like a mathematician

5 Work with a partner to answer this question.

a Work out the first three terms of this sequence.

First term is 3. Term-to-term rule is square and subtract 6.

What do you notice about the terms in the sequence?

b Make up two sequences of your own where all terms are the same. You must choose the first term and the term-to-term rule. The term-to-term rule must include a square.

Tip

'Square and subtract 6' means the same as 'square, then subtract 6'.

Continued

Your rules can look like this:
square and subtract … OR subtract … and square

c Is it possible to have a term-to-term rule that makes a sequence where all the terms are the same that looks like this:

i square and add … **ii** add … and square

Explain your answers.

d Compare your answers to parts **a** to **c** with other learners in your class.

6 Copy these linear sequences and fill in the missing terms.

a $2, 3\frac{2}{7}, \square, 5\frac{6}{7}, \square, 8\frac{3}{7}, 9\frac{5}{7}$ **b** $90, 84\frac{3}{4}, \square, 74\frac{1}{4}, \square, 63\frac{3}{4}, \square$

c $-4, \square, \square, -3.1, -2.8, \square, \square$ **d** $\square, \square, 18.6, 12.4, \square, \square, -6.2$

7 The first three terms of a sequence are 2, 10, 106, …

a Which of these cards, **A**, **B** or **C**, shows the correct term-to-term rule?

A cube and add 2 **B** multiply by 7 and subtract 4 **C** square and add 6

b Which is the first term in this sequence to be greater than one million? Show how you worked out your answer.

8 Write down the first four terms of each non-linear sequence.

a first term is 3 term-to-term rule is add 1, add 2, add 3, …

b first term is 6 term-to-term rule is add 2, add 4, add 6, …

c first term is 20 term-to-term rule is subtract 1, subtract 3, subtract 5, …

d first term is 100 term-to-term rule is subtract 10, subtract 15, subtract 20, …

Activity 9.1

On a piece of paper, write two questions similar to those in Question **2**, two questions similar to those in Question **4**, and two questions similar to those in Question **8**.

Work out the answers on a separate piece of paper.

Give your questions to a partner. Work out the answers to your partner's questions.

Swap back and mark each other's work.

If you think your partner has made a mistake, discuss with them where they have gone wrong.

Think like a mathematician

9 Zara makes her own sequence. This is what she writes.

First term is 3, term-to-term rule is cube and subtract ∗.

Zara says:

Is Zara correct? Justify your answer.

Discuss your answer with other learners in your class.

10 Work out the first three terms in these sequences.

- a first term is 4 term-to-term rule is subtract 2 and cube
- b first term is −6 term-to-term rule is add 4 and cube
- c first term is 2 term-to-term rule is power 4 and subtract 12

> **Tip**
>
> For part **c**:
>
> 2nd term = $2^4 - 12 = \square$

11 This is part of Tania's homework.

Question

The 6th term of a sequence is 486.

The term-to-term rule is multiply by 3.

What is the 3rd term of the sequence?

Answer

3rd term = 6th term ÷ 2 = 486 ÷ 2 = 243

Is Tania's method correct? Explain your answer.
Show all your working.

12 The fifth term of a sequence is 11.5. The term-to-term rule is: divide by 2 and add 6.

Show that the second term in the sequence is 8.

13 The fourth term of a sequence is 116. The term-to-term rule is: square and subtract 5.
What is the first term of the sequence?

Look back at your answers to questions **12** and **13**.
Write a short explanation of the method you used to solve these problems.
Discuss your method with a partner. Did they use the same method?
Can you think of a better method?

Summary checklist

☐ I can make sequences of numbers from a given term-to-term rule.

9.2 Using the *n*th term

In this section you will ...

- use the *n*th term rule for a number sequence
- work out the *n*th term rule for a number sequence.

Key word

quadratic sequence

You already know how to use the *n*th term rule of a linear sequence.

Example: Write the first three terms of the sequence with *n*th term $3n - 1$.

$1\text{st term} = 3 \times 1 - 1 = 2$, $2\text{nd term} = 3 \times 2 - 1 = 5$,
$3\text{rd term} = 3 \times 3 - 1 = 8$

First three terms are: 2, 5, 8.

Tip

Remember:

$3n$ means $3 \times n$

You also know how to work out the *n*th term rule of a linear sequence.

Example: Work out the *n*th term rule for the sequence 6, 8, 10, 12, …

The term-to-term rule is 'multiply by 2', so add a row to the table which shows $2n$.

When you work out $2n + 4$, you get the terms of the sequence.

position number (n)	1	2	3	4
term	6	8	10	12
$2n$	2	4	6	8
$2n + 4$	6	8	10	12

*n*th term is $2n + 4$

You can use similar methods to work out the nth term rules for more difficult linear sequences as well as for non-linear sequences.

Tip

This sequence is a **quadratic sequence** because the highest power in the nth term rule is 2 (squared).

Worked example 9.2

a The nth term rule of a sequence is $n^2 + 4$.
Work out the first three terms and the tenth term of the sequence.

b The nth term rule of a sequence is $\frac{n}{4}$
Work out the fifth term and the eighth term of the sequence.

Answer

a 1st term $= 1^2 + 4 = 5$	To find the first term, substitute $n = 1$ into the rule.
2nd term $= 2^2 + 4 = 8$	To find the second term, substitute $n = 2$ into the rule.
3rd term $= 3^2 + 4 = 13$	To find the third term, substitute $n = 3$ into the rule.
10th term $= 10^2 + 4 = 104$	To find the tenth term, substitute $n = 10$ into the rule.
b 5th term $= \frac{5}{4} = 1\frac{1}{4}$	Substitute $n = 5$ into the rule. Leave the answer as an improper fraction or write as a mixed number.
8th term $= \frac{8}{4} = 2$	Substitute $n = 8$ into the rule. Write the answer as a whole number.

Exercise 9.2

1 Copy and complete the workings to find the first four terms of these sequences.

a nth term is $4n - 5$
1st term $= 4 \times 1 - 5 = -1$
2nd term $= 4 \times 2 - 5 = \square$
3rd term $= 4 \times 3 - 5 = \square$
4th term $= 4 \times 4 - 5 = \square$

b nth term is $n^2 + 1$
1st term $= 1^2 + 1 = 2$
2nd term $= 2^2 + 1 = \square$
3rd term $= 3^2 + 1 = \square$
4th term $= 4^2 + 1 = \square$

c nth term is $\frac{n}{3}$
1st term $= \frac{1}{3}$
2nd term $= \frac{\square}{3}$
3rd term $= \frac{\square}{3} = \square$
4th term $= \frac{\square}{3} = \square\frac{\square}{3}$

d nth term is n^3
1st term $= 1^3 = 1$
2nd term $= 2^3 = \square$
3rd term $= 3^3 = \square$
4th term $= 4^3 = \square$

2 Work out the first three terms and the 10th term of the sequences with these nth terms.

a $4n + 3$ b $2n - 5$ c $\frac{1}{2}n + 3$ d $\frac{n}{5}$ e $n^2 - 1$

3 Match each yellow sequence card with the correct blue nth term expression card.

A	1, 4, 9, 16, …	**B**	$\frac{1}{2}, 1, \frac{3}{2}, 2, \ldots$	**C**	1, 8, 27, 64, …	**D**	1, 2, 3, 4, …
i	n^3	**ii**	n	**iii**	$\frac{n}{2}$	**iv**	n^2

4 The cards show one term from two different sequences.

A 8th term in the sequence nth term is $n^2 - 14$

B 20th term in the sequence nth term is $\frac{4}{5}n + 33$

a Without doing any calculations, conjecture which card you think has the greater value, **A** or **B**? Explain why you chose this card.

b Work out which card has the greater value. Show your working.

c Did you choose the correct card in part **a**? If not, can you see why?

Think like a mathematician

5 Work with a partner to answer this question.

a Write down the first six terms of this sequence:
First term is 7. Term-to-term rule is add 1, add 3, add 5, …

b This is the sequence you should have for part **a**:
7, 8, 11, 16, 23, 32, …

Take another look at the sequence:

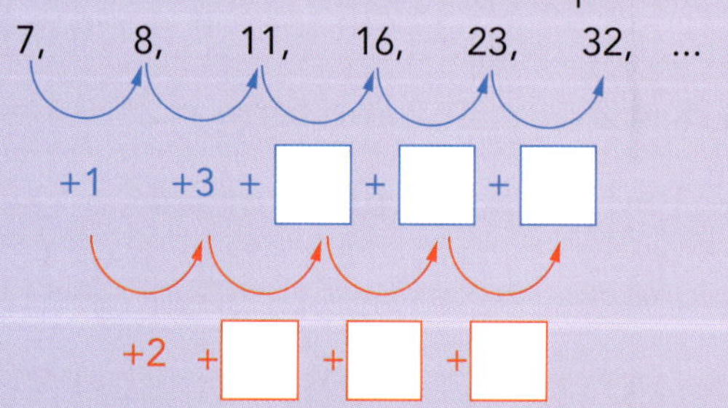

Copy and complete the first differences in the blue boxes.
Copy and complete the second differences in the red boxes.

c What do you notice about the second differences?

Tip

The first differences are the differences between the terms of the sequence.

The second differences are the differences between the first differences.

Continued

d Work out the first differences and the second differences for each of these sequences.

i 5, 7, 11, 17, 25, 35, … **ii** 2, 7, 13, 20, 28, 37, …

iii 3, 5, 11, 21, 35, 53, …

What do you notice about the second differences?

> When the second differences in a sequence are the same, the sequence is called a quadratic sequence.

e Decide if each of these sequences is linear, quadratic or neither.

i 6, 10, 15, 21, 28, 36, … **ii** 9, 12, 15, 18, 21, 24, …

iii 2, 4, 8, 16, 32, 64, … **iv** 20, 18, 16, 14, 12, 10, …

v 60, 30, 15, 7.5, 3.75, … **vi** 25, 24, 22, 19, 15, 10, …

f Discuss your answers to parts **c**, **d** and **e** with other learners in your class.

Tip

Look back at the quadratic sequence in part **a** of Worked example 9.2 to check that the second differences follow this rule.

6 This is how Serge works out the *n*th term rule for the sequence 2, 5, 10, 17, 26, 37, …

Sequence: 2, 5, 10, 17, 26, 37, …

First differences: +3 +5 +7 +9 +11

Second differences: +2 +2 +2 +2

As the second differences are the same, it is a quadratic sequence, so the nth term rule contains n^2.

Make a table of values.

position number (n)	1	2	3	4
term	2	5	10	17
n^2	1	4	9	16
$n^2 + 1$	2	5	10	17

Adding 1 on to the n^2 values gives the exact terms in the sequence.

Use Serge's method to work out the nth term rules for these sequences.

a 4, 7, 12, 19, 28, … **b** 11, 14, 19, 26, …

c 0, 3, 8, 15, 24, … **d** −8, −5, 0, 7, 16, …

7 Look at this number sequence: −1, 2, 7, 14, 23, …

Just by looking at the numbers in the sequence, explain why you can tell that the nth term rule for this sequence cannot be $n^2 + 5$.

Think like a mathematician

8 Work with a partner to answer this question.

a What is the nth term rule for each of these sequences?

i $\frac{1}{7}, \frac{2}{7}, \frac{3}{7}, \frac{4}{7}, \frac{5}{7}, \frac{6}{7}, \ldots$ **ii** $\frac{1}{8}, \frac{1}{4}, \frac{3}{8}, \frac{1}{2}, \frac{5}{8}, \frac{3}{4}, \ldots$ **iii** $\frac{1}{6}, \frac{1}{3}, \frac{1}{2}, \frac{2}{3}, \frac{5}{6}, 1, \ldots$

b Compare your answers with other pairs in the class. Discuss the different methods you used, then decide on the best method. Explain why this is the best method.

9 The cards **A**, **B** and **C** show one term from three different sequences.

A 12th term in the sequence nth term is $\frac{n}{15}$

B 14th term in the sequence nth term is $\frac{n}{18}$

C 9th term in the sequence nth term is $\frac{n}{12}$

a Work out the term for each card.

b Write your answers to part **a** in order of size, starting with the smallest.

10 Taki and Miyo use different methods to work out the answer to this question.

The nth term rule for a sequence is $n^2 + 9$. Is the number 263 a term in this sequence?

Taki's method

Work out the terms in the sequence:

$n = 1,\ 1^2 + 9 = 10$

$n = 2,\ 2^2 + 9 = 13$

$n = 3,\ 3^2 + 9 = 18$, etc.

so the sequence is 10, 13, 18, 25, 34, 45, 58, 73, 90, 109, 130, 153, 178, 205, 234, 265, ...

No, 263 is not in the sequence. 234 and 265 are consecutive terms in the sequence and 263 is between these terms.

Miyo's method

Make an equation and solve it to find n:

$n^2 + 9 = 263$

$n^2 = 263 - 9$

$n^2 = 254$

$n^2 = \sqrt{254} = 15.93...$

No, 263 is not in the sequence, because the value for n is not a whole number.

a Critique Taki's and Miyo's methods.

b Can you think of a different method? If you can, explain this method.

c Which method do you prefer? Explain why.

d Use your favourite method to work out the answers to these questions.

 i The *n*th term rule for a sequence is $n^2 - 76$. Is the number 93 a term in this sequence?

 ii The *n*th term rule for a sequence is n^3. Is the number 4896 a term in this sequence?

11 Arun and Marcus are looking at this number sequence:

$4, 3\frac{1}{2}, 3, 2\frac{1}{2}, 2, \ldots$

Read what they say.

Is either of them correct? Explain your answer.

12 Work out an expression for the *n*th term for each sequence.

a $9\frac{1}{4}, 9, 8\frac{3}{4}, 8\frac{1}{2}, \ldots$

b 20, 19.8, 19.6, 19.4, …

c $-1\frac{1}{2}, -2, -2\frac{1}{2}, -3, \ldots$

d −5, −6.5, −8, −9.5, …

Summary checklist

- [ ] I can use the *n*th term rule for a number sequence.
- [ ] I can work out the *n*th term rule for a number sequence.

9.3 Representing functions

In this section you will …

- work out output values of function machines that use indices
- work out input values of function machines that use indices
- write a function as an equation.

You have already worked with one-step and two-step function machines and you have used input and output numbers which are integers, decimals and fractions. In this section, you will use function machines that include indices.

Worked example 9.3

a Copy and complete the table of values for this two-step function machine.

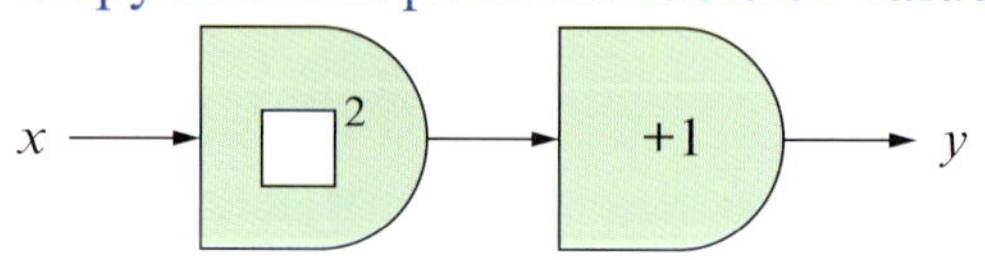

x	0	1	2	3
y				

b Draw a mapping diagram to show the function in part **a**.

c Write the function in part **a** as an equation.

Continued

Answer

a

x	0	1	2	3
y	1	2	5	10

To work out the y-values, **square** the x-values, then add 1.

$0^2 + 1 = 1$, $1^2 + 1 = 2$, $2^2 + 1 = 5$, $3^2 + 1 = 10$

b

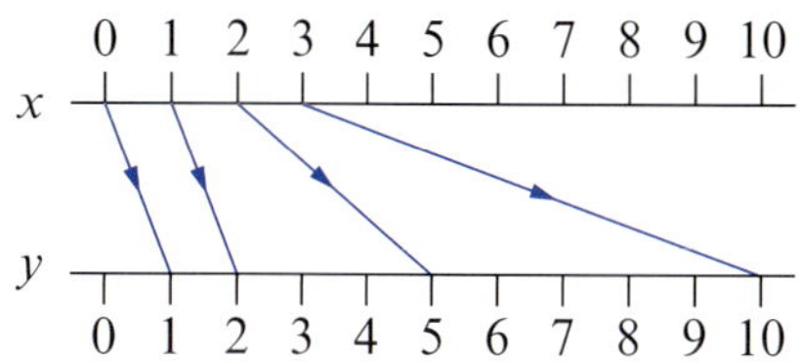

Draw a line connecting each x-value to its y-value.

Draw an arrow on each line to show that 0 maps to 1, 1 maps to 2, 2 maps to 5 and 3 maps to 10.

c $x^2 + 1 = y$, so $y = x^2 + 1$

Write the equation with the '$y =$' on the left.

Exercise 9.3

1 **a** Copy and complete the table of values for each one-step function machine.

i

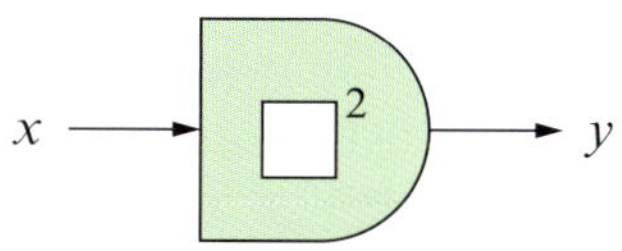

x	0	1	2	3
y				

ii

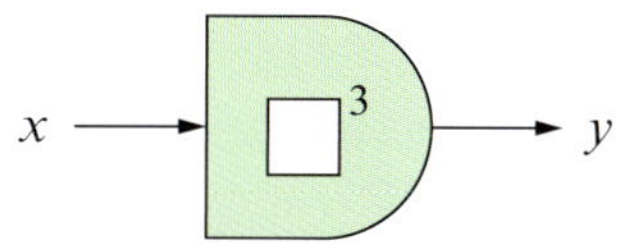

x	0	1	2
y			

b Draw a mapping diagram for each function in part **a**.

c Write each function in part **a** as an equation.

2 **a** Copy and complete the table of values for each two-step function machine.

i

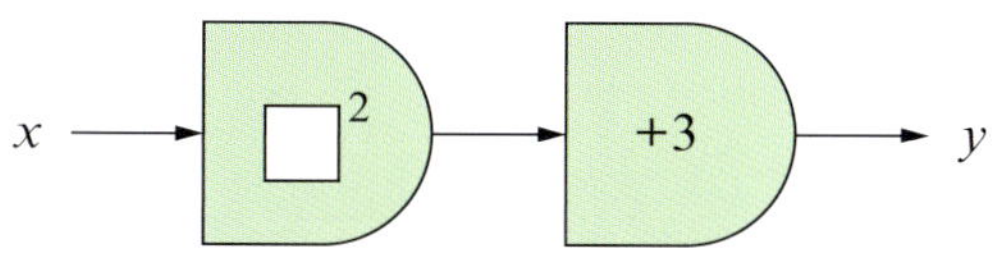

x	2	5	9	11
y				

ii

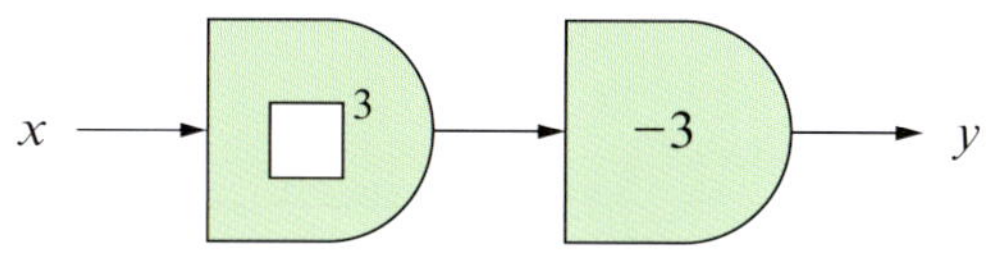

x	1	3	5	10
y				

b Write each function in part **a** as an equation.

Think like a mathematician

3 Work with a partner to answer these questions.

a Copy and complete the table of values for each two-step function machine.

i

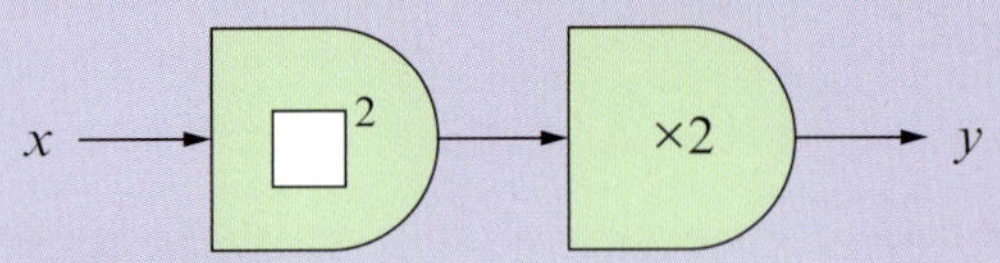

x	−3	$\frac{1}{3}$	$\frac{1}{2}$
y			

ii

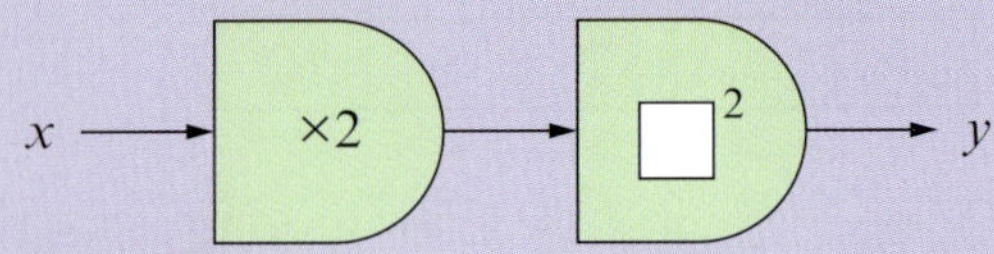

x	−5	$\frac{1}{4}$	$\frac{1}{2}$
y			

iii

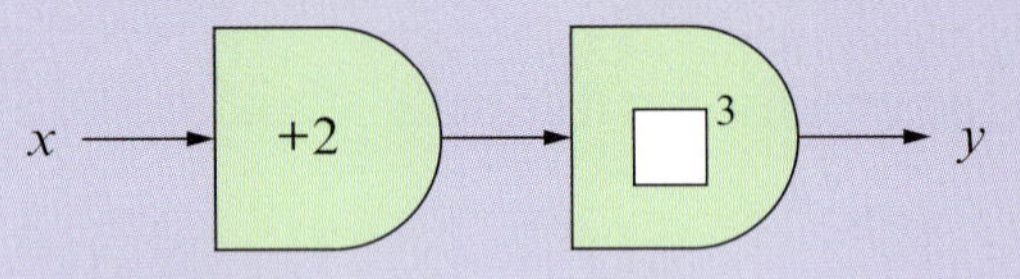

x	−4	0	3
y			

b Discuss your answers to part **a** with other learners in your class.
Did you all get the same y-values? Do you think it is easier to work out the fraction answers as fractions or decimals? Explain why.

c Write each function in part **a** as an equation.

d Discuss your answers to part **c** with other learners in your class. Did you all write the function equations in the same way? If not, decide which is the best way to write them.

4 a Copy and complete the table of values for each two-step function machine.

i

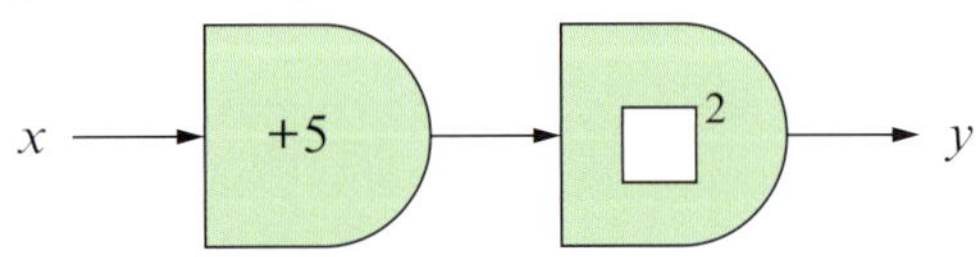

x	−8	−4	15
y			

ii

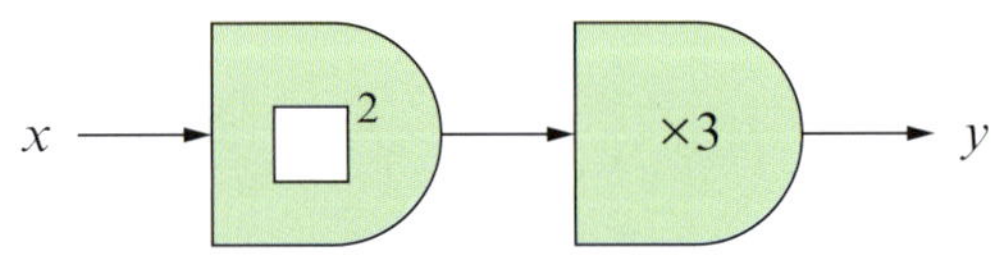

x	−2	$\frac{1}{3}$	$\frac{1}{2}$
y			

iii

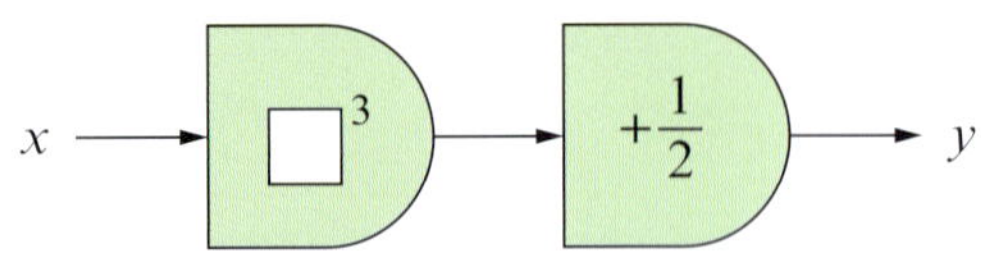

x	−2	$\frac{1}{4}$	$\frac{1}{2}$
y			

b Write each function in part **a** as an equation.

5 **a** Draw a function machine for the equation $y = 4x^2$.

b Draw a table of values for $x = \frac{1}{4}, \frac{1}{3}, \frac{1}{2}$ and 1.

Work out the values of y for the function $y = 4x^2$.

> **Tip**
>
> Which step comes first, multiplying by 4 or squaring?

Think like a mathematician

6 Work with a partner to answer these questions.

a **i** Copy and complete the table of values for this function machine.

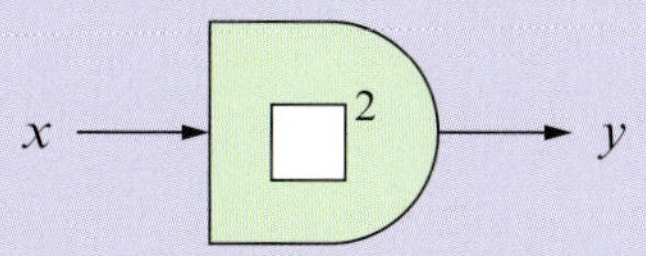

x	−4	−3	3	4
y				

ii What do you notice about the y-values in your table?

iii Will the y-values for $+x$ and $-x$ be the same for all values of x?

Compare and discuss your answers with other learners in the class.

b **i** Copy and complete the table of values for this function machine.

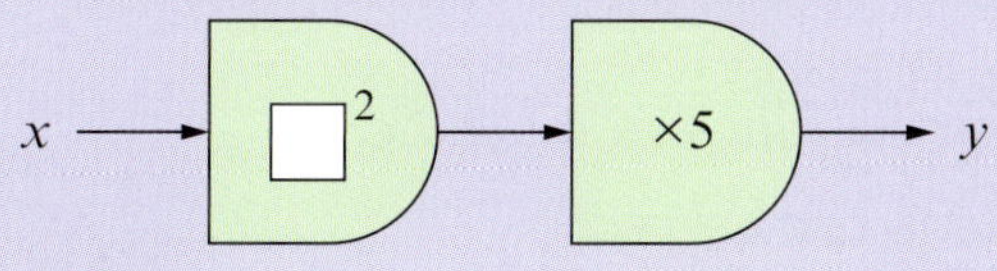

x				
y	5	20	80	500

> **Tip**
>
> Remember to use inverse operations to find the x-values.

ii What do you notice about the values for x in your table?

iii What could you add to the question to make sure you have only one x-value for each y-value?

Compare and discuss your answers with other learners in the class.

7 Work out the missing values in the tables for these function machines.
The x-values are all positive.

i

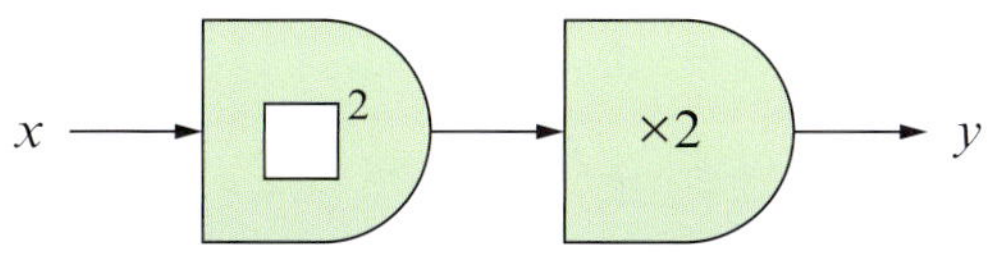

x	2			
y		32	50	288

ii

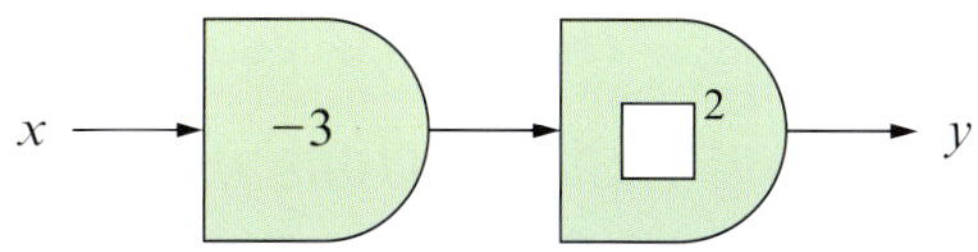

x	7			
y		49	64	100

b Write each function in part **a** as an equation.

Activity 9.3

a On a piece of paper draw two function machines of your own, similar to those in Question **7**.

Draw tables for the function machines and give two x-values and two y-values.

On a different piece of paper, write the missing x-values and y-values.

Swap function machines with a partner and work out their missing x-values and y-values.

b Swap back and mark each other's work.

Discuss any mistakes.

8 This is part of Lara's classwork.

<u>*Question*</u>

i *Write the equation for this function machine.*

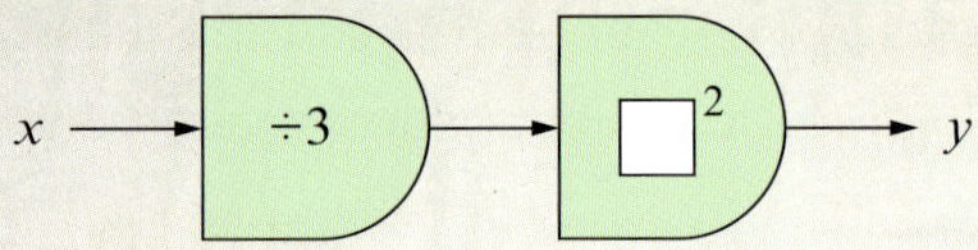

ii *Work out the reverse equation for the function machine.*

iii *Show how to check your equations are correct.*

<u>*Answer*</u>

i *The function machine is:*

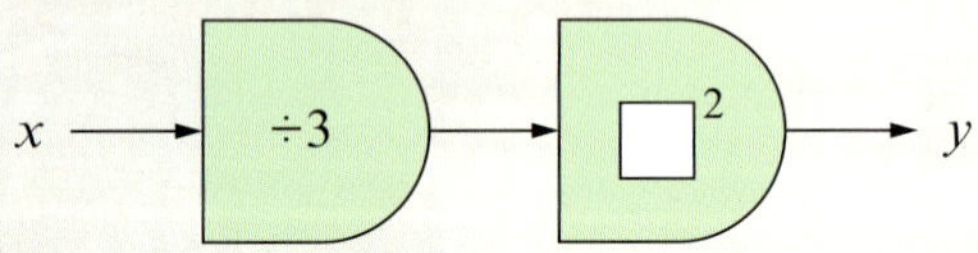

so the equation is $y = \left(\frac{x}{3}\right)^2$

ii *Reverse the machine:*

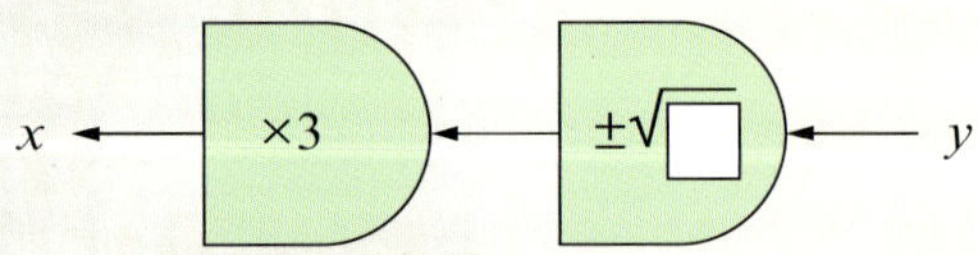

The reverse equation is $\pm\sqrt{y} \times 3 = x$ *or* $x = \pm 3\sqrt{y}$

iii *Check: Using the machine* → *when* $x = \pm 6$, $\pm 6 \div 3 = \pm 2$ *and* $(\pm 2)^2 = 4$

Using the equation → *when* $x = \pm 6$, $y = \left(\frac{\pm 6}{3}\right)^2 = (\pm 2)^2 = 4$ ✓

Using the reverse equation → *when* $y = 4$,

$x = \pm 3\sqrt{4} = \pm 3 \times 2 = \pm 6$ ✓

> **Tip**
>
> The ± symbol means the number can be positive or negative.

For each of these function machines, use Lara's method to

i write the equation
ii work out the reverse equation
iii check your equations are correct.

a

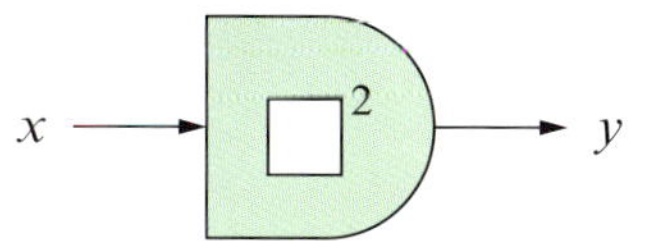

b

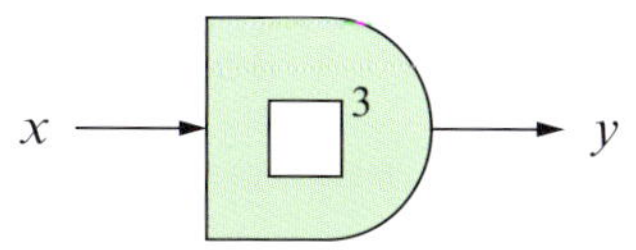

c

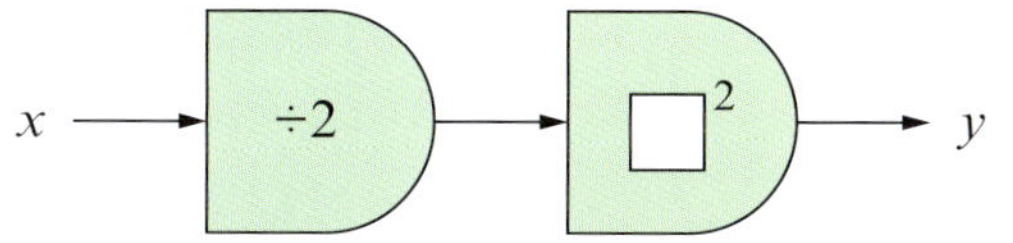

d

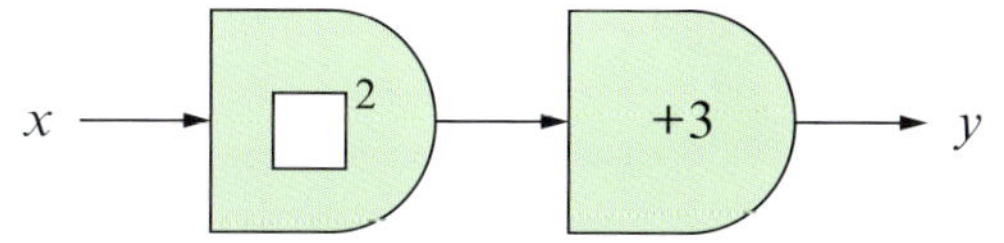

e

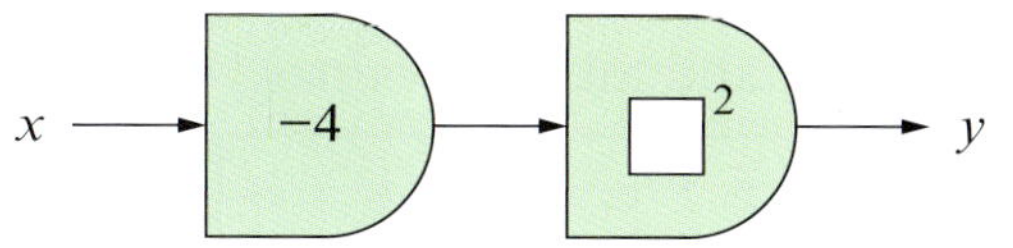

f

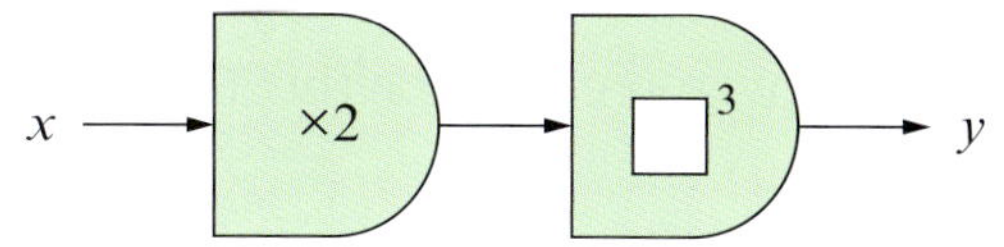

9 Match each function equation with the correct reverse equation.
You can draw function machines to help you if you want to.
The first one has been done for you: **A** and iii.

A 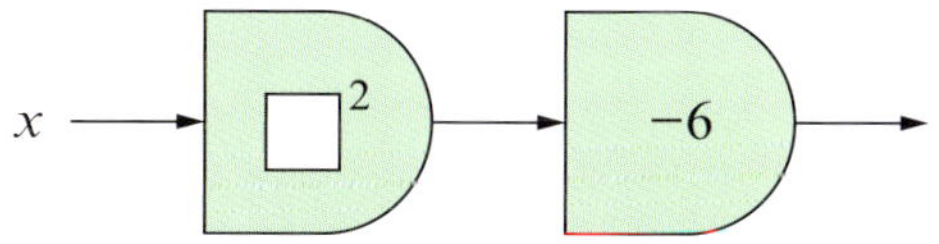

$y \rightarrow$ equation is $y = x^2 - 6$

iii 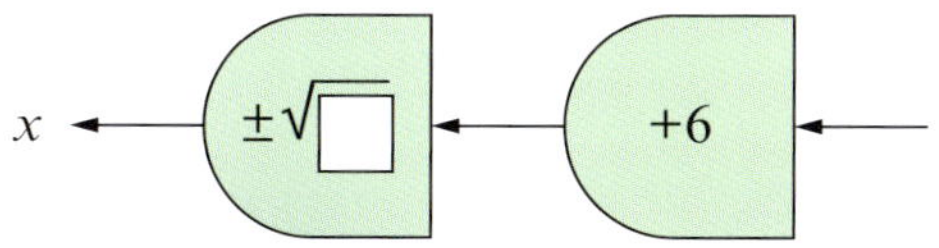

$y \rightarrow$ equation is $x = \pm\sqrt{y+6}$

A $y = x^2 - 6$ **B** $y = \left(\frac{x}{6}\right)^2$ **C** $y = \frac{x^3}{6}$

D $y = 6x^2$ **E** $y = (x+6)^2$ **F** $y = (6x)^3$

i $x = \pm 6\sqrt{y}$ **ii** $x = \frac{\sqrt[3]{y}}{6}$ **iii** $x = \pm\sqrt{y+6}$

iv $x = \pm\sqrt{y} - 6$ **v** $x = \sqrt[3]{6y}$ **vi** $x = \pm\sqrt{\frac{y}{6}}$

10 Sofia and Zara are looking at this function machine and table of values.

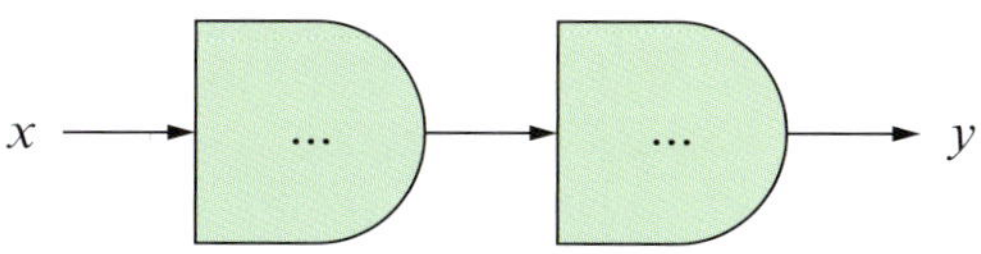

x	−2	3	5
y	16	36	100

Sofia says:

Zara says:

Is either of them correct? Explain your answer. Show all your working.

11 Copy and complete this function machine, its equation and table of values.

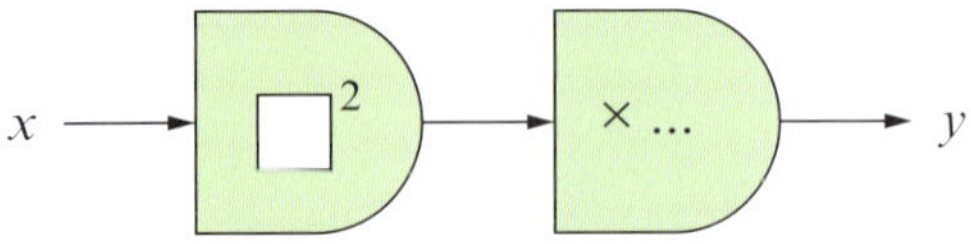

x	$\frac{1}{4}$	$\frac{1}{2}$	
y	$\frac{1}{2}$		72

Explain how you worked out your answer.

12 Arun is looking at the two functions $y = 2x^4$ and $y = \frac{1}{2}x^3$.

Arun makes this conjecture.

Is Arun correct? Show working to justify your answer.

How well do you think you understand functions that include indices?

Summary checklist

- ☐ I can work out output values of function machines that use indices.
- ☐ I can work out input values of function machines that use indices.
- ☐ I can write a function as an equation.

Check your progress

1 Work out the first four terms of these sequences.

a first term 3 term-to-term rule is square, then subtract 5

b first term −3 term-to-term rule is add 2 and square

c first term is 5 term-to-term rule is add 1, add 3, add 5, …

d first term is 40 term-to-term rule is subtract 2, subtract 4, subtract 6, …

2 Work out the first three terms and the 10th term of the sequences with the given nth terms.

a $\frac{n}{2}$ **b** $n^2 + 7$

3 Work out the nth term rules for these sequences.

a 1, 4, 9, 16, 25, … **b** −1, 2, 7, 14, 23, … **c** $\frac{1}{9}, \frac{2}{9}, \frac{1}{3}, \frac{4}{9}, \frac{5}{9}, \frac{2}{3}, \ldots$

4 The nth term rule for a sequence is $n^2 + 32$. Is the number 178 a term in this sequence? Show your working.

5 **a** Work out the missing values in the tables for these function machines.
The x-values are all positive.

i

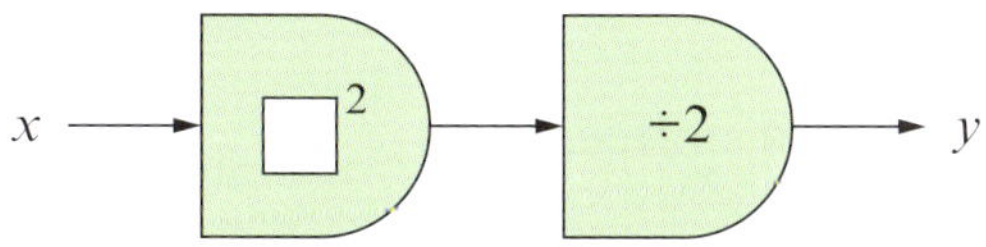

x	−2		5	
y		8		$40\frac{1}{2}$

ii

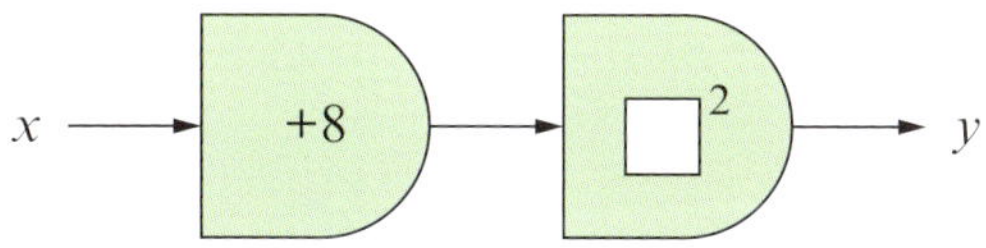

x	−15	$-8\frac{1}{2}$		
y			81	144

b Write each function in part **a** as an equation.

10 Graphs

Getting started

1. The cost of hiring a van is \$35 plus \$20 per day.
   a. Work out the cost of hiring the van for 6 days.

   It costs c dollars to hire the van for d days.

   b. Write a function for c.
2. Here is a function: $y = 2x - 1$
   a. Copy and complete this table of values.

x	−2	−1	0	1	2	3
y	−5				3	

   b. Use the table to draw a graph of $y = 2x - 1$
   c. Write the gradient of the graph.
   d. Write the y-intercept.
3. This graph shows the temperature of a cup of coffee.
   a. Find the initial temperature of the coffee.
   b. Find the temperature after 10 minutes.
   c. When is the coffee cooling most quickly?

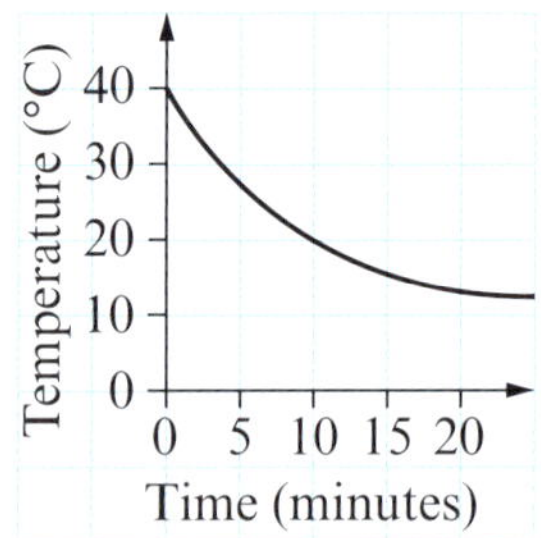

Here are some examples of linear graphs.

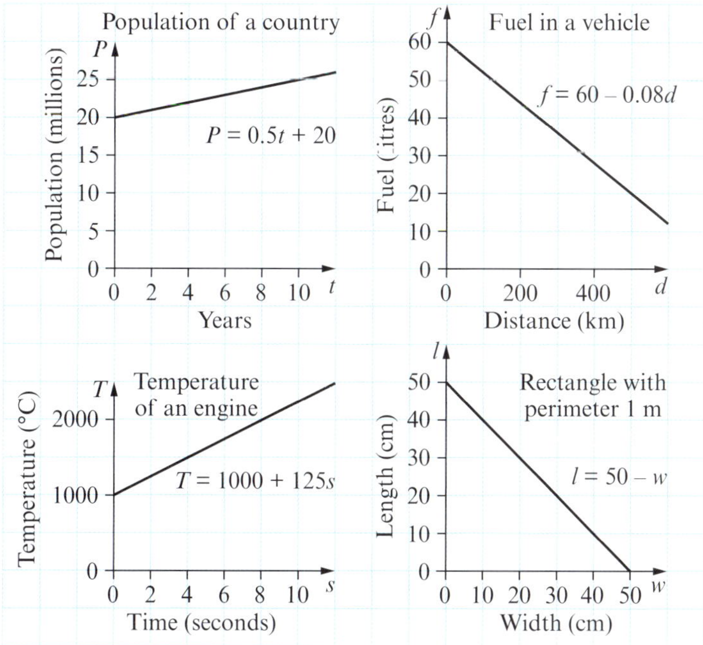

You can use the equation to make a table of values. The values give you coordinates of points to plot. In a linear graph, the points will be in a straight line.

Often a graph is not a straight line.

The 'Population of a country' graph might not continue in the same way in the future. The population might increase more quickly or more slowly or it might decrease in future years. What will the graph look like if this happens?

In this unit you will look in more detail at linear graphs. You will also look at some simple graphs that are not linear.

10.1 Functions

In this section you will …

- describe situations either in words or using functions
- use functions of two different types.

Ali and Bella both have some money. The total amount is \$37.
Ali has a dollars and Bella has b dollars. You can write $a + b = 37$
For example, when Ali has \$25, $a = 25$ and $b = 12$ because $25 + 12 = 37$

Worked example 10.1

Fatima buys some pens and pencils.

Pencils cost \$2 and pens cost \$6.

Fatima spends \$30.

a Show that Fatima could buy 9 pencils and 2 pens.

b Suppose Fatima buys c pencils and k pens.
Write a function to show what she spends.

Answer

a $9 \times 2 + 2 \times 6 = 18 + 12 = 30$ which is correct.

One pencil costs \$2, so 9 pencils cost $9 \times 2 = \$18$. One pen costs \$6, so 2 pens cost $2 \times 6 = \$12$.

b The pencils cost $2c$ dollars and the pens cost $6k$ dollars.
Fatima spends \$30, so $2c + 6k = 30$

Exercise 10.1

1 The cost of hiring a ladder is a fixed charge of \$10 plus \$3 per day.

a Work out the cost of hiring the ladder for one week.

b Explain why $y = 3x + 10$ where x is the number of days' hire and y is the total cost in dollars.

2 The cost of hiring a chainsaw is a fixed charge of \$15 plus \$10 per day.

a Aran pays \$45. For how many days does he hire the chainsaw?

b If t is the total cost in dollars for n days, write a function to show the cost.

3 A boy's mass is 3 kg less than twice his sister's mass.

a His sister's mass is 15 kg. Work out the boy's mass.

b If the boy's mass is b kg and his sister's mass is g kg, write a function to show the relationship between b and g.

4 Shen is s years old and his father is f years old.

The total age of Shen and his father is 50.

a Write a function to show this.

b Write a function to show the relation between their ages after one year.

c Write a function to show the relation between their ages after 5 years.

5 Kasia has some \$5 notes and \$10 notes. She has a total of \$90.

a Show that she could have 6 notes of each type.

b Suppose Kasia has f \$5 notes and t \$10 notes. Write a function to show that she has \$90.

c What is the largest number of \$10 notes Kasia could have?

6 There are large and small tables in a restaurant. Large tables have 6 seats and small tables have 4 seats.

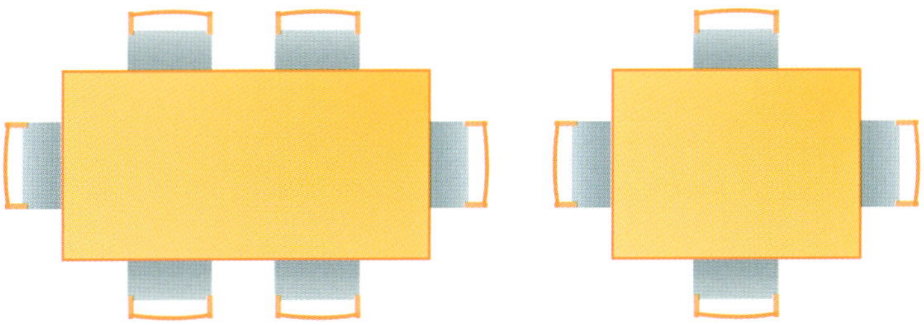

There is a total of 120 seats.

a Show that there could be 12 tables of each type.

b There are l large tables and s small tables. Write a function connecting l and s.

c Suppose the number of small tables is double the number of large tables. Write a function to show this.

7 Erin has a 2-cent coins and b 5-cent coins.

a She writes $2a + 5b = 80$. What does this tell you?

b Erin is given some more 5-cent coins. Now she writes $2a + 5b = 100$. How many 5-cent coins was she given?

8 There are two types of sofa in a lounge. x sofas have 3 seats and y sofas have 2 seats.

There is a total of 50 seats.

a Write a function to show this.

b Explain why x cannot be 7.

Think like a mathematician

9 Work with a partner to answer this question.

Here is a function: $s = 5t + 12$

a Write a possible interpretation of s and t.

b Write another possible interpretation of s and t.

Here is another function: $3h + 4k = 48$

c Write a possible interpretation of h and k.

d Write a different interpretation of h and k.

10 In a collection of tiles, there are two shapes: triangles and squares.

a Work out the total number of edges of 4 triangles and 5 squares.

A collection of tiles has a total number of 100 edges.

b There are r triangles and q squares. Write a function to show that there are 100 edges.

c There are 20 triangles. Work out the number of squares.

d Work out the largest possible number of triangles.

e Can there be an equal number of triangles and squares? Give a reason for your answer.

f The number of squares is 5 less than the number of triangles multiplied by 3. Write a function to show this.

Here is a function: $x + 2y = 20$

Can you write the function in a different way?

Summary checklist

- [ ] I can understand a relationship written either in words or as a function.
- [ ] I can interpret functions such as $y = 3x + 12$ or $4x + 3y = 24$.

10.2 Plotting graphs

In this section you will …

- use a function to complete a table of values
- use a table of values to draw a graph
- draw straight-line graphs and simple curves.

Key word

linear function

$y = 2x + 3$ and $2x + 3y = 12$ are examples of **linear functions**. The graph of a linear function is a straight line.

You know how to find coordinate pairs for $y = 2x + 3$. Choose some values for x and use them to find values of y. Put them in a table.

x	−2	−1	0	1	2	3
y	−1	1	3	5	7	9

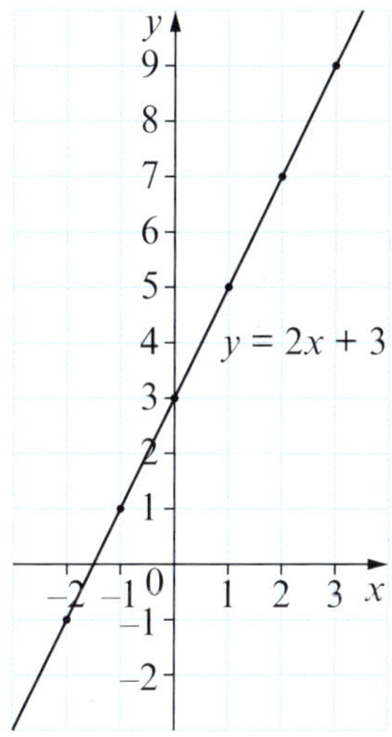

Plot the points (−2, −1), (−1, 1), (0, 3) and so on. Draw a straight line through the points. The line continues beyond the points you have plotted.

For a function such as $2x + 3y = 12$, you can choose a value for x or y and then work out the corresponding value of y or x.

Worked example 10.2

a Copy and complete this table of values for $2x + 3y = 12$.

x	0		3	
y		3		0

b Draw a graph of $2x + 3y = 12$

Answer

a When $x = 0$, then $0 + 3y = 12$ so $y = 4$

When $y = 3$, then $2x + 9 = 12$ so $2x = 3$ and $x = 1.5$

When $x = 3$, then $6 + 3y = 12$ so $3y = 6$ and $y = 2$

When $y = 0$, then $2x = 12$ so $x = 6$

x	0	1.5	3	6
y	4	3	2	0

Substitute each value of x or y into the equation to find the corresponding value of y or x.

Continued

b

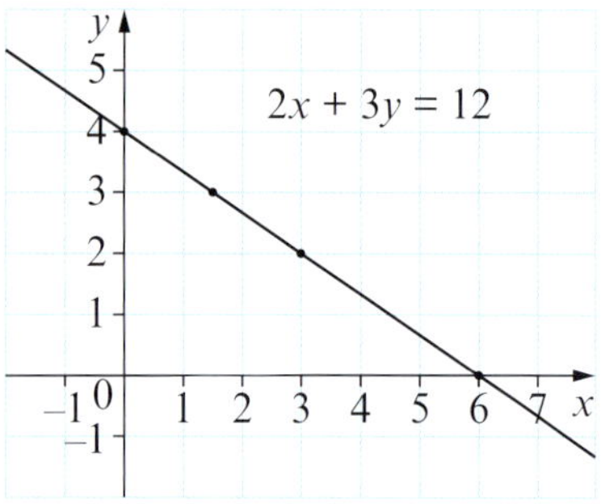

It is a good idea to use $x = 0$ for one point and $y = 0$ for another point. This allows you to find the intercepts on the axes.

For other types of function, the graph might not be a straight line.

Worked example 10.3

a Copy and complete the table of values for $y = x^2 - 3$.

x	−3	−2	−1	0	1	2	3
y	6			−3		1	

b Use the table to draw a graph of $y = x^2 - 3$.

Answer

a When $x = -3$, then $y = x^2 - 3 = (-3)^2 - 3 = 9 - 3 = 6$, and so on.

The square of any negative number is positive.

x	−3	−2	−1	0	1	2	3
y	6	1	−2	−3	−2	1	6

b

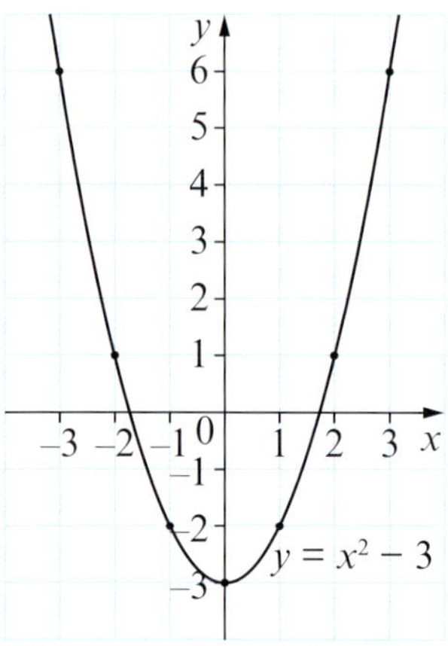

When the points are not in a straight line, join them with a smooth curve. If you have graphing software, you can use it to check that you have drawn the curve correctly.

Exercise 10.2

1 a Copy and complete this table for the function $y = 10x + 15$.

x	−1	0	1	2	3
y		15			

b Show that the point (5, 65) is on the graph of $y = 10x + 15$.

2 a Copy and complete this table for the function $y = 2x - 10$.

x	−10	0	10	20	30
y			10		

b Where does the graph of $y = 2x - 10$ cross the y-axis?

c Is the point (23, 36) on the graph of $y = 2x - 10$? Give a reason for your answer.

3 Here is a function: $4x + y = 20$

a Copy and complete this table of values for the function.

x	0	1			6
y			8	0	

b Where does a graph of $4x + y = 20$ cross the axes?

4 Here is a function: $2x + 5y = 60$

a Copy and complete this table of values for the function.

x	0	10	20	30	40
y					

b Show that the point (15, 6) is on the graph of $2x + 5y = 60$.

5 a Copy and complete this table of values for the function $y = x^2 + 6$.

x	−2	0	2	4	6
y			10		

b Show that the point (5, 31) is on the graph of $y = x^2 + 6$.

6 a Copy and complete this table of values for the function $2x + 4y = 32$.

x	0	2		10	
y			5		0

b Write the coordinates of the point where the graph of $2x + 4y = 32$ crosses

i the x-axis

ii the y-axis.

7 Here is a function: $3x + 2y = 18$

a Copy and complete this table of values for this function.

x	0		2	4	
y		7.5			0

b Write the coordinates of the point where the graph of $3x + 2y = 18$ crosses

i the x-axis

ii the y-axis.

c Use the table to draw a graph of $3x + 2y = 18$.

8 Here is a function: $x + 5y = 15$

a Copy and complete this table of values for $x + 5y = 15$.

x				
y	0	1	2	3

b Draw a graph of $x + 5y = 15$.

9 Draw all the graphs in this question on the same axes.

a Copy and complete this table of values for $x + y = 10$.

x	0	2	4	6	8	10
y						

b Draw a graph of $x + y = 10$.

c Draw a graph of $x + y = 7$.

d Copy and complete this table of values for $x + y = 4$.

x	−1	0	1	2	3	4	5
y	5						

e Draw a graph of $x + y = 4$.

f Describe the graph of $x + y = c$ when c is a number.

g Draw a graph of $x + y = 0$.

10 Draw all the graphs in this question on the same axes.

a Draw a graph of $x + y = 12$.

b Copy and complete this table of values for $2x + y = 12$.

x	0	1	2	3	4	5	6
y				6			

c Draw a graph of $2x + y = 12$.

d Draw a graph of $3x + y = 12$.

e Draw a graph of $4x + y = 12$.

f Describe the graph of $kx + y = 12$ when k is a positive integer.

11 a Draw a graph of $x + 2y = 14$.

b Describe the graph of $x + 2y = n$ when n is a positive integer.

12 a Copy and complete this table of values for the function $y = x^2$.

x	−3	−2	−1	0	1	2	3
y		4					

b Draw a graph of $y = x^2$.

c Copy and complete this table of values for the function $y = x^2 + 2$.

x	−3	−2	−1	0	1	2	3
y	11						

d Draw a graph of $y = x^2 + 2$.

e Copy and complete this table of values for the function $y = x^2 - 4$.

x	−3	−2	−1	0	1	2	3
y	5						

f Draw a graph of $y = x^2 - 4$.

g Describe the graph of $y = x^2 + c$ when c is a number.

13 Match each graph with the correct equation.

i
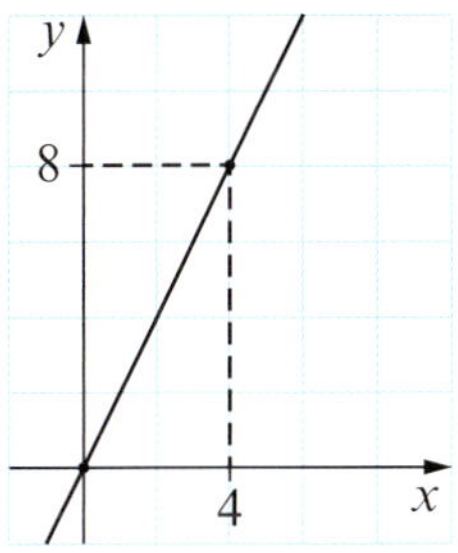

ii
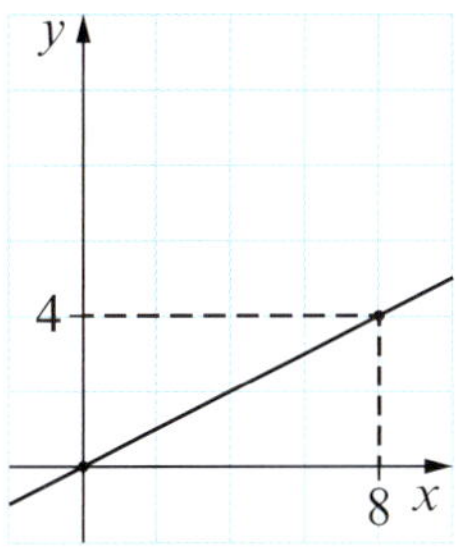

iii
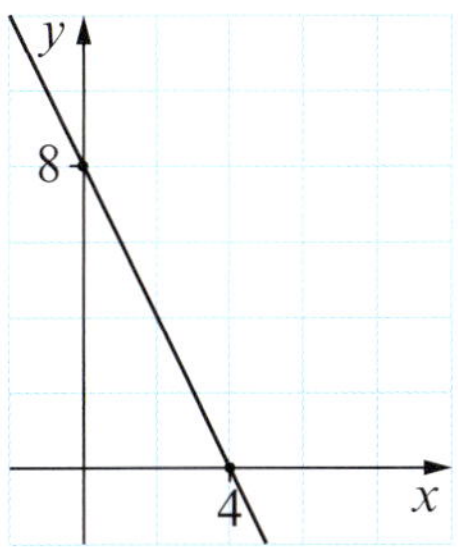

iv
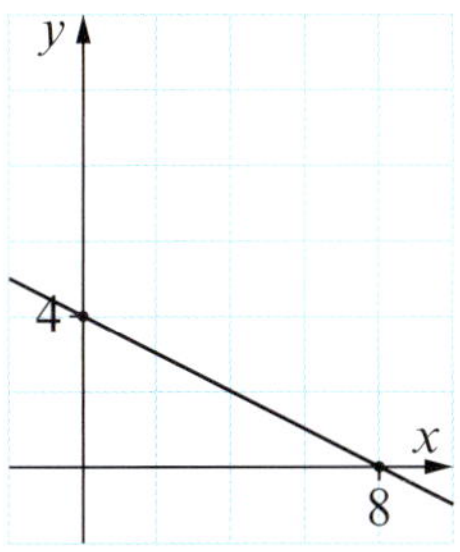

A $2x + y = 8$ B $2y + x = 8$ C $y = 2x$ D $x = 2y$

14 **a** Copy and complete this table of values for $y = x^2 - 9$.

x	−5	−4	−3	−2	−1	0	1	2	3	4	5
y	16					−9			0		

b Draw a graph of $y = x^2 - 9$.

c These points are on a graph of $y = x^2 - 9$. Find the missing coordinate for each point.

i (−10, ☐) **ii** (8, ☐) **iii** (20, ☐)
iv (☐, 0) **v** (☐, 27)

Summary checklist

☐ I can complete a table of values for a function in the form $ax + by = c$ or $y = x^2 + c$.
☐ I can draw a graph of a function from a table of values.

10.3 Gradient and intercept

In this section you will ...

- find the gradient and y-intercept of a straight line from an equation
- rearrange the equation of a straight line to find the gradient and the y-intercept.

You saw this graph of $y = 2x + 3$ at the start of Section 10.2. The gradient is 2 and the y-intercept is 3. For any graph in the form $y = mx + c$, the gradient is m and the y-intercept is c.

You saw in the last section that a graph of $ax + by = c$ is a straight line. To find the gradient and intercept, rewrite the function with y as the subject.

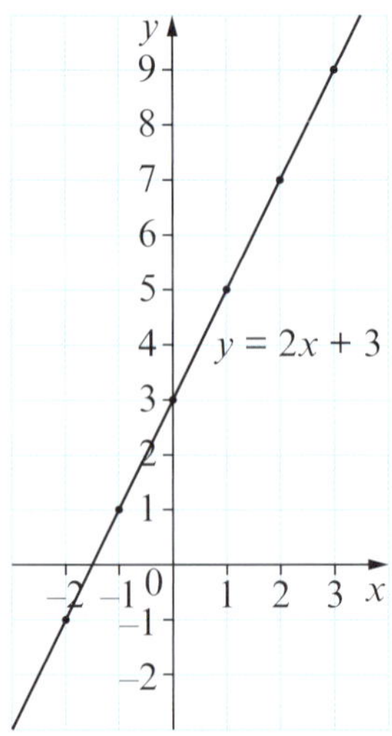

Worked example 10.4

A graph of $2x + 3y = 12$ is a straight line. Work out the gradient and the y-intercept.

Answer

$2x + 3y = 12$
$3y = 12 - 2x$
$y = 4 - \frac{2}{3}x$

You need to rewrite $2x + 3y = 12$ in the form $y = \ldots$

First, subtract $2x$ from both sides.

Then divide both sides by 3.

gradient $= -\frac{2}{3}$, y-intercept $= 4$

In an equation with the form $y = mx + c$, m is the gradient and c is the y-intercept.

In Worked example 10.2 you saw that the graph of $2x + 3y = 12$ crosses the y-axis at (0, 4). This shows that the y-intercept is 4.

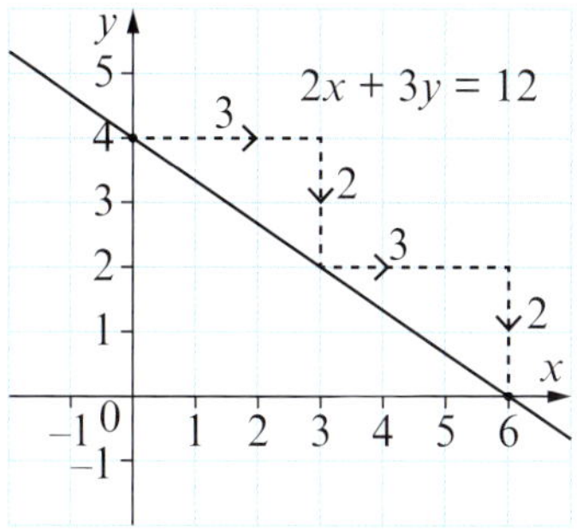

The line slopes downwards from left to right so the gradient is negative. Imagine you are moving along the line from left to right.

- As the x-coordinate **increases** by 3, the y-coordinate **decreases** by 2.
- As the x-coordinate **increases** by 1, the y-coordinate **decreases** by $\frac{2}{3}$.

The gradient is $-\frac{2}{3}$.

Exercise 10.3

1 Write the gradient and the y-intercept of each of these straight lines.

   a $y = 4x - 6$ b $y = 6x + 4$ c $y = 4 - 6x$

2 Write the gradient and the y-intercept of each of these straight lines.

   a $y = 0.5x + 3$ b $y = -x + 8$ c $y = \frac{1}{4}x$

3 Find the gradient of each line.

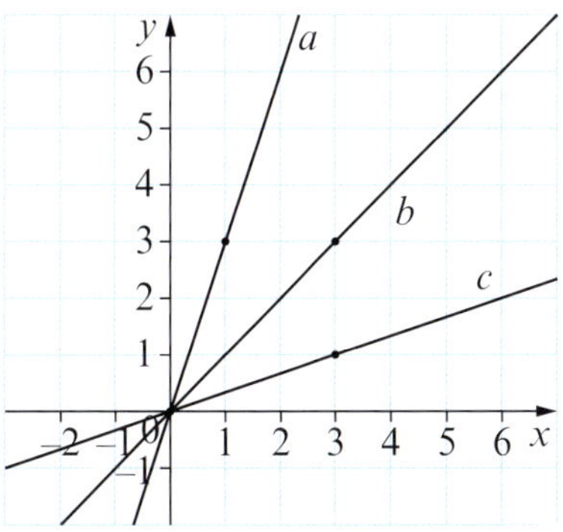

4 Find the gradient of each line.

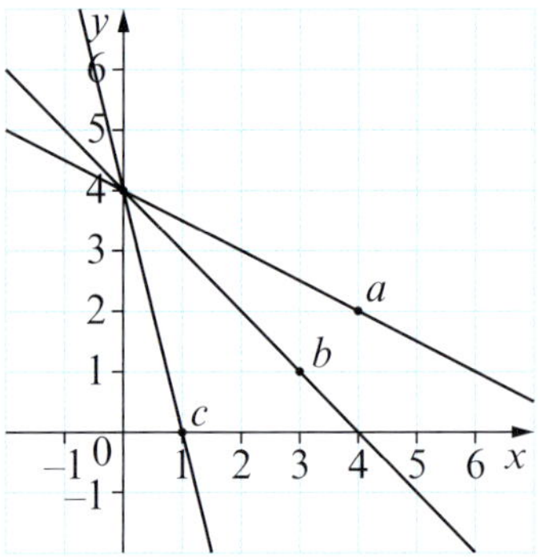

Tip

All the gradients are negative.

5 a Copy and complete this table of values for $x + 2y = 10$.

x	0	2	4	6	8	10
y						

b Draw a graph of $x + 2y = 10$.

c Make y the subject of $x + 2y = 10$.

d Use your answer to part **c** to find the gradient and y-intercept of a graph of $x + 2y = 10$.

e Use your graph to check that your answer to part **d** is correct.

Tip

'Make y the subject' means 'write in the form $y = \ldots$'.

6 a Rewrite $3x + y = 15$ to make y the subject.

b Write the gradient and the y-intercept of a graph of $3x + y = 15$.

c Copy and complete this table of values for $3x + y = 15$.

x	0		2	4
y		0		

d Draw a graph of $3x + y = 15$.

e Use your graph to check your answers to part **b**.

7 a Rewrite $3x + 4y = 24$ to make y the subject.

b Write the gradient and the y-intercept of the line $3x + 4y = 24$.

c Copy and complete this table for $3x + 4y = 24$. Add your own values for the empty column.

x	0		4	
y		0		

d Draw a graph of $3x + 4y = 24$.

e Use the graph to check your answers to part **b**.

8 a Make y the subject of each of these equations.

i $2x + y = 18$ ii $x + 2y = 18$

iii $4x + 2y = 18$ iv $3x + 6y = 18$

b Copy and complete this table.

line	gradient	y-intercept
$2x + y = 18$		
$x + 2y = 18$		
$4x + 2y = 18$		
$3x + 6y = 18$		

c Can you make a general statement about the gradient and the y-intercept of $ax + by = 18$ when a and b are positive integers?

9 a Rearrange the equation $y - 4x + 2 = 10$ to make y the subject.

b Describe the line with equation $y - 4x + 2 = 10$.

10 For each graph work out

i the y-intercept ii the gradient iii the equation.

a

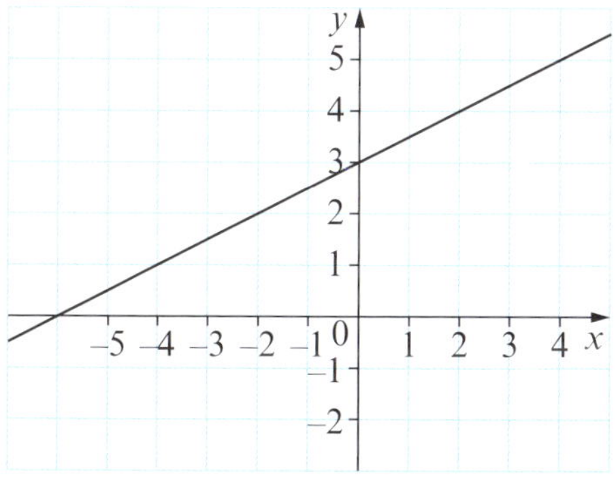

b

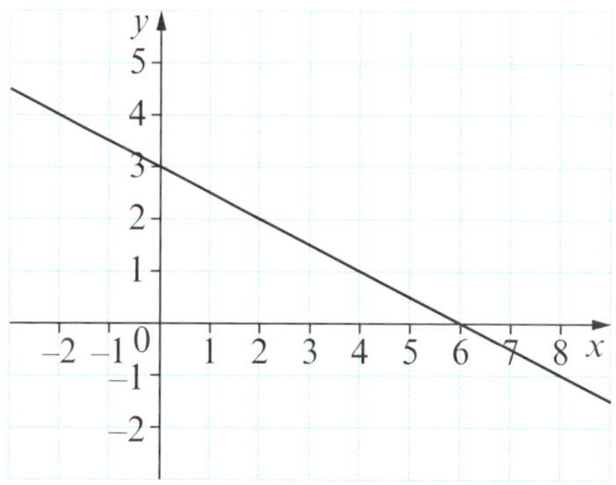

Summary checklist

- ☐ I can find the gradient and y-intercept of the line $y = mx + c$.
- ☐ I can rearrange $ax + by = c$ to find the gradient and y-intercept.

10.4 Interpreting graphs

In this section you will …

- read and interpret graphs.

This graph shows the distance travelled by a runner. The graph is a straight line. This means the runner is travelling at a constant speed. The point (100, 240) is on the line. This tells us the runner travels 240 m in 100 s. The speed is $\frac{240}{100} = 2.4$ m/s

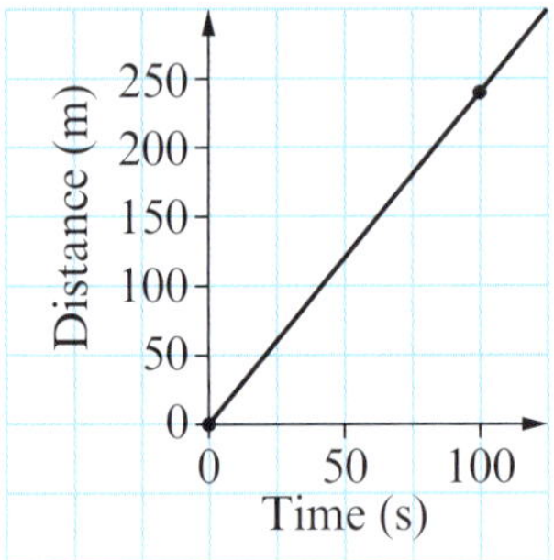

> **Tip**
> The distance is in metres and the time is in seconds, so the speed is in m/s.

The speed is the gradient of the distance–time graph. If the runner travels d m in t s, the equation of the line is $d = 2.4t$.

> **Tip**
> The line passes through the origin, so the y-intercept is 0.

You can use the equation of the line to find distances or times. For example:

1 How far does the runner travel in 15 minutes?

15 minutes = 15 × 60 = 900 s

When $t = 900$, then $d = 2.4 \times 900 = 2160$

Distance = 2160 m = 2.16 km.

2 How long does it take the runner to travel 5 km at this speed?

5 km = 5000 m and so $d = 5000$

$d = 2.4t$ and so $5000 = 2.4t$ and so $t = \frac{5000}{2.4} = 2083$

It takes the runner 2083 s or nearly 35 minutes to travel 5 km.

> **Tip**
> $2083 \div 60 = 34.7$

Worked example 10.5

This graph shows how the temperature of a metal bar changes over 50 minutes.

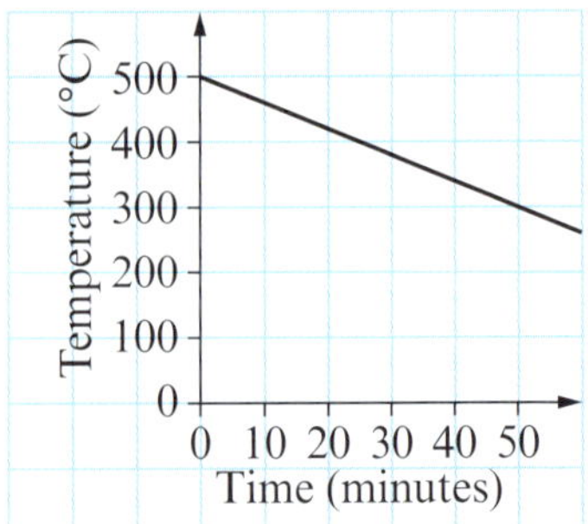

a How does the graph show that the rate of cooling is constant?

b Find the gradient of the line.

c What does the gradient tell you?

d The temperature is y°C after t minutes. Find the equation of the line.

e The bar continues to cool at the same rate. Find the temperature after $1\frac{1}{2}$ hours.

Continued

Answer

a The graph is a straight line so the rate of cooling is constant.

b The graph line goes through (0, 500) and (50, 300).

The gradient is $\frac{300-500}{50-0} = \frac{-200}{50} = -4$

c The rate of cooling is 4°C/minute.

d The y-intercept is 500 so the equation is $y = 500 - 4t$

e $1\frac{1}{2}$ hours = 90 minutes and so $t = 90$ and $y = 500 - 4 \times 90 = 140$

The temperature after $1\frac{1}{2}$ hours is 140 °C.

Exercise 10.4

1 This graph shows the distance travelled by a car.

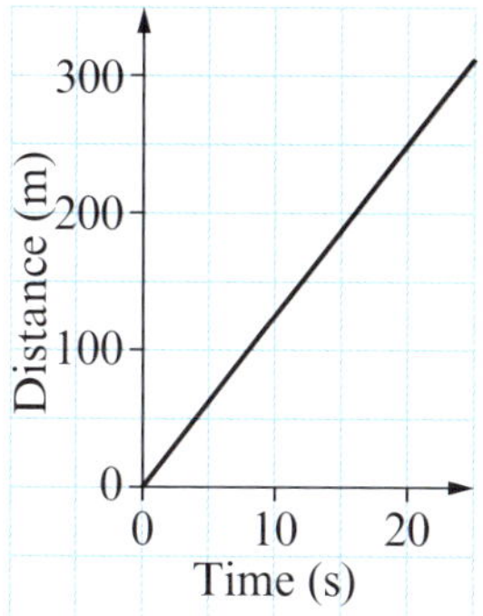

- a Find the distance travelled after 20 seconds.
- b Find the time taken to travel 200 m.
- c Find the speed of the car in m/s.
- d The car travels d m in t s. Write an equation for d in terms of t.
- e Work out how far the car travels in 50 seconds.

2 This graph shows the exchange rate between US dollars and HK dollars.

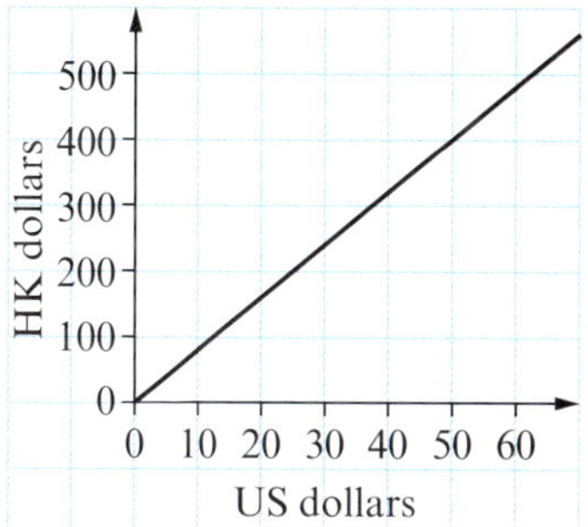

- a How many HK dollars can you buy for 50 US dollars?
- b How many US dollars can you buy for 160 HK dollars?
- c i Work out the gradient of the line.
  - ii What does the gradient tell you?
- d You can buy y HK dollars for x US dollars. Write an equation for y in terms of x.
- e Jan has 115 US dollars. How many HK dollars can Jan buy?

3 This graph shows the cost of petrol.

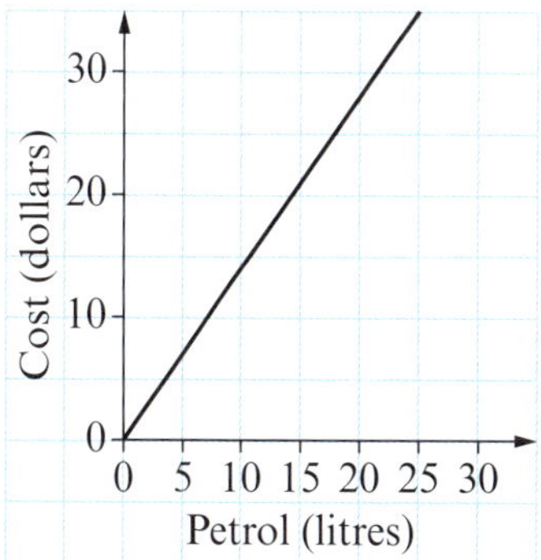

- a Find the cost of 20 litres.
- b How many litres can you buy for 21 dollars?
- c Find the cost of 1 litre of petrol.
- d x litres cost y dollars. Write an equation linking x and y.
- e Find the cost of 45.8 litres of petrol.
- f Hassan pays 51.1 dollars for petrol. How many litres does Hassan buy?

4 This graph shows the increasing height of a bamboo plant.

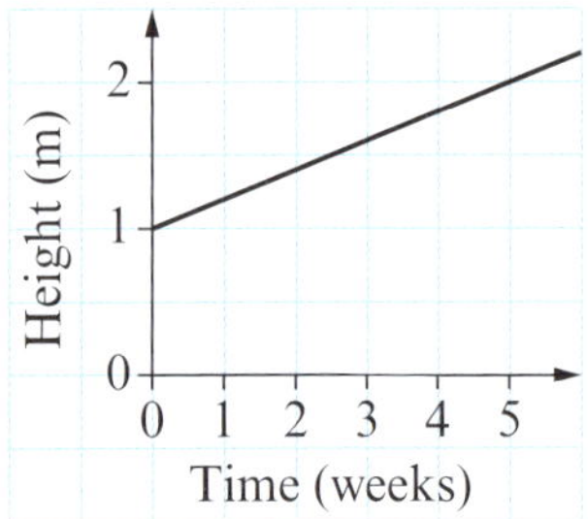

a Write the initial height of the bamboo.

b Copy and complete this table.

weeks	0	1	2	3	4	5
height (m)						

c By how much does the height of the bamboo increase each week?

d The height is y m after t weeks. Write an equation for y in terms of t.

e Find the height of the bamboo after 11 weeks.

5 Luca is walking home from school. The graph shows the distance Luca is from home.

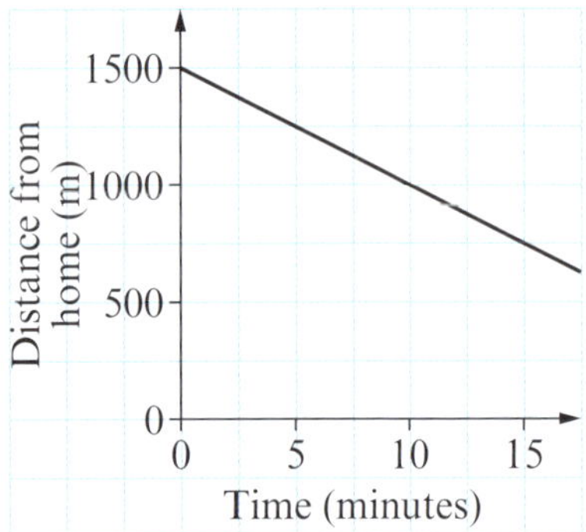

a How far from home was Luca when he started walking?

b How far from home was Luca after 15 minutes?

c Find Luca's speed in metres/minute.

d After x minutes, Luca is y m from home. Write an equation for y.

e Assuming Luca continues to walk at a constant speed, how far from home is he after 23 minutes?

f How long does Luca take to walk home?

6 Ali has 50 dollars and uses them to buy 45 euros.

a Draw a graph to show the exchange rate between dollars and euros. Put dollars on the x-axis.

b Use your graph to copy and complete this table.

dollars	50	20		
euros	45		27	13.5

c **i** Work out the gradient of your graph.

ii What does the gradient tell you?

d x dollars will buy y euros. Write an equation for y in terms of x.

e How many euros can you buy for 280 dollars?

f Shen spends 153 euros buying dollars. How many dollars does he buy?

Tip

Plot the point (50, 45) and join it to the origin.

7 Seed is sold by mass.

A farmer buys 25 kg of seed and pays 40 dollars.

- **a** Draw a graph to show the price of seed. Put mass on the horizontal axis and price on the vertical axis.
- **b** Use the graph to find the cost of 15 kg of seed.
- **c** Work out the gradient of the graph.
- **d** Find the cost per kilogram of seed.
- **e** x kg costs y dollars. Write a formula for y in terms of x.
- **f** Work out the cost of 95 kg of seed.
- **g** How many kg of seed can you buy for 100 dollars?

8 The temperature of some water is initially 20 °C.

The temperature increases at a constant rate. After 30 seconds, the temperature is 32 °C.

- **a** Draw a graph to show how the temperature increases. Put time on the horizontal axis.
- **b** Use your graph to find the temperature after 10 seconds.
- **c** Find the rate of increase of temperature in degrees/second.
- **d** The temperature is y °C after t seconds. Write an equation for y in terms of t.
- **e** Work out the temperature after 1 minute.
- **f** The temperature continues to increase at the same rate. Work out the time until the temperature is 100 °C.
- **g** Compare your graph and your answers with a partner. Have you drawn the same graph? Check that you have the same answers.

9 Water is leaking from a tank at a constant rate. Initially there are 100 litres of water in the tank. After 8 hours there are 72 litres of water in the tank.

- **a** Draw a graph to show the amount of water in the tank over time.
- **b** Use your graph to find the amount of water in the tank after 6 hours.
- **c** Find the rate at which water is leaking in litres/hour.
- **d** There are y litres left in the tank after h hours. Write an equation for y.

10 This graph shows the exchange rate between euros and Japanese yen.

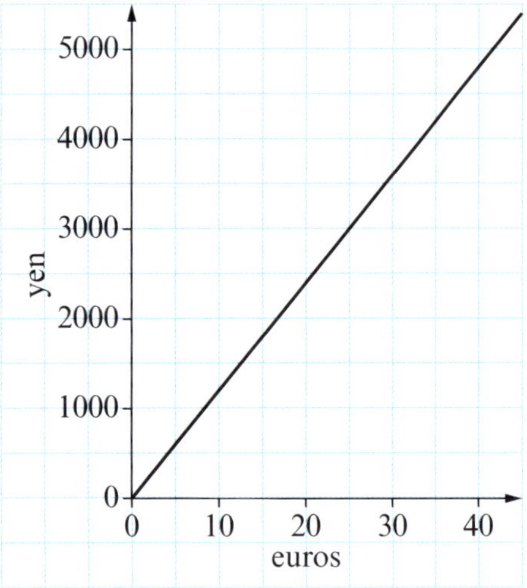

a Work out the number of Japanese yen you can exchange for 40 euros.

b A computer costs 275 euros. Work out the cost in Japanese yen. Show your method.

11 This graph shows the population of a town over a number of years.

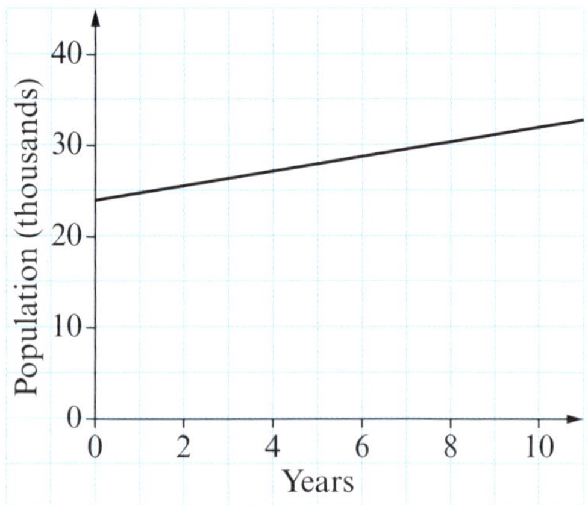

a The population after t years is p thousand people.

Show that $p = 0.8t + 24$

b The population continues to increase at the same rate. How long will it be until the population is 36 000? Show your method.

12 Marcus and Arun are running. Here is a distance–time graph for each person.

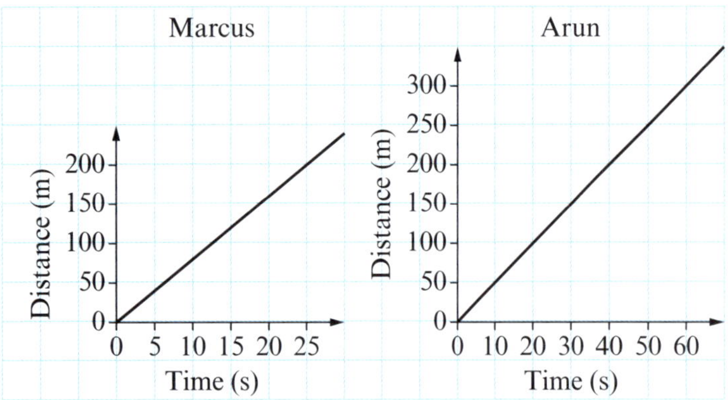

a Work out Marcus' speed.

b Who runs faster, Marcus or Arun? Give a reason for your answer.

13 Water is flowing out of two tanks, A and B. The graphs show how the depth of water in each tank is changing.

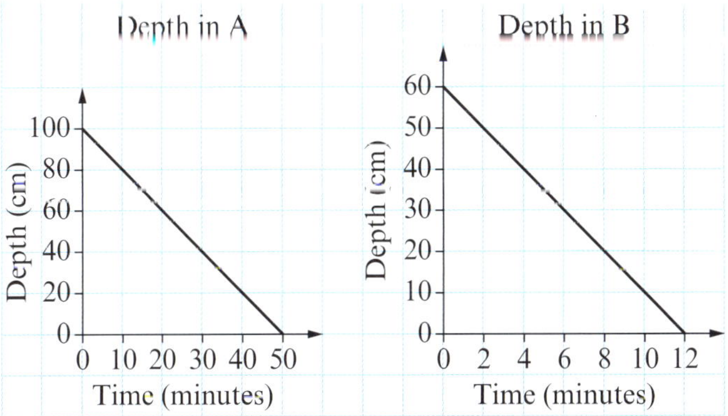

Sofia says:

Show that Sofia is not correct.

14 This graph shows the distance travelled by a car in 25 seconds.

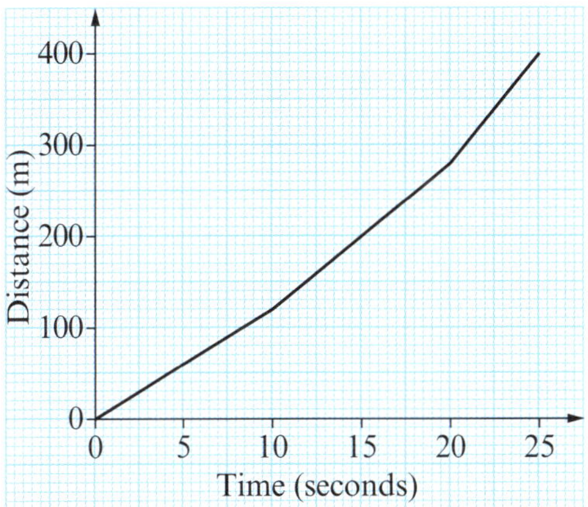

Work out

a the speed for the first 10 seconds

b the speed between 10 seconds and 20 seconds

c the speed for the last 5 seconds.

15 An engine runs on diesel.

This graph shows the amount of diesel in the tank.

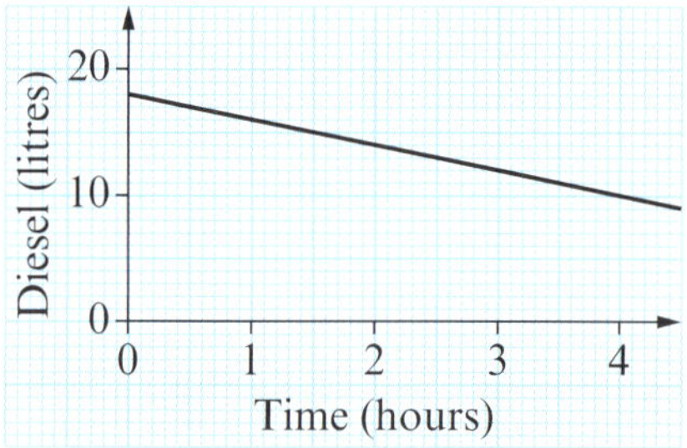

a Describe how the amount of diesel in the tank is changing.

b Work out an equation to show the number of litres in the tank after t hours.

c Work out the length of time before the engine runs out of diesel.

Think like a mathematician

16 You can work with a partner to answer this question.

Here is a graph.

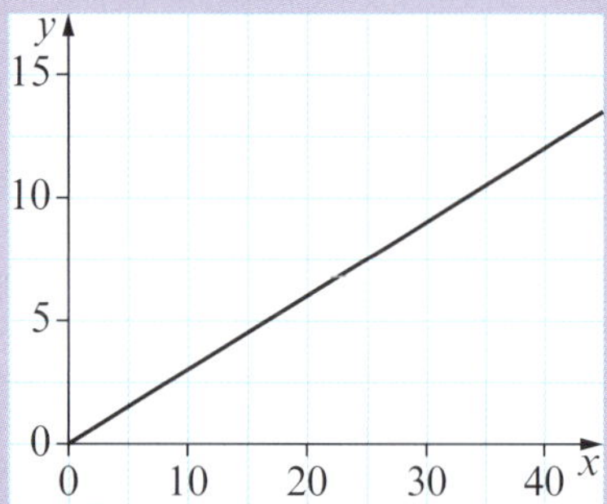

Describe **two** different situations this graph could represent.

In each case, say what x and y represent and what the gradient shows.

Summary checklist

- ☐ I can draw and interpret linear graphs.
- ☐ I can calculate a gradient to find a rate of change.

Check your progress

1 Amin has x 5-dollar bills and y 10-dollar bills.
The total value is 100 dollars.
  a Write an equation to show this.
  b Show that the equation can be written as $y = 10 - \frac{1}{2}x$.
  c Write the gradient of a graph of $y = 10 - \frac{1}{2}x$.

2 a Copy and complete this table of values for $3x + y = 15$.

x	0	1	2	3	4	5
y	15					

  b Draw a graph of $3x + y = 15$.
  c Work out the gradient of the graph.

3 a Draw a graph of $y = x^2 + 5$ with values of x between −3 and 3.
  b The point $(a, 30)$ is on the graph. Work out the possible values of a.

4 This graph shows the height of a tree.
  a Find the height after 5 years.
  b Find the rate of growth of the tree.
  c The height after x years is y metres.
  Write an equation for y.
  d The tree continues to grow at the same rate. Work out the height after 9 years.

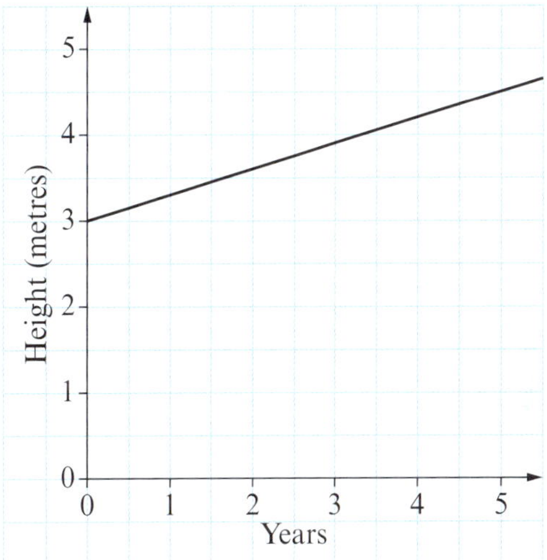

Project 4

Cinema membership

At the local cinema, you can choose to become a Gold, Silver or Bronze member.

- **Gold membership** costs **$80 for three months**. Gold membership entitles you to **free tickets** to as many films as you want to see.
- **Silver membership** costs **$50 for three months**, but you have to pay **$2.50 for each ticket**.
- **Bronze membership** costs **$20 for three months**, but you have to pay **$8.50 for each ticket**.
- **Non-members** have to pay **$18 for each ticket**.

Which membership would you choose?

Perhaps it depends on how many films you plan to see …

Create a table, a graph and a formula to represent the cost of buying tickets for each membership scheme.

How could you advise someone on the best membership option if they tell you how many films they plan to see?

Imagine you are the manager of a rival cinema. You want to set up your own membership scheme, in which:

- Basic membership is best for customers who want to see between 4 and 9 films every three months
- Premium membership is best for customers who want to see 10 or more films every three months.

Design some pricing schemes that satisfy these criteria.

11 Ratio and proportion

Getting started

1 Simplify these ratios.

a 8 cm : 4 mm

b 15 seconds : 1 minute

c 300 mL : 1.5 L

2 In a tennis club there are men, women and children members in the ratio 5 : 6 : 4.

The tennis club has 270 members.

How many members of the tennis club are

a men b women c children?

3 A school maths club has 56 members. The ratio of boys to girls is 3 : 4.

a What fraction of the club members are girls?

b How many girls are in the club?

4 Sam mixes two shades of blue paint using the following ratios of blue : white.

Sky blue 1 : 3	Ocean blue 2 : 5

a What fraction of each shade of blue paint is white?

b Which shade of blue paint is lighter? Show all your working. Justify your choice.

5 Six packets of potato chips cost $5.10. Work out the cost of eight packets of potato chips.

Tip

Make sure both measurements in each ratio are in the same units before you start to simplify.

Tip

The blue paint with the greater fraction of white paint will be lighter.

Every musical note has a frequency. This frequency is measured in hertz (Hz). The frequency tells you how many times a string playing that note vibrates every second. This table shows the frequency of some of the notes in the musical scale, rounded to one decimal place.

Note	C	D	E	F	G	A	B
Frequency (Hz)	261.6	293.7	329.6	349.2	392.0	440.0	493.9

There are some very simple ratios between the frequencies of some of these notes.

- Frequency of G : frequency of C = 3 : 2
  because $392.0 \div 261.6 = 1.50$ or $\frac{3}{2}$ or 3 : 2
- Frequency of A : frequency of D = 3 : 2
  because $440.0 \div 293.7 = 1.50$ or $\frac{3}{2}$ or 3 : 2
- Frequency of A : frequency of E = 4 : 3
  because $440.0 \div 329.6 = 1.33$ or $\frac{4}{3}$ or 4 : 3

The frequencies of G and C are in the same proportion as the frequencies of A and D; these pairs of notes both have the same ratio, 3 : 2. Can you find some other ratios from the table that are equivalent to 3 : 2?

The frequencies of A and E are in the ratio 4 : 3. Can you find some other pairs of notes in the same proportion, with a ratio of 4 : 3? Can you find any pairs of notes with frequencies in the ratio 5 : 4?

Many situations in real life use ratios. Getting better at ratios is similar to playing the piano: you need to practise, practise, practise!

11.1 Using ratios

In this section you will …

- use ratios in a range of contexts.

You already know the method to share an amount in a given ratio. For example:

Question

Share \$120 between Ali, Bea and Cas in the ratio 4 : 5 : 6.

Answer

4 + 5 + 6 = 15 and 120 ÷ 15 = 8

Ali gets 4 × 8 = \$32

Bea gets 5 × 8 = \$40

Cas gets 6 × 8 = \$48

Check: 32 + 40 + 48 = \$120 ✓

You also need to be able to reverse this method to solve similar problems when you are given different pieces of information. For example:

Question

Ali, Bea and Cas share some money in the ratio 4 : 5 : 6.

Ali gets \$32.

What is the total amount of money that they share?

Worked example 11.1

A fruit drink contains orange juice and mango juice in the ratio 2 : 3.

There are 500 mL of orange juice in the drink.

a How much mango juice is in the drink?

b How much fruit juice is in the drink altogether?

Continued

Answer

a	1 part is worth $500 \div 2 = 250$ mL	2 parts of the drink is orange juice, so use division to work out the number of millilitres in 1 part (1 unit) first.
	mango juice: $3 \times 250 = 750$ mL	3 parts of the drink is mango juice, so use multiplication to work out the number of millilitres in 3 parts.
b	Total: $500 + 750 = 1250$ mL	Add the number of millilitres of orange and mango juice.
	$= 1.25$ litres	Change your answer into litres.

Exercise 11.1

1 To make a cake, Marco uses sultanas and cherries in the ratio 5 : 2.
Marco uses 80 g of cherries to make the cake.
Copy and complete the working to answer these questions.

- **a** What mass of sultanas does Marco use?
  Cherries: 2 parts = 80 g, so 1 part = 80 ÷ 2 = □
  Sultanas: 5 parts = 5 × □ = □ g
- **b** What is the total mass of sultanas and cherries in the cake?
  Total = 80 + □ = □ g

2 A fruit dessert contains raspberries and strawberries in the ratio 1 : 2. There are 400 g of strawberries in the dessert.
Copy and complete the working to answer these questions.

- **a** How many grams of raspberries are there in the dessert?
  Strawberries: 2 parts = 400 g, so 1 part = 400 ÷ 2 = □
  Raspberries: 1 part = □ g
- **b** How much fruit is there altogether in the dessert?
  Total = 400 + □ = □ g

3 Xavier and Alicia share some money in the ratio 3 : 5.
Xavier gets $75.

a How much money does Alicia get?

b What is the total amount of money that they share?

4 Kaya and Akiko share their electricity bills in the ratio 3 : 4.
In January Akiko pays $24.

a How much does Kaya pay?

b What is their total bill?

5 When Jerry makes concrete, he uses cement, sand and gravel in the ratio 1 : 2 : 4.
For one wall he uses 15 kg of sand.
Copy and complete the working to answer these questions.

a How much cement and gravel does he use?

Sand: 2 parts = 15 kg so 1 part = $15 \div 2 = \square$

Cement: 1 part = $\square$ kg

Gravel: 4 parts = $4 \times \square = \square$ kg

b What is the total mass of the concrete he makes?

Total = $15 + \square + \square = \square$ kg

6 Three children share some sweets in the ratio 4 : 7 : 9.
The child with the most sweets gets 54 sweets.

a How many sweets does each of the other children get?

b What is the total number of sweets that they share?

Think like a mathematician

7 Nia and Rhys use different methods to answer this question.

Question

Jan, Kai and Li share a water bill in the ratio 2 : 3 : 5.

Li pays $36.25.

How much is the total bill?

Continued

> *Nia writes:*
> *Total number of parts = 2 + 3 + 5 = 10*
> *Li: 5 parts = \$36.25*
> *so 1 part = 36.25 ÷ 5 = \$7.25*
> *so 10 parts = 7.25 × 10 = \$72.50*

> *Rhys writes*
> *Li: 5 parts = \$36.25 so 1 part = 36.25 ÷ 5 = \$7.25*
> *Jan: 2 parts = 7.25 × 2 = \$14.50*
> *Kai: 3 parts = 7.25 × 3 = \$21.75*
> *Total = 36.25 + 14.50 + 21.75 = \$72.50*

a Critique their methods.

b Can you think of a better method to use? If you can, write down your method.

c Compare and discuss your answers to parts **a** and **b** with other learners in the class.

8 Xavier makes some green paint.
He mixes yellow, blue and white paint in the ratio 4 : 5 : 1.
He uses 600 mL of yellow paint.

a How much blue paint does he use?

b How much green paint does he make?
Give your answer in litres.

9 The cards show the steps Ahmad uses to solve this problem.

> *Purple gold is made from gold and aluminium in the ratio 4 : 1.*
> *A purple gold bracelet has 39 g more gold than aluminium.*
> *What is the mass of the bracelet?*

Total mass = 13 + 52 = 65 g

3 parts = 39 g

1 part = 39 ÷ 3 = 13 g

Difference in number of parts = 4 − 1 = 3

4 parts = 13 × 4 = 52 g

The cards are not in the correct order.

Write the cards in the correct order.

Check all the steps to make sure the solution makes sense.

10 Moira and Non share some money in the ratio 3 : 7.

Non gets $28 more than Moira.

a What is the total amount of money that they share?

b How much money do they each get?

Think like a mathematician

11 Work with a partner to answer this question.

a Two numbers are in the ratio 2 : 3.
One of the numbers is 6.
What is the other number?

b Look back at your solution to part **a**.

i Were you able to answer the question or did you need more information?

ii How many possible answers are there to the question? Explain why.

iii Show how to check that your answers are correct.

c Discuss your answers to parts **a** and **b** with other pairs of learners in your class. Consider which Thinking and Working Mathematically characteristics you have used to answer this question.

12 Two numbers are in the ratio 8 : 3. One of the numbers is 0.48.

Work out the two possible values for the other number.

Show how to check that your answers are correct.

13 When Sofia makes oat biscuits, she uses syrup, butter and oats in the ratio 1 : 2 : 4.

Sofia makes as many oat biscuits as she can with these ingredients.

How much of each ingredient does she use? Show how you worked out your answer.

14 White gold is made from gold, palladium, nickel and zinc in the ratio 15 : 2 : 2 : 1.

A white gold ring contains 9 g of gold.

What is the mass of the ring?

15 The largest angle in a triangle is 75°.

The difference between the two other angles is 15°.

Write the ratio of the angles from smallest to biggest in its simplest form.

16 The table shows the child-to-staff ratios in a kindergarten. It also shows the number of children in each age group.

Age of children	Child : staff ratios	Number of children
up to 18 months	3 : 1	10
18 months up to 3 years	4 : 1	18
3 years up to 5 years	8 : 1	15
5 years up to 7 years	14 : 1	24

At the kindergarten there are four rooms, one for each age group in the table.

Erin thinks that 12 members of staff are needed to look after the children in this kindergarten.

What do you think? Show all your working and explain your answer.

Tip

The child : staff ratios show the maximum number of children allowed in the room for each member of staff.

So a ratio of 3 : 1 shows that there can be no more than three children for one member of staff.

Look back at the questions in this exercise.

a Which questions have you found

i the easiest **ii** the most difficult?

Explain why.

b How can you improve your skills in using ratios in different contexts?

Summary checklist

☐ I can use ratios in a range of contexts.

11.2 Direct and inverse proportion

In this section you will …

- understand the relationship between two quantities when they are in direct or inverse proportion.

Key word

inverse proportion

You already know that two quantities are in direct proportion when their ratios stay the same as they increase or decrease. For example, when you buy bottles of milk, the more bottles you buy, the more it will cost you. The two quantities, number of bottles and total cost, are in direct proportion.

When two quantities are in **inverse proportion**, as one quantity increases the other quantity decreases in the same ratio. For example, suppose it takes two people 20 minutes to wash a car. If you increase the number of people, the time taken to wash the car will decrease.

Worked example 11.2

Answer these questions and state whether the quantities are in direct or inverse proportion.

a One tin of tomatoes costs \$0.65. How much do 5 tins cost?

b It takes two people 20 minutes to wash a car. How long will it take four people to wash the car?

Answer

a Direct proportion

×5 (1 tin = \$0.65) ×5
5 tins = \$3.25

The quantities are in direct proportion because five tins of tomatoes will cost five times as much as one tin of tomatoes.

b Inverse proportion

×2 (2 people = 20 minutes) ÷2
4 people = 10 minutes

The quantities are in inverse proportion because the more people washing the car, the less time it will take. The number of people is doubled, so the time taken is halved.

Exercise 11.2

Think like a mathematician

1 Work with a partner to decide if these quantities are in direct proportion, inverse proportion or neither.

a The total cost of packets of potato chips and the number of packets bought.

b The value of a house and the age of a house.

c The time it takes to run a certain distance and the speed of the runner.

d The total mass of packets of sultanas and the number of packets.

e The number of runs scored by a cricket team and the number of players in the team.

f The time it takes to paint a fence and the number of people who are painting the fence.

g The value of a car and the age of a car.

Discuss your answers with other learners in your class.

2 Two litres of fruit juice cost \$3.50. Work out the cost of

a 4 litres

b 10 litres

c 1 litre

d 5 litres of fruit juice.

3 Here is a recipe for rice pudding.

a How much sugar is needed for 8 people?

b How much rice is needed for 6 people?

c How much milk is needed for 10 people? Give your answer in litres.

Rice pudding
(Serves 4 people)
100 g rice
25 g sugar
750 ml milk

4 Four horses can eat a bale of hay in two days.
Copy and complete the working for these questions.

a How long does it take one horse to eat a bale of hay?

÷4 (4 horses = 2 days) ×4
1 horse = □ days

b How long does it take eight horses to eat a bale of hay?

×2 (4 horses = 2 days) ÷2
8 horses = □ days

5 It takes Dieter 36 seconds to run a certain distance.

Copy and complete the working for these questions.

a Dieter halves his speed. How long will it take him to run the same distance?

$\div 2$ normal speed = 36 seconds $\times 2$

$\frac{1}{2}$ speed = ☐ seconds

b Dieter runs three times as fast. How long will it take him to run the same distance?

$\times 3$ normal speed = 36 seconds $\div 3$

$3 \times$ speed = ☐ seconds

6 It takes Julia 40 minutes to drive to work at an average speed of 60 km/h.

a Julia drives at an average speed of 120 km/h. How long will it take Julia to drive to work?

b It takes Julia 80 minutes to drive to work. What is Julia's average speed?

7 It costs a fixed amount to hire a villa in Spain. Up to 12 people can stay in the villa.

Antonio hires the villa for his family of four people. The cost per person is €300.

Copy and complete the table.

Number of people	4	12	2	1	6	10	5
Cost per person (€)	300						

Think like a mathematician

8 Work with a partner to answer this question.

Bengt and Susu are working out the answer to this question.

Question

9 men can build a house in 28 days.

How long will it take 12 men to build the house?

Continued

Bengt writes:

$\div 9$ (9 men : 28 days) $\times 9$

1 man : 252 days

$\times 12$ (12 men : 21 days) $\div 12$

Susu writes:

$12 \div 9 = \frac{12}{9} = \frac{4}{3}$

$28 \div \frac{4}{3} = 28 \times \frac{3}{4} = 21$ days

a Critique their methods.

b Can you think of a different method to use? If you can, write it down.

c What is your favourite method?

d Compare and discuss your answers to parts **a** to **c** with other pairs of learners in the class.

9 It takes 6 people 4 hours to sort and pack a load of eggs.

How long will it take 10 people to sort and pack the same number of eggs?

Give your answer in hours and minutes.

10 Arun and Marcus are looking at this question.

Question

At a theme park, there are 36 people on a roller coaster.

The ride takes 4 minutes.

How long does the ride take when there are 18 people on the roller coaster?

Arun says:

Marcus says:

a What do you think? Justify your answer.

b Discuss your answer to part **a** with a partner.

Activity 11.2

Work with a partner for this activity.

a Take it in turns to choose one of these information cards.

It takes 2 people 6 days to paint a house.	A recipe uses 200 g of flour to make 12 biscuits.
With \$1 (USA) you can buy €0.8 (euros).	80 chickens eat a bag of corn in one day.
Tim can cycle to school in 30 minutes.	4 cleaners clean a holiday home in $2\frac{1}{2}$ hours.

b Use the information card you have chosen to write a question for your partner. Make sure you work out the answer. Write the answer on a separate piece of paper.

c Ask your partner to answer your question, then check their answer and working. Discuss any mistakes that have been made.

d Do this three times each, so you use all the cards.

11 In a science experiment, Camila measures how far a ball bounces when she drops it from different heights. The table shows her results.

Height when dropped (cm)	50	100	150	200	250
Height of bounce (cm)	40	80	120	160	200

a Do Camila's results show that the height of the drop and the height of the bounce are in direct proportion? Explain your answer.

b How high does the ball bounce when it is dropped from a height of 120 cm?

c i Make a copy of this coordinate grid and plot the points in the table on the grid.

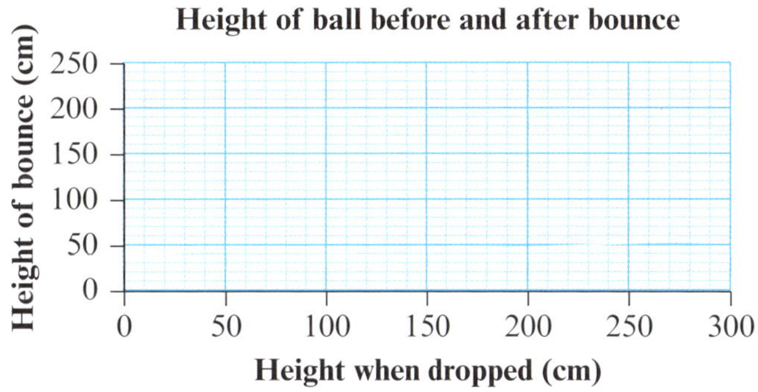

ii What do you notice about the points?

iii Is it possible to draw a straight line through all the points?

iv Camila drops the ball and it bounces back up 180 cm. Use your graph to work out the height from which she dropped the ball.

12 In a science experiment, Abnar measures the increase in the length of a string when it has different masses attached. The table shows his results.

Mass (g)	20	30	40	50
Increase in length (mm)	12	18	24	30

a What type of proportion do Abnar's results show? Explain your answer.

b Draw a graph to show Abnar's results. Draw a straight line through all the points.

c Use your graph to work out

i the increase in length when a mass of 45 g is attached

ii the mass attached when the increase in length is 20 mm.

d Is the following statement true or false? Explain your answer.

'When two quantities are in direct proportion, you can draw a straight-line graph to show the relationship between the two quantities.'

Summary checklist

☐ I can understand the relationship between two quantities when they are in direct or inverse proportion.

Check your progress

1 A fruit conserve contains blackcurrants and redcurrants in the ratio 5 : 2.

There are 300 g of redcurrants in the conserve.

a How many grams of blackcurrants are in the conserve?

b How much fruit is in the conserve altogether?

2 Four children share some strawberries in the ratio 6 : 8 : 10 : 14.

The child with the fewest strawberries gets 18 strawberries.

a How many strawberries does each of the other children get?

b What is the total number of strawberries that they share?

3 To make scones, Arun uses sugar, butter and flour in the ratio 1 : 2 : 8.

Arun makes as many scones as he can with these ingredients.

How much of each ingredient does he use?

4 Lian delivers leaflets. She is paid \$12 for delivering 400 leaflets.

How much is she paid for delivering

a 200 leaflets b 600 leaflets c 150 leaflets?

5 It takes 3 people 4 days to build a garage.

a How long does it take one person to build the garage?

b How long does it take four people to build the garage?

c How many people are needed to build the garage in 2 days?

12 Probability

Getting started

1 The probability it will rain tomorrow is 0.15.
Work out the probability it will not rain tomorrow.

2 A coin is flipped and a dice is rolled.

a Copy and complete this table of outcomes.

H 1			H 4		
T 1					T 6

b Work out the probability of

i head and 6

ii tail and an odd number.

3 A spinner has 5 different coloured sectors. In 50 spins it lands on red 13 times.

a Work out the experimental probability of landing on red.

b If each colour is equally likely, work out the theoretical probability of landing on red.

4 Work out

a $\frac{1}{5} + \frac{3}{5}$

b $\frac{1}{5} \times \frac{3}{5}$

c $\frac{3}{8} + \frac{1}{4}$

d $\frac{3}{8} \times \frac{1}{4}$

Tip

H 1 = head and 1,
T 6 = tail and 6

On Sunday 3 June 2012 there was a Jubilee Pageant in London. One thousand boats travelled down the River Thames through the city of London. The pageant was held to celebrate the fact that Queen Elizabeth II had been on the throne for 60 years. The pageant started at 14:30 and lasted about 3 hours. The chart shows a weather forecast for London on that day.

City of London Youth Hostel
Sun 3 Jun

UK local time	Regional warnings	Weather	Temperature (°C)	Wind speed & direction (mph)	Wind gusts (mph)	Visibility	Humidity (%)	Precipitation Probability (%)	Feels like (°C)	UV index	Air Quality index [BETA]
0100	No warnings		10	11	24	Moderate	91	80	8	0	
0400	No warnings		10	12	26	Moderate	95	80	8	0	
0700	No warnings		10	11	24	Moderate	95	80	7	1	
1000	No warnings		10	10	No gusts	Moderate	93	80	8	1	2
1300	No warnings		10	8	No gusts	Moderate	94	80	8	1	
1600	No warnings		10	7	No gusts	Moderate	92	80	8	1	
1900	No warnings		10	6	No gusts	Moderate	91	60	8	1	
2200	No warnings		9	5	No gusts	Moderate	93	60	8	0	

Issued at 0900 on Fri 1 Jun 2012

The forecast was made on Friday morning, two days before the pageant. It predicted the weather every three hours through the day. One column shows the probability of precipitation – that means rain or snow. The probability is given as a percentage. The forecast reported an 80% chance of heavy rain during the pageant. The thousands of spectators were advised to take umbrellas. The forecast predicted no gusts of wind during the pageant.

Weather forecasts are produced by complicated computer programs. They are available for thousands of places throughout the world. Weather forecasts are updated regularly. You can easily find them on the internet. Try to find a weather forecast for a place near where you live.

On the day of the pageant, it was dry until about 16:00. After that it rained steadily. There were no gusts of wind. In this unit, you will learn more about predicting probabilities.

12.1 Mutually exclusive events

In this section you will …

- learn how to use addition to find probabilities
- use the fact that the total probability of all possible mutually exclusive events is 1.

Key word

mutually exclusive

There are 25 balls, numbered from 1 to 25, in a bag.

1 2 3 4 5 6 7 8 9 10 11 12 13 14 15 16 17 18 19 20 21 22 23 24 25

One ball is taken out at random. Here are some possible events:

- F: The number on the ball is a multiple of 5
- S: The number on the ball is a multiple of 7
- N: The number on the ball is a multiple of 9

These events are **mutually exclusive**. This means only one of them can happen at one time. The multiples of 5 in the bag are 5, 10, 15, 20 and 25, so the probability of event F, P(F) = $\frac{5}{25} = \frac{1}{5}$. Similarly, the probability of S, P(S) = $\frac{3}{25}$ and the probability of N, P(N) = $\frac{2}{25}$.

Tip

P(F) means the probability of event F.

The probability that F does **not** happen is $1 - \frac{1}{5} = \frac{4}{5}$. The probability that S does **not** happen is $1 - \frac{3}{25} = \frac{22}{25}$.

What is the probability that F **or** S happens? This means you get 5, 10, 15, 20, 25, 7, 14 **or** 21. There are 8 numbers, so the probability of F or S, P(F or S) = $\frac{8}{25}$. There is an easier way to work this out: just add the probabilities of the separate events.

Tip

This works because the events are mutually exclusive.

- P(F or S) = P(F) + P(S) = $\frac{5}{25} + \frac{3}{25} = \frac{8}{25}$
- P(S or N) = P(S) + P(N) = $\frac{3}{25} + \frac{2}{25} = \frac{5}{25} = \frac{1}{5}$
- P(F or S or N) = $\frac{5}{25} + \frac{3}{25} + \frac{2}{25} = \frac{10}{25} = \frac{2}{5}$

The probability that none of F or S or N happens is $1 - \frac{2}{5} = \frac{3}{5}$

Worked example 12.1

A spinner has sections in different colours.

The probability of landing on red is 0.35. The probability of landing on blue is 0.2.
The probability of landing on gold is 0.1.

Work out the probability of landing on

a red or blue

b neither blue nor gold.

Answer

a Probability of red or blue = probability of red + probability of blue = 0.35 + 0.2 = 0.55

b Probability of blue or gold = 0.2 + 0.1 = 0.3

So the probability of neither is 1 − 0.3 = 0.7

Exercise 12.1

1 The probability a football team will win its next match is 60%.
The probability it will draw is 15%.
Work out the probability it will lose.

2 You roll a fair dice.
Work out the probability of rolling

a a 3 **b** an even number

c a 3 or an even number.

3 Here are 10 numbered cards.

2	2	2	2	3	3	4	5	5	5

A card is chosen at random.
Find the probability that the number on the card is

a 2 **b** 5

c 2 or 5 **d** neither 2 nor 5.

4 A bag contains a large number of coloured balls. The balls are yellow, green, brown, blue and pink.

P(yellow) = 0.1 P(green) = 0.25 P(brown) = 0.35 P(blue) = 0.05

A ball is taken out of the bag at random.
Work out the probability that the ball is

a green or blue **b** brown or yellow

c yellow, green or brown **d** pink

5 You roll 2 dice and find the total.

The probability of a total of 2 is 0.028

The probability of a total of 3 is 0.056

Work out the probability that the total is

a 2 or 3

b more than 3.

6 The temperature each day at midday can be low, average, high or very high.

The forecast for Monday is

P(low) = 0.15 P(average) = 0.55 P(high) = 0.25

Work out the probability that the temperature on Monday is

a not low

b low or average

c very high.

7 There are 50 people in a room. There are 7 girls, 13 boys and 19 women. The rest of the people are men.

One person is chosen at random.

Work out the probability that the person is

a a child

b a female

c an adult

d a male.

8 The letters of the word MUTUALLY are written on separate cards. One card is chosen at random. Work out the probability that the letter on the card is

a M

b U

c L

d M, U or L

e not M, U or L.

9 There are red, white, green and black counters in a box.

A counter is taken out at random.

The probability the counter is red is 0.55.

The other three colours are all equally likely.

Find the probability the counter is

a not red

b red or white.

10 A spinner has three sectors labelled A, B and C.

The probability of landing on A is twice the probability of landing on B.

The probability of landing on B is twice the probability of landing on C.

Work out the probability of landing on each letter.

11 There are counters of four different colours in a bag. A counter is taken out at random.

This table shows the probabilities of different colours.

Colour	gold	silver	bronze	white
Probability	0.05	0.15		0.55

Find the probability that the counter is

a gold or silver **b** not gold

c silver or bronze.

12 A calculator generates a random number between 1 and 100 inclusive.

Find the probability the number is

a a multiple of 10 **b** a multiple of 11

c a multiple of 10 or 11 **d** not a multiple of 10 or 11.

Tip

'Between 1 and 100 inclusive' means 1 and 100 are included in the possible numbers.

Think like a mathematician

13 You want to put black, white and yellow counters in a bag.

One counter will be chosen at random.

You want P(black) = $\frac{1}{4}$ and P(white) = $\frac{2}{3}$

a Work out P(yellow).

b What is a suitable number of counters of each colour to put in the bag? Give a reason for your answer.

Summary checklist

- [ ] I can use addition to work out probabilities of mutually exclusive events.
- [ ] I can use the fact that the total probability for mutually exclusive events is 1.

12.2 Independent events

In this section you will ...

- learn about independent events
- use probabilities to show whether two events are independent or not.

Key word

independent events

You flip a coin and then you roll a dice. Here are two events.

- A: a head on the coin
- B: a 4 on the dice

If A happens, the coin lands on a head. Then the probability of 4, P(4) = $\frac{1}{6}$. If A does **not** happen, the coin lands on a tail. Then the probability of 4, P(4), is still $\frac{1}{6}$. Whether A happens or not does not affect the probability of B. You say that A and B are **independent events**.

Now suppose you have 10 balls, numbered from 1 to 10, in a bag. You take out one ball at random. Here are two events.

- C: the number is odd
- D: the number is less than 4

Suppose C happens. The number is 1, 3, 5, 7 or 9. Two of these numbers are less than 4, and so P(D) = $\frac{2}{5}$. Now suppose C does **not** happen. The number is 2, 4, 6, 8 or 10. Only one of these numbers is less than 4, so now P(D) = $\frac{1}{5}$. The probabilities are **not** the same and so C and D are **not** independent events. Whether C happens or not **does** affect the probability of D.

Worked example 12.2

You roll a fair dice.

Here are three events.

- X: the number is even
- Y: the number is more than 2
- Z: the number is a prime number

a Show that X and Y are independent events.

b Show that X and Z are not independent events.

Continued

Answer

a Suppose X happens. The number is 2, 4 or 6.
Two of these three numbers are more than 2, and so $P(Y) = \frac{2}{3}$
Suppose X does not happen. Then the number is 1, 3 or 5.
Two of these three numbers are more than 2, and so $P(Y) = \frac{2}{3}$
P(Y) has not changed, and so X and Y are independent.

b Suppose X happens. The number is 2, 4 or 6.
Only one of these numbers is a prime number, and so $P(Z) = \frac{1}{3}$
Suppose X does not happen. Then the number is 1, 3 or 5.
Two of these numbers (3 and 5) are prime numbers, and so $P(Z) = \frac{2}{3}$
P(Z) is not the same in both cases, and so the events X and Z are not independent.

Exercise 12.2

1 A coin is flipped twice. Here are two events.
F: the first flip is a head S: the second flip is a head
Explain why F and S are independent events.

2 A fair dice is rolled. Here are two events.
A: the number is 2, 3 or 4 B: the number is 1 or 2
Show that A and B are independent events.

3 A coin is flipped three times. Here are two events.
X: the first two flips are tails Y: all three flips are tails
Are X and Y independent events? Give a reason for your answer.

4 A fair coin is flipped ten times.
Here are two events.
A: the first nine flips are heads B: the tenth flip is a head
Are A and B independent? Give a reason for your answer.

5 Here are two events.
A: there is fog at the airport B: the flight to Dubai leaves on time
Explain why these events are not independent.

6 There are ten cards in a pack.

Six cards have the numbers 1, 2, 3, 4, 5, 6 in red.

Four cards have the numbers 1, 2, 3, 4 in black.

1	4	3	6	3	1	2	4	5	2

a Here are two events.

R: the number is red E: the number is even

Are these independent events? Give a reason for your answer.

b Here are two events.

B: the number is black T: the number is 2

Are these independent events? Give a reason for your answer.

7 There are ten balls in a bag. Three balls are black and seven balls are white.

a One ball is chosen at random and then replaced. Then a second ball is chosen at random.

Here are two events.

F: the first ball is black S: the second ball is black

Are F and S independent? Give a reason for your answer.

b The situation is the same as in part **a**, but this time the first ball is **not** replaced.

Are F and S independent in this case? Give a reason for your answer.

8 Arun and Sofia attend the same school. Here are two events.

A: Arun is late for school S: Sofia is late for school

a Describe how A and S could be independent events.

b Describe how A and S could be events that are not independent.

9 Here are five cards.

A	B	C	D	E

A card is chosen at random.

Here are two events.

X: the letter is in the word CARD Y: the letter is in the word CODE

Are these events independent? Give a reason for your answer, using probabilities.

Summary checklist

☐ I can explain whether two events are independent or not.

12.3 Combined events

In this section you will …

- calculate the probability that two independent events both happen
- use a tree diagram to calculate the probabilities of different outcomes.

If two events are independent, you can find the probability that **both** events will happen by **multiplying** the separate probabilities. Suppose you flip a coin and roll a fair dice.

- The probability of a head on the coin, P(head) = $\frac{1}{2}$
- The probability of more than 2 on the dice, P(more than 2) = $\frac{4}{6} = \frac{2}{3}$
- The probability of both, P(head and more than 2) = $\frac{1}{2} \times \frac{2}{3} = \frac{2}{6} = \frac{1}{3}$

When you have two independent events, you can use a tree diagram to show the outcomes and to calculate the probabilities.

Worked example 12.3

Here are two spinners. Each spinner is spun once.

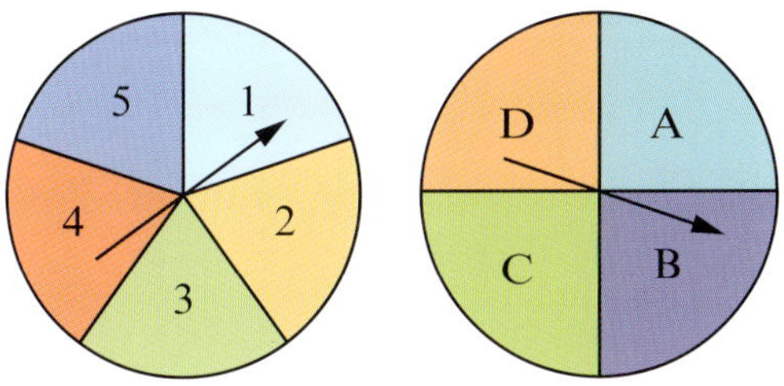

Find the probability of landing on

a an odd number and the letter A

b neither an odd number nor the letter A.

Answer

P(odd) = $\frac{3}{5}$ P(A) = $\frac{1}{4}$

P(not odd) = P(even) = $\frac{2}{5}$ P(not A) = $1 - \frac{1}{4} = \frac{3}{4}$

Continued

You can draw a tree diagram to show the four possible outcomes:

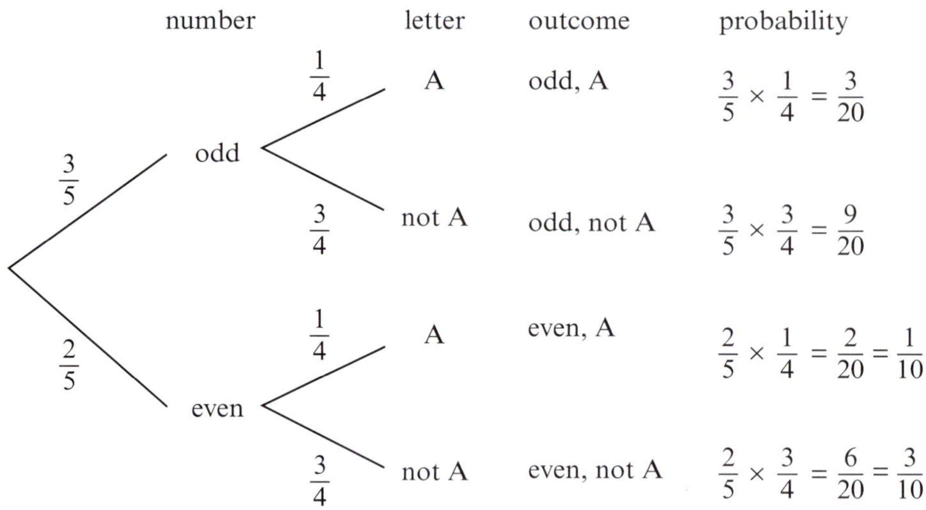

Write the probabilities on the branches and multiply them to find the probability of the outcome.

a P(odd and A) = P(odd) × P(A) = $\frac{3}{5} \times \frac{1}{4} = \frac{3}{20}$

b P(even and not A) = P(even) × P(not A) = $\frac{2}{5} \times \frac{3}{4} = \frac{6}{20} = \frac{3}{10}$

You can see in the tree diagram in Worked example 12.3 that there are four possible outcomes. The probability of each outcome is the product of the probabilities on the branches. The sum of the four probabilities is 1:

$\frac{3}{20} + \frac{9}{20} + \frac{2}{20} + \frac{6}{20} = \frac{20}{20} = 1$

Exercise 12.3

1 An unbiased coin is flipped twice. Work out the probability of

a 2 heads **b** 2 tails

c a head and then a tail.

2 A fair dice is rolled twice. Find the probability of

a a 5 and then a 3

b an even number and then a 6

c a 2 and then an odd number.

3 A fair dice is rolled twice. Work out the probability of

a a multiple of 3 and then an even number

b a multiple of 3 both times

c not getting a 6 either time.

4 A spinner has two colours, red and green.
P(red) = 0.3 and P(green) = 0.7
The spinner is spun twice. Work out the probability of landing on

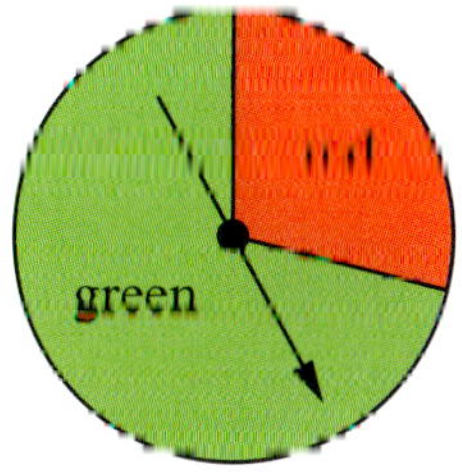

a red both times **b** green both times
c red and then green **d** green and then red.

5 City and United are football teams.
The probability that City will win their next match is 0.8.
The probability that United will win their next match is 0.6.
They are not playing each other in their next match.
Work out the probability that

a both teams win their next match **b** City wins but United does not
c United wins but City does not **d** neither team wins its next match.

6 The probability that Arun is late for school is 0.1.
The probability that Marcus is late for school is 0.15.
These are independent events.

a Work out the probability that
   i they are both late for school
   ii Arun is late but Marcus is not
   iii Marcus is late but Arun is not
   iv neither of them is late for school.

b Check that the sum of your four answers in part **a** is 1. Why is this?

7 When you roll two dice and add the two numbers, the probability of a total of 5 is $\frac{1}{9}$.
Sofia rolls two dice twice. She is trying to get a total of 5 each time.

a Use Resource sheet 12.3 to complete this tree diagram. Put probabilities on the branches.

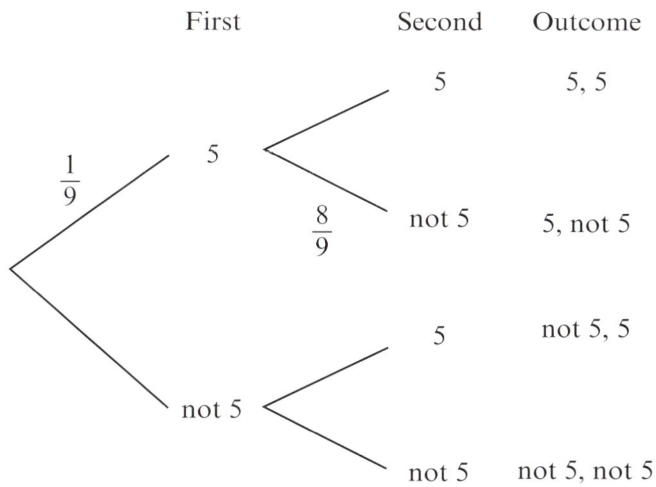

b Find the probabilities of the following events.

  i Sofia gets 5 both times.

  ii Sofia does not get a 5 either time.

  iii Sofia gets a 5 the first time but not the second time.

  vi Sofia does not get a 5 the first time but does get a 5 the second time.

c There are four possible outcomes on the tree diagram. Which of those four outcomes is the most likely? Explain your answer.

8 A driver goes through two sets of traffic lights on the way to work.

The probability the first light is red is 0.3

The probability the second light is red is 0.6

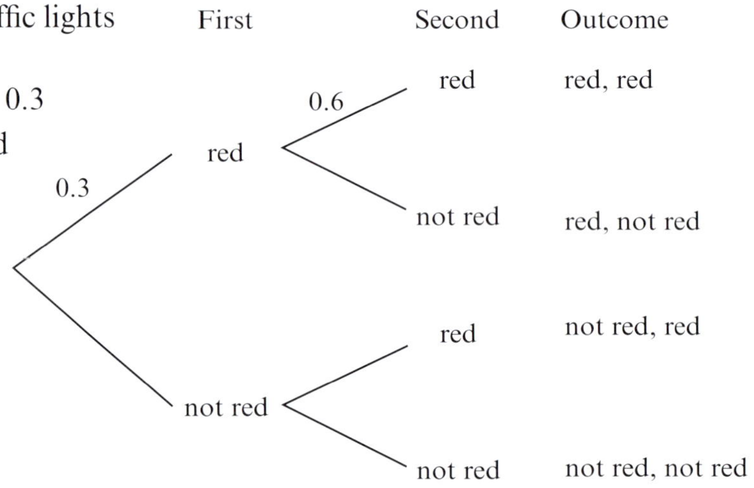

a Complete this tree diagram on Resource sheet 12.3.

b Find the probability that

  i both lights are red

  ii neither light is red

  iii the first light is red but the second light is not red

  iv only the second light is red.

c Show that the sum of the probabilities in part **b** is 1. Why is this?

9 Zara is birdwatching.

The probability she sees a blackbird is 0.9.

The probability she sees a robin is 0.8.

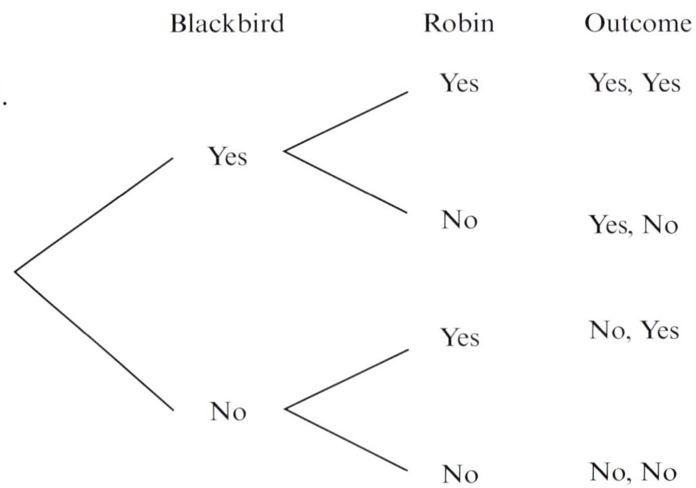

a Complete this tree diagram on Resource sheet 12.3. It shows whether she sees each type of bird.

b Work out the probability that Zara sees

  i both birds

  ii neither bird.

c Work out the probability that Zara sees at least one of the birds.

10 Here are two spinners. The spinners show the probability of landing on each colour.

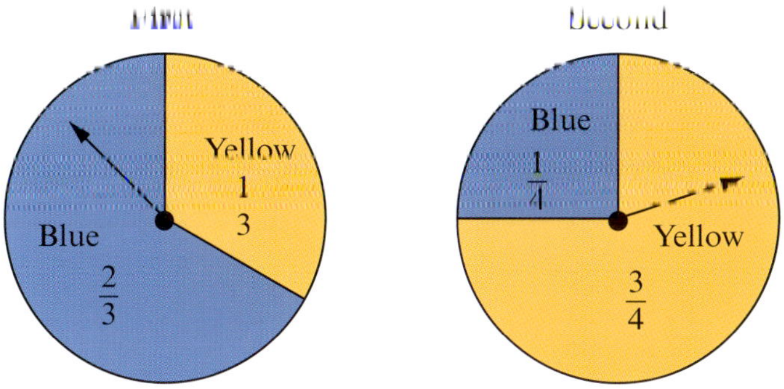

Each spinner is spun once.

a Complete the tree diagram on Resource sheet 12.3.

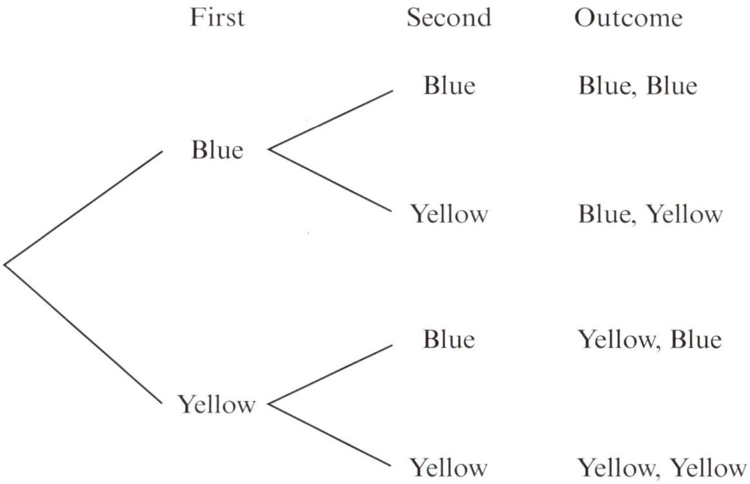

b Work out the probability of landing on

i blue both times **ii** yellow both times **iii** blue and then yellow

iv blue at least once **v** yellow at least once.

11 Zara throws a ball at a basketball hoop twice.

The probability that she gets a basket the first time is 0.4.

The probability that she gets a basket the second time is 0.9.

a Zara could get a basket either time. Show the probabilities of the different possible outcomes in a diagram.

b What is the most likely outcome?

c Find the probability that Zara gets at least one basket.

Summary checklist

- ☐ I can calculate the probability of two events by multiplying probabilities.
- ☐ I can use a tree diagram to find probabilities.

12.4 Chance experiments

In this section you will …

- carry out and analyse experiments involving chance
- look at experiments with large and small sample sizes
- compare relative frequencies with probabilities.

Key word

relative frequency

Zara rolls a dice 50 times. She is looking for sixes. Here are the results.

2	1	6	5	3	3	1	6	4	4
6	1	3	3	5	6	5	5	3	6
6	3	4	4	5	6	1	4	1	2
3	2	3	6	6	6	5	3	5	3
3	5	5	4	5	6	3	1	5	1

The top row shows the first ten rolls. The frequency of a 6 in the top row is 2. The **relative frequency** of a 6 after the first ten rolls is $\frac{2}{10} = 0.2$. After 20 rolls, the frequency of a 6 is 5 and the relative frequency is $\frac{5}{20} = 0.25$. This table shows the changing relative frequency:

Rolls	10	20	30	40	50
Frequency	2	5	7	10	11
Relative frequency	0.2	0.25	0.233	0.25	0.22

You can show these values on a graph:

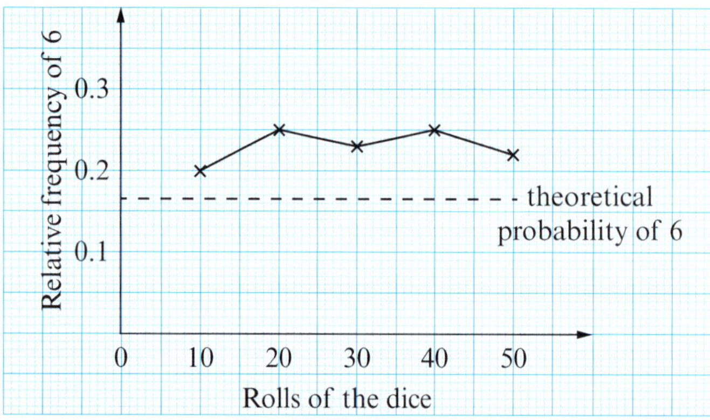

The theoretical probability of getting a 6 when you roll a dice is $\frac{1}{6} = 0.167$ to 3 d.p. The relative frequency will keep changing as Zara rolls the dice more times.

Exercise 12.4

1 Two coins are flipped together 25 times. Both coins land on tails 3 times.

a Work out the relative frequency of two tails.

The experiment is repeated. This time both coins land on tails 7 times.

b Work out the relative frequency of two tails for the second experiment.

c Put the two sets of results together and work out the relative frequency of two tails.

2 Here is a spinner. The spinner is spun 200 times.

This table gives the frequencies of each colour:

Colour	red	white	blue
Frequency	78	54	68

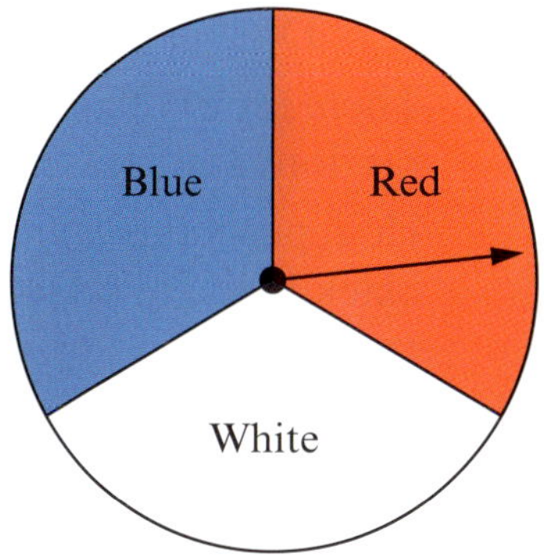

a Work out the relative frequency of each colour. Give your answers as decimals.

b Each colour is equally likely. Compare the relative frequencies with the probability of each colour.

3 Marcus rolls a dice 100 times. He counts the total number of sixes after each set of 10 rolls. Here are his results:

Rolls	10	20	30	40	50	60	70	80	90	100
Total frequency	2	4	5	8	9	10	11	16	17	18
Relative frequency	0.2	0.2	0.167							0.18

a Copy and complete the table. Round the relative frequencies to 3 decimal places if necessary.

b Draw a graph to show how the relative frequency changes.

c Draw a horizontal line to show the probability of a 6.

4 Sofia flips a coin 100 times. She records the frequency of heads every 20 flips.

Here are the results:

Flips	20	40	60	80	100
Frequency of heads	8	19	30	38	44
Relative frequency	0.4				

a Calculate the missing relative frequencies. Copy and complete the table.

b Draw a graph to show the changing relative frequencies.

c Compare the relative frequencies with the probability of the coin landing on a head.

5 You can answer this question with a partner. You will need two dice.

a Roll two dice. Record whether the total is 7 or more. Repeat this 50 times. After each 10 rolls, work out the relative frequency of 7 or more. Record your results in a table as shown.

Rolls of two dice	10	20	30	40	50
Frequency of 7 or more					
Relative frequency					

b Show your relative frequencies on a graph.

c Use your graph to estimate the probability of a total of 7 or more.

d Compare your results with another pair. Do you have similar graphs? Do you have the same estimate for the probability?

6 There are 20 black and white balls in a bag. Arun takes out one ball at random and records the colour. Then he replaces the ball in the bag.

He repeats this 200 times. After every 20 balls, he counts the frequency of a black ball.

Here are his results:

Draws	20	40	60	80	100	120	140	160	180	200
Frequency	10	14	27	36	42	50	55	62	70	79
Relative frequency	0.5									

a Calculate the relative frequencies. Copy and complete the table.

b Show the relative frequencies on a graph.

c Estimate the numbers of black and white balls in the bag.

7 A calculator generates random digits between 0 and 9.

Arun generates 100 digits.

After each 20 digits he counts the number of 0s.

Digits	20	40	60	80	100
Frequency of 0	2	5	7	7	8
Relative frequency					

a Calculate the relative frequencies. Copy and complete the table.

b Show Arun's relative frequencies on a graph.

Marcus carries out the same experiment. Here are his results:

Digits	20	40	60	80	100
Frequency of 0	2	6	8	9	15
Relative frequency					

c Calculate the relative frequencies for Marcus. Copy and complete the table.

d Show Marcus' expected frequencies on the same graph as Arun's.

Sofia generates 500 digits. She finds the frequency of 0 after every 100 digits. Here are Sofia's results:

Digits	100	200	300	400	500
Frequency of 0	11	27	40	52	60
Relative frequency					

e Work out Sofia's relative frequencies. Copy and complete the table.

f Show Sofia's relative frequencies on a graph.

g What is the probability that a digit is 0? Compare this probability with the relative frequencies in the three experiments.

Think like a mathematician

8 You can work with a partner on this question.

Here is a table of 500 random digits between 0 and 9 generated by a spreadsheet.

5 0 2 1 3	4 4 5 0 1	2 0 3 2 4	2 9 1 7 3	6 7 8 5 8
3 0 0 3 5	9 1 5 8 8	0 7 5 1 3	8 7 0 8 4	8 2 6 6 6
7 5 7 9 1	5 7 3 0 6	0 5 9 1 0	2 6 5 0 2	8 1 9 7 4
9 5 1 7 7	3 5 0 1 7	6 4 2 1 6	4 1 9 3 8	0 4 5 7 4
9 0 2 6 9	8 5 1 7 4	4 3 2 1 2	9 1 6 8 5	9 8 2 4 1
4 1 0 5 3	5 5 0 7 9	4 7 0 9 0	7 7 6 2 6	6 9 5 0 4
1 9 2 8 2	2 0 0 2 7	9 9 0 7 5	4 0 3 1 7	0 3 5 2 8
2 2 8 5 0	2 2 1 8 1	5 3 0 7 4	9 2 3 8 6	3 9 2 4 6
9 0 5 4 2	0 4 8 1 6	4 3 9 9 2	9 2 3 0 6	5 3 6 6 4
3 2 1 9 6	0 8 7 5 2	4 1 1 6 3	2 0 3 4 4	7 1 6 0 6
9 2 4 6 2	6 0 0 7 2	9 8 8 6 4	7 6 4 8 5	7 6 8 2 2
2 4 0 7 0	2 9 6 2 9	2 4 1 9 7	6 8 8 2 1	3 0 7 3 1
2 5 0 4 7	2 9 8 1 6	5 6 7 0 4	9 9 4 2 1	4 7 2 2 6
6 1 9 7 7	6 6 3 9 7	4 6 8 1 3	9 4 1 5 2	2 2 4 1 5
3 7 7 0 8	6 0 9 4 1	1 2 7 5 9	2 6 8 2 8	7 7 0 9 0
5 6 3 9 4	7 6 1 7 0	0 3 3 8 7	4 6 3 0 6	8 1 9 9 6
8 8 8 2 7	1 3 2 3 4	2 9 7 3 3	7 8 2 6 9	7 7 3 8 5
7 1 8 0 0	2 4 1 4 0	0 4 4 0 3	0 9 2 0 3	7 5 2 6 2
9 1 9 3 8	9 5 8 4 8	7 6 9 9 6	1 8 4 5 8	5 0 0 5 9
2 1 9 1 2	4 6 5 1 3	8 5 3 6 6	9 5 6 6 5	8 9 5 0 7

The probability that a digit has a particular value is 0.1.

Continued

a Choose a sample of digits and find the relative frequency of one digit. You can choose the digit and the sample size.

b Repeat the experiment with a different sample of digits. Use the same digit and the same sample size.

c Compare the results of your experiments and the probability.

d Design a similar experiment of your own. You can choose your own sample size. You could look at the combined frequency of several digits instead of just one digit. Compare your relative frequency with an appropriate probability.

Summary checklist

- [ ] I can analyse the results of an experiment involving chance.
- [ ] I can calculate relative frequencies and compare them with a probability.

Check your progress

1 Two fair dice are rolled and the sum of the two numbers is found.

  a Describe two mutually exclusive events.

  b Describe two events that are not mutually exclusive.

2 A fair dice is rolled. Here are three events.

  X: even number Y: multiple of 3 Z: less than 4

  a Show that X and Y are independent events.

  b Show that X and Z are not independent events.

3 A bag contains ten balls. Six of the balls are green.

  A ball is chosen at random.

  The ball is replaced and then a second ball is chosen at random.

  Work out the probability that

  a both balls are green b neither ball is green.

4 A spinner has five equal sectors coloured red, green, black, yellow and white.

  The spinner is spun 20 times. It lands on black 4 times.

  a Work out the relative frequency of black.

  The spinner is spun another 30 times. It lands on black another 7 times.

  b Work out the relative frequency of black for all 50 spins.

  c Compare the relative frequency with the probability of black.

13 Position and transformation

Getting started

1 Draw diagrams to show these bearings of B from A.
For each bearing start with the diagram shown.

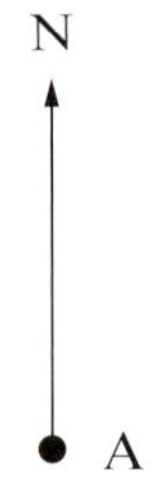

a 060° b 155°
c 220° d 305°

2 A map has a scale of 1 : 200 000.
a On the map, the distance between two villages is 8 cm.
What is the distance, in km, between the two villages in real life?
b The distance between two towns is 60 km in real life.
What is the distance, in cm, between the two towns on the map?

3 Work out the midpoint of the line segments joining these pairs of points.
a (4, 8) and (12, 8) b (3, 10) and (7, 6)

4 The diagram shows shapes A and B on a coordinate grid.

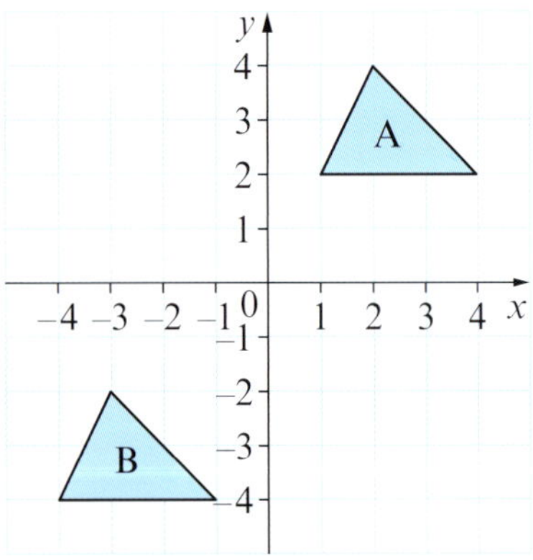

Write the column vector that translates
a shape A to shape B b shape B to shape A.

Continued

5 Make a copy of this diagram.

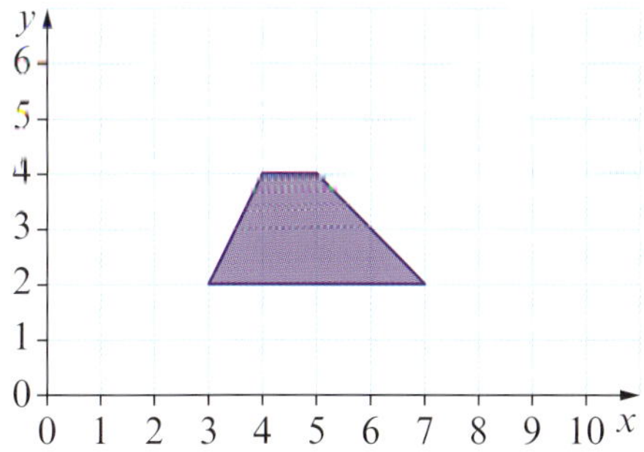

a Reflect the shape in the line $y = 4$. Label the image (a).

b Reflect the shape in the line $x = 6$. Label the image (b).

6 The diagram shows triangles P and Q.

Describe the rotation that takes P to Q.

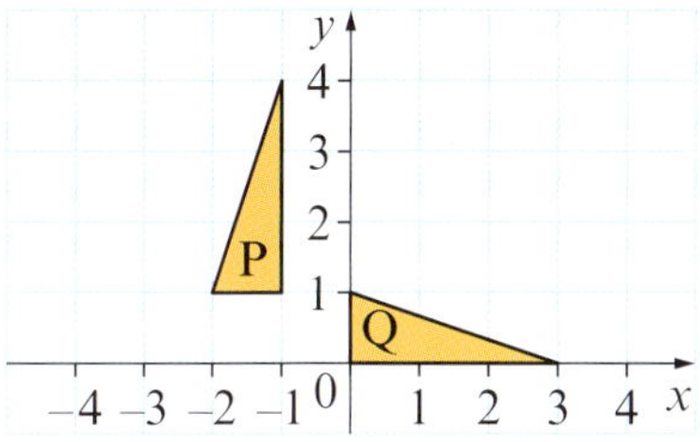

7 Copy this shape on to squared paper.

Enlarge the shape by scale factor 2 using the centre of enlargement shown.

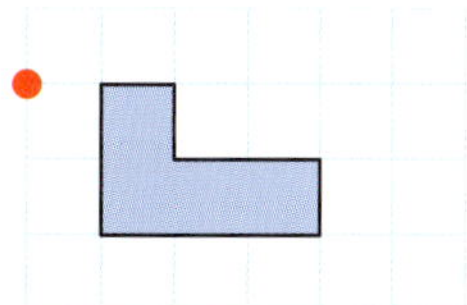

In stages 7 and 8 you transformed 2D shapes by reflecting, translating or rotating them. Look at this repeating wallpaper pattern:

- There is a pattern with three flowers on the left. What symmetry does this pattern have?
- The three-flower pattern on the left is rotated to form the middle three-flower pattern. Where is the centre of rotation? What is the angle of rotation?

- The three-flower pattern on the left can be reflected or translated to give the three-flower pattern on the right. Where is the mirror line for the reflection?

With any of these three transformations, the shape only changes its position. It does not change its shape or size. The object and its image are always identical in shape and size. They are congruent.

When you draw an enlargement of a 2D shape, the object and its image are **not** congruent because you change the size of the shape.

Tip

Remember:

- reflection, rotation and translation → congruent shapes
- enlargement → not congruent shapes

13.1 Bearings and scale drawings

In this section you will ...

- use bearings and scaling to interpret position on maps and plans.

In Stage 7 you did some work on scale drawings. You know that you can write a scale in three ways:

- using the word 'represents', for example, '1 cm represents 100 cm'
- using the word 'to', for example, '1 to 100'
- using a ratio sign, for example, '1 : 100'.

In Stage 8 you did some work on bearings. You know that:

- a bearing describes the direction of one object from another
- a bearing is an angle measured from north in a clockwise direction
- a bearing can have any value from 0° to 360°
- a bearing is always written with three figures.

You can use bearings in scale drawings to help you to solve problems. When you make a scale drawing, make sure you always measure the lengths and angles accurately.

Worked example 13.1

a Tia cycles on a bearing of 280° for 20 km.
Make a scale drawing of Tia's journey. Use a scale of 1 cm represents 5 km.

b A ship leaves a harbour and sails 120 km on a bearing of 085°. The ship then sails 90 km on a bearing of 135°.
Make a scale drawing of the ship's journey. Use a scale of 1 cm represents 10 km.

Answer

a

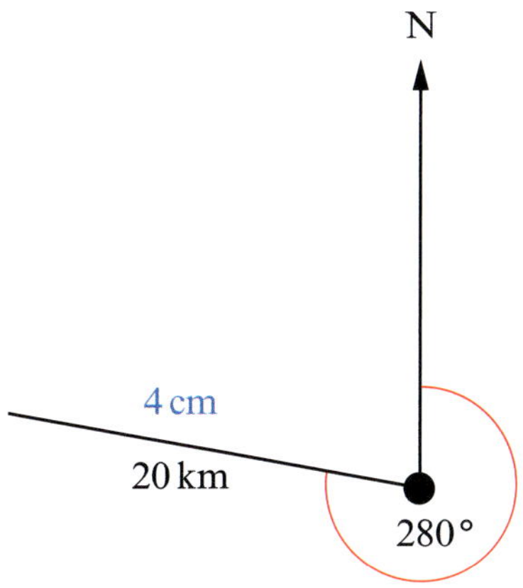

First use the scale of 1 cm represents 5 km to work out the distance Tia cycles on the scale drawing:

$20 \div 5 = 4$

1 cm represents 5 km. The distance on the scale drawing will be 4 cm.

Draw a north arrow, then measure the angle 280° clockwise from north. Draw a 4 cm line on this bearing. This line shows all the possible locations of Tia during her journey.

b

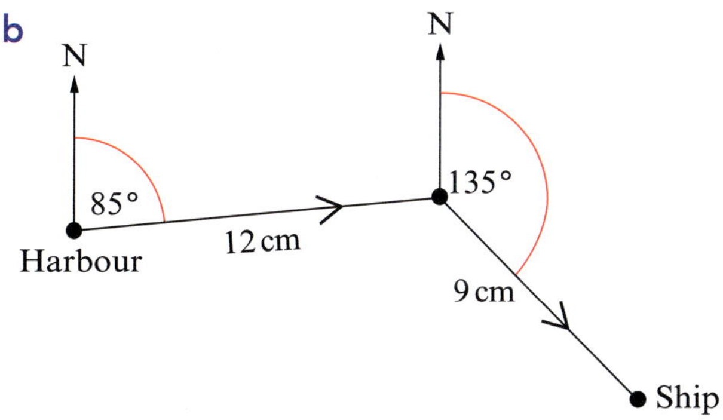

First, draw a north arrow and measure a bearing of 085°. Use the scale of 1 cm represents 10 km to work out the distance on the scale drawing.

$120 \div 10 = 12$

Draw a line 12 cm long to represent the first part of the journey.

Now draw another north arrow at the end of the first line, and measure a bearing of 135°. Again, use the scale to work out the distance on the scale drawing.

$90 \div 10 = 9$

Draw a line 9 cm long to represent the second part of the journey.

Exercise 13.1

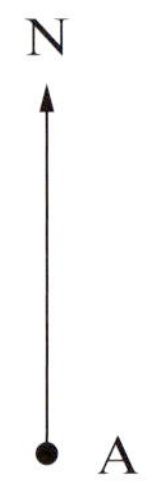

1 Firash walks on a bearing of 050° for 800 m.

Copy and complete the working and scale drawing to show Firash's journey.

Use a scale of 1 cm represents 100 m.

Distance on scale drawing = 800 ÷ 100 = □ cm

2 Jahia and Rafiki stand by a tree.

Jahia walks on a bearing of 140° for 50 m.

Rafiki walks on a bearing of 230° for 70 m.

a Show both their journeys on the same scale drawing.

Use a scale of 1 cm represents 10 m.

b On your scale drawing, measure the distance between the girls at the end of their walk.

How far apart are the girls in real life?

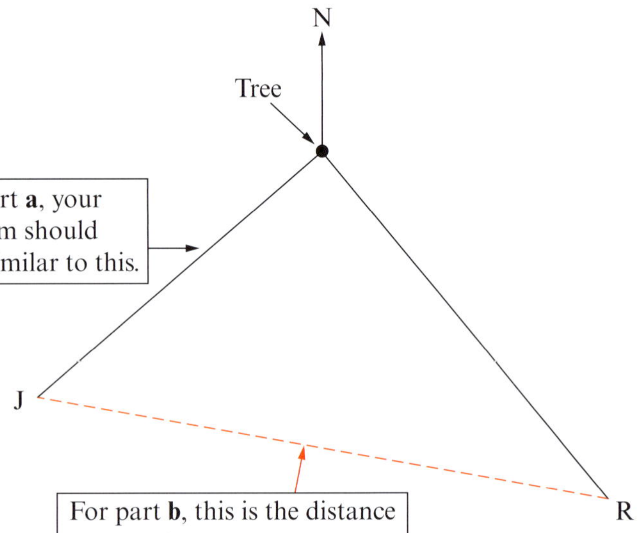

For part **a**, your diagram should look similar to this.

For part **b**, this is the distance you must measure.

Think like a mathematician

3 Work with a partner to answer this question.

A yacht is 70 km west of a speedboat.

The yacht sails on a bearing of 082°.

The speedboat travels on a bearing of 285°.

Could the yacht and the speedboat meet? Explain your answer.

Discuss and compare your methods and answers with other pairs of learners in your class.

4 Two lighthouses are 160 km apart.

Lighthouse A is north of lighthouse B.

A ship is on a bearing of 152° from lighthouse A and 042° from lighthouse B.

Draw a scale diagram to show the position of the ship.

Use a scale of 1 : 2 000 000.

> **Tip**
>
> Remember:
>
> '1 : 2 000 000' means 1 cm on the diagram represents 2 000 000 cm on the ground, so start by changing 2 000 000 cm into km.

5 This is part of Teshi's classwork.

> *Question*
> Jun lives 8 km south of Yue.
> Jun leaves home and walks 6 km to a lake.
> She walks on a bearing of 070°.
> Yue leaves home and walks to meet Jun at the lake.
> i Draw a scale drawing to represent the problem.
> ii How far, and on what bearing, must Yue walk?
>
> *Sketch:*

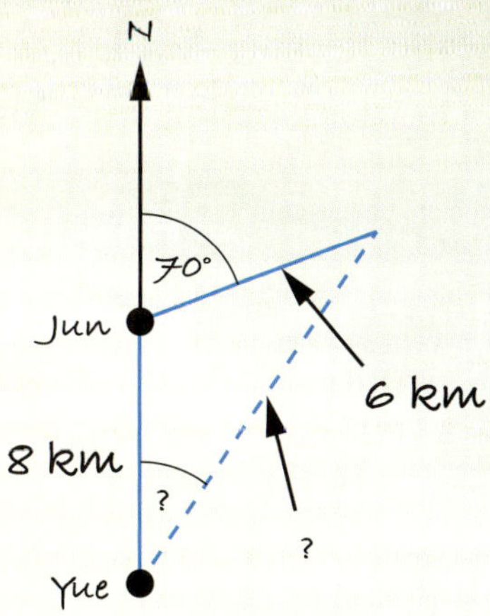

Teshi draws a sketch before he draws the scale drawing.

a Is Teshi's sketch correct? Explain your answer.

b Show that Yue must walk 8.2 km on a bearing 137°.

Think like a mathematician

6 Work with a partner to answer this question.

A ship leaves a harbour and sails 80 km on a bearing of 120°. The ship then sails 100 km on a bearing of 030°.

a Make a scale drawing of the ship's journey. Choose a sensible scale.

b What distance must the ship now sail to return to the harbour?

c On what bearing must the ship now sail to return to the harbour?

d Discuss and compare your answers to parts **b** and **c** with other pairs of learners in your class.
Did you all get the same answers? Compare the methods you used.
Discuss any mistakes that were made and suggest ways to avoid making those mistakes.

7 Mark leaves his tent and walks 12 km on a bearing of 045°.
He then walks 16 km on a bearing of 275°.

a Make a scale drawing of Mark's walk.
Use a scale of 1 cm represents 2 km.

b How far must Mark now walk in a straight line to return to his tent?

c On what bearing must Mark now walk to return in a straight line to his tent?

Activity 13.1

Work with a partner for this activity.

a With your partner, on a piece of paper, write a question similar to question **6** or **7**.

b On a different piece of paper, answer your question by drawing a diagram and measuring the distance and bearing for the return journey.

c Swap your question with another pair of learners in your class. Work out the answer to their question.

d Mark each other's work and discuss any mistakes that have been made.

8 The diagram shows two radio masts P and Q.

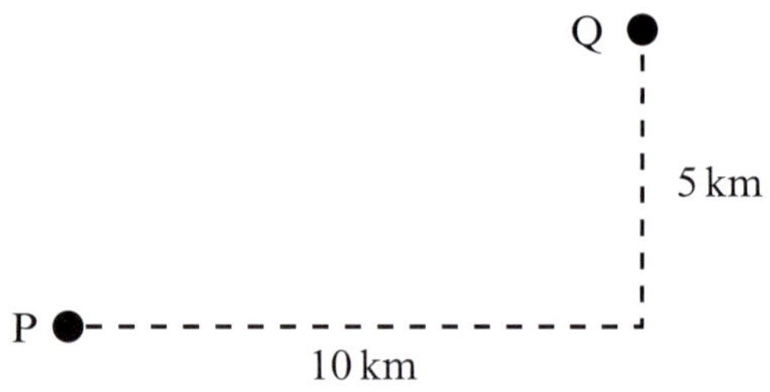

a Make a scale drawing of the diagram. Use a scale of 1 : 200 000.

b A farmhouse is 8 km on a bearing of 330° from P.

i Draw the position of the farmhouse on your diagram.

ii Measure the distance and bearing of the farmhouse from Q.

c A shop is 12 km on a bearing of 210° from Q.

i Draw the position of the shop on your diagram.

ii Measure the distance and bearing of the shop from P.

d A cafe is on a bearing of 070° from P and 135° from Q.

i Draw the position of the cafe on your diagram.

ii Measure the distance of the cafe from P and Q.

Tip

In parts **b ii**, **c ii** and **d ii** make sure you give the real life distances.

9 A lighthouse is 75 km east of a port.
The captain of a ship knows he is on a bearing of 315° from the lighthouse.
He also knows he is on a bearing of 052° from the port.

a Draw a scale diagram to show the position of the ship.
Use a scale of 1 : 1 000 000.

b How far is the ship from the lighthouse?

c How far is the ship from the port?

10 Alicia is participating in a charity sailing race on the Mar Menor.
The map shows the route she takes.

a On what bearing must she sail to get from

i the start to A **ii** A to B

iii B to the finish.

The map has a scale of 1 : 250 000.

b What is the total distance that Alicia sails?

Alicia earns $56 for charity, for every kilometre she sails.

c What is the total amount that Alicia raises for charity?

In this exercise you have used scale drawings in these situations:

- with one bearing to show the position of something
- with two bearings to show the position of something
- to work out the bearing and distance of a return journey.

a Which of these did you find the easiest? Explain why.

b Which of these did you find the most difficult? Explain why.
What could you do to help you to improve this skill?

Summary checklist

☐ I can use bearings and scaling to interpret position on maps and plans.

13.2 Points on a line segment

In this section you will …

- use coordinates to find points on a line segment.

In Stage 8 you learned how to find the midpoint of a line segment. The diagram shows a line segment AB. You can see from the diagram that the midpoint of AB is (3, 3).

In this section you will find the coordinates of different points along a line segment. For example, how can you work out the coordinates of the point that lies one third, two thirds, one quarter or three quarters of the way along line segment AB?

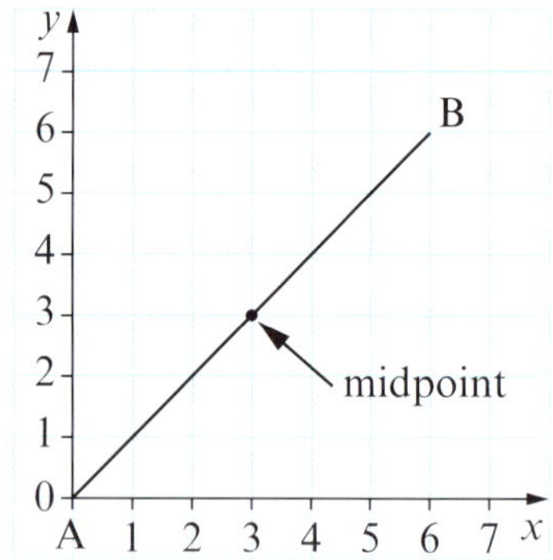

Worked example 13.2

The diagram shows two line segments LM and PQ.

Write the coordinates of the points that lie

a one third of the way along LM

b one quarter of the way along PQ.

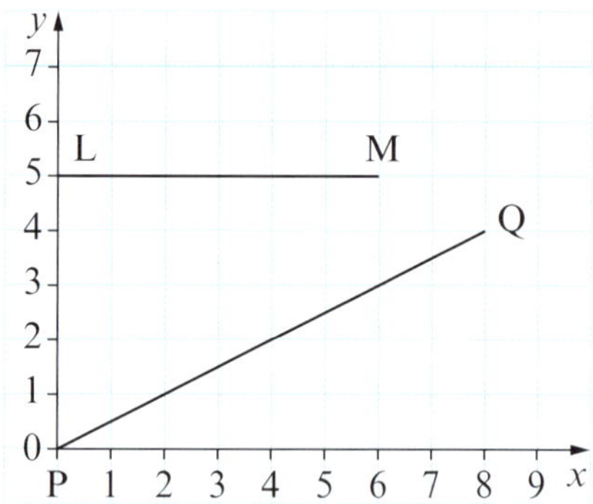

Answer

a (2, 5)

x-coordinate: L is 0 and M is 6, so $\frac{1}{3}$ of the way across is $6 \div 3 = 2$

Line LM is horizontal, so you know all the y-coordinates are 5.

b (2, 1)

x-coordinate: P is 0 and Q is 8, so $\frac{1}{4}$ of the way across is $8 \div 4 = 2$

y-coordinate: P is 0 and Q is 4, so $\frac{1}{4}$ of the way up is $4 \div 4 = 1$

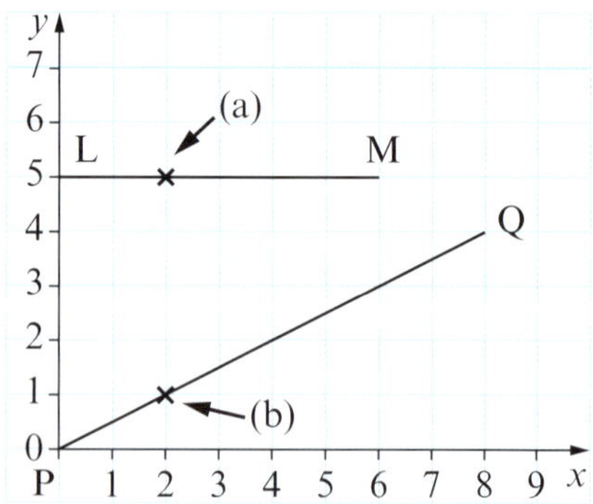

Exercise 13.2

1 Make a copy of this diagram.

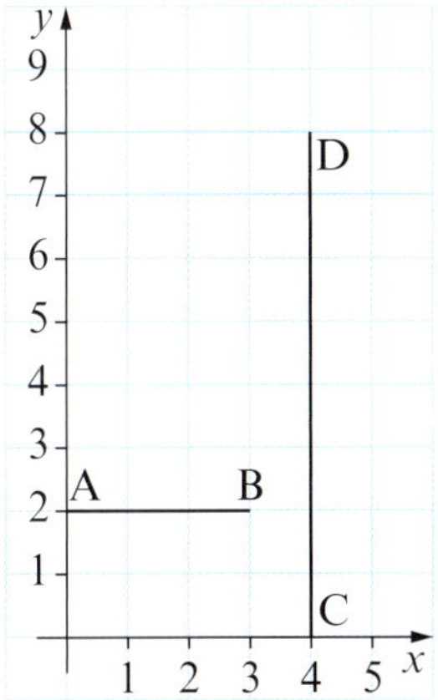

- **a** Write the coordinates of the points A and B.
- **b** Work out the coordinates of the point that lies one third $\left(\frac{1}{3}\right)$ of the way along AB.
  Mark this point on your diagram and label it (b).
- **c** Work out the coordinates of the point that lies two thirds $\left(\frac{2}{3}\right)$ of the way along AB.
  Mark this point on your diagram and label it (c).
- **d** Write the coordinates of the points C and D.
- **e** Work out the coordinates of the point that lies one quarter $\left(\frac{1}{4}\right)$ of the way along CD.
  Mark this point on your diagram and label it (e).
- **f** Work out the coordinates of the point that lies three quarters $\left(\frac{3}{4}\right)$ of the way along CD.
  Mark this point on your diagram and label it (f).

2 The diagram shows the line segment PQ.

Cards **A** to **F** show a fraction of the way along PQ.

Cards **i** to **vi** show coordinates.

Match each card **A** to **F** with the correct card **i** to **vi**.

The first one has been done for you: **A** and **v**.

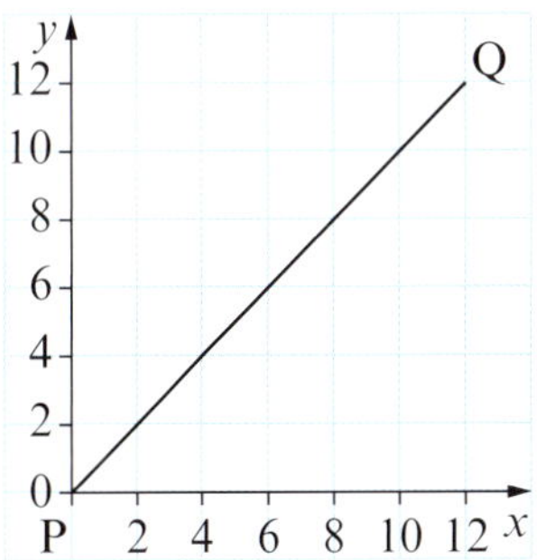

A	$\frac{1}{6}$	**i**	(10, 10)
B	$\frac{1}{4}$	**ii**	(9, 9)
C	$\frac{1}{3}$	**iii**	(3, 3)
D	$\frac{3}{4}$	**iv**	(8, 8)
E	$\frac{2}{3}$	**v**	(2, 2)
F	$\frac{5}{6}$	**vi**	(4, 4)

Think like a mathematician

3 Work with a partner to answer these questions.

Chesa and Tefo use different methods to find the coordinates of the point that lies $\frac{2}{5}$ of the way along the line segment ST. S is at (0, 0) and T is at (10, 5).

Chesa's method

Draw a diagram.

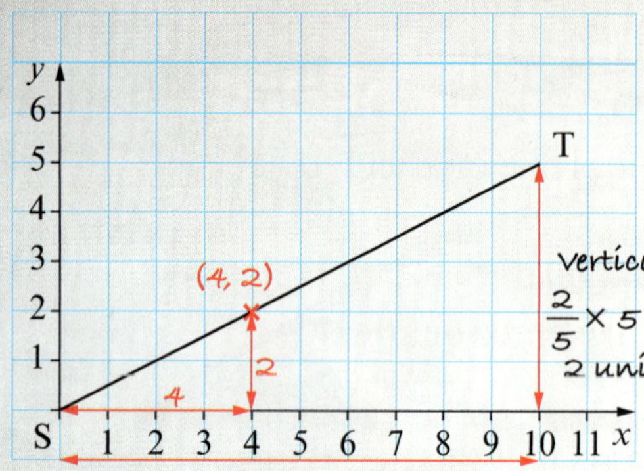

Vertical distance = 5

$\frac{2}{5} \times 5 = 2$, so the point is 2 units from S vertically.

Horizontal distance = 10

$\frac{2}{5} \times 10 = 4$, so the point is 4 units from S horizontally.

Tefo's method

$\left(\frac{2}{5} \times 10, \frac{2}{5} \times 5\right) = (4, 2)$

Coordinate of the point is (4, 2)

- **a** Critique Chesa's method.
- **b** Critique Tefo's method.
- **c** Whose method do you prefer? Explain why.
- **d** Can you think of a better method?
- **e** Will both Chesa's and Tefo's methods work when S is not at the point (0, 0)?
- **f** Discuss your answers with other pairs of learners in your class.

4 O is at the point (0, 0), M is at (16, 12) and N is at (10, 15).
Write whether **A**, **B** or **C** is the correct answer.
Use your favourite method.

a	$\frac{1}{4}$ of the way along OM is	**A**	(3, 4)	**B**	(4, 3)	**C**	(4, 4)
b	$\frac{3}{4}$ of the way along OM is	**A**	(12, 9)	**B**	(12, 8)	**C**	(9, 12)
c	$\frac{1}{5}$ of the way along ON is	**A**	(5, 3)	**B**	(2, 5)	**C**	(2, 3)
d	$\frac{4}{5}$ of the way along ON is	**A**	(12, 8)	**B**	(8, 12)	**C**	(8, 10)

5 Ω (omega) is the point (0, 0) and A is the point (2, 3).

a Points A and B are equally spaced along the same line such that the distance ΩA is equal to the distance AB. What are the coordinates of point B?

> **Tip**
> You could draw a diagram to help you.

b C is the next point along the same line such that the distance BC is equal to distances ΩA and AB. What are the coordinates of point C?

c The points continue along the line, equally spaced. Each point is labelled with a letter of the alphabet, in order from A to Z. Show that point J has coordinates (20, 30).

> **Tip**
> J is the 10th letter in the alphabet.

d What are the coordinates of point P?

Show how you worked out your answer.

> **Tip**
> P is the 16th letter in the alphabet.

e What are the coordinates of the point labelled with the 20th letter in the alphabet?

Show how you worked out your answer.

f Write an expression for the coordinates of the point along the same line labelled with the *n*th letter of the alphabet.

> **Tip**
> You could write your expression as: *n*th letter is (□, □).

6 O is the point (0, 0) and D is the point (3, 7).

D lies $\frac{1}{4}$ of the way along the line segment OE.

Sofia says:

Marcus says:

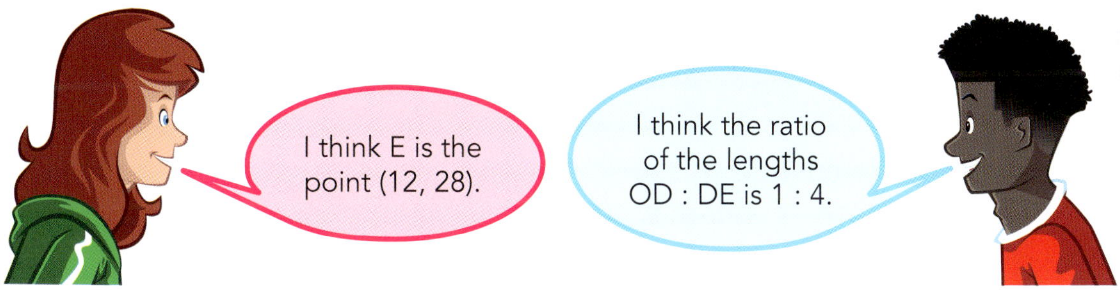

a Is Sofia correct? Justify your answer.

b Is Marcus correct? Justify your answer.

7 O is the point (0, 0) and T is the point (20, 25). The points P, Q, R and S are equally spaced along the line OT. Work out the coordinates of R.

Think like a mathematician

8 Work with a partner to answer these questions.

Briana tries to answer this question.

Question

The diagram shows points A (3, 2) and B (8, 12).

Point C lies $\frac{1}{5}$ of the way along the line segment AB.

Work out the coordinates of point C.

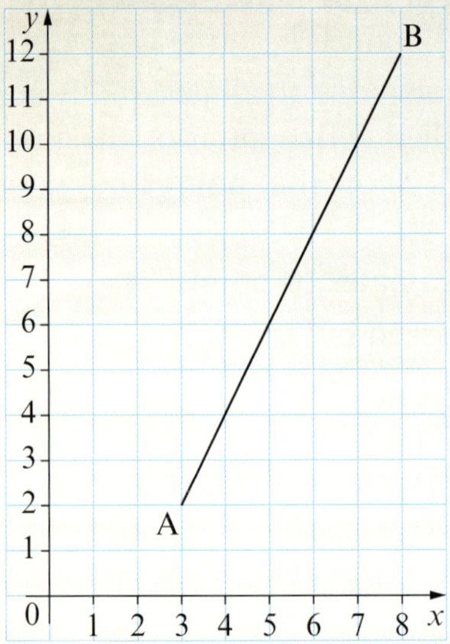

Briana writes:

Difference in x-coordinates = 8 − 3 = 5 $\quad \frac{1}{5} \times 5 = 1$

Difference in y-coordinates = 12 − 2 = 10 $\quad \frac{1}{5} \times 10 = 2$

Coordinates of C are (1, 2).

a Only by looking at the diagram, explain why Briana's coordinates for C must be incorrect.

b Look carefully at Briana's solution. Explain the extra steps Briana must do to get the correct answer.

c Work out the correct coordinates for C. Use a diagram to check that your coordinates are correct.

d Write the ratio of the length of

   i AC : AB   **ii** AC : BC.

e Discuss your answers to parts **a** to **d** with other learners in your class.

9 F is the point (3, 4) and G is the point (9, 13). H is the point that lies $\frac{2}{3}$ of the way along FG.

Show that H has coordinates (7, 10).

10 J is the point (1, 5) and K is the point (13, 13). L is the point that lies $\frac{3}{4}$ of the way along JK.

a Work out the coordinates of L.

b Use a diagram to show that your answer to part **a** is correct.

11 A kite has vertices at A (1, 1), B (2, 5), C (5, 5) and D (5, 2).

a Draw a diagram of kite ABCD on a coordinate grid.

b On your diagram, draw the diagonals AC and BD.

c Line segments AC and BD cross at point E. Write the coordinates of E.

d Show, using calculations, that E is the midpoint of BD.

e Show, using calculations, that E lies $\frac{5}{8}$ of the way along AC.

12 F is the point (5, 1) and L is the point (17, 19). Points G, H, I, J, K and L are equally spaced along the line FL.

Which of the points G, H, I, J, K and L is the only point to have the same x and y coordinate?

Show all your working.

Summary checklist

☐ I can use coordinates to find points on a line segment.

13.3 Transformations

In this section you will ...

- transform shapes by a combination of reflections, translations and rotations
- identify and describe a transformation
- explain that after a combination of transformations the object and the image are congruent.

You already know how to describe the transformation that maps an object on to its image. Here is a quick reminder:

To describe a reflection you must give:	• the equation of the mirror line.
To describe a translation you must give:	• the column vector.
To describe a rotation you must give:	• the centre of rotation • the angle of the rotation • the direction of the rotation (clockwise or anticlockwise).

Tip

Remember that when a rotation is 180° you do not need to give the direction of the rotation. The image of the object will be the same whether you rotate it clockwise or anticlockwise.

You can use a **combination** of reflections, translations and rotations to transform a shape.

Worked example 13.3

The diagram shows triangles A, B, C and D.

a Copy the diagram and draw the image of triangle A after a reflection in the y-axis followed by a rotation 90° clockwise, centre $(-1, 1)$.
Label the image E.

b Are triangle A and triangle E congruent or not congruent?

c Describe the transformation that transforms

i triangle A to triangle B

ii triangle B to triangle C

iii triangle C to triangle D.

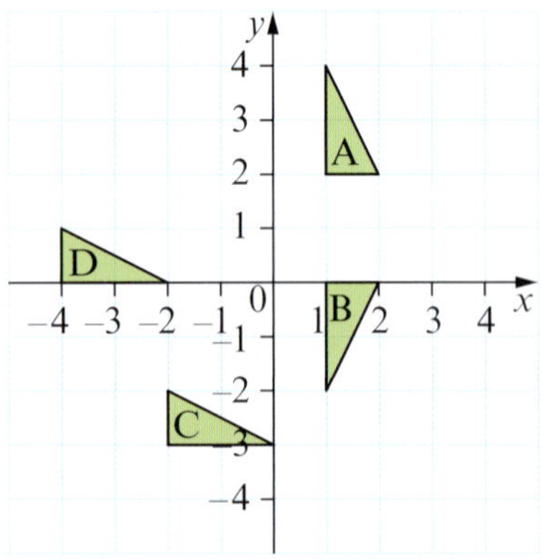

Continued

Answer

a

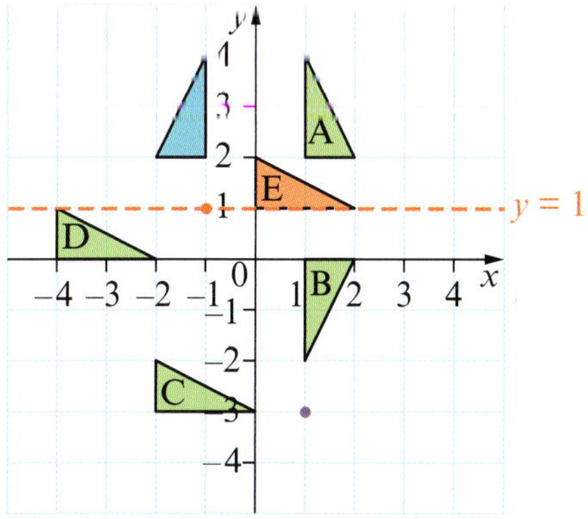

First, reflect triangle A in the y-axis to give the blue triangle shown in the diagram.

Then rotate the blue triangle 90° clockwise about $(-1, 1)$, shown by an orange dot, to give the final image.

Remember to label the final triangle E.

b congruent

Triangles A and E are identical in shape and size.

c **i** Triangle A to triangle B is a reflection in the line $y = 1$, shown in orange in the diagram in the solution to part **a**.

ii Triangle B to triangle C is a rotation 90° anticlockwise, centre $(1, -3)$, shown by a purple dot in the diagram in the solution to part **a**.

iii Triangle C to triangle D is a translation two squares left and three squares up, so the column vector is $\begin{pmatrix} -2 \\ 3 \end{pmatrix}$.

Exercise 13.3

1 The diagram shows triangle A.
Cards **a**, **b** and **c** show three combinations of transformations.
Diagrams **i**, **ii** and **iii** show triangle A and its image, triangle B.
Match each card with the correct diagram.

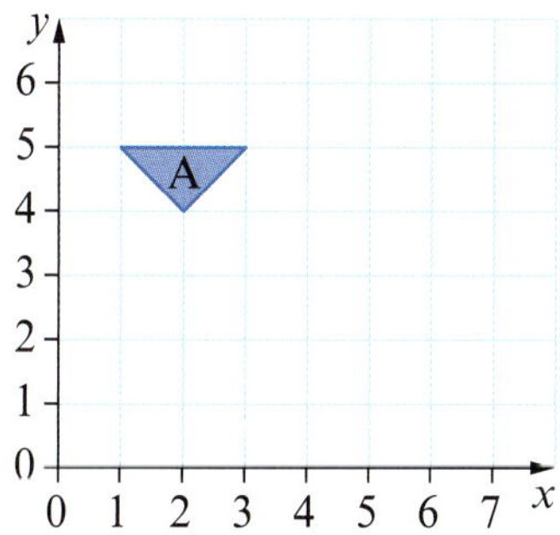

a A translation $\begin{pmatrix} 2 \\ -1 \end{pmatrix}$ followed by a reflection in the line $y = 3$.

b A rotation of 90° anticlockwise, centre (3, 5) followed by a translation $\begin{pmatrix} 3 \\ -2 \end{pmatrix}$.

c A reflection in the line $x = 4$ followed by a rotation of 180°, centre (6, 4).

i
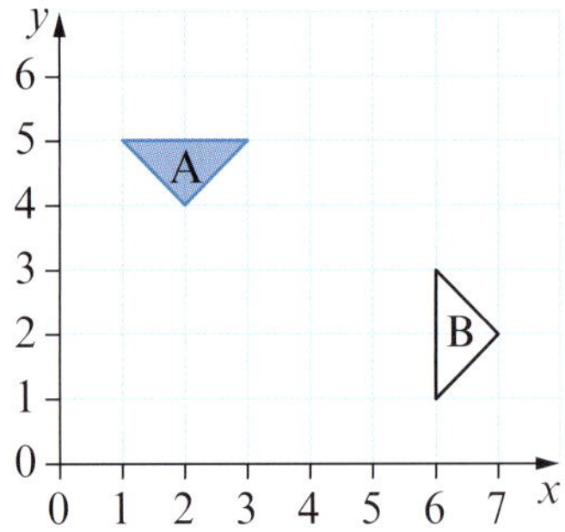

ii
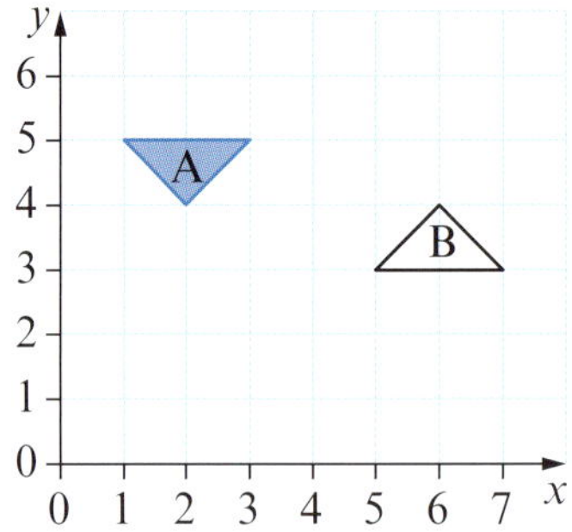

iii
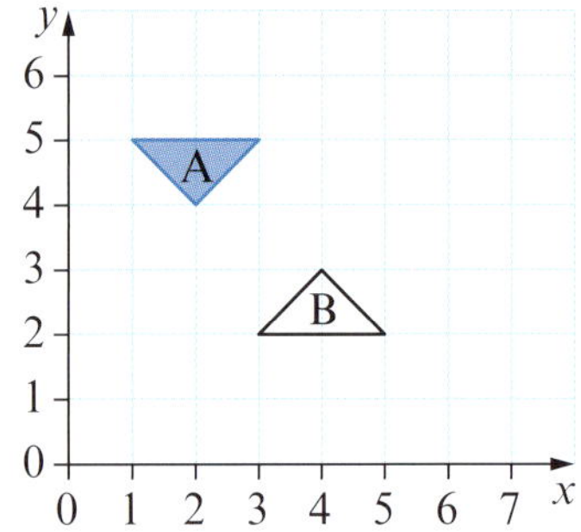

2 The diagram shows shape A on a coordinate grid.

Make two copies of the diagram.

On different copies of the diagram, draw the image of A after each combination of transformations.

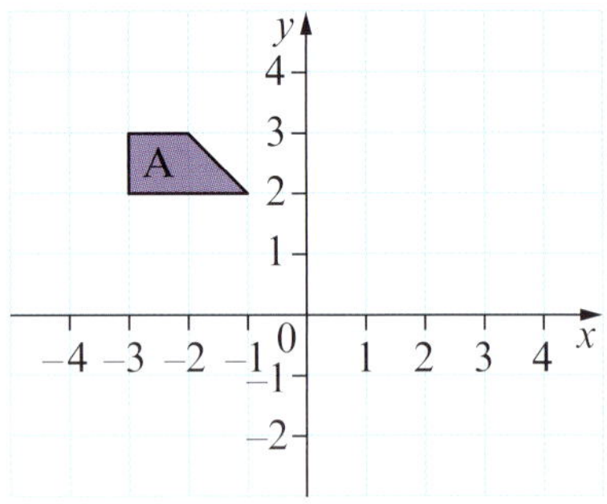

- **a** Reflection in the y-axis followed by the translation $\begin{pmatrix} 1 \\ -2 \end{pmatrix}$.
- **b** Rotation of 90° anticlockwise, centre $(-1, 2)$, followed by reflection in the line $x = 1$.
- **c** Look at your answers to parts **a** and **b**. In each part, are the object and the image congruent or not congruent? Explain your answers.

3 The diagram shows triangle B on a coordinate grid.

Make four copies of the diagram.

On different copies of the diagram, draw the image of B after each combination of transformations.

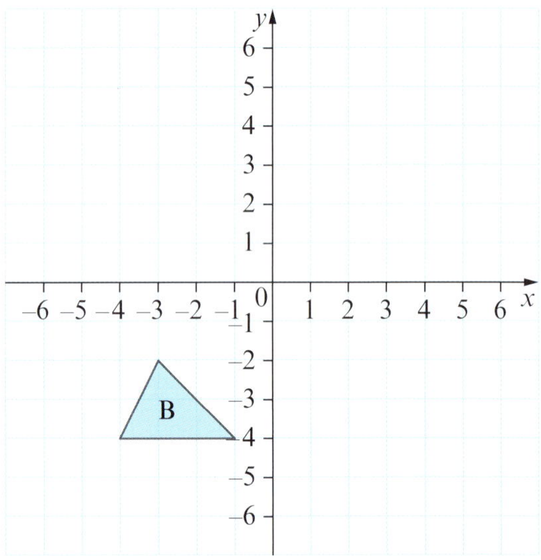

- **a** Translation $\begin{pmatrix} 5 \\ 1 \end{pmatrix}$, followed by reflection in the x-axis.
- **b** Rotation of 180°, centre $(-3, -2)$, followed by reflection in the x-axis.
- **c** Translation $\begin{pmatrix} -1 \\ 5 \end{pmatrix}$, followed by rotation 90° clockwise, centre $(-2, 1)$.
- **d** Reflection in the line $y = -1$, followed by rotation 90° anticlockwise, centre $(2, 2)$.

Think like a mathematician

4 The diagram shows three shapes, X, Y and Z, on a coordinate grid.

Make three copies of the grid.

On the first grid draw shape X, on the second grid draw shape Y and on the third grid draw shape Z.

Continued

a On the first grid, draw the image of X after the combination of transformations

 i reflection in the line $y = 1$ followed by rotation 90° anticlockwise, centre (2, −3)

 ii rotation 90° anticlockwise, centre (2, −3), followed by reflection in the line $y = 1$.

b On the second grid, draw the image of Y after the combination of transformations

 i reflection in the line $x = -1$ followed by translation $\begin{pmatrix} 2 \\ -5 \end{pmatrix}$

 ii translation $\begin{pmatrix} 2 \\ -5 \end{pmatrix}$ followed by reflection in the line $x = -1$.

c On the third grid, draw the image of Z after the combination of transformations

 i rotation 180°, centre (0, 0), followed by reflection in the line $y = 2$

 ii reflection in the line $y = 2$ followed by rotation 180°, centre (0, 0).

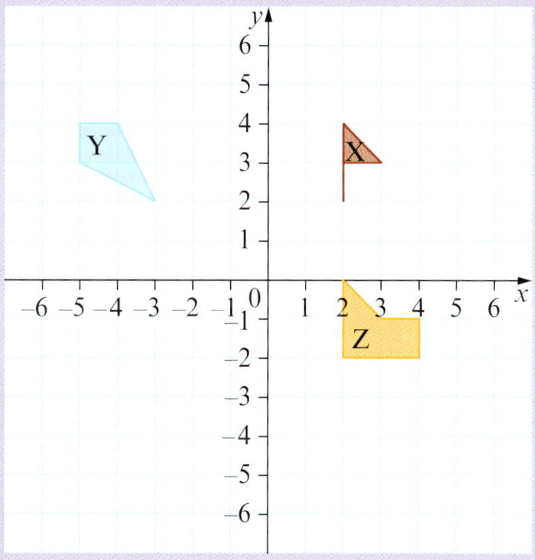

d **i** What do you notice about your answers to **i** and **ii** in parts **a**, **b** and **c**?

 ii Does it matter in which order you carry out combined transformations? Explain your answer.

 iii Discuss your answers to part **d** **i** and **ii** with other learners in your class.

 iv Write two different transformations you can carry out on shape Z so the final image is the same, in whatever order you do the transformations.

 v Ask a partner to check your answer to part **d iv** is correct.

5 The diagram shows shapes G, H, I, J and K on a coordinate grid.

Describe the transformation that transforms

a shape G to shape H **b** shape G to shape K

c shape H to shape J **d** shape J to shape I.

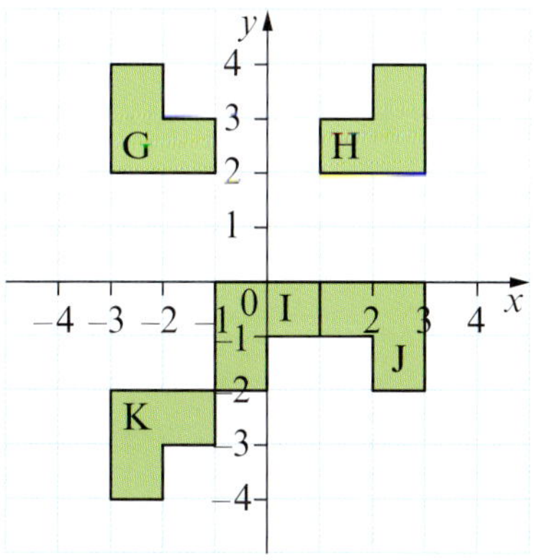

Tip

Remember, for a reflection you need to write 'Reflection' and give the equation of the mirror line.

6 The diagram shows shapes L, M, N, P and Q on a coordinate grid.
Describe the transformation that transforms

a shape L to shape M
b shape M to shape N
c shape N to shape P
d shape P to shape Q
e shape Q to shape M
f shape P to shape M.

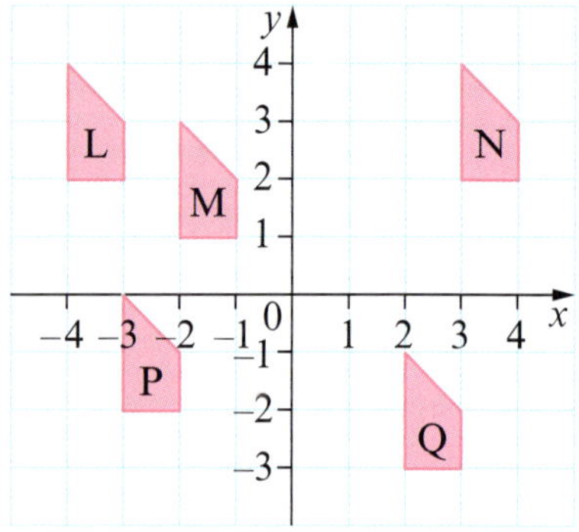

Tip

Remember, for a translation you need to write 'Translation' and give the column vector.

7 The diagram shows triangles R, S, T, U, V and W on a coordinate grid.
Describe the transformation that transforms

a triangle S to triangle R
b triangle R to triangle T
c triangle R to triangle U
d triangle V to triangle T
e triangle V to triangle W.

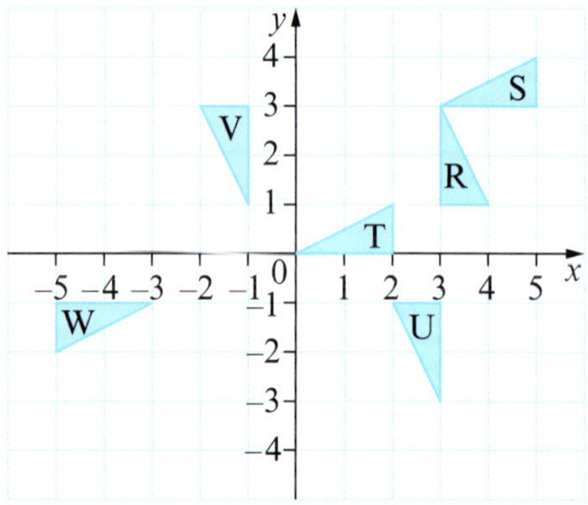

Tip

Remember, for a rotation you need to write 'Rotation' and give the centre of rotation as well as the angle of rotation and the direction of rotation.

Think like a mathematician

8 Work with a partner to answer these questions.
The diagram shows shapes A, B, C, D and E on a coordinate grid.

a Describe the single transformation that transforms
   i shape A to shape E
   ii shape B to shape C
   iii shape C to shape D.

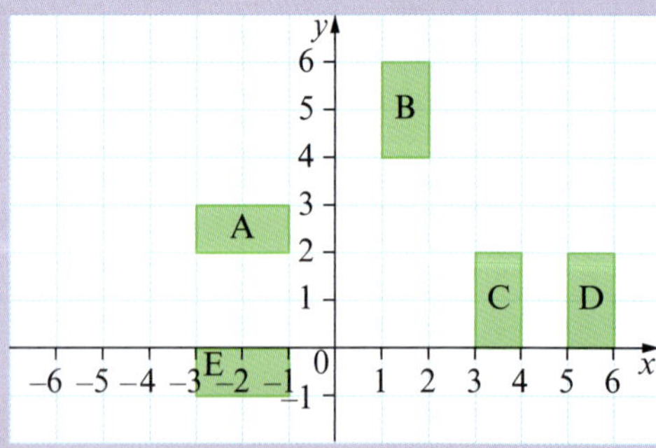

b Discuss and compare your answers to part **a** with other pairs of learners in your class.
Did you all get the same answers? Is it possible to have more than one answer for each transformation? Discuss why.

Continued

c Describe a combined transformation that transforms

i shape B to shape D　　ii shape B to shape E

iii shape C to shape A

d Discuss and compare your answers to part **c** with other pairs of learners in your class.

Did you all get the same answers? Is it possible to have more than one answer for each combined transformation? Discuss why.

9 The vertices of triangle G are at (1, 3), (3, 3) and (1, 4).
The vertices of triangle H are at (−1, 1), (−3, 1) and (−1, 2).

Sofia says:

I think the combined transformation to take G to H is: reflection in the line $x = -1$ then translation $\begin{pmatrix} 2 \\ -2 \end{pmatrix}$.

Zara says:

I think the combined transformation to take G to H is: translation $\begin{pmatrix} 0 \\ -2 \end{pmatrix}$ then reflection in the y-axis.

a Who is correct? Explain your answer.

b Write two different combined transformations that take G to H.

c How many more different combined transformations are there that take G to H? Explain your answer.

10 The diagram shows shape A on a coordinate grid.
Make two copies of the grid.

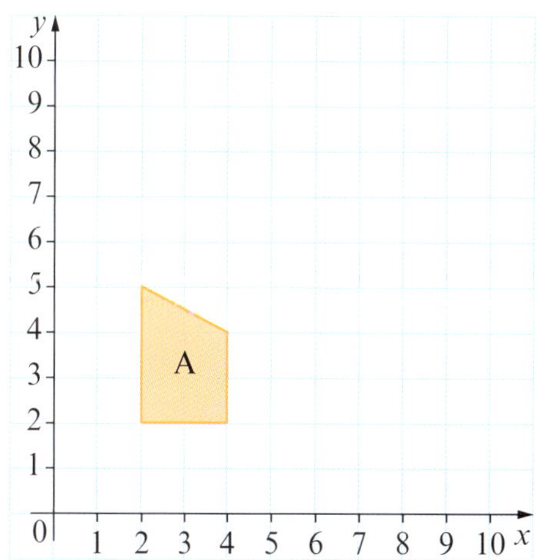

a i On the first copy, reflect shape A in the line $x = 5$ and label the image B. Then rotate shape B 180°, centre (5, 5), and label the image C.

ii Describe the single transformation that takes shape A to shape C.

b i On the second copy, rotate shape A 90° anticlockwise, centre (2, 8), and label the image D.

Then translate shape D $\begin{pmatrix} -3 \\ -3 \end{pmatrix}$ and label the image E.

ii Describe the single transformation that takes shape A to shape E.

Activity 13.3

Work with a partner for this activity.

Here are three shapes on a coordinate grid.

Make three copies of this grid: grid **1** with only the square, grid **2** with only the rectangle and grid **3** with only the triangle.

Here are eight different transformations.

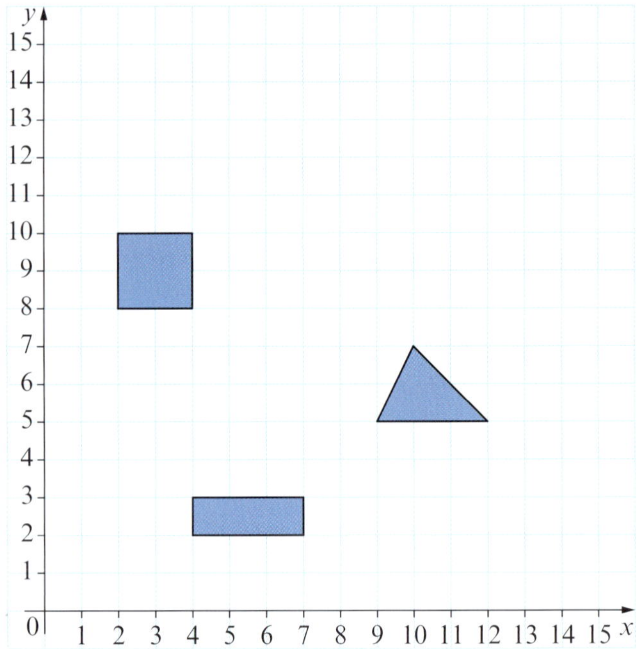

① Reflection in the line $x = 6$	② Reflection in the line $y = 5$
③ Rotation 180° centre (6, 6)	④ Rotation 90° clockwise, centre (5, 7)
⑤ Rotation 90° anticlockwise, centre (8, 8)	⑥ Translation $\begin{pmatrix} 2 \\ 3 \end{pmatrix}$
⑦ Translation $\begin{pmatrix} 4 \\ -1 \end{pmatrix}$	⑧ Translation $\begin{pmatrix} -1 \\ -3 \end{pmatrix}$

a On grid **1**, choose any two of the transformations and work out the position of the square after the combined transformation. Can you describe a single transformation that takes the image back to the object? Repeat with two more sets of two transformations.

b Repeat part **a** with grid **2**, and then grid **3**.

c With which shape – the square, rectangle or triangle – did you find it easiest to describe a single transformation that takes the image back to the object? Discuss why.

d After which transformations did you find it easiest to describe a single transformation that takes the image back to the object? Discuss why.

e Compare and discuss your answers with other pairs of learners in the class.

11 The diagram shows five triangles, A to E.

Here are four transformations.

a translation $\begin{pmatrix} 3 \\ -1 \end{pmatrix}$ followed by reflection in the line $y = 3$

b reflection in the line $x = 4$ followed by reflection in the line $y = 2$

c rotation 90° anticlockwise, centre (4, 5), followed by translation $\begin{pmatrix} -2 \\ -2 \end{pmatrix}$

d reflection in the line $y = 4$ followed by rotation 90° anticlockwise, centre (7, 6)

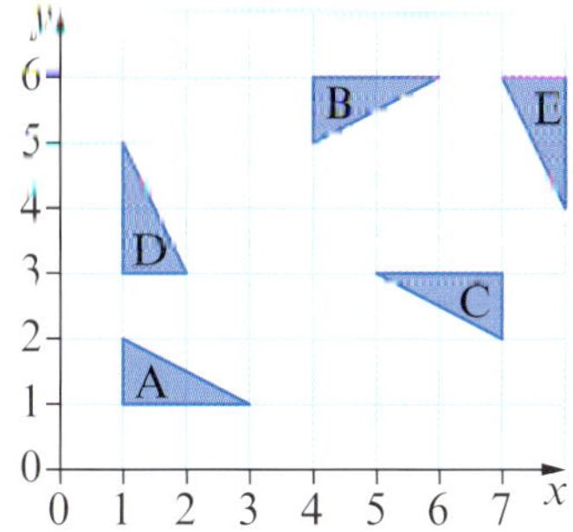

Work out which triangle is transformed to which other triangle by each of the combined transformations.

Look back at the questions in this exercise.

a What do you notice about an object and its image after a single or combined transformation?

b Write the missing words in these statements.

Choose from the words in the box.

longer	shorter	equal
different	congruent	not congruent

When you compare an object and its image after any single or combined transformation:

- corresponding lengths are ....
- corresponding angles are ....
- the object and the image are ....

Summary checklist

- ☐ I can transform shapes by a combination of reflections, translations and rotations.
- ☐ I can identify and describe a transformation.
- ☐ I can explain that after a combination of transformations, the object and the image are congruent.

13.4 Enlarging shapes

In this section you will ...

- enlarge shapes using a positive whole number scale factor from a centre of enlargement
- identify and describe enlargements
- describe changes in the perimeter and area of squares and rectangles when the side lengths are enlarged.

Key word

ray lines

You already know that when you enlarge a shape:

- all the lengths of the sides of the shape increase in the same proportion
- all the angles in the shape stay the same size.

In Stage 8, you enlarged shapes using a centre of enlargement outside or on the shape. In this section you will enlarge shapes using a centre of enlargement inside the shape. You will also look at the effect of an enlargement on the perimeter and area of squares and rectangles.

Remember that when you describe an enlargement you must give:

- the scale factor of the enlargement
- the position of the centre of enlargement.

Worked example 13.4

a The diagram shows a trapezium.

Draw an enlargement of the trapezium, with scale factor 2, centre of enlargement shown.

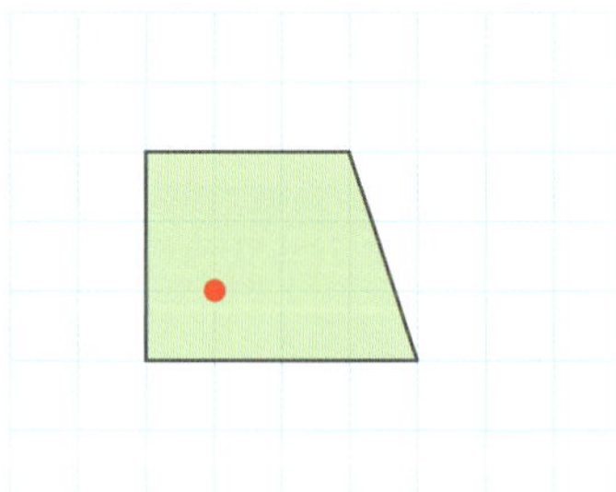

b The diagram shows two triangles, A and B.

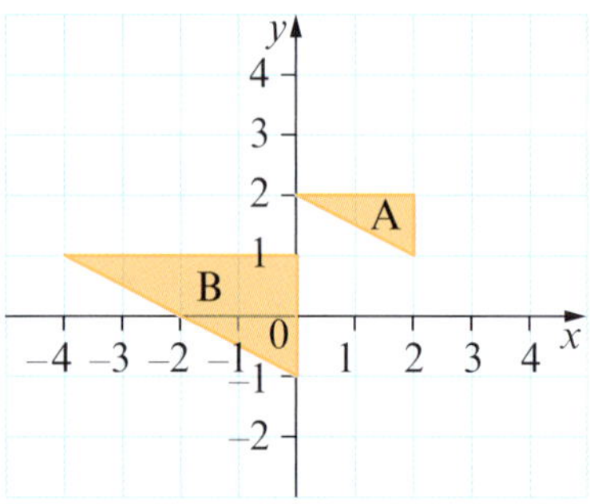

Triangle B is an enlargement of triangle A.

Describe the enlargement.

Continued

Answer

a

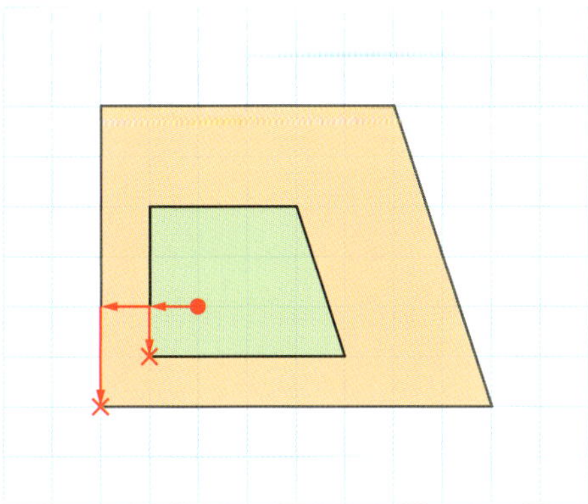

The closest vertex of the trapezium is one square left and one square down from the centre of enlargement. On the enlarged trapezium, this vertex will be two squares left and two squares down from the centre of enlargement (shown by the red arrows).

Mark this vertex on the diagram, then complete the trapezium. The length of each side is twice the length of that side in the original shape.

b

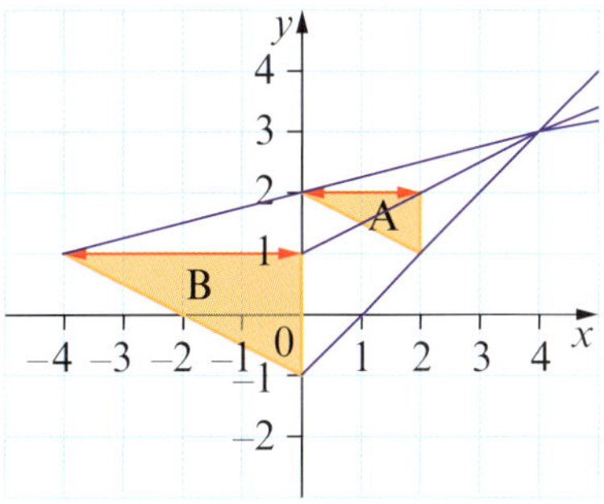

The enlargement has scale factor 2, centre (4, 3).

First, work out the scale factor of the enlargement.

Compare matching sides of the triangles – for example, the two sides marked with red arrows. In triangle A, the length is 2 squares and in triangle B the length is 4 squares.

$4 \div 2 = 2$, so the scale factor is 2.

Now find the centre of enlargement by drawing **ray lines** through the corresponding vertices of the triangles, shown by the purple lines. The purple lines meet at (4, 3).

Exercise 13.4

1 Copy and complete this enlargement with scale factor 3 and centre of enlargement shown.

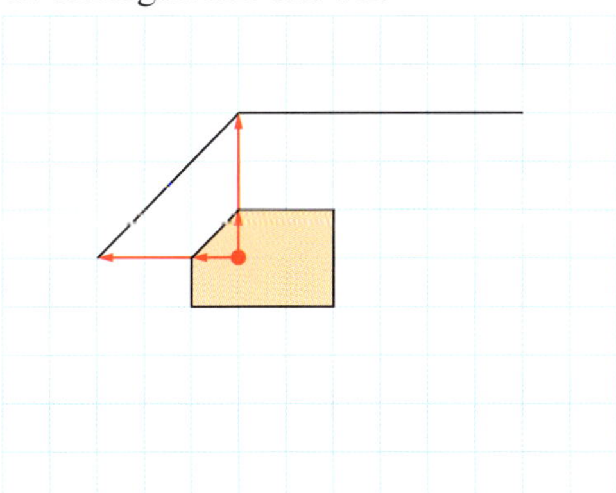

2 Copy each of these shapes on to squared paper.
Enlarge each shape using the given scale factor and centre of enlargement shown.

a scale factor 2

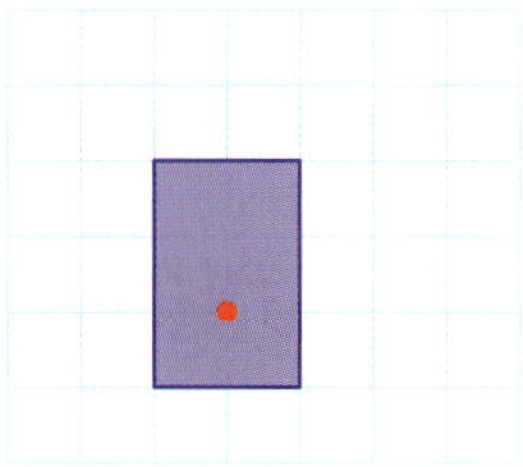

b scale factor 3

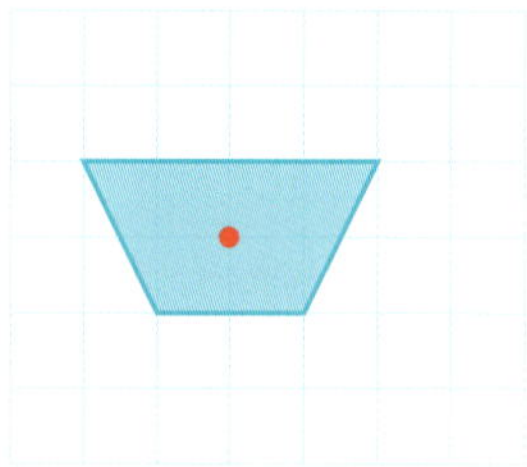

c scale factor 4

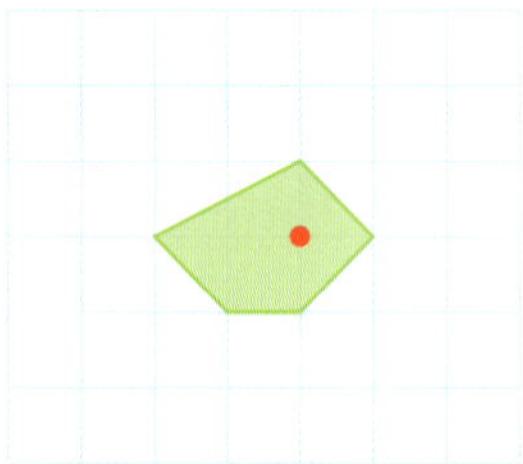

> **Tip**
> Make sure you leave enough space around your shape to complete the enlargement.

3 This is part of Tasha's homework.

Question
Enlarge this triangle using scale factor 2 and centre of enlargement shown.

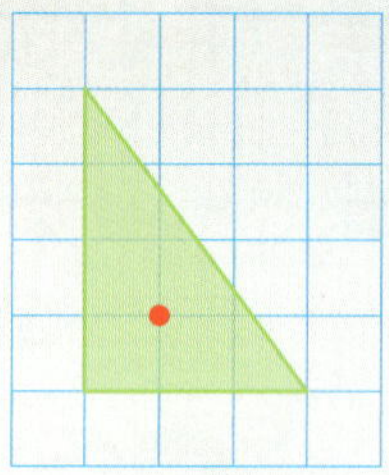

Answer

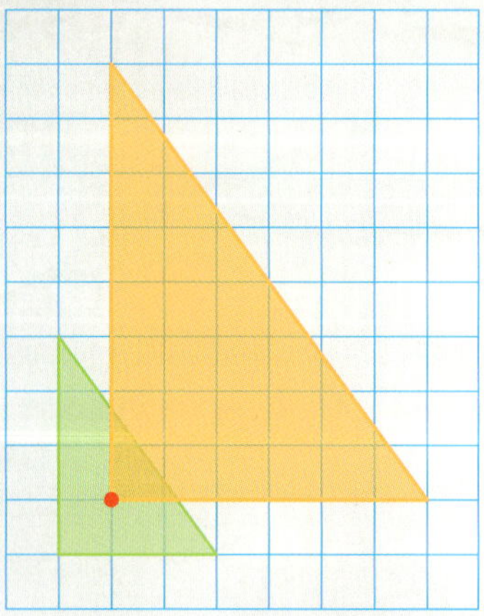

a Explain the mistake Tasha has made.

b Make a copy of the triangle on squared paper.
Draw the correct enlargement.

Activity 13.4

Work with a partner to answer this question. Read the instructions before you start.

a On squared paper, draw a quadrilateral of your choice.

b Ask your partner to enlarge your quadrilateral by a scale factor of your choice.
Mark, with a dot, the centre of enlargement, which must be somewhere **inside** the quadrilateral.
You **must** make sure the enlarged shape will fit on the paper.

c Check each other's work and discuss any mistakes that have been made.

4 The diagram shows square A on a coordinate grid.
Make three copies of the diagram on squared paper.

a On the first copy, draw an enlargement of the shape with scale factor 2, centre (7, 5). Label the image B.

b On the second copy, draw an enlargement of the shape with scale factor 3, centre (5, 6). Label the image C.

c On the third copy, draw an enlargement of the shape with scale factor 4, centre (5, 5). Label the image D.

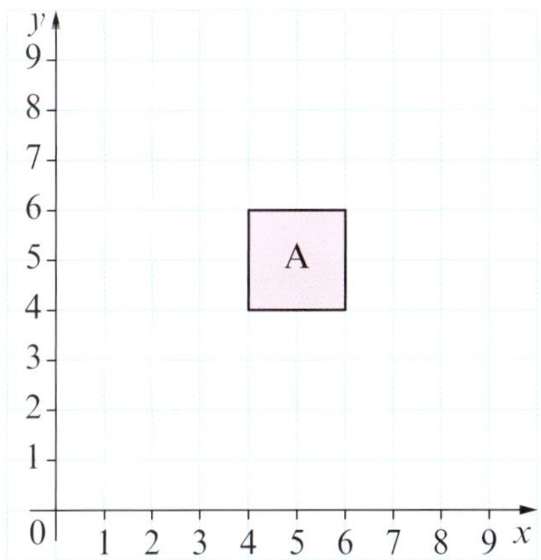

Think like a mathematician

5 Work with a partner to answer these questions.

a Look back at your diagrams in Question **4**.

i Work out the perimeter of each square A, B, C and D.

ii Work out the area of each square A, B, C and D.

b Copy and complete this table.
Write all the ratios in their simplest form.

Squares	Scale factor of enlargement	Ratio of lengths	Ratio of perimeters	Ratio of areas
A:B	2	1:2		
A:C				
A:D				

Continued

c Write a rule that connects the ratio of lengths to the ratio of perimeters.

d Write a rule that connects the ratio of lengths to the ratio of areas.

e Will these rules work for any scale factor of enlargement?
Will these rules work for any shape?

f Compare your answers with other pairs of learners in your class. Discuss any differences.

Tip

In part **d**, remember the square numbers: $1^2 = 1$, $2^2 = 4$, $3^2 = 9$, $4^2 = 16$, etc.

6 A rectangle, R, has a perimeter of 14 cm and an area of 10 cm^2.
The rectangle is enlarged by a scale factor of 3 to become rectangle T.
Copy and complete the workings to find the perimeter and area of rectangle T.
Perimeter of R = 14 cm → Perimeter of T = 14 × 3 = ☐ cm
Area of R = 10 cm^2 → Area of T = 10 × 3^2 = ☐ cm^2

7 A triangle, G, has a perimeter of 12 cm and an area of 6 cm^2.
The triangle is enlarged by a scale factor of 5 to become triangle H.
Work out the perimeter and area of triangle H.

8 The diagram shows shapes F and G on a square grid.
Copy and complete this statement:
Shape G is an enlargement of shape F, scale factor ☐ and centre of enlargement (☐, ☐).

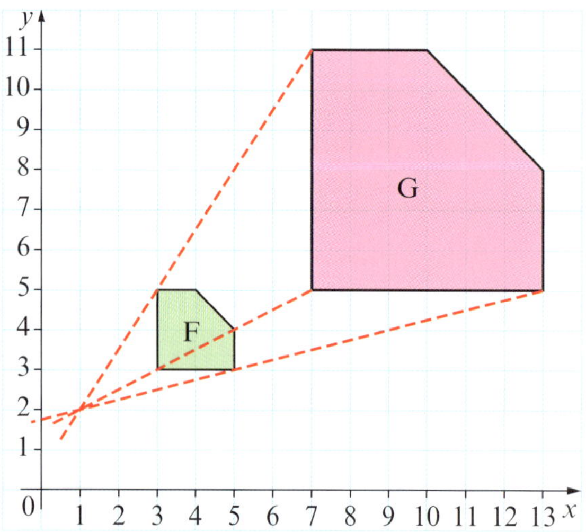

Tip

Some ray lines have been drawn on the diagram to help you.

9 The diagram shows three triangles, A, B and C, on a coordinate grid.

a Triangle B is an enlargement of triangle A. Describe the enlargement.

b Triangle C is an enlargement of triangle A. Describe the enlargement.

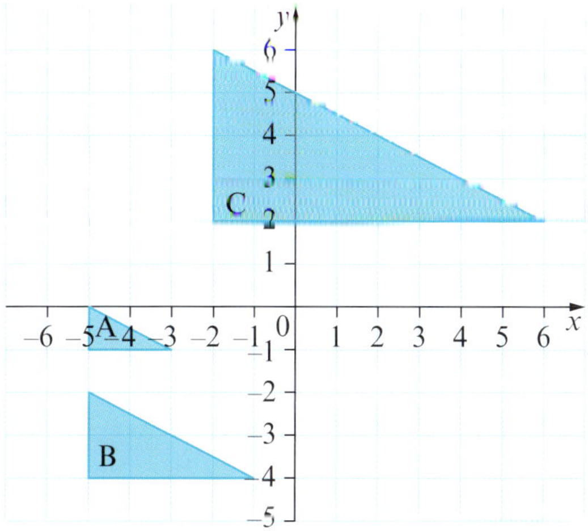

Tip

Remember: to describe an enlargement, you need to write 'Enlargement' and give the scale factor and the centre of enlargement.

10 The vertices of rectangle X are at (1, −2), (1, −3), (3, −3) and (3, −2).
The vertices of rectangle Y are at (−5, 4), (−5, 1), (1, 1) and (1, 4).
Rectangle Y is an enlargement of rectangle X.
Describe the enlargement.

Think like a mathematician

11 Work with a partner to answer this question.
Arun makes this conjecture:

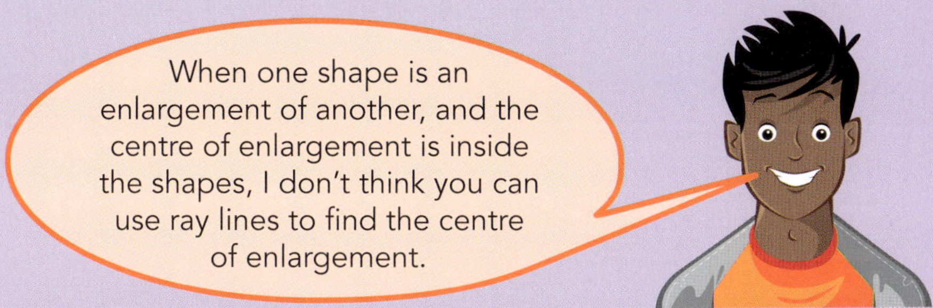

What do you think? Show working to justify your answer.

12 The vertices of shape K are at (4, 7), (7, 7), (7, 4) and (5, 5).
The vertices of shape L are at (0, 11), (9, 11), (9, 2) and (3, 5).
Shape L is an enlargement of shape K. Describe the enlargement.

13 The diagram shows two shapes, A and B. Shape B is an enlargement of shape A. Describe the enlargement.

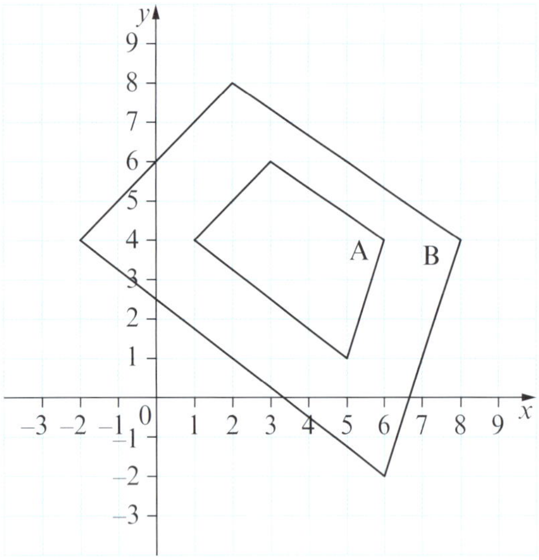

Summary checklist

- ☐ I can enlarge shapes using a positive whole number scale factor from a centre of enlargement.
- ☐ I can identify and describe an enlargement.
- ☐ I can describe changes in the perimeter and area of squares and rectangles when the side lengths are enlarged.

Check your progress

1 A ship leaves a harbour and sails 90 km on a bearing of 140°. The ship then sails 120 km on a bearing of 050°.

- a Make a scale drawing of the ship's journey. Use a scale where 1 cm represents 10 km.
- b How far must the ship now sail to return to the harbour?
- c On what bearing must the ship now sail to return to the harbour?

2 O is the point (0, 0), M is (20, 12) and N is (9, 15).

Work out the coordinates of the point that lies

- a $\frac{1}{4}$ of the way along OM
- b $\frac{2}{3}$ of the way along ON.

3 J is the point (2, 7) and K is the point (12, 22). L is the point that lies $\frac{1}{5}$ of the way along JK.

Work out the coordinates of L.

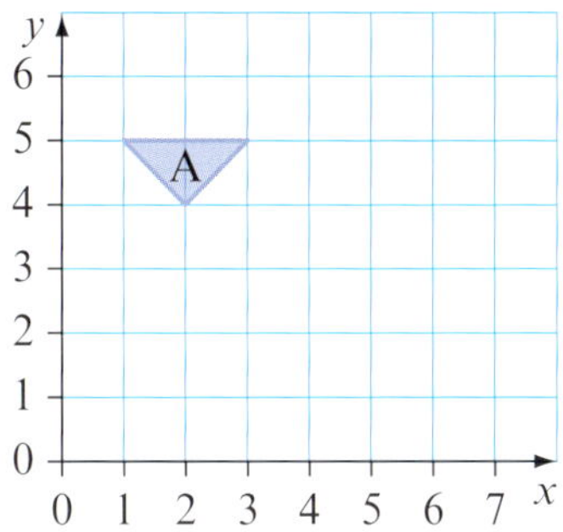

4 The diagram shows a triangle A.

Make two copies of the diagram.

- a Draw the image of A after each combination of transformations. Use a different copy of the diagram for each part.
  - i Translation $\begin{pmatrix} 2 \\ -2 \end{pmatrix}$ followed by reflection in the line $y = 3$. Label the image B.
  - ii Rotation 90° clockwise, centre (3, 3), followed by translation $\begin{pmatrix} -1 \\ -1 \end{pmatrix}$. Label the image C.
- b Describe the single transformation that transforms:
  - i triangle B to triangle A
  - ii triangle C to triangle A.

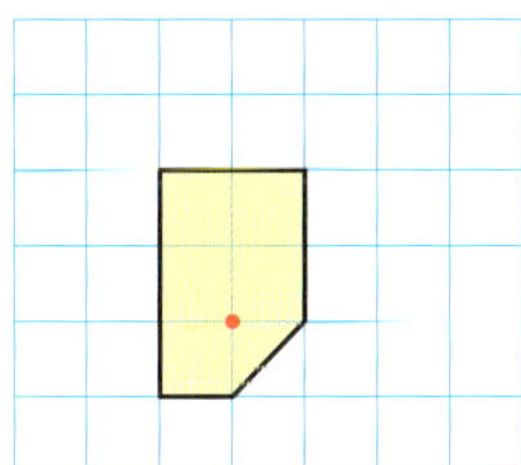

5 Copy the diagram.

Enlarge the shape using a scale factor of 3 and the centre of enlargement shown.

6 The vertices of trapezium T are at (7, 3), (12, 3), (10, 5) and (8, 5).

The vertices of trapezium U are at (1, 1), (4, 7), (10, 7) and (16, 1).

Trapezium U is an enlargement of trapezium T.

Copy and complete this statement:

Trapezium U is an enlargement of trapezium T, scale factor ☐ and centre of enlargement (☐, ☐).

7 A shape, V, has perimeter 18 cm and area 20 cm^2.

The shape is enlarged by a scale factor of 3 to become shape W.

Work out the perimeter and area of shape W.

Project 5

Triangle transformations

Zara drew the blue triangle with vertices at (1, 1), (1, 3) and (2, 1).

She then performed three transformations, one after the other, and ended up with the red triangle, with vertices at (3, 3), (9, 3) and (3, 6).

Finally, Zara performed three more transformations, one after the other, and ended up with the pink triangle, with vertices at (1, 1), (1, −1), and (2, 1).

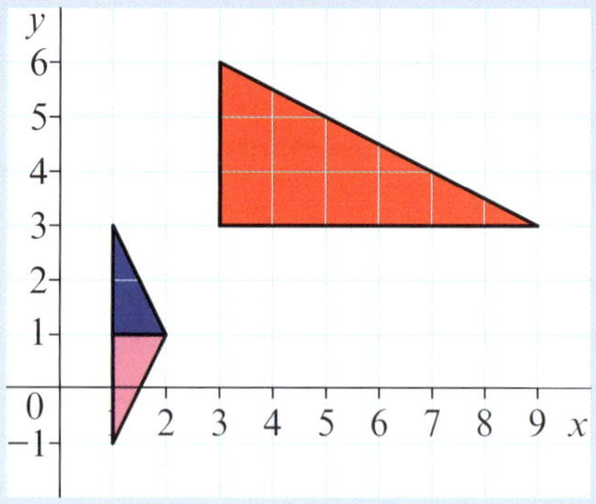

All the transformations Zara performed were chosen from this set of cards:

Rotate 90° clockwise, centre (0, 0)	Rotate 90° anticlockwise, centre (0, 0)	Rotate 180°, centre (0, 0)
Reflect in the line $x = 0$	Reflect in the line $y = 0$	Reflect in the line $y = x$
Reflect in the line $y = -x$	Enlarge by scale factor 3, centre of enlargement (0, 0)	Enlarge by scale factor $\frac{1}{3}$, centre of enlargement (0, 0)
Enlarge by scale factor 2, centre of enlargement (0, 0)	Enlarge by scale factor $\frac{1}{2}$, centre of enlargement (0, 0)	Translate by $\begin{pmatrix} 2 \\ 0 \end{pmatrix}$
Translate by $\begin{pmatrix} 0 \\ 2 \end{pmatrix}$	Translate by $\begin{pmatrix} -2 \\ 0 \end{pmatrix}$	Translate by $\begin{pmatrix} 0 \\ -2 \end{pmatrix}$

- Can you find a set of three transformations that Zara could have performed to get from the **blue** triangle to the **red** triangle?
- Can you find a set of three transformations that Zara could have performed to get from the **red** triangle to the **pink** triangle?
- Can you find a set of three transformations that Zara could have performed to get from the **blue** triangle to the **pink** triangle?
- Can you find **more than one** set of three transformations for any of these?
- Can you get from one triangle to another using **only two** transformations?

Create a triangle transformation of your own using three or more cards of your choice. Write the coordinates of the vertices of your first and last triangles and give them to a partner to see if they can work out which transformation cards you used.

14 Volume, surface area and symmetry

Getting started

1 Work out the circumference of a circle with radius 4 cm. Use the π button on your calculator. Give your answer correct to two decimal places.

2 Work out the area of each shape. Give your answer to part **c** correct to one decimal place.

a 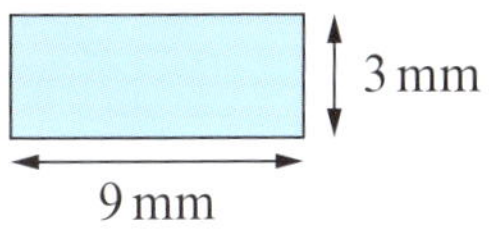

b 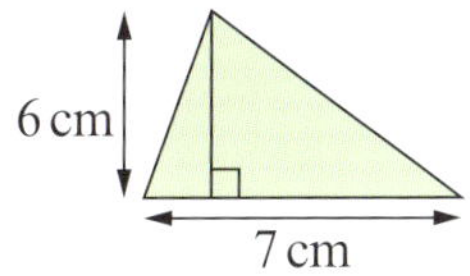

c 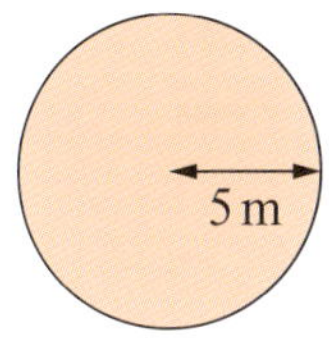

3 The diagram shows a cuboid.

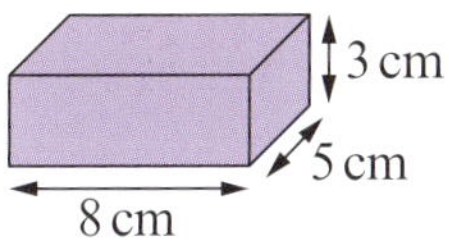

Work out

a the volume of the cuboid

b the surface area of the cuboid.

4 The diagram shows a triangular prism.

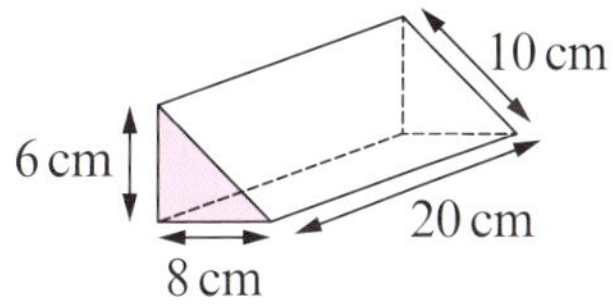

a Work out the volume of the prism.

b Sketch a net of the prism.

c Work out the surface area of the prism.

5 Write the number of lines of symmetry for each of these shapes.

a 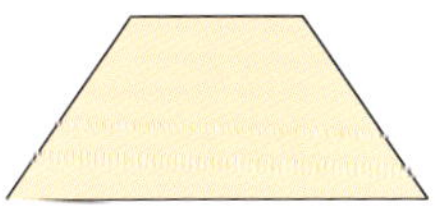

b 

c 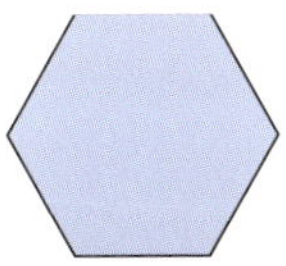

d 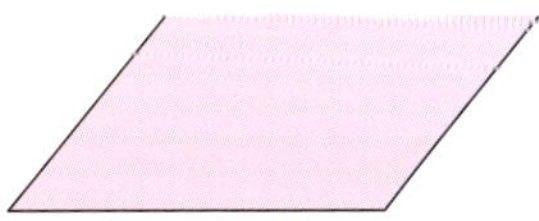

Prisms, pyramids and cylinders are common in everyday life. Most boxes are cuboids, but you will also see different shaped boxes. To make their products look good, manufacturers often use interesting shaped containers to try to encourage customers to buy them. Have you ever thought about:

- the amount of cardboard, tin or paper for labels needed to make different containers?
- the amount of product a container holds?
- the most cost-effective shape and size of container to use?

Manufacturers have to decide how to make their products and packaging as attractive as possible, while keeping costs as low as possible.
This is not an easy thing to do!

14.1 Calculating the volume of prisms

In this section you will ...

- derive and use the formulae for the volume of prisms and cylinders.

You already know that a prism is a 3D shape that has the same cross-section along its length. Here are some examples of prisms. The cross-section of each shape is shaded.

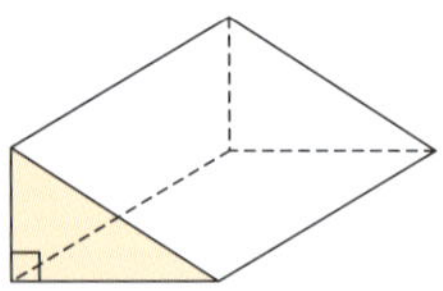

Cross-section is a right-angled triangle.

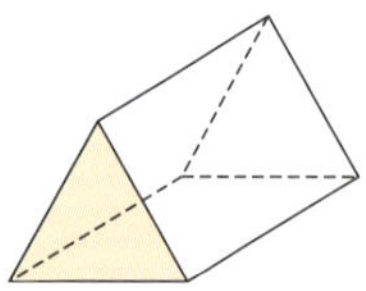

Cross-section is an equilateral triangle.

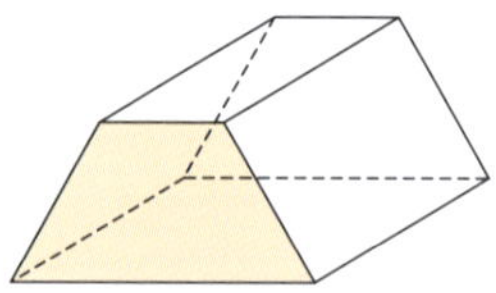

Cross-section is a trapezium.

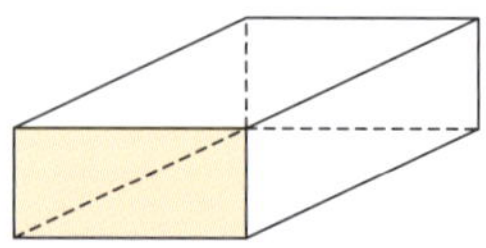

Cross-section is a rectangle.

You can work out the volume of a prism using the formula:

volume = area of cross-section × length

Worked example 14.1

a Work out the volume of this prism.

b A prism has a volume of $135\,\text{cm}^3$.
The area of the cross-section of the prism is $15\,\text{cm}^2$.
What is the length of the prism?

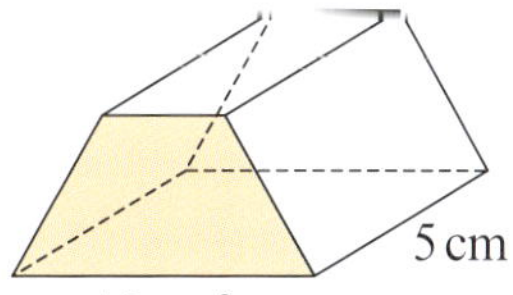

Answer

a V = area of cross-section × length	The area of the cross-section of the prism is $12\,\text{cm}^2$. The length is 5 cm.
$= 12 \times 5$	Substitute these values into the formula for volume.
$= 60\,\text{cm}^3$	Work out the answer and remember the units, cm^3.
b V = area of cross-section × length	Write the formula for the volume of a prism.
$135 = 15 \times$ length	Substitute the values for volume and area into the formula.
length $= 135 \div 15$	Use inverse operations to work out the length of the prism.
$= 9\,\text{cm}$	Work out the answer and remember the units, cm.

Exercise 14.1

In this exercise when you need to use π, use the π button on your calculator.

1 Work out the volume of each prism.

a

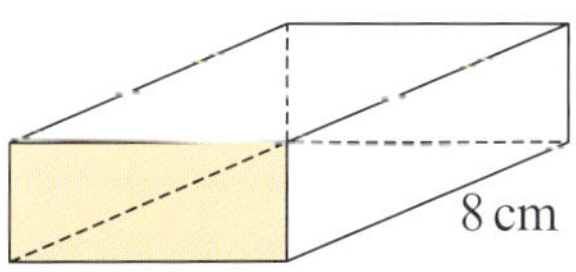

b

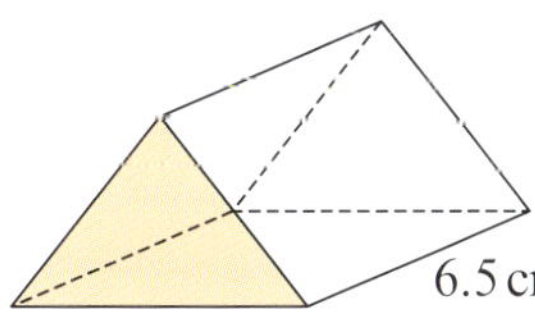

c

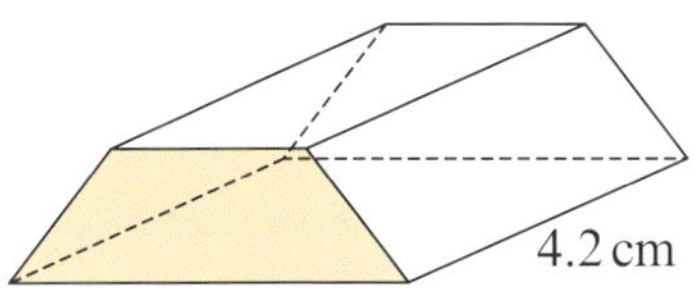

> **Tip**
> Remember to use the formula:
> volume = area of cross-section × length

2 Copy and complete this table.

	Area of cross-section	Length of prism	Volume of prism
a	12 cm^2	10 cm	☐ cm^3
b	24 cm^2	☐ cm	204 cm^3
c	☐ m^2	6.2 m	114.7 m^3

Tip

In parts **b** and **c**, you will need to use inverse operations.

3 This is part of Yusaf's homework.

Question

Work out the volume of this shape.

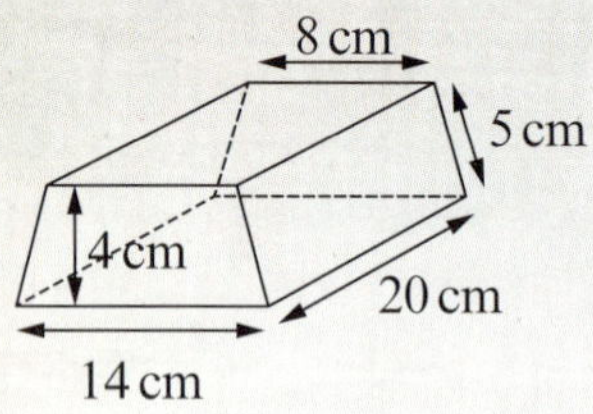

Answer

Area of rectangle $= 20 \times 5 = 100\ cm^2$

Volume = *area of cross-section* × *length*

$= 100 \times 14 = 1400\ cm^3$

a Explain the mistakes Yusaf has made.

b Write out the correct solution.

Think like a mathematician

4 Work with a partner to answer these questions.

The diagram shows a cylinder.

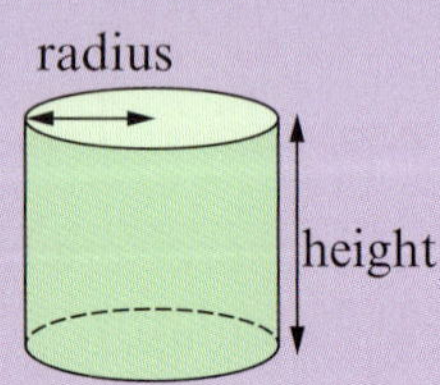

a Is a cylinder a prism? Justify your answer.

b How can you work out the volume of a cylinder?

c Write a formula you can use to work out the volume of a cylinder.

Write your formula in its simplest form. Use r for radius and h for height.

d Discuss your answers to parts **a**, **b** and **c** with other pairs of learners in your class.

5 This is part of Sara's homework.

Question

Work out the volume of this cylinder.

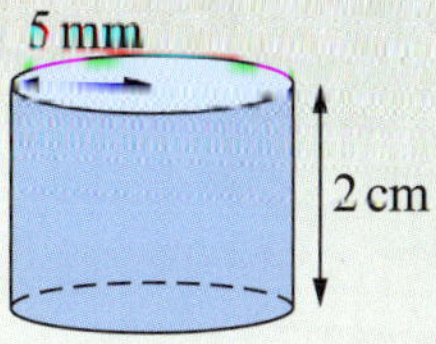

Answer

$V = \pi r^2 h = \pi \times 5^2 \times 2 = \pi \times 25 \times 2$

$= 157\ cm^3$ (3 s.f.)

Sara has got the answer wrong.

Explain the mistake Sara has made and work out the correct answer.

6 Work out the volume of each cylinder.

Give your answers correct to one decimal place (1 d.p.).

a

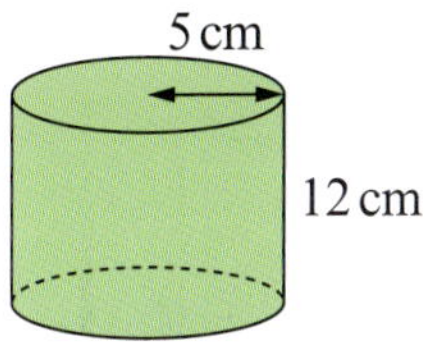

b

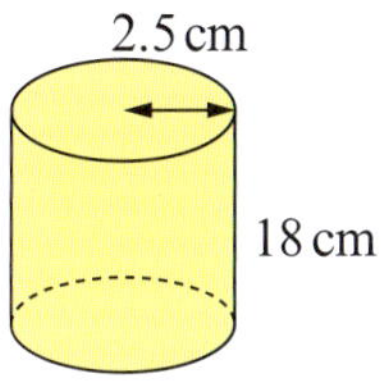

c

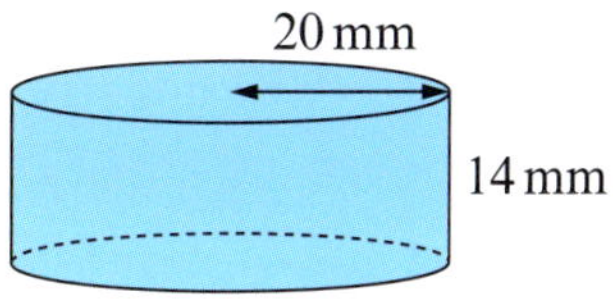

Activity 14.1

Work with a partner to answer this question.

On a piece of paper, draw two cylinders, similar to those in Question **6**. For one of the cylinders write the radius of the circle. For the other cylinder write the diameter of the circle. For both cylinders write the height.

- a On a different piece of paper, work out the volume of each cylinder, correct to two decimal places (2 d.p.). Do not let your partner see your working.
- b Swap pieces of paper with your partner and work out the volumes of their cylinders.
- c Swap back and mark each other's work. Discuss any mistakes that have been made.

7 Copy and complete this table. Give your answers correct to two decimal places (2 d.p.).

	Radius of circle	Area of circle	Height of cylinder	Volume of cylinder
a	2.5 m	☐ m^2	4.2 m	☐ m^3
b	6 cm	☐ cm^2	☐ cm	507 cm^3
c	☐ m	20 m^2	2.5 m	☐ m^3
d	☐ mm	☐ mm^2	16 mm	1044 mm^3

8 Each of these prisms has a volume of $256\,cm^3$.

Work out the length marked x in each diagram. Give your answers correct to one decimal place (1 d.p.).

a

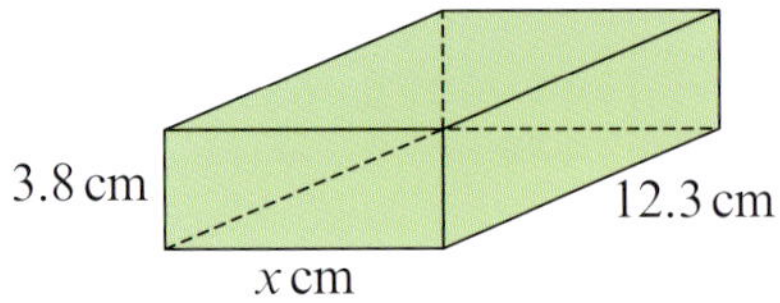

b

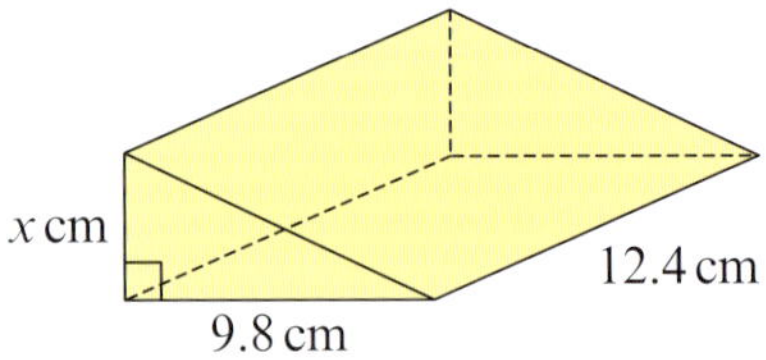

c

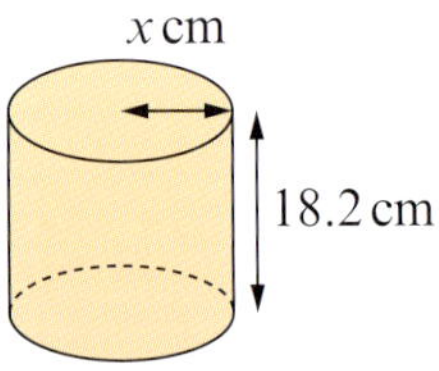

Think like a mathematician

9 Work with a partner to answer this question.

The diagram shows an empty cylindrical container.

Ana puts a solid cube of side length 8 cm into the container.

She then pours 1.5 litres of water into the container.

Will the water come over the top of the container?

Explain your answer and show all your working.

Discuss your methods and answers with other pairs of learners in your class.

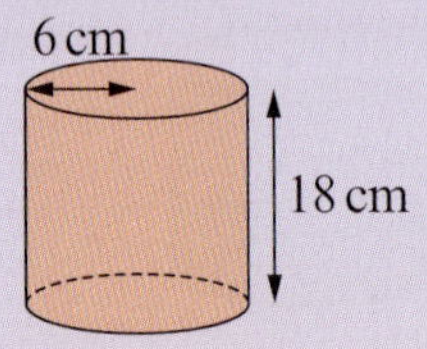

Tip

$1\,cm^3 = 1\,mL$

a Imagine you are a maths teacher. The students in your class have never seen a prism before. Give answers to the following questions:

i What is a prism?

ii What is the cross-section of a prism?

iii How do you work out the volume of a prism?

b Give your explanations to another learner. Do they understand your explanations?

c Do you feel confident in being able to explain about prisms to another person?

Summary checklist

☐ I can derive and use the formulae for the volume of prisms and cylinders.

14.2 Calculating the surface area of triangular prisms, pyramids and cylinders

In this section you will …

- calculate the surface area of triangular prisms, pyramids and cylinders.

You already know how to draw the net of a triangular prism and of a pyramid. You also know how to use nets to work out the surface area of these shapes. You can use the same method to work out the surface area of a cylinder.

Worked example 14.2

The diagram shows a cylinder.

a Sketch a net of the cylinder.

b Work out the surface area of the cylinder.

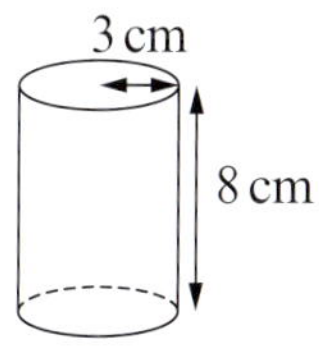

Answer

a

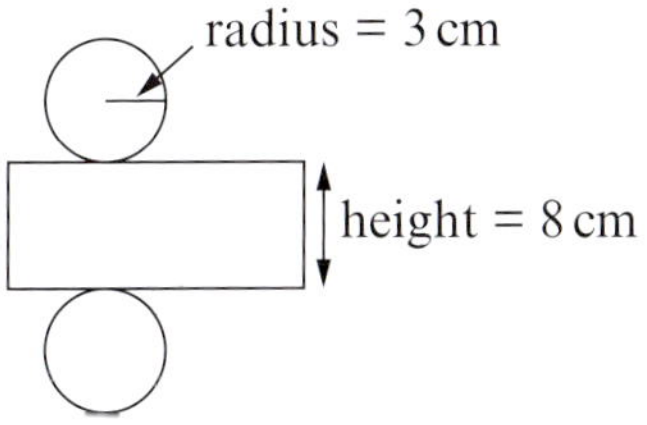

The net of the cylinder is made up of two circles, one for the top and one for the bottom of the cylinder.

When you 'unfold' the curved surface of a cylinder it is a rectangle. The height of the rectangle is the height of the cylinder. The length of the rectangle is the circumference of the circle.

b Area of circle $= \pi r^2$

$= \pi \times 3^2$

$= 28.27 \text{ cm}^2$

Work out the area of one of the circular ends. Substitute the radius measurement into the formula for the area of a circle and write the answer to at least two decimal places.

Continued

Circumference of circle $= \pi d$

$= \pi \times 6$

$= 18.85$ cm

The curved surface of a cylinder is a rectangle. The length of this rectangle is the circumference of the circle.

Work out the diameter first: $r = 3$ cm so $d = 6$ cm.

Then work out the circumference.

Area of rectangle $= 18.85 \times 8$

$= 150.80\text{ cm}^2$

Finally, work out the area of the curved surface (length × height) and write the answer to at least two decimal places.

Total area $= 2 \times 28.27 + 150.80$

$= 207.3\text{ cm}^2$

Add together the areas of the two ends and the curved surface.

Write the final answer correct to one decimal place.

Exercise 14.2

In this exercise when you need to use π, use the π button on your calculator.

1 Copy and complete the workings to find the surface area of this cylinder.

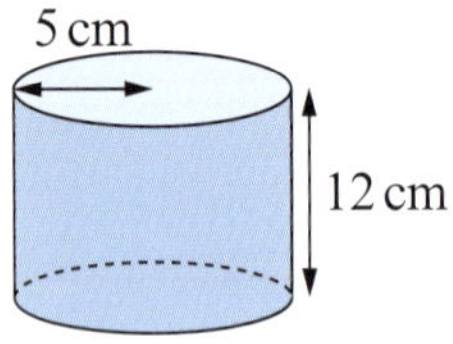

Area of circle $= \pi r^2$

$= \pi \times 5^2$

$= \square\text{ cm}^2$ (2 d.p.)

Circumference of circle $= \pi d$

$= \pi \times \square$

$= \square$ cm (2 d.p.)

Area of rectangle $= \square \times 12$

$= \square\text{ cm}^2$ (2 d.p.)

Total area $= 2 \times \square + \square$

$= \square\text{ cm}^2$ (3 s.f.)

Tip

Sketch the net of the cylinder, like this.

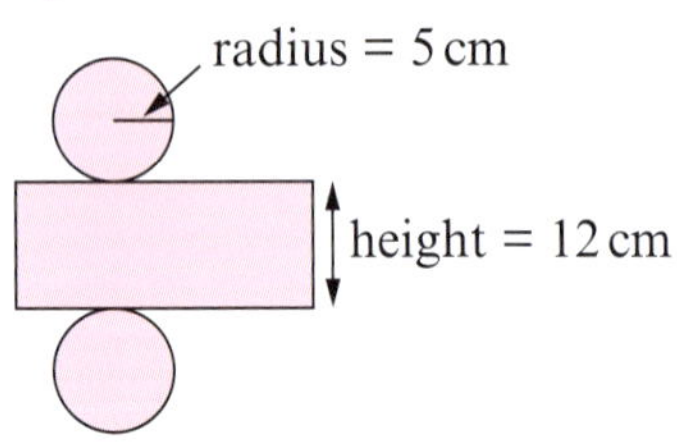

2 Work out the surface area of each cylinder.
Give your answers correct to one decimal place (1 d.p.).

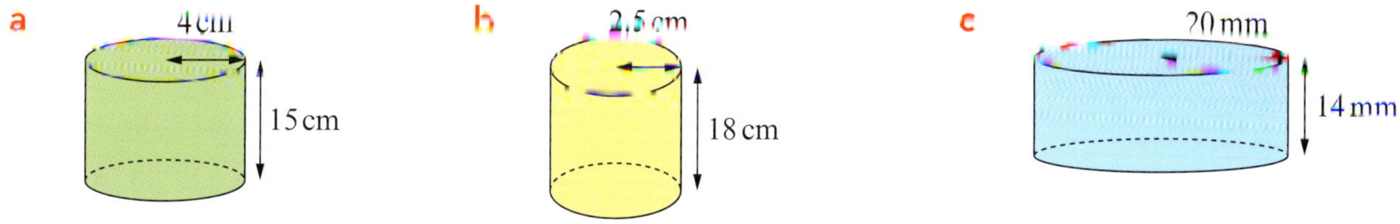

3 The diagram shows a square-based pyramid and a cylinder.
Which shape has the greater surface area? Show your working.

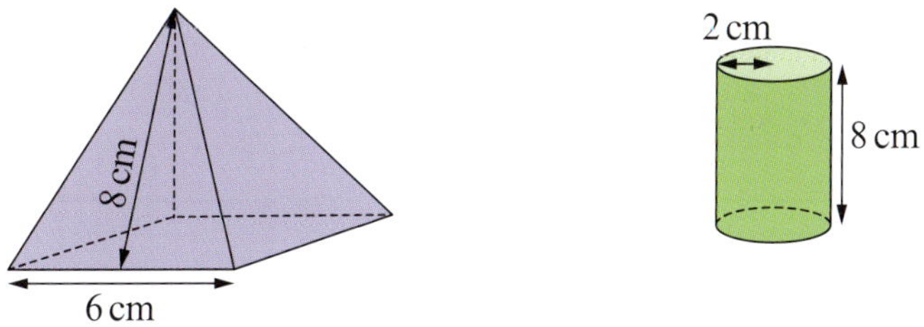

Think like a mathematician

4 Work with a partner to answer this question.
The diagram shows a cylinder.
The circular cross-section has radius r cm.
The height of the cylinder is h cm.

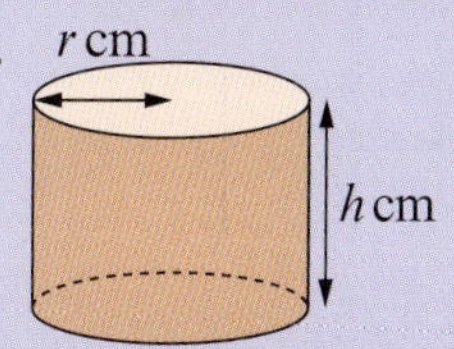

- **a** Write a formula, using r and h, for the surface area (SA) of the cylinder.
- **b** Show that you can simplify the formula in part **a** to $SA = 2\pi r(r + h)$.
- **c** When the height is twice the radius, show that the formula for the surface area of the cylinder can be simplified to $SA = 6\pi r^2$.
- **d** Simplify the formula for the surface area of the cylinder when
  - **i** $h = 3r$ **ii** $h = 4r$ **iii** $h = 5r$
- **e** Can you spot a pattern in your answers to part **d**? Use this pattern to write the formula for the surface area of the cylinder when $h = 19r$.
- **f** Discuss your methods and answers to parts **a** to **e** with other pairs of learners in your class.

Tip

For part **c**, replace h with $2r$ in the formula from part **b** and then simplify.

5 The circular cross-section of a cylinder has radius 3 cm. The height of the cylinder is three times the radius. Work out the surface area of the cylinder correct to three significant figures.

Think like a mathematician

6 Work with a partner to answer this question.
The diagram shows a triangular prism.
The triangular cross-section is a right-angled triangle.

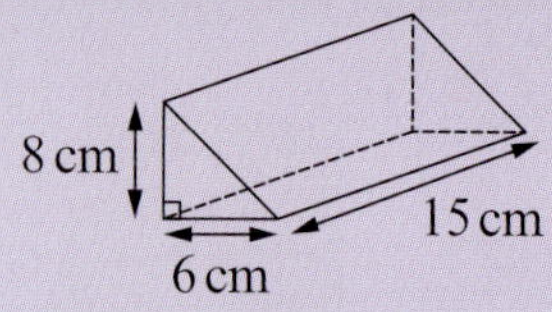

a Before you work out the surface area of the prism, answer these questions:
   i Which length that you need to use is missing from the diagram?
   ii How can you work out this missing length?

b Discuss your answers to part **a** with other pairs of learners in your class.

c Work out the surface area of the prism. Compare your answers with other pairs of learners in your class. Discuss any mistakes that have been made.

7 Work out the surface area of these triangular prisms.
The triangular cross-section of each prism is a right-angled triangle.
Give your answer to part **c** correct to one decimal place (1 d.p.).

a
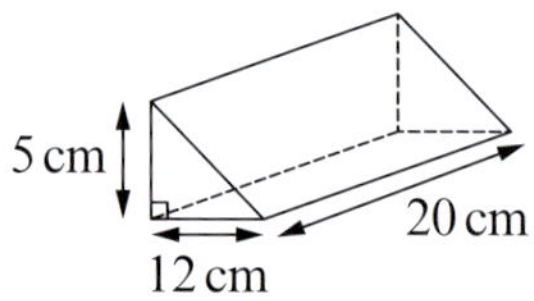

b
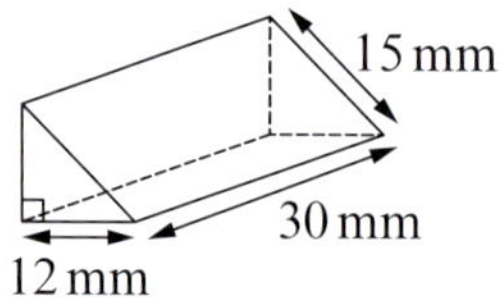

c
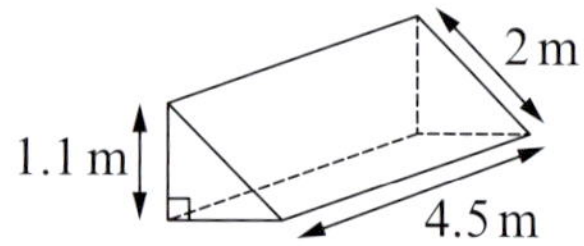

Activity 14.2

Work with a partner for this activity.

A manufacturer wants to design different shaped boxes to hold sweets. The volume of each box must be about 800 cm^3.

a Design some different boxes with a volume of approximately 800 cm^3. Try to include a cuboid, a triangular prism and a cylinder.

b Work out the surface area of each of your boxes.

c Which box would you recommend for the manufacturer to use? Explain why.

d Discuss your methods, answers and decisions with other pairs of learners in your class.

8 The diagram shows a cardboard tube.
Work out the area of cardboard needed to make the tube.
Give your answer correct to three significant figures (3 s.f.).

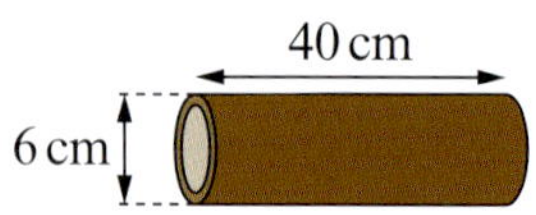

9 The diagram shows a tin of beans.

A label is cut to the exact size of the curved surface of the tin and glued on to the tin.

Labels are cut from a rectangular piece of paper that measures 35 cm by 120 cm.

What is the maximum number of labels that can be cut from one piece of paper? Show all your working.

Summary checklist

- ☐ I can calculate the surface area of triangular prisms.
- ☐ I can calculate the surface area of pyramids.
- ☐ I can calculate the surface area of cylinders.

14.3 Symmetry in three-dimensional shapes

In this section you will …

- identify reflective symmetry in 3D shapes.

Key words

isometric paper

plane of symmetry

Three-dimensional shapes can be symmetrical. For example, this chair is symmetrical. Instead of a line of symmetry, a 3D shape has a **plane of symmetry**. In three dimensions, a plane of symmetry divides a solid into two congruent parts.

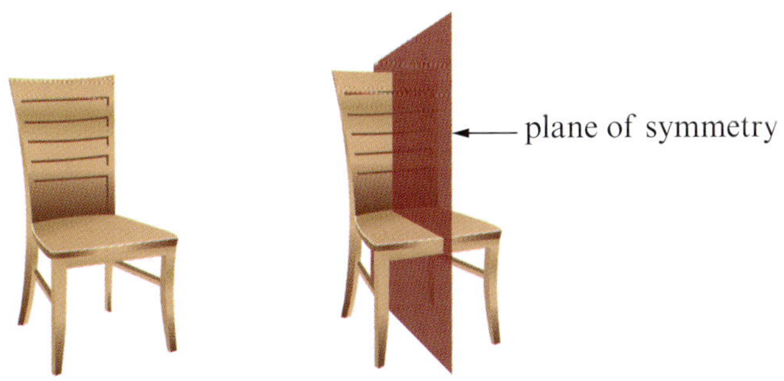

Tip

If you imagine a mirror on the plane, one half of the chair is a reflection of the other half of the chair.

Worked example 14.3

How many planes of symmetry does this cuboid have?

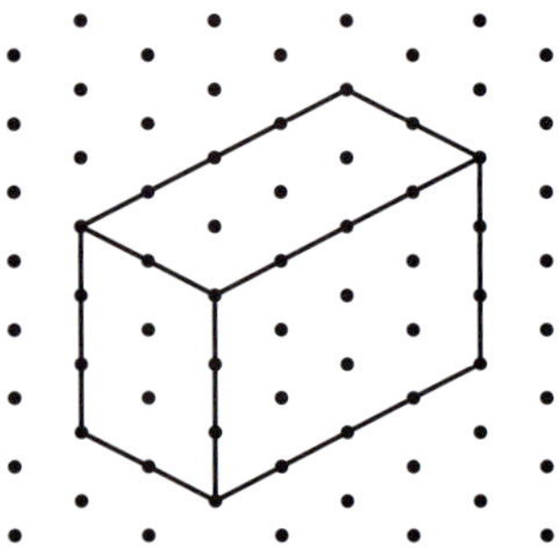

Answer

The cuboid has three planes of symmetry: two vertical planes of symmetry and one horizontal plane of symmetry. Each plane of symmetry divides the cuboid into two congruent parts which are the mirror image of each other.

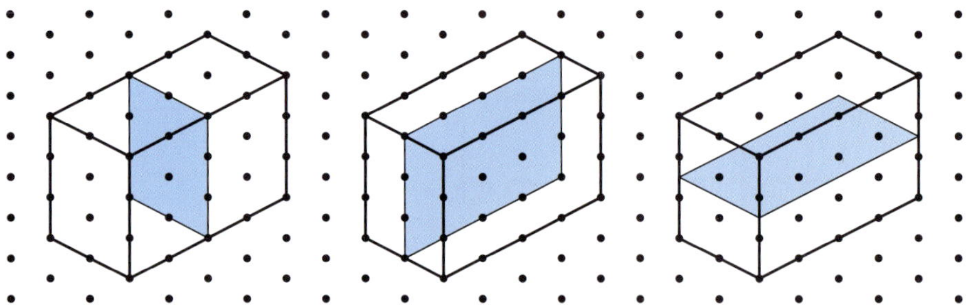

Exercise 14.3

1 These shapes are drawn on **isometric paper**.

Each shape has one plane of symmetry.

Copy the diagrams and draw the plane of symmetry on each shape.

a

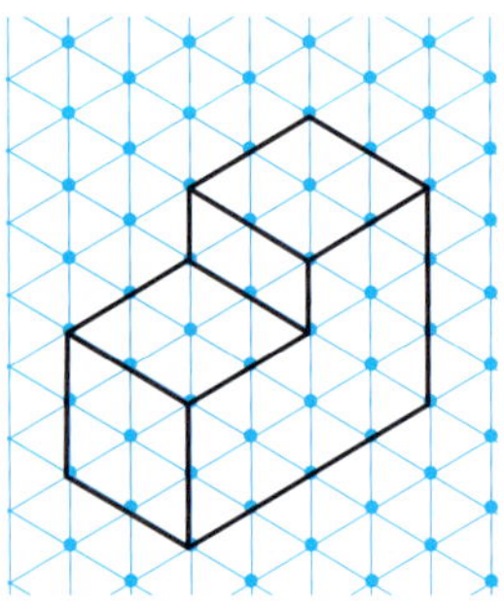

b

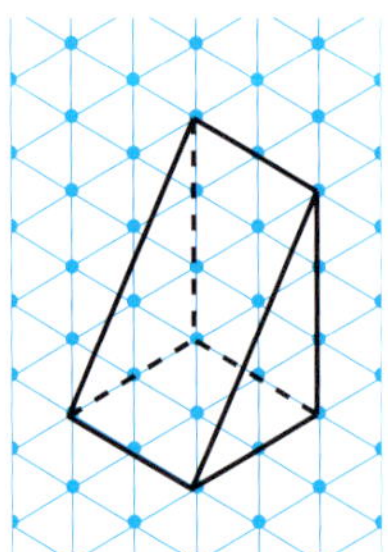

c

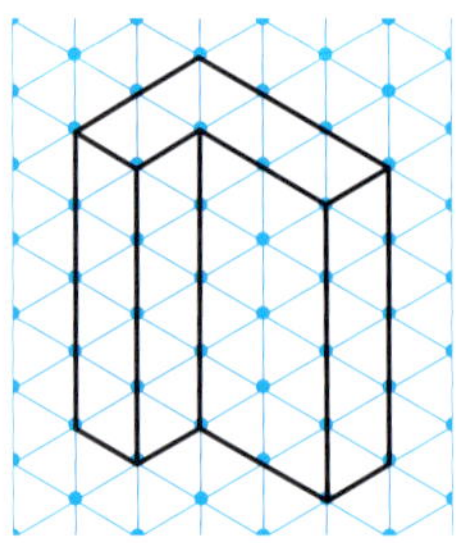

Tip

Shapes **a** and **b** have a vertical plane of symmetry and shape **c** has a horizontal plane of symmetry.

2 Shape **a** has two planes of symmetry. Shape **b** has three planes of symmetry.

Copy the diagrams and draw the planes of symmetry on each shape.

a 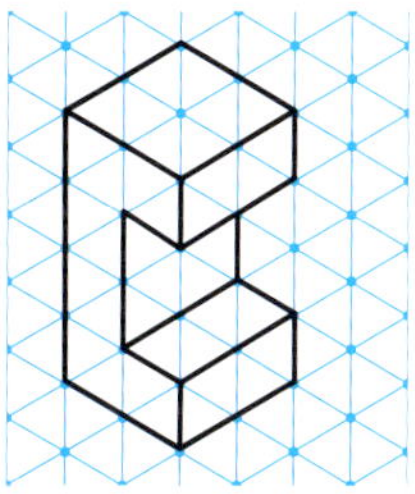

b 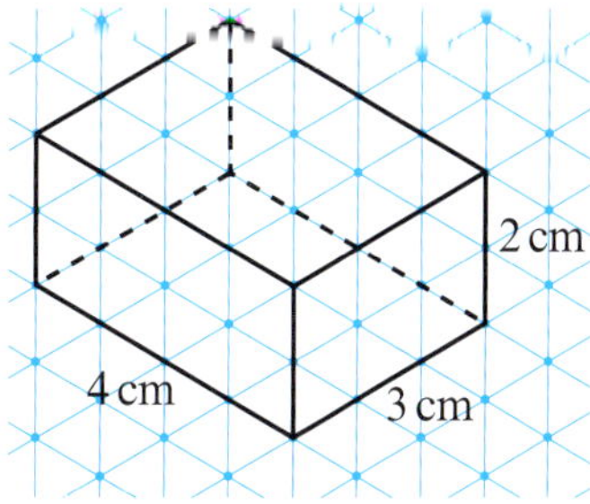

Tip

Shape **a** has one vertical and one horizontal plane of symmetry. Shape **b** has two vertical planes and one horizontal plane of symmetry.

3 The diagram shows an L-shaped prism.

a Draw the object on isometric paper.

b The prism has one plane of symmetry.

Draw the plane of symmetry on your isometric drawing.

c Describe the plane of symmetry.

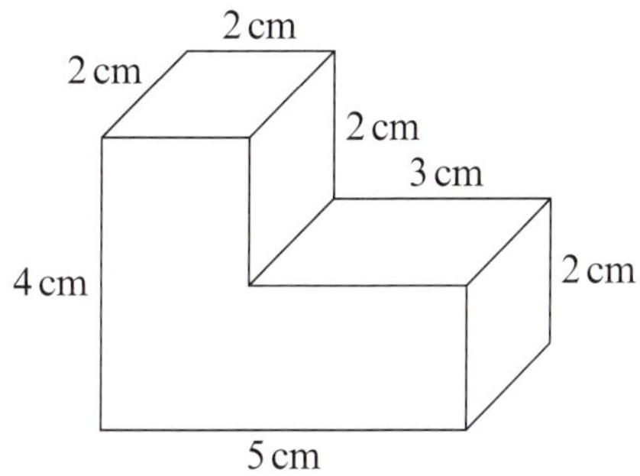

Tip

For part **c**, is the plane of symmetry horizontal, vertical or diagonal?

Think like a mathematician

4 a Draw a cube. Draw a plane of symmetry that passes through four edges but no vertices.

b Draw the cube again. Draw a plane of symmetry that passes through four vertices of the cube.

c Copy and complete this statement: A cube has a total of ☐ planes of symmetry.

d Draw diagrams to justify your answer to part **c**.

e Compare your answers and diagrams for parts **a** to **d** with other learners in your class.

5 The diagram shows a 3D shape.

a Describe the planes of symmetry for this shape.

b Copy the shape and draw on the planes of symmetry.

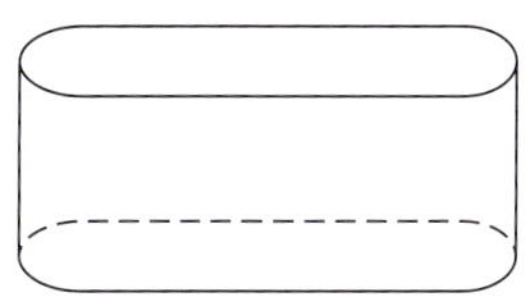

Think like a mathematician

6 Here are some regular polygons.

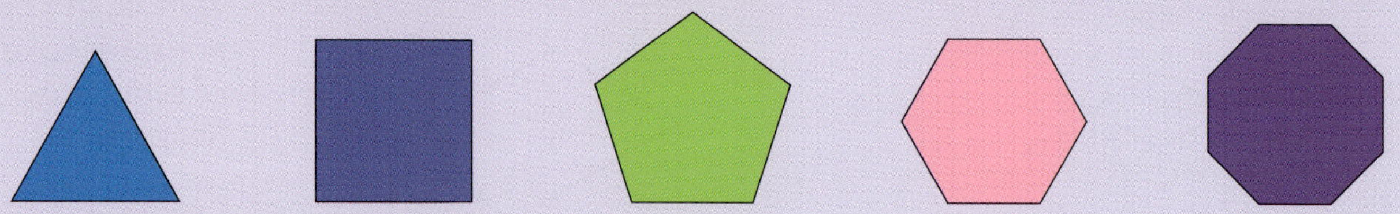

Equilateral triangle | Square | Pentagon | Hexagon | Octagon

Each regular polygon is made into a prism as shown.

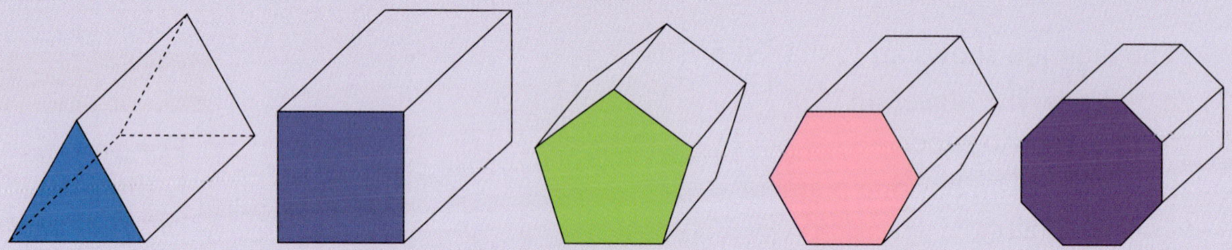

Triangular prism | Square prism | Pentagonal prism | Hexagonal prism | Octagonal prism

a Copy and complete this table.

2D regular polygon	Number of lines of symmetry	3D prism	Number of planes of symmetry
triangle		triangular	
square		square	
pentagon		pentagonal	
hexagon		hexagonal	
octagon		octagonal	

b What is the connection between the number of lines of symmetry of a regular 2D polygon and the number of planes of symmetry of its matching 3D prism? Explain why this connection occurs.

c Use your answer to part **b** to write the number of planes of symmetry of a regular

i decagonal prism

ii dodecagonal prism.

d Discuss your answers to parts **a** to **c** with other learners in your class.

> **Tip**
>
> A decagon has 10 sides and a dodecagon has 12 sides.

7 a Draw a cylinder.
b Draw a plane of symmetry that passes through the circular ends of the cylinder.
c Draw a plane of symmetry that does **not** pass through the circular ends of the cylinder.
d How many planes of symmetry does a cylinder have? Explain your answer.

Discuss with a partner

a the similarities between a line of symmetry and a plane of symmetry

b the differences between a line of symmetry and a plane of symmetry.

Tip

Use words such as congruent, 2D, 3D, mirror, etc.

Summary checklist

- [ ] I can identify reflective symmetry in 3D shapes.

Check your progress

1 Work out the volume of this prism.

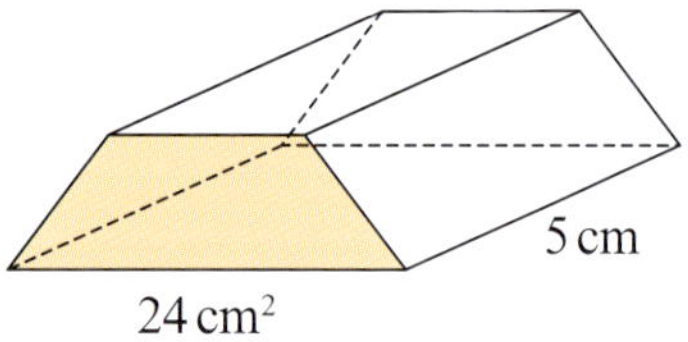

2 A prism has a volume of $112\,m^3$. It has a length of 8 m.
Work out the area of the cross-section of the prism.

3 A cylinder has a height of 9 cm. The radius of the circular cross-section is 4 cm.
Work out the volume of the cylinder correct to three significant figures (3 s.f.).

4 The diagram shows a square-based pyramid and a cylinder.
Which shape has the greater surface area? Show your working.

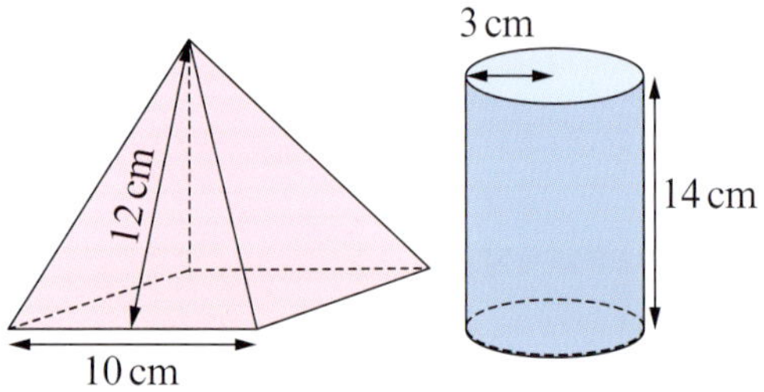

5 The diagram shows a 3D shape.

a Describe the planes of symmetry for this shape.

b Copy the shape and draw on the planes of symmetry.

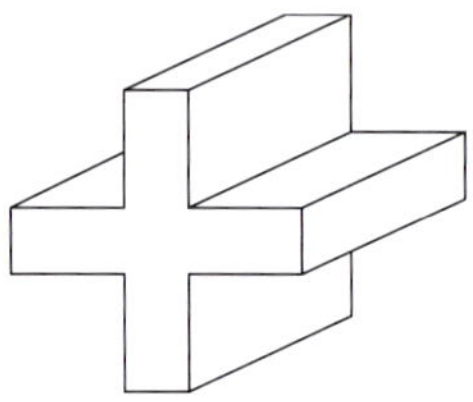

15 Interpreting and discussing results

Getting started

1 Here are the ages, to the nearest year, of the members of a sailing club.

16	13	18	20	23	29	20	21	14	25
28	24	16	12	29	21	25	22	20	27

a Record this information in a frequency table.
Use the classes $10 < a \leqslant 15$, $15 < a \leqslant 20$, $20 < a \leqslant 25$ and $25 < a \leqslant 30$.

b Draw a frequency diagram to show the data.

c How many of the members are more than 20 years old?

2 The students in class 9P took a test. The table shows the results, out of 40.

18	12	40	22	17	39	16	27	28	30	39	26	36
40	14	23	8	24	38	31	19	39	24	3	9	

a Draw an ordered stem-and-leaf diagram showing their scores out of 40.

b What percentage of the students had a score greater than 30?

c What fraction of the students had a score less than 15?

d Any student scoring less than 60% fails the test. How many students did not fail the test?

3 The test marks, out of 20, of two groups of students are shown.

History: 12, 16, 14, 9, 10, 16, 12, 15, 16, 9

Chemistry: 15, 20, 8, 18, 5, 18, 11, 17

a Copy and complete this table.

	Mean	Median	Mode	Range
History				
Chemistry				

Continued

b Does the history group or the chemistry group have better marks on average? Justify your answer.

c Does the history group or the chemistry group have more consistent marks? Justify your answer.

Here are the results for the soccer teams FC Barcelona, Real Madrid and Sevilla in La Liga one year. The table shows how many games were won, drawn or lost by each team.

	Won	Drawn	Lost
FC Barcelona	28	5	5
Real Madrid	18	10	10
Sevilla	14	10	14

A group of students used computer software to draw charts of these results. Here are some of the charts they drew.

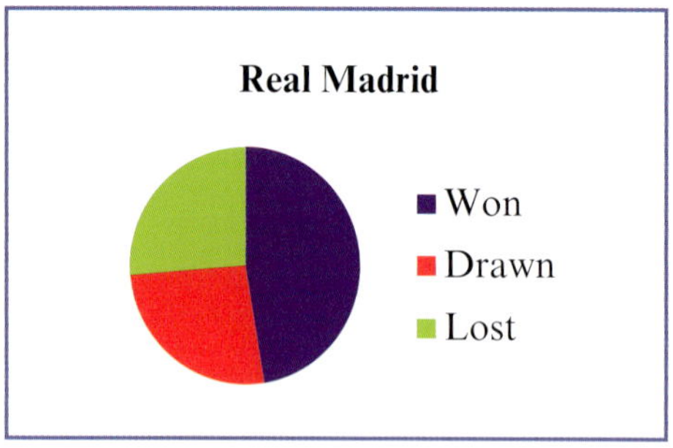

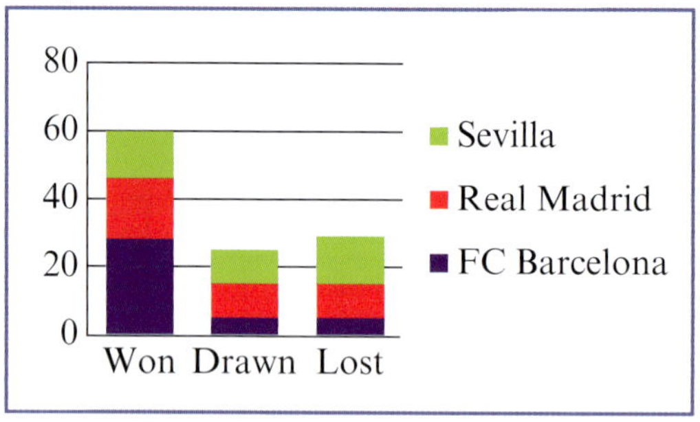

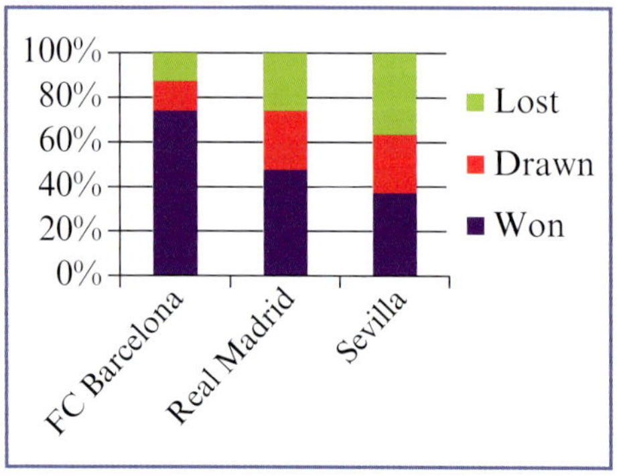

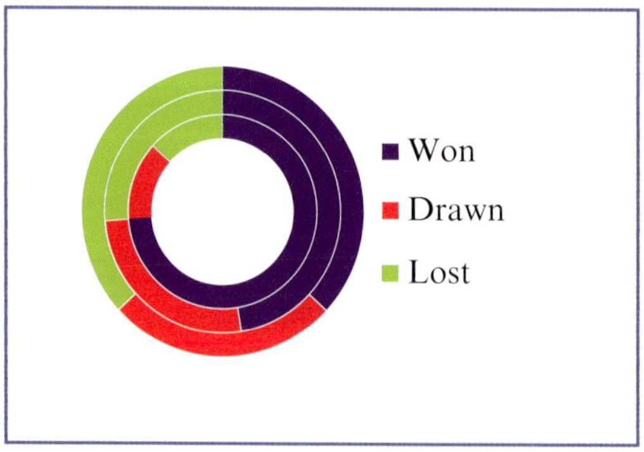

- What do you think of these charts?
- Which is the best chart?
- Which chart is not very useful?
- How could you improve the charts?
- What chart would you draw to best show the results in the table?

It is important to draw charts which effectively show the data you are given. A chart that does not effectively show the data is not very useful.

15.1 Interpreting and drawing frequency polygons

In this section you will …

- draw and interpret frequency polygons for discrete and continuous data.

Key words

frequency polygon
midpoint

You already know how to draw frequency diagrams for discrete and continuous data. You can also draw a **frequency polygon** for continuous data. Drawing a frequency polygon is a useful way to show patterns, or trends, in the data. When you draw a frequency polygon, you plot the frequency against the **midpoint** of the class interval.

Worked example 15.1

The frequency table shows the masses of 20 teachers.

Draw a frequency polygon to show the data.

Mass, m (kg)	Frequency
$60 \leqslant m < 70$	4
$70 \leqslant m < 80$	5
$80 \leqslant m < 90$	9
$90 \leqslant m < 100$	2

Answer

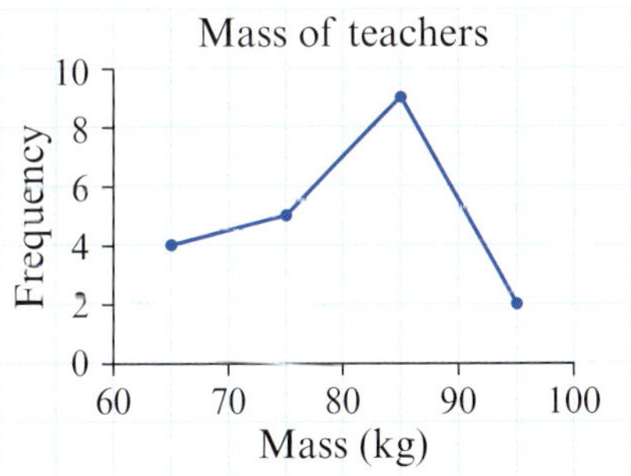

Add a column to the frequency table to show the midpoint of each class interval.

Mass, m (kg)	Frequency	Midpoint
$60 \leqslant m < 70$	4	65
$70 \leqslant m < 80$	5	75
$80 \leqslant m < 90$	9	85
$90 \leqslant m < 100$	2	95

Plot each frequency against its midpoint, then join the points with straight lines.

Exercise 15.1

1 The table shows the heights of the students in class 9R.

a Copy and complete the table.

b Copy and complete the frequency polygon.

Height, h (cm)	Frequency	Midpoint
$140 \leqslant h < 150$	7	
$150 \leqslant h < 160$	13	
$160 \leqslant h < 170$	6	
$170 \leqslant h < 180$	2	

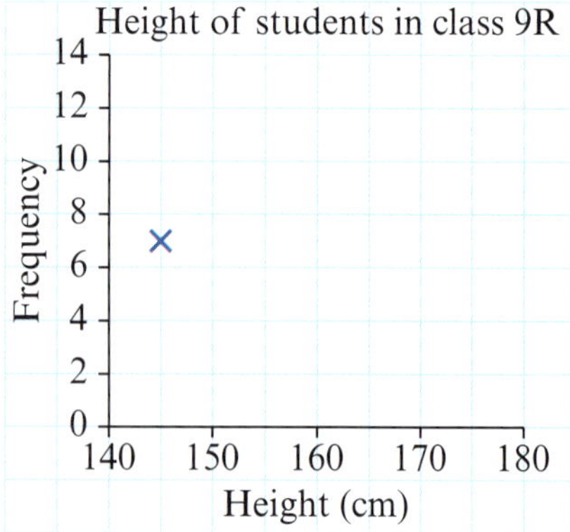

2 The table shows the masses of the students in class 9T.

a Copy and complete the table.

b Draw a frequency polygon for this data.

c How many students are there in class 9T?

d What fraction of the students have a mass less than 60 kg?

e Arun says:

Mass, m (kg)	Frequency	Midpoint
$40 \leqslant m < 50$	4	
$50 \leqslant m < 60$	12	
$60 \leqslant m < 70$	8	

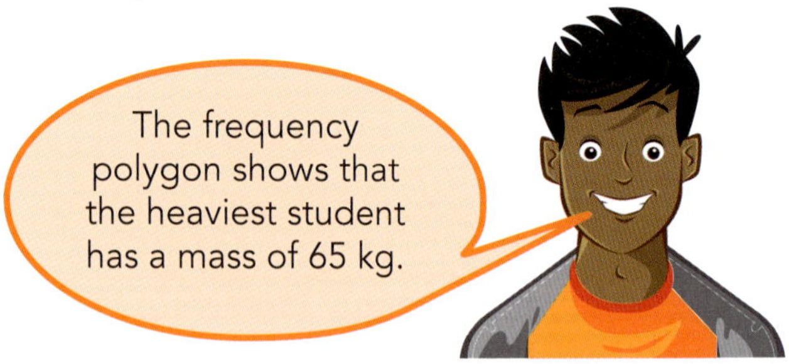

Is Arun correct? Explain your answer.

Think like a mathematician

3 Work with a partner or in a small group to answer this question.
Evan recorded the ages of the members of a cycling club.
Here are his results:

25	30	44	18	33	13	43	32	54	49	35	29	60	72
61	10	75	69	52	32	27	16	36	22	47	58	41	21

a Record this information in a frequency table. Choose your own suitable classes. Make sure you have equal class intervals.

b Draw a frequency polygon to show the data.

c Compare your frequency table and polygon with other groups.
Discuss the classes you used. Which classes do you think are best to show this data? Explain why.

4 Here are the times, in minutes, it took 24 people to complete a puzzle.

17	21	28	27	13	28	14	33	37	22	44	38
35	42	30	32	25	34	36	22	26	39	17	48

a Record this information in a frequency table. Choose your own suitable classes.

b Draw a frequency polygon to show the data.

5 Ahmad carried out a survey on the length of time patients waited to see a doctor at two different doctors' surgeries. The tables show the results of his survey.

Oaklands Surgery		
Time, t (minutes)	Frequency	Midpoint
$0 \leqslant t < 10$	25	
$10 \leqslant t < 20$	10	
$20 \leqslant t < 30$	12	
$30 \leqslant t < 40$	3	

Birchfields Surgery		
Time, t (minutes)	Frequency	Midpoint
$0 \leqslant t < 10$	8	
$10 \leqslant t < 20$	14	
$20 \leqslant t < 30$	17	
$30 \leqslant t < 40$	11	

a How many people were surveyed at each surgery?

b Copy and complete the tables.

c On the same grid, draw a frequency polygon for each set of data.

Make sure you show clearly which frequency polygon represents which surgery.

d Compare the two frequency polygons. What can you say about the waiting times at the two surgeries?

Think like a mathematician

6 Sofia and Zara use different methods to draw a frequency polygon for the data in this table.

Time, t (hours)	Frequency
$0 \leqslant t < 2$	6
$2 \leqslant t < 4$	8
$4 \leqslant t < 6$	2

Continued

Sofia writes:

I draw a frequency diagram first, then join the midpoints of the bars.

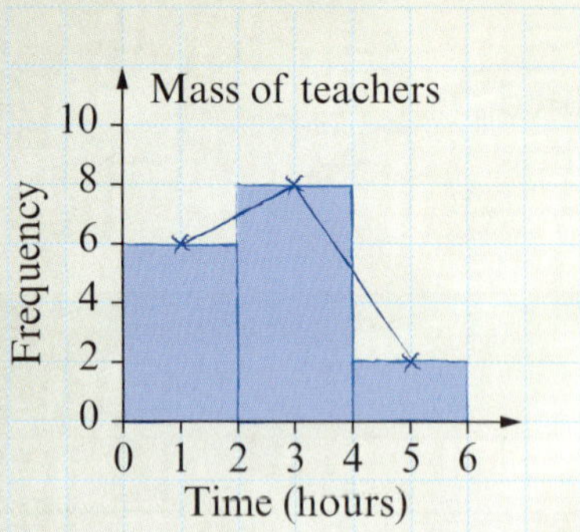

Zara writes:

I work out the midpoints first, plot the points and then join them.

The midpoints are at 1, 3 and 5.

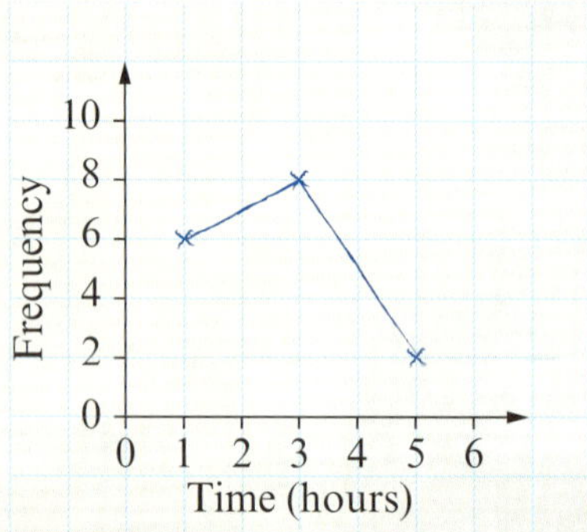

a Critique their methods.

b Whose method do you prefer and why?

c Discuss your answers to parts **a** and **b** with other learners in your class.

7 Jeff grew 40 plants. He grew 20 plants in a greenhouse and 20 plants outdoors.

The heights of the 20 plants grown in the greenhouse are shown in the table.

Height, h (cm)	Frequency
$0 \leqslant h < 10$	2
$10 \leqslant h < 20$	4
$20 \leqslant h < 30$	8
$30 \leqslant h < 40$	6

a Draw a frequency polygon for the data in the table.

b This frequency polygon shows the heights of the 20 plants grown outdoors.

Compare the two frequency polygons (the diagram shown here and the diagram you drew in part **a**). What can you say about the heights of the two sets of plants?

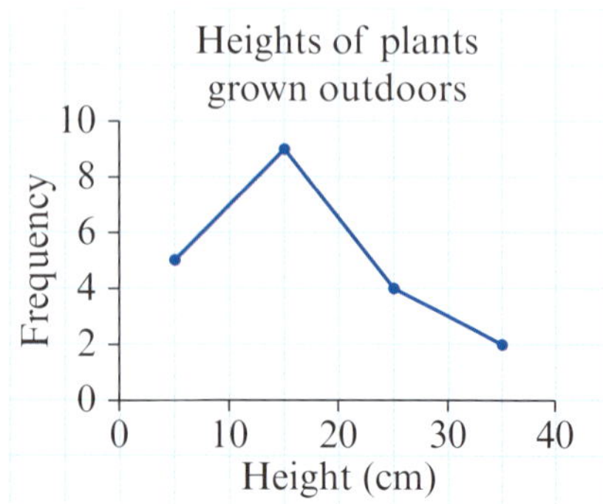

8 Liza carried out a survey on the number of hours that some learners spent doing homework each week. The frequency diagrams show the results of her survey.

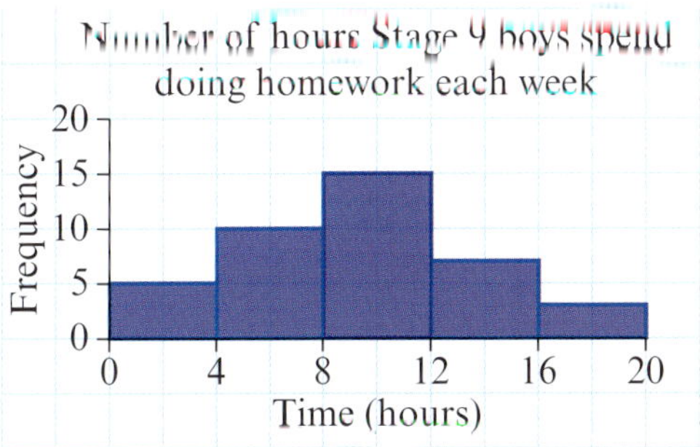

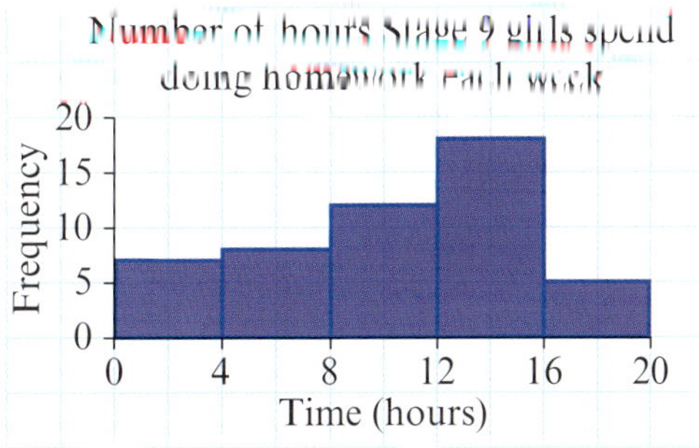

a On the same grid, draw a frequency polygon for each set of data.

b Compare the two frequency polygons.

What can you say about the amount of time that boys and girls spend doing homework?

c How many boys and how many girls were surveyed?

d Do you think it is fair to make a comparison using these sets of data? Explain your answer.

9 The table shows the lengths of 40 sea turtles.

Length, l (cm)	Frequency
$190 \leqslant l < 210$	5
$210 \leqslant l < 230$	8
$230 \leqslant l < 250$	11
$250 \leqslant l < 270$	7
$270 \leqslant l < 290$	5
$290 \leqslant l < 310$	4

a Draw a frequency polygon for the data in the table.

b Marcus wants to draw a frequency table with fewer groups. He regroups the data and draws this frequency table:

i Copy and complete Marcus' frequency table.

ii Draw a frequency polygon for the data in Marcus' table.

Length, l (cm)	Frequency
$190 \leqslant l < 230$	
$230 \leqslant l < 270$	
$270 \leqslant l < 310$	

c Compare your frequency polygons in parts **a** and **bi**. Which frequency polygon gives you better information on the length of the sea turtles? Explain your answer.

Tip

bi Use the frequencies in the table at the start of the question.

d Arun wants to draw a frequency table with more groups. This is the table he starts to draw:

i How many groups will there be in Arun's frequency table?

ii Can Arun fill in the correct frequencies in his table, using the frequencies in the table at the start of the question? Explain your answer.

Length, l (cm)	Frequency
$190 \leqslant l < 200$	
$200 \leqslant l < 210$	
$210 \leqslant l < 220$	
$220 \leqslant l < 230$	

Summary checklist

☐ I can draw and interpret frequency polygons for continuous data.

15.2 Scatter graphs

In this section you will …

- draw and interpret scatter graphs.

Key words

correlation
line of best fit
scatter graph

A **scatter graph** is a useful way to compare two sets of data. You can use a scatter graph to find out whether there is a **correlation**, or relationship, between the two sets of data. Two sets of data could have:

- **positive correlation** – as one value increases, the other value also increases. For example, as the age of a car increases, the distance it has travelled also increases. This scatter graph shows what this graph could look like.

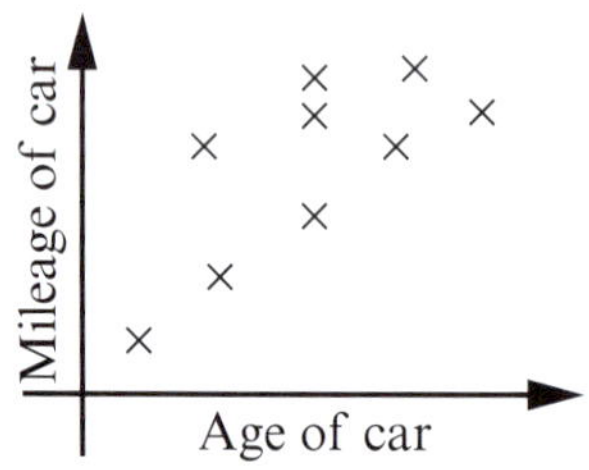

- **negative correlation** – as one value increases, the other value decreases. For example, as the age of a car increases, the value of the car decreases. This scatter graph shows what this graph could look like.

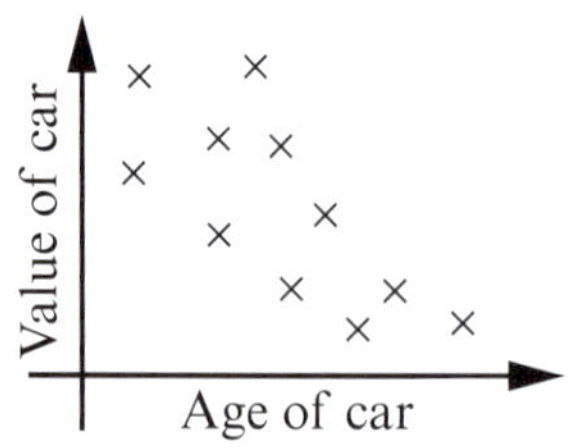

- **no correlation** – there is no relationship between one set of values and the other set of values. For example, adults' heights do not relate to their ages. This scatter graph shows what this graph could look like.

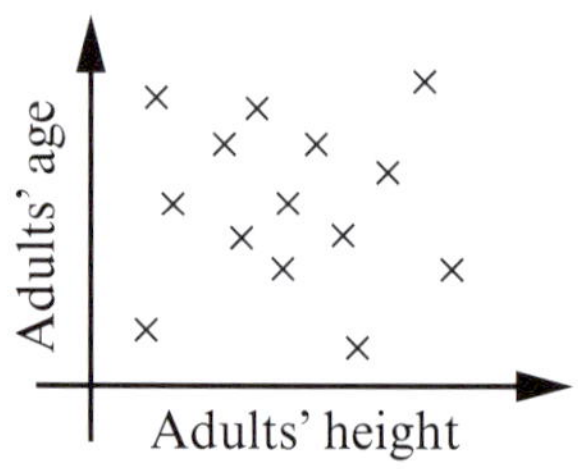

When two sets of data have positive or negative correlation, you can draw a **line of best fit** on the scatter graph. The line of best fit shows the relationship between the two sets of data. You can use the line of best fit to estimate other values. If two sets of data have a strong correlation, most of the data points will be close to the line of best fit. If most of the data points are not close to the line of best fit, the two sets of data have a weak correlation. The diagrams below show examples of the different strengths of correlation.

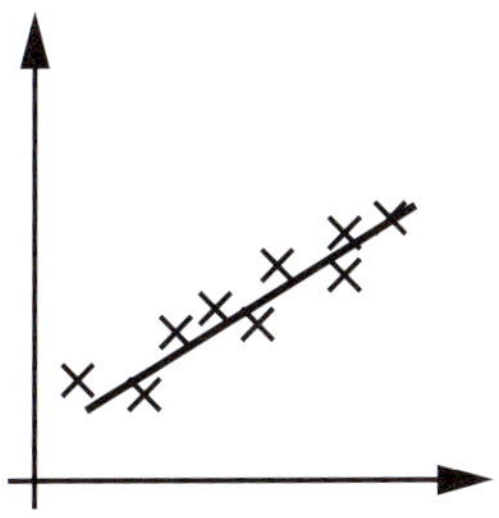

Strong positive correlation

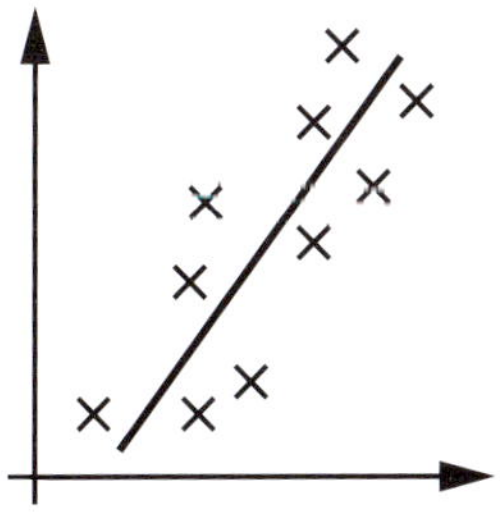

Weak positive correlation

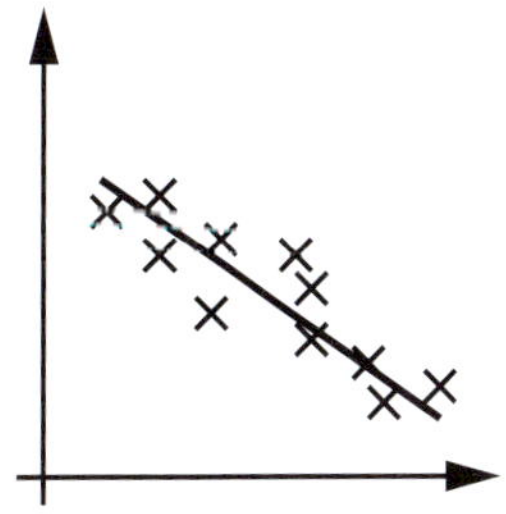

Strong negative correlation

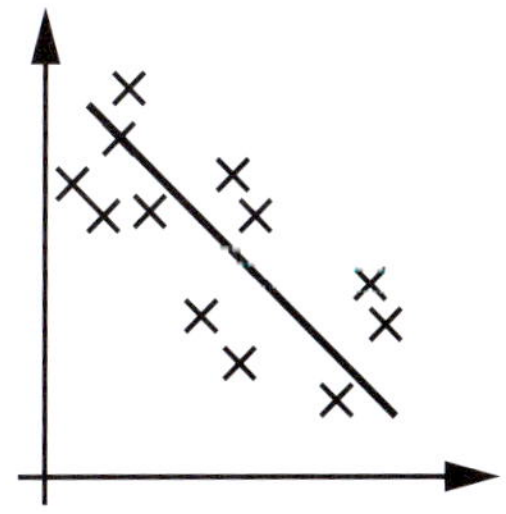

Weak negative correlation

Worked example 15.2

The table shows the maths and science test results of 12 students. Each test was marked out of 10.

Maths result	8	5	2	10	5	8	9	3	6	6	7	3
Science result	7	4	3	9	6	8	8	4	5	4	8	2

a Draw a scatter graph to show this data.

b Draw a line of best fit on your graph.

c What strength of positive correlation does the scatter graph show? Explain your answer.

d Maddie scored 7 in the maths test. She was ill for the science test. Use your line of best fit to estimate a score for Maddie in her science test.

Continued

Answer

a

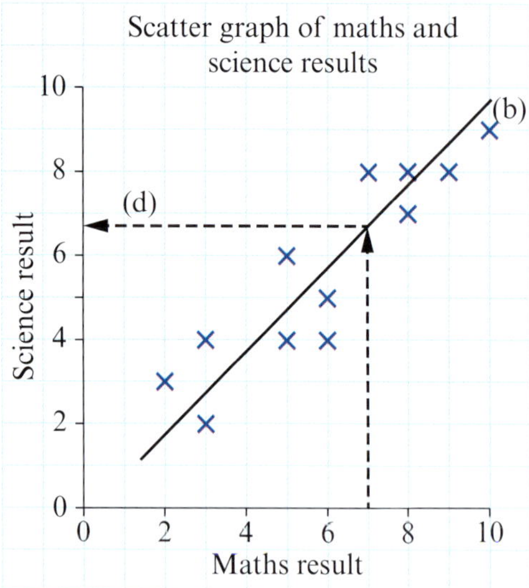

Mark each axis with a scale from 0 to 10. Take the horizontal axis as the maths result and the vertical axis as the science result.
Plot each point and mark it with a cross. Start with point (8, 7), then (5, 4), etc.
Make sure you plot all the points: there should be 12 crosses on the scatter graph, one for each student.
Remember to give the graph a title.

b Added to graph.

Draw the line of best fit approximately through the middle of all the crosses.

c The graph shows a weak positive correlation, because most of the data points are not close to the line of best fit.

For the correlation to be strong most of the data points need to be a lot closer to the line of best fit.

d 6.7 rounded to the nearest whole number is 7, so an estimated score for Maddie in her science test is 7.

Read up from a maths test score of 7 to the line of best fit, then read across to the science test score, as shown on the graph.

Exercise 15.2

1 Hassan carried out a survey on 15 students in his class. He asked them how many hours a week they spend doing homework, and how many hours a week they spend watching TV.
The table shows the results of his survey.

Hours doing homework	14	11	19	6	10	3	9	4	12	8	6	15	18	7	12
Hours watching TV	7	12	4	15	11	18	15	17	8	14	16	7	5	16	10

a Draw a scatter graph to show this data. Mark each axis with a scale from 0 to 20. Show 'Hours doing homework' on the horizontal axis and 'Hours watching TV' on the vertical axis.

b Does the scatter graph show positive or negative correlation? Explain your answer.

c Draw a line of best fit on your graph and describe the strength of the correlation.

d Hassan spends 6 hours watching TV one week. Use your line of best fit to estimate how many hours he spends doing homework that week.

Think like a mathematician

2 Work with a partner to answer this question.

The table shows the maximum daytime temperature in a town over a period of 14 days.

It also shows the number of cold drinks sold at a store each day over the same 14-day period.

Maximum daytime temperature (°C)	28	26	30	31	34	32	27	25	26	28	29	30	33	27
Number of cold drinks sold	25	22	26	28	29	27	24	23	24	27	26	29	31	23

a Without looking at the values in the table, do you think there will be positive, negative or no correlation between the maximum daytime temperature and the number of cold drinks sold? Explain your answer.

b Draw a scatter graph to show the data.

Show 'Maximum daytime temperature' on the horizontal axis, with a scale from 25 to 45.

Show 'Number of cold drinks sold' on the vertical axis, with a scale from 20 to 40.

c What type of correlation does the scatter graph show? Explain your answer.

d Was your conjecture in part **a** correct?

e Draw a line of best fit on your graph.

f Is it possible to estimate the number of cold drinks sold at the store when the temperature is 44 °C? Explain your answer.

g Discuss and compare your answers to parts **a** to **f** with other pairs of learners in your class.

3 The table shows the history and music exam results of 15 students.

The results for both subjects are given as percentages.

History result	12	15	22	25	32	36	45	52	58	68	75	77	80	82	85
Music result	25	64	18	42	65	23	48	24	60	45	68	55	42	32	76

a Without looking at the percentages or drawing a graph, do you think there will be positive, negative, or no correlation between the history and music exam results of the students? Explain your answer.

b Draw a scatter graph to show the data. Mark a scale from 0 to 100 on each axis.

Show 'History result' on the horizontal axis and 'Music result' on the vertical axis.

c What type of correlation does the scatter graph show? Explain your answer.

d Was your conjecture in part **a** correct? Explain your answer.

4 The scatter graph shows the distance travelled and the time taken by a taxi driver for the 12 journeys he made on one day.

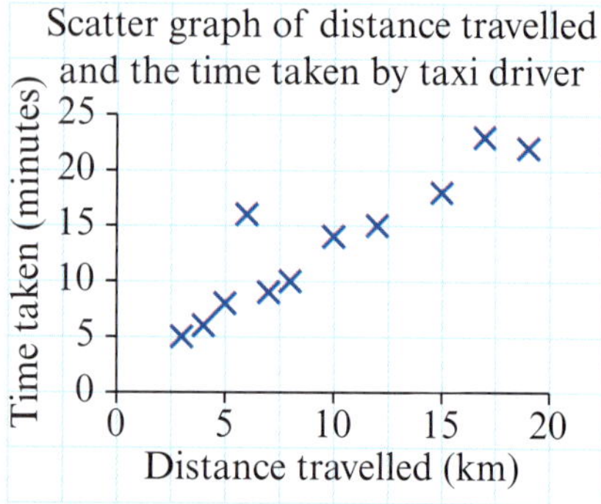

a What type and strength of correlation does the scatter graph show? Explain your answer.

b One of the journeys doesn't seem to fit the correlation. Which journey is this?

Explain why you think this journey might be different from the other journeys.

Think like a mathematician

5 Work with a partner to answer this question.

The scatter graph shows the body length and wingspan of 10 birds.

Marcus has drawn a line of best fit on the scatter graph in red.

Arun has drawn a line of best fit on the scatter graph in black.

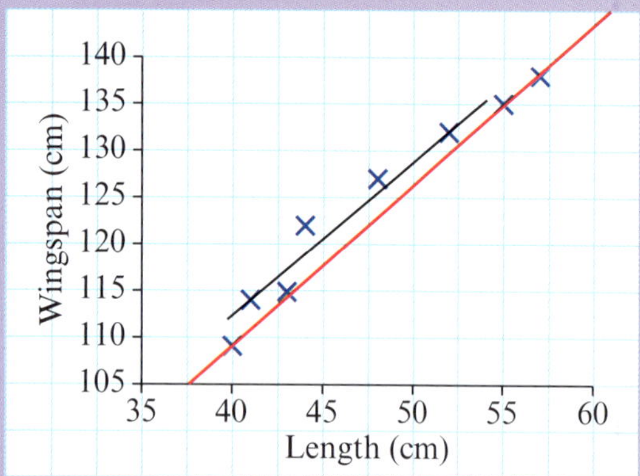

a Critique Marcus and Arun's lines of best fit.

b Suggest a method someone could follow to draw a good line of best fit.

c Discuss your answers to parts **a** and **b** with other pairs of learners in your class.

d In your groups discuss the answer to this question.

Is it a good idea to use the line of best fit to make predictions outside the range of the data? For example, estimating the wingspan of a bird with a body length of 75 cm.

6 The table shows the number of fish recorded at 10 different points in the Red Sea. It also shows the temperature of the sea at each point.

Sea temperature (°C)	25	26	21	20	22	24	20	23	21	19
Number of fish	102	75	122	129	120	92	76	95	138	146

a Draw a scatter graph to show this data.

b Describe the type and strength of the correlation between the number of fish and the temperature of the sea.

c Draw a line of best fit on your scatter graph. Use your line of best fit to estimate the number of fish at a point where the temperature is 27 °C.

d Do you think it is a good idea to use your line of best fit to predict the number of fish in the Red Sea when the temperature of the sea is 30 °C, 35 °C or even higher? Explain your answer.

e Scientists estimate that the sea temperature in the world is increasing every year. Use your graph to predict what will happen to the fish population in the sea as temperatures increase.

Look back at your answer to Question **6**, part **e**.
How confident do you feel in your prediction?
Do you think you have enough data to make this prediction?
What other information do you think you would need to support or contradict your prediction? Discuss the answers to these questions with other learners in your class.

7 Twenty learners in a school completed the same maths test. The length of their right foot was also measured. This scatter graph shows the results:

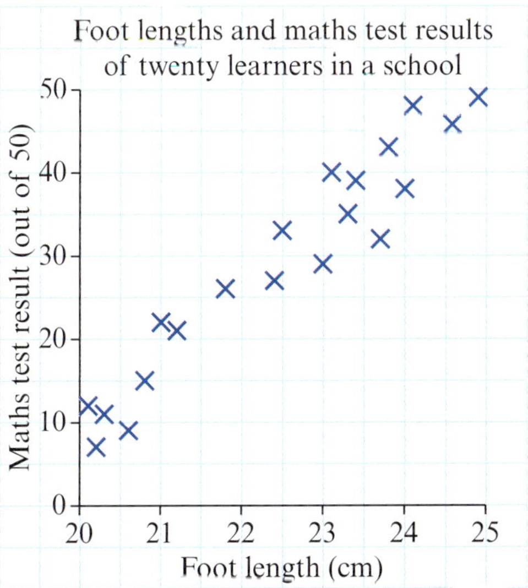

Sofia says: Zara says:

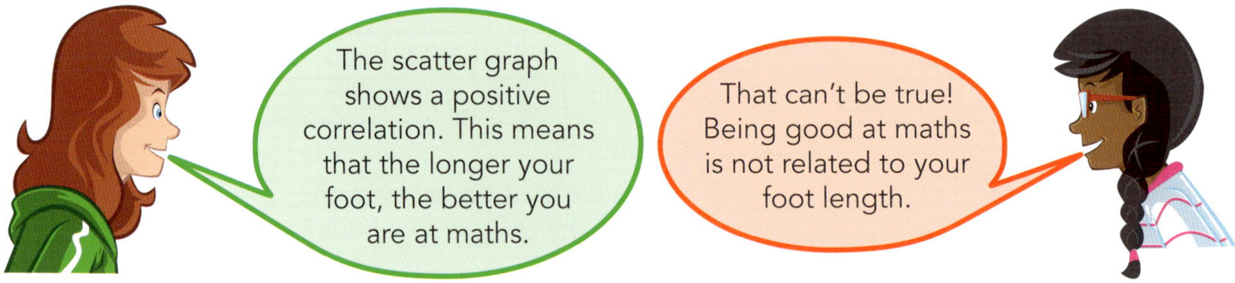

a Explain why Zara is correct.

b Discuss your answer to part **a** with other learners in your class.

Summary checklist

☐ I can draw and interpret scatter graphs.

15.3 Back-to-back stem-and-leaf diagrams

In this section you will …

- draw and interpret back-to-back stem-and-leaf diagrams.

Key word

back-to-back stem-and-leaf diagram

You already know how to use ordered stem-and-leaf diagrams to display one set of data. You can use a **back-to-back stem-and-leaf diagram** to display two sets of data. In a back-to-back stem-and-leaf diagram, you write one set of data with its 'leaves' to the right of the stem. Then you write the second set of data with its 'leaves' to the left of the stem. Both sets of numbers count from the stem, so you write the second set of numbers 'backwards'.

Tip

Remember, when you draw an ordered stem-and-leaf diagram, you should:

- write the numbers in order of size, smallest nearest the stem
- write a key to explain what the numbers mean
- keep all the numbers in line, vertically and horizontally.

Worked example 15.3

The results of a maths test taken by classes 9A and 9B are shown:

Class 9A test results									
10	33	6	26	14	25	4	23	5	39
7	15	8	26	34	8	15	26	34	14

Class 9B test results									
12	21	8	17	32	19	9	21	7	33
8	13	20	18	32	21	33	18	25	14

a Draw a back-to-back stem-and-leaf diagram to show this data.

b For each set of test results, work out

i the mode **ii** the median **iii** the range **iv** the mean.

c Compare and comment on the test results of the two classes.

Answer

a

Class 9A test results		Class 9B test results
8 8 7 6 5 4	0	7 8 8 9
5 5 4 4 0	1	2 3 4 7 8 8 9
6 6 6 5 3	2	0 1 1 1 5
9 4 4 3	3	2 2 3 3

Key: For class 9A, 4 | 0 means 04 marks
For class 9B, 0 | 7 means 07 marks

The test results vary between 4 and 39, so 0, 1, 2 and 3 need to form the stem. The leaves for class 9A come out from the stem, in order of size, to the left. The leaves for class 9B come out from the stem, in order of size, to the right. Write a key for each set of data to explain how the diagram works.
You will need to draw an unordered stem-and-leaf diagram first, before you draw the ordered stem-and-leaf diagram.

b i Class 9A mode = 26
Class 9B mode = 21

Look for the test result that appears most often in each set of data. This is the mode.

ii 20 students:
median = 21 ÷ 2 = 10.5th value
Class 9A: 10th = 15, 11th = 15, so median = 15
Class 9B: 10th = 18, 11th = 19, so median = 18.5

There are 20 students in each class, so the median is the mean of the 10th and 11th students' results.

iii Class 9A range = 39 − 4 = 35
Class 9B range = 33 − 7 = 26

Range is the difference between the highest result and the lowest result.

iv Class 9A mean = 372 ÷ 20 = 18.6
Class 9B mean = 381 ÷ 20 = 19.05

To work out the mean, add all the scores together, then divide by the number of scores (20).

Continued

c On average, class 9B had better results than class 9A as their median and mean were higher. The median shows that in class 9B 50% of the students had a result greater than 18.5 compared with 15 for class 9A. Class 9A had a higher modal (most common) score than class 9B. Class 9A had more variation in their scores as they had a higher range.

Write a few sentences comparing the test results of the two classes. Use the modes, medians, ranges and means you have worked out and explain what they mean.

Decide which class you think had the better results and give reasons for your answer.

Exercise 15.3

1 The ages of 16 people in two different clothes shops, A and B, are shown:

Shop A							
9	30	18	12	8	29	23	16
24	14	31	17	21	17	10	19

Shop B							
36	33	29	25	8	32	35	19
24	36	30	19	31	27	32	27

a Copy and complete the unordered back-to-back stem-and-leaf diagram to show this data.

Shop A		Shop B
9	0	
2 8	1	
	2	9 5
0	3	6 3

Key: 9 | 0 means 9 years old   Key: 3 | 6 means 36 years old

b Copy and complete the ordered back-to-back stem-and-leaf diagram to show this data.

Shop A		Shop B
9 8	0	8
2 0	1	9 9
	2	4
	3	

Key: 9 | 0 means 9 years old   Key: 3 | 6 means 36 years old

c Check your stem-and-leaf diagram is correct by comparing it with another learner's diagram. If your diagrams are not the same, try to find the mistake.

d Use your stem-and-leaf diagram to answer these questions:

i Which shop has the younger shoppers?

ii Which shop has the older shoppers?

e Make one conclusion about the types of clothes sold in the two different shops.

Think like a mathematician

2 An ice-cream vendor sells ice-creams. They record the numbers of ice-creams they sell at different locations.

The values in the tables show how many ice-creams the vendor sold each day over a two-week period at two different locations.

Beach car park						
56	46	60	47	57	46	62
60	57	45	61	46	59	62

City car park						
68	54	45	45	56	30	69
39	42	45	59	68	47	34

a Draw a back-to-back stem-and-leaf diagram to show this data.

b For each set of data, work out

i the mode ii the median iii the range.

c Compare and comment on the ice-cream sales at the different locations. Use your diagram in part **a** and your answers in part **b**.

d The vendor thinks their sales are better at the City car park. Do you agree or disagree? Explain why.

e Discuss your answers to parts **c** and **d** with other learners in your class.

3 The stem-and-leaf diagram shows the times taken by the students in a Stage 9 class to run 100 m.

		Boys' times						**Girls' times**		
	7	5	5	1	15	9				
8	3	2	2	0	16	7	8	8	8	
6	4	4	4	3	17	3	5	5	6	7
				0	18	1	4	4	5	
					19	6	9			

Key: For the boys' times, 1 | 15 means 15.1 seconds
For the girls' times, 15 | 9 means 15.9 seconds

a For each set of times, work out

i the mode ii the median

iii the range iv the mean.

b Compare and comment on the times taken by the boys and the girls to run 100 m.

c Zara says:

Do you agree? Explain your answer.

4 The stem-and-leaf diagram shows the mass of 12 desert hedgehogs in two different locations.

Location A				Stem	Location B				
				38	2	3	5	5	9
	8	5	4	39	4	6	8		
9	9	6	5	40	5	8			
	8	5	2	41	0	3			
		5	0	42					

Key: 4 | 39 means 394 g   Key: 38 | 0 means 380 g

a What fraction of the hedgehogs from each location had a mass less than 400 g?

b What percentage of the hedgehogs from each location had a mass greater than 415 g?

c Which location, A or B, had the most variation in the mass of the hedgehogs?

d Work out the mean and median mass of hedgehogs for each location.

e Which location, A or B, do you think has more food available for the hedgehogs to eat? Explain your answer.

Think like a mathematician

5 Work with a partner to answer this question.

Two websites record the number of 'hits' they have over a period of 21 days.

The tables show the number of hits per day on each website.

> **Tip**
>
> A 'hit' is when a person uses the website.

Website A						
141	152	134	161	130	153	142
130	158	159	145	133	145	147
145	148	153	155	146	160	152

Website B						
134	129	145	156	145	128	138
166	136	146	154	146	157	145
148	158	169	157	168	155	167

a Draw a back-to-back stem-and-leaf diagram to show this data.

b Compare and comment on the number of hits on each website.

c Marcus thinks website A is better because the number of hits for website A is more consistent than the number of hits for website B.

Do you agree or disagree? Explain your answer.

d Discuss your answers to parts **b** and **c** with other pairs of learners in your class.

> **Tip**
>
> Use the mode, median, range and mean to compare the hits on each website.

Summary checklist

☐ I can draw and interpret back-to-back stem-and-leaf diagrams.

15.4 Calculating statistics for grouped data

In this section you will …

- use mode, median, mean and range to compare sets of grouped data.

You already know how to work out the mode, median, mean and range for individual data and also for data represented in a frequency table. When data is grouped, you cannot work out exact values for the mode, median, mean and range, because you do not have the individual data. However, you can write the modal class interval and the class interval where the median lies, and you can work out estimates for the mean and the range.

Worked example 15.4

The frequency table shows the masses of 20 teachers.

Mass, m (kg)	Frequency
$60 < m \leqslant 70$	4
$70 < m \leqslant 80$	7
$80 < m \leqslant 90$	6
$90 < m \leqslant 100$	3

a Write

  i the modal class interval

  ii the class interval where the median lies.

b Work out an estimate for

  i the range **ii** the mean.

c Explain why your answers to part **b** are estimates.

Answer

a i $70 < m \leqslant 80$

This is the class with the greatest frequency (7).

ii $20 \div 2 = 10$, so the median is half way between the 10th and 11th values. The class containing the median is $70 < m \leqslant 80$

The first four values are in the class $60 < m \leqslant 70$, then the 5th to 11th values are in the class $70 < m \leqslant 80$. As the 10th and 11th values are both in the class $70 < m \leqslant 80$, the median must be in this class.

b i Estimate of range = $100 - 60 = 40$ kg

To work out an estimate of the range, find the difference between the highest possible mass and the lowest possible mass.

Continued

ii

Midpoint	Frequency	Midpoint × frequency
65	4	260
75	7	525
85	6	510
95	3	285
Totals:	20	1580

estimate of mean = $\frac{1580}{20}$ = 79 kg

First find the midpoint for each class. Multiply each midpoint by the frequency for that class and add the results to estimate the total mass of the teachers.

Divide this total by the number of teachers to find an estimate of the mean mass.

c The answers are estimates because the data is grouped and you do not know the individual values.

Give a short explanation that shows you understand that, when data is grouped, you do not know the individual values and so you cannot use the individual values to work out accurate answers.

Exercise 15.4

1 The table shows the heights of the students in class 9R.

Height, h (cm)	Frequency
$140 \leqslant h < 150$	7
$150 \leqslant h < 160$	13
$160 \leqslant h < 170$	6
$170 \leqslant h < 180$	2

a Write

i the modal class interval

ii the class interval where the median lies.

b Explain why you can only give class intervals for the mode and median, and not exact values.

c Work out an estimate for the range.

d Copy and complete the table and workings to find an estimate of the mean.

Give your answer correct to the nearest centimetre.

Midpoint	Frequency	Midpoint × frequency
145	7	145 × 7 = 1015
155	13	155 × 13 = ☐
☐	6	☐ × 6 = ☐
☐	2	☐ × 2 = ☐
Totals:	28	☐

Estimate of mean = $\frac{\square}{28}$ = ☐ cm

2 The table shows the masses of the students in class 9T.

Mass, m (kg)	Frequency
$40 \leqslant m < 50$	4
$50 \leqslant m < 60$	12
$60 \leqslant m < 70$	8

a Write

i the modal class interval

ii the class interval where the median lies.

b Work out an estimate for

i the mean **ii** the range.

c Explain why your answers to part **b** are estimates.

Think like a mathematician

3 Look back at the method you used to work out an estimate of the mean in questions **1** and **2**.

Marcus says: Arun says:

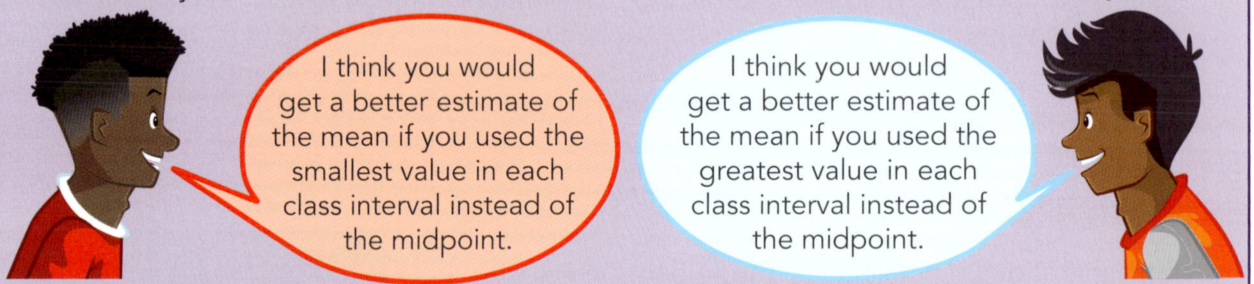

a What do you think? Explain your answer.

b Discuss Marcus' and Arun's statements and your answer to part **a** with other learners in your class.

4 Anita carried out a survey on the length of time patients waited to see a doctor at two different hospitals. The tables show the results of her survey.

The Heath	
Time, t (minutes)	Frequency
$0 \leqslant t < 10$	5
$10 \leqslant t < 20$	23
$20 \leqslant t < 30$	10
$30 \leqslant t < 40$	2

Moorlands	
Time, t (minutes)	Frequency
$0 \leqslant t < 10$	16
$10 \leqslant t < 20$	8
$20 \leqslant t < 30$	14
$30 \leqslant t < 40$	12

a How many people were surveyed at each hospital?

b Copy and complete this table.

Hospital	Modal class interval	Class interval where the median lies	Estimate of mean
The Heath			
Moorlands			

c Compare and comment on the average waiting times for the two hospitals.

d Which hospital would you prefer to go to, based only on the waiting times? Explain your answer.

Think like a mathematician

5 Hank has a six-sided spinner, showing the numbers 1 to 6.

He also has a seven-sided spinner, showing the numbers 1 to 7.

Hank spins the spinners and adds the numbers the spinners land on to give the score.

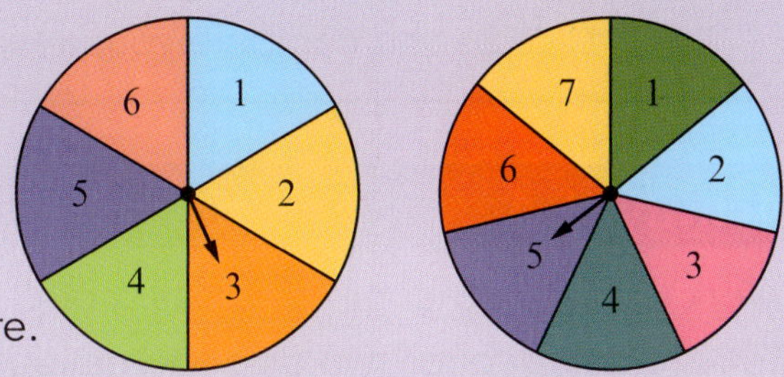

a What is the smallest score Hank could get?

b What is the greatest score Hank could get?

c Hank spins the spinners 20 times. Here are the scores he gets:

10	3	13	8	3	12	7	2	9	3
9	6	2	10	6	8	3	8	11	10

Work out the mean, median and mode for this data.

d Hank decides to group the data. He is not sure which groups to use, so he draws two frequency tables.

Table A		
Score	Tally	Frequency
2 – 4		
5 – 7		
8 – 10		
11 – 13		

Table B		
Score	Tally	Frequency
2 – 5		
6 – 9		
10 – 13		

Copy and complete both tables for the data in part **c**.

Continued

e Copy and complete this table using table A and table B in part **d**.

	Modal class interval	Class interval where the median lies	Estimate of mean
Table A			
Table B			

f i Compare the accurate mean in part **c** with the estimates you found in part **e**. What do you notice?

ii Compare the accurate median in part **c** with the class intervals you found in part **e**. What do you notice?

iii Compare the accurate mode in part **c** with the class intervals you found in part **e**. What do you notice?

g Discuss and compare your answers to parts **a** to **f** with other learners in your class.

Activity 15.4

Work with a partner or in a small group to answer this question.

You are going to roll two dice and multiply the numbers on the dice to give the score. For example, if you roll a 1 and a 6, you get a score of 6.

a What is the smallest score you can get?

b What is the largest score you can get?

c Roll the dice 40 times. Note all your scores.

d Work out

i the mode ii the median iii the mean score for your data.

e Which average best represents your data? Give a reason for your choice.

f You are now going to group your data.

Draw a frequency table similar to one of the tables in Question **5**, part **d**. Decide on the groups you are going to use.

g Use your table in part **f** to work out

i the modal class interval ii the class interval where the median lies

iii an estimate of the mean.

h Comment on the differences and similarities between your answers to parts **d** and **g**.

i Compare and discuss your answers to parts **d**, **g** and **h** with other learners in your class.

6 The table shows the masses of 50 meerkats.

Mass, m (g)	Frequency
$600 \leqslant m < 650$	2
$650 \leqslant m < 700$	5
$700 \leqslant m < 750$	7
$750 \leqslant m < 800$	12
$800 \leqslant m < 850$	10
$850 \leqslant m < 900$	8
$900 \leqslant m < 950$	4
$950 \leqslant m < 1000$	2

Tip

A meerkat is a small mongoose that lives in Africa.

a Write
   i the modal class interval
   ii the class interval where the median lies.

b Work out an estimate for
   i the mean
   ii the range.

c Zara decides to regroup the data, using larger group sizes. Copy and complete this table.

Mass, m (g)	Frequency
$600 \leqslant m < 700$	
$700 \leqslant m < 800$	
$800 \leqslant m < 900$	
$900 \leqslant m < 1000$	

Tip

Use the frequencies in the table at the start of the question to complete this table.

d Write
   i the modal class interval
   ii the class interval where the median lies.

e Work out an estimate for
   i the mean
   ii the range.

f Compare your answers to parts **a** and **b** with your answers to parts **d** and **e**.
   i Do you think the answers in parts **a** and **b** or the answers in parts **d** and **e** are more accurate? Explain why.
   ii Were the answers in parts **a** and **b** or the answers in parts **d** and **e** quicker to work out? Explain why.

Summary checklist

☐ I can use mode, median, mean and range to compare sets of grouped data.

15.5 Representing data

In this section you will …

- choose how to represent data.

Before you can represent data using a diagram, graph or chart, you need to decide which type of diagram, graph or chart is best to use. There are many you can choose from such as:

- Venn and Carroll diagrams
- line graphs and time series graphs
- stem-and-leaf diagrams
- frequency polygons
- infographics
- dual and compound bar charts
- scatter graphs
- tally charts and frequency tables
- two-way tables
- pie charts.

In this section, instead of an exercise, you have an activity to do. You can work with a partner or on your own. You can represent the data in any way you choose, but first you should ask yourself these questions:

- Is the data discrete or continuous?
- Is the data individual pieces of data or grouped data?
- What type of chart or graph is suitable for this data?
- What type of chart or graph will best represent this data?

Project Australia!

In the following text, there are lots of facts, figures and tables giving you information about Australia.

a Choose some of the information to represent using diagrams, graphs or charts.

b Write a brief explanation about what your diagrams, graphs or charts show.

c Make a poster to display your diagrams, graphs and charts. It is up to you how you design your poster – for example, you could

- include a map of Australia
- add photos or drawings
- find out some other information you would like to include.

d Compare your posters with other learners in your class. Discuss these questions:

i Did you all use the same methods to display the same data?

ii Do the posters display the data in a way that is quick and easy to understand?

iii Choose your favourite poster from all the posters (not including yours!) and explain why you like this poster the best.

iv Now you have seen all the posters, could you improve your poster? Explain your answer.

Australia facts and figures

Geography

Australia is the largest country in the Southern Hemisphere, the sixth-largest country in the world and the largest country without land borders. Australia also has the third longest land mountain range in the world.

Here are some facts about Australia's geography:

- land area: 7682300 km^2
- length of coastline: 25760 km
- capital city: Canberra
- largest city: Sydney
- highest point: Mt. Kosciusko (2.23 km)
- lowest point: Lake Eyre (−12 m)
- longest river: Murray River (2520 km)
- total length of railways: 33343 km

Here are some approximate percentages:

- land area of Australia: 53% agriculture, 16% forest, 31% other
- gauge of the railways used in Australia: 53% standard, 37% narrow, 10% broad.

Tip

The 'gauge' of a railway is the width of the railway.

Population

In 2018, Australia had an estimated population of 23.47 million. Approximately 86% of these people live in the towns and cities. The rest of the people live in the countryside. The table shows the age structure of the population.

Age	Percentage (nearest 1%)	Number of males (millions)	Number of females (millions)
0–14	18	2.14	2.03
15–24	13	1.52	1.44
25–54	41	4.94	4.76
55–64	12	1.38	1.40
65+	16	1.79	2.07

	Median age (years)
Male	38.1
Female	39.7

The approximate percentages of main language spoken at home are: English 73%, Mandarin 3%, Arabic 2%, Cantonese 1%, Vietnamese 1%, Italian 1%, Greek 1%, other 18%.

Energy

Electricity production comes from: 72% fossil fuels, 11% hydroelectric, 17% other renewable sources.

Crude oil (measured in barrels per day): production 284 000, exports 192 500, imports 341 700.

Natural gas (measured in m^3 per year): production 105.2 billion, exports 68.0 billion, imports 5.8 billion.

Nature

The Great Barrier Reef marine park stretches over 3000 km. The Great Barrier Reef is between 15 km and 150 km offshore and around 65 km wide in some parts. The Great Barrier Reef is made up of around 3000 individual reefs and 900 islands.

Here are some facts about the Great Barrier Reef:

- 30 species of whales, dolphins and porpoises have been recorded in the reef.
- 6 species of sea turtles come to the reef to breed.
- Around 20 species of reptiles live on the reef.
- 215 species of birds visit the reef or nest on the islands.
- 17 species of sea snake live on the reef.
- More than 1500 fish species live on the reef.
- Around 10% of the world's total fish species can be found within the reef.
- There are more than 400 different types of coral on the reef.

The east coast of Australia is home to the koala bear. Koala bears generally live an average of 13–17 years. Female koala bears tend to live longer than male koala bears. The life expectancy of a male koala bear is often less than 10 years due to injuries caused by fights, attacks by dogs and being hit by traffic. Koala bears eat approximately 1 kg of food a day and sleep for up to 19 hours each day. There are only 2000 to 8000 koala bears left in the wild. The population of koala bears has dropped by 90% in less than 10 years due to the destruction of the koala bears' natural habitat.

The table shows the length and mass of 12 koala bears.

Length (cm)	76	80	72	78	88	70	81	83	71	84	90	74
Mass (kg)	5.4	6.3	5.2	6.0	8.3	4.0	6.9	8.0	4.6	7.1	8.9	4.9

Tourism

The table shows the number of tourists visiting Australia in 2018 from five different countries. It also shows the total amount spent by those tourists, and the average number of nights they stayed.

Country	Japan	USA	UK	New Zealand	China
Number of tourists (thousands)	272	381	145	534	773
Total spend ($ billion)	2	4	3.3	2.6	12
Average number of nights' stay	24	17	32	10	43

This table shows the international visitor numbers each month in 2018.

Month	Jan	Feb	Mar	Apr	May	Jun	Jul	Aug	Sep	Oct	Nov	Dec
Number of visitors (thousands)	730	914	872	680	609	647	774	741	690	754	800	1000

The approximate percentages of reasons for visiting Australia were: holiday 45%, visiting friends and relatives 11%, business 39% and other 5%.

Summary checklist

- [ ] I can choose how to represent data.

Check your progress

1 Marina carried out a survey on the length of time it took employees to travel to work at two different supermarkets. The tables show the results of her survey.

Kabayan Supermarket		
Time, t (minutes)	Frequency	Midpoint
$0 \leqslant t < 15$	5	7.5
$15 \leqslant t < 30$	8	
$30 \leqslant t < 45$	38	
$45 \leqslant t < 60$	9	

Shoprite Supermarket		
Time, t (minutes)	Frequency	Midpoint
$0 \leqslant t < 15$	32	7.5
$15 \leqslant t < 30$	13	
$30 \leqslant t < 45$	10	
$45 \leqslant t < 60$	5	

a How many people were surveyed at each supermarket?

b Copy and complete the tables.

c On the same grid, draw a frequency polygon for each set of data.

d Compare the travelling times to the two supermarkets. Use the frequency polygons to help you.

Tip

Make sure you show clearly which frequency polygon represents which supermarket.

2 The table shows the age and value of 10 different cars for sale at a garage.

Age of car (years)	8	10	2	3	15	1	12	5	9	4
Value of car ($)	8500	6000	13 500	12 500	3500	15 000	4000	10 000	6500	12 000

a Draw a scatter graph to show this data.

b Describe the correlation between the age and the value of a car.

c Draw a line of best fit on your scatter graph. Use your line of best fit to estimate the value of a car that is six years old.

3 Some Stage 9 students were asked to estimate a time of 60 seconds.

Each student had to close their eyes and raise their hand when they thought 60 seconds had passed.

The stem-and-leaf diagram shows the actual times estimated by the students.

Boys' times						Girls' times				
					4	9				
		6	5	3	5	6	6	7	9	
9	7	7	4	3	6	0	1	3	4	7
8	6	5	3	2	7	2	3	4	5	
			5	4	8	1				

Key: For the boys' times, 3 | 5 means 53 seconds
For the girls' times, 4 | 9 means 49 seconds

a For each set of times, work out
- **i** the mode
- **ii** the median
- **iii** the range
- **iv** the mean.

b Compare and comment on the boys' and the girls' estimates for 60 seconds.

c Arun says:

Do you agree? Explain your answer.

4 The table shows the number of hours one week that the students in class 9T spent doing homework.

Time, t (hours)	Frequency
$4 \leqslant t < 6$	6
$6 \leqslant t < 8$	14
$8 \leqslant t < 10$	10

a Write
- **i** the modal class interval
- **ii** the class interval where the median lies.

b Work out an estimate for
- **i** the mean
- **ii** the range.

Project 6

Cycle training

Marcus is training for a cycle race. He goes for a ride every day to track his progress. He cycles along a straight, flat road all the way to a shop where he stops for ten minutes to rest. Marcus then cycles home again.

Yesterday, Marcus used his Smart Watch to note the time, to the nearest half minute, after every 5 km he travelled.

Here is the data for his outward journey:

Distance (km)	5	10	15	20
Time (minutes)	10.5	21	30.5	40

Here is the data for his return journey:

Distance (km)	5	10	15	20
Time (minutes)	10	20.5	31	40

Draw a distance–time graph to represent this information.

Today, Marcus recorded his progress slightly differently. Every ten minutes, he used his Smart Watch to note how far he had travelled.

Here is the data for his outward journey:

Time (minutes)	10	20	30	40	50
Distance (km)	3.8	7.9	12.1	15.9	20

Here is the data for his return journey (including the time when he completed his ride):

Time (minutes)	10	20	30	33 minutes, 20 seconds
Distance (km)	5.9	12.2	18	20

On the same set of axes as before, draw a distance–time graph to represent Marcus' second ride.

- What do you notice when you compare yesterday's journey with today's journey?
- Work out the average speed for the outward and return journeys of each ride.
- How do the average speeds on today's ride compare with the average speeds on yesterday's ride?
- Can you suggest any reasons why the journeys might be different?

In fact, Marcus' performance today was affected by the wind, which reduced his speed on the outward journey but increased his speed on the return journey. Explore what would happen on days when the wind was even stronger (so, for example, his average speed might be 20 km per hour on the outward journey and 40 km per hour on the return journey).

How does wind affect Marcus' total journey time?

Glossary

algebraic fraction	a fraction that contains an unknown variable, or letter	43
back-to-back stem-and-leaf diagram	a way of displaying two sets of data on one stem-and-leaf diagram	330
bias	selectivity when choosing a sample that makes the results unrepresentative	133
brackets	used to enclose items that are to be seen as a single expression	38
cancelling common factors	dividing the numerator and denominator of a fraction by a common factor	173
changing the subject	rearranging a formula or equation to get a different letter on its own	48
compound percentage	when a percentage increase or decrease is followed by another percentage increase or decrease	68
construct (algebra)	use given information to write an equation, draw a diagram or draw a graph	84
construct (geometry)	use given information to draw shapes, angles or lines in diagrams using compasses and a ruler	114
correlation	the relationship between two variable quantities	324
counter-example	an example that shows a statement is not true	22
difference of two squares	an expression of the form $a^2 - b^2$. It can be written as $(a + b)(a - b)$	38
equivalent calculation	a different calculation than the one you have to do but which gives exactly the same answer	63
equivalent decimal	a decimal number that has the same value as a fraction	163
expand	to multiply the terms inside one bracket by the terms inside the other bracket	38
exterior angle of a polygon	the angle outside a polygon between an extension of one side and an adjacent side	111
frequency polygon	a chart made up of straight-line segments that shows frequencies	319
hypotenuse	the longest side of a right-angled triangle, opposite the right angle	118

in terms of	refers to the letters you use to represent unknown numbers in an expression	27
independent events	if the probability that event B happens is the same, whether event A happens or not, then A and B are independent events	256
inequality	a relationship between two expressions that are not equal	97
inscribe	when you inscribe a polygon in a circle, every vertex is on the circle	114
inverse proportion	two quantities are in inverse proportion if, when one quantity increases the other quantity decreases in the same ratio	243
irrational number	a number on the number line that is not a rational number	10
isometric paper	paper covered with lines or dots that form congruent equilateral triangles	311
line of best fit	a line on a scatter graph that shows the relationship between the two sets of data	324
linear function	a function with a straight-line graph	217
linear sequence	a sequence of numbers in which the difference between consecutive terms is the same	193
lower bound	the smallest value that a rounded number could have been before it was rounded	75
method of elimination	a method for solving simultaneous equations when the number of xs or ys is the same, so you add or subtract the two equations to eliminate the xs or the ys	89
method of substitution	a method for solving simultaneous equations where you write one of the equations in the form '$y = \ldots$' or '$x = \ldots$' and then substitute this into the other equation	89
midpoint	the middle value in a class interval	319
misleading	information that leads you to an incorrect conclusion	133
mutually exclusive	events are mutually exclusive if only one of them can happen at one time	252
non-linear sequence	a sequence of numbers in which the difference between consecutive terms is not the same	193
perfect square	a perfect square is a number, or expression, that can be written as the product of two equal factors e.g. $3 \times 3 = 9$, $x \times x = x^2$, $(x + 1)(x + 1) = x^2 + 2x + 1$	38
plane of symmetry	a plane that divides a 3D shape into two congruent halves that are mirror images of each other	311
prefix	a set of letters that you put in front of a word	153
Pythagoras' theorem	a relationship between the three sides of a right-angled triangle	118

quadratic sequence	a sequence of numbers in which the second difference between consecutive terms is the same; the highest power in the *n*th term rule is 2 (squared)	190
rational number	any number that can be written as a fraction	10
ray lines	lines that start at a fixed point and continue forever	292
recurring decimal	in a recurring decimal, a digit or group of digits is repeated forever	163
regular polygon	a polygon where all the sides are the same length and all the interior angles are the same size	107
relative frequency	if an action is repeated, the relative frequency of a particular outcome is the fraction of times when that outcome occurs	264
scatter graph	a graph showing linked values of two variables, plotted as coordinate points, that might or might not be related	324
scientific notation	the same as standard form	14
sector	a part of a circle formed by two radii and the part of the circumference joining their ends	87
simultaneous equations	two or more equations, each containing several variables	89
solution set	the set of numbers that form a solution to a problem	97
solve	calculate the value of any unknown letter(s) in an equation	84
standard form	a way of writing very large or very small numbers in the form $a \times 10^n$, where $1 \leqslant a < 10$ and n is an integer	14
strategies	methods	184
subject of a formula	the letter that is on its own on one side (usually the left) of a formula	48
surd	an irrational square root or cube root	10
terminating decimal	a decimal number that does not go on forever	163
tonne	a unit of mass such that 1 tonne = 1000 kilograms	153
upper bound	the largest value that a rounded number could have been before it was rounded	75